THE YAMASEE INDIANS

"This impressive anthology tells the remarkable story of the Yamasee Indians and, in the telling, reveals the opportunities, upheavals, and strategies for survival of Native communities living on the edge of an expanding European empire."

—ROBBIE ETHRIDGE, professor of anthropology at the University of Mississippi and author of *From Chicaza to Chickasaw: The European Invasion and the Transformation of the Mississippian World, 1540–1715*

"A much-needed, remarkably thorough, and impressively interdisciplinary investigation of a critically important but all-too-often misunderstood Native nation. Anyone with an interest in the early American South and its people should read this book."

—JOSHUA PIKER, editor of the *William and Mary Quarterly*, Omohundro Institute of Early American History and Culture, and professor of history at the College of William and Mary

"This anthology makes a fine addition to the extant scholarship on the Yamasee people, offers a balanced juxtaposition of disciplinary and thematic approaches to the subject, and builds on the scholarship that has come before while casting an eye toward what might be some promising areas for future study. The chapters all interconnect in ways that bespeak a kind of collective and collaborative approach to the topic at hand."

—JAMES TAYLOR CARSON, professor and head of the School of Humanities, Languages, and Social Science at Griffith University in Brisbane and author of *The Columbian Covenant: Race and the Writing of American History*

THE YAMASEE INDIANS
From Florida to South Carolina

Edited and with an introduction by DENISE I. BOSSY
Foreword by ALAN GALLAY

University of Nebraska Press
LINCOLN

© 2018 by the Board of Regents of the University of Nebraska

Acknowledgments for the use of copyrighted material appear on page 157, which constitutes an extension of the copyright page.

All rights reserved

Library of Congress Cataloging-in-Publication Data
Names: Bossy, Denise I., editor, writer of introduction.
Title: The Yamasee Indians: from Florida to South Carolina / edited and with an introduction by Denise I. Bossy; foreword by Alan Gallay.
Description: Lincoln: University of Nebraska Press, [2018] | Includes bibliographical references and index.
Identifiers: LCCN 2018006597
ISBN 9781496207609 (cloth: alk. paper)
ISBN 9781496230386 (paperback)
ISBN 9781496212276 (epub)
ISBN 9781496212283 (mobi)
ISBN 9781496212290 (pdf)
Subjects: LCSH: Yamassee Indians—History.
Classification: LCC E99.Y22 Y36 2018 | DDC 975.7/01—dc23 LC record available at https://lccn.loc.gov/2018006597

Set in Adobe Caslon Pro by E. Cuddy.

Dedicated to Yamasee peoples, past, present, and future.

Contents

List of Illustrations ix
List of Tables xi
Foreword, by Alan Gallay .xiii
Acknowledgments xvii

Introduction: Recovering Yamasee History 1
    DENISE I. BOSSY

PART 1. Yamasee Identity

1. Living at Liberty: The Ungovernable Yamasees of Spanish Florida . . . 27
    AMY TURNER BUSHNELL

2. Yamasee Migrations into the Mocama and Timucua Mission Provinces of Florida, 1667–1683: An Archaeological Perspective 55
    KEITH ASHLEY

3. Yamasee Material Culture and Identity: Altamaha/San Marcos Ceramics in Seventeenth- and Eighteenth-Century Yamasee Indian Settlements, Georgia and South Carolina 81
    ERIC C. POPLIN AND JON BERNARD MARCOUX

4. Cultural Continuity and Change: Archaeological Research at Yamasee Primary Towns in South Carolina 99
    ALEXANDER Y. SWEENEY

PART 2. Yamasee Networks

5. Spiritual Diplomacy: Reinterpreting the Yamasee Prince's Eighteenth-Century Voyage to England. 131
    DENISE I. BOSSY

6. Yamasee-African Ties in Carolina and Florida 163
   JANE LANDERS

7. The Long Yamasee War: Reflections on Yamasee Conflict in the
Eighteenth Century 191
   STEVEN C. HAHN

PART 3. **Surviving the Yamasee War**

8. The Persistence of Yamasee Power and Identity at the Town of
San Antonio de Pocotalaca, 1716–1752 221
   AMANDA HALL

9. Refuge among the Spanish: Yamasee Community Coalescence in
St. Augustine after 1715 251
   ANDREA P. WHITE

10. Chief Francisco Jospogue: Reconstructing the Paths of a
Guale-Yamasee Indian Lineage through Spanish Records 281
    SUSAN RICHBOURG PARKER

11. The Yamasee in West Florida 309
    JOHN E. WORTH

List of Contributors 339
Index 343

Illustrations

Figures

1. View of Yamasee house from Altamaha Town 106
2. Yamasee burial, Altamaha Town 115
3. The Euhaw Prince's letter to the SPG 143
4. Well profile, La Punta 266
5. Excavation of barrel well, La Punta 267
6. Decorated ceramics, La Punta 271
7. Mission red filmed bowl, La Punta 272
8. Cacique Jospogue's signature 283

Maps

1. The colonial Southeast 56
2. Yamasee sites, Amelia Island 68
3. Yamasee regions along the St. Johns River 72
4. Location of the Upper and Lower Yamasee in South Carolina . . . 101
5. General location of Yamasee migrations from the 1660s to 1715 . . . 104
6. General location and sketch plan view of late Mississippian and Yamasee houses 107
7. Lower Yamasee settlements, ca. 1732 110
8. Yamasee slaving into Florida as depicted by Thomas Nairne 122
9. Euhaw and Yamasee worlds 135
10. Pocotalaca community, ca. 1737 225
11. Map of the Duero site units, features, and structure 241
12. La Punta refugee community 253
13. La Punta excavations 264
14. The Jospo home, St. Augustine 298
15. The Yamasee in West Florida 311

Tables

1. San Marcos series pottery from the Riverbend site 73
2. Yamasee calculated household sizes 109
3. The Duero site assemblage. .232
4. Count and percentage of San Marcos surface treatments from
the Duero site 234
5. Stamped and plain San Marcos surfaces from the Duero and
Oneida sites 234
6. Comparison of Pocotalaca, La Punta, and Altamaha/San Marcos
stamped and plain surfaces. .235
7. Faunal remains from the Duero site 240
8. Pocotalaca's population 1717 to 1752 245
9. La Punta population estimates. 260

Foreword

ALAN GALLAY

The Yamasee Indians played an enormous role in the geopolitics of early America along the Atlantic Seaboard. Yet we know so little about them. The Yamasee lived on lands that ranged from northern Florida to southern South Carolina. Sometimes they located on the sea islands and at other times on the mainland. In the mid-seventeenth century Yamasees filtered into the Spanish mission system of northern Florida but usually did not convert to Christianity. Unable to obtain adequate protection from the Spanish against slave raiders—both Native and European—in the third quarter of the seventeenth century many Yamasees migrated to the mainland north of the Savannah River, where they became neighbors of the recently established English colony of Carolina. The Yamasees partnered with English and Scots to conduct slave raids in the Southeast. Having themselves been victimized in previous decades, the Yamasee informed the Creek Indians of the stark alternative they faced: if they did not become slavers allied with the English, they would continue to be enslaved. The Creeks followed the Yamasees in conducting slave raids that extended all the way to the Florida Keys. In a whirlwind of violence that engulfed the South, thousands were enslaved by the English and allied Indians.

These were not the only relationships that Yamasees had with Europeans. They provided military assistance, both offensive and defensive, including as rangers and scouts. Many hunted deer, processed the pelts, and exchanged the skins and meat for British trade goods. The Yamasees never assumed subservience in their relations with the Europeans. To maintain their independence they continuously adapted to the rapidly changing southern landscape, which included in- and out-migrations of peoples of diverse cultures, including Iroquoian

Westo from the Great Lakes, Shawnee from the Ohio River Valley, French from Canada and Europe, and Africans from various locales in Africa and the West Indies.

Yamasee adaptability was recognized throughout the region. At one point the governor of Carolina negotiated to employ three hundred Yamasees to produce silk and cotton, revealing not only European respect for Yamasee agricultural practices but Yamasee ability to cultivate new crops under European market conditions. Yamasees employed diplomacy, military power, and mobility to great effect. Europeans and Indians turned to them for military assistance, mediation, goods, and information. The relative ease with which Yamasees traversed the coastal region meant they often were the first to know important news, and they used that knowledge to their benefit.

Yamasee mobility formed a dialectic with their adaptability. They forged ties with a variety of people, often under difficult circumstances. Yamasees grew resentful of the Spanish and of Apalachee Indians and other Natives on the missions—yet Yamasees established a wide range of positive relations with the Spanish and with Florida Natives through the years, including military alliance. Having been victimized by slavers, and later become slavers, Yamasees then liberated African slaves of the English and brought them to freedom in Spanish Florida. Yamasees incorporated African, Indian, and other refugees into their towns. This ability to move from one role to another and from relationships of hostility to friendship is remarkable, but it also demonstrates how important adaptability and mobility were to survival in the American Southeast. The Yamasees excelled in these skills.

Decades of living on the Spanish missions and as military and economic partners of the English made the Yamasee informed, feared, powerful, and wary. The decline of potential slaves in Florida, and of deer herds in South Carolina, led the Yamasees into great debt with British traders. This diminished trade led some English to devalue the Yamasee relationship, as they coveted Yamasee lands to turn into rice plantations. The Yamasee were not alone in their resentment. Many southeastern Native peoples who had been slaving allies of the British shared Yamasee dismay over the growing imbalance in their economic relations with Carolina traders. In April 1715 Yamasees struck at the British, igniting a pan-Indian war in the American Southeast against Carolina known as "the Yamasee War." This conflict brought South Carolina to the brink of destruction and led to an exodus of Yamasees to Florida and Georgia, and ultimately to points east and west—Yamasees migrated in significant numbers to Cuba and Mexico, and many others joined the Creeks and eventually suffered the same forced removal to Oklahoma.

Yamasee history has received little scholarly attention outside recent studies of the Yamasee War. Although Yamasees frequently appear in the written colonial records, individuals and towns can be difficult to identify. Unlike the Christianized Apalachee, who co-inhabited with Yamasees on Florida missions and frequently wrote letters and petitions to the king of Spain and others, the Yamasees remained outsiders at the missions. They are discussed in the Spanish documents, but their voice is generally heard through the filter of others reporting what they said or did. The English records are generally less helpful than the Spanish, but provide important "news" about Yamasee activities, and offer some detail as Yamasees forged closer relations with Carolina. To enlarge the story of the Yamasee it is necessary to analyze the non-written archaeological sources—and this volume goes a long way in showing what archaeologists have uncovered through the material record of Yamasee life. Some of the questions they pose include: Who were the Yamasee? Where did they live at various times and what were the patterns of their migrations? How did Yamasee histories influence their subsequent lives in various places?

The collection of essays presented here is the product of many years of research, analysis, and discussion by historians and archaeologists, all of whom to varying degrees are ethnohistorians both in their methodologies and in their attempt to understand the Yamasees as a collection of peoples who developed their own unique culture. The authors place the Yamasee in a multiplicity of contexts and situations in early America. They seek a more holistic understanding of these unique people and their history in the colonial era. Earlier versions of the essays were presented at the first-ever conference devoted to Yamasee history, in St. Augustine, Florida, in the spring of 2015. This well-attended conference, "The Yamasee Indians from Florida to South Carolina," generated deep discussions of the Yamasee. The essays of this volume, which are expertly edited by Denise Bossy, one of the organizers of the conference, are foundational to Yamasee studies. Together, the conference and this volume provide the best model yet for how scholars of varying interests and methodologies can come together to help one another recover the history and lives of Native peoples. Ironically, like the Yamasees, these scholars' own mobility and adaptability has created a greater history than they would have produced as disconnected individuals from different disciplines—establishing a foundation for Yamasee history required the diversity of skills that this collective has brought forth and applied to an array of issues about Yamasee life. The stories told in this book, the questions raised, and the answers offered provide us the basis for moving forward in reconstructing Yamasee history through the centuries.

Acknowledgments

It was Eric Poplin who first brought together a small group of us with interest in the Yamasees and Guales. Presenting at the Society of Early Americanists and Ethnohistory conferences with Eric, Chester DePratter, David Hurst Thomas, and Amanda Hall laid the intellectual groundwork for the larger conference that Chester and I subsequently organized. I am particularly grateful for the constant support that Chester has given to this project. He and I set out to bring archaeologists and historians together to spark greater interest in and understanding of the Yamasees. Over the course of these years, we have not only done so but also become close friends. I am grateful to the scholars who participated in the Yamasee Conference and contributed to this volume, especially for their willingness to embark on the daunting task of returning the Yamasees to their rightful place in southern history. Alan Gallay has been both my sounding board and an unfailing source of encouragement throughout this project. Alan, John Worth, Charles Cobb, and Gifford Waters provided invaluable comments at the conference, helping to shape and improve these essays. Thank you also to Carl Halbirt and Bill Ramsey, whose contributions made the conference that much richer. Historian Donald Grinde (Yamasee) opened the conference with an insightful talk in which he encouraged us to think about the Yamasee past in light of Yamasee survival to the present day. Elders from the Okelevueha Band of Yamassee Seminoles and the Yamassee Nation of South Carolina attended the conference, and I am grateful for their continued support of my work, especially Chief LorenAshley Buford, Coe Buford, Chief Matriarch Brenda Red Crow, and Chief Se'khu Hadjo Gentle. Chief Little Buck Buford passed away before he could see this work come to fruition; his comments at the conference inspired and challenged all of us. Generous funding for the Yamasee conference was provided by the University of South Carolina's Institute of Archaeology and Anthropology, the University of North Florida's College of Arts and Science and Department of History, the St. Augustine Historical Society, and Flagler College. The conference was a success thanks to the hard work of Marianne Roberts, Michael Boyles, Charles Closmann, Magen Wilson, Laura Stevenson, and Patti Bibb. Students in my spring 2015 Southeastern Indians seminar were instrumental in helping to run the conference, especially Brittany Arias, Brittany Cohill, Allison Gordon, Shenice McField, Samantha Mizeras, and Will Pate. Our editor at the University of Nebraska Press, Matt Bokovoy, has been a source of consummate support and counsel. Finally, my family is unfailingly supportive of my work. Giles, Sabine, Kathy, and Michel-André, you make all of this possible.

THE YAMASEE INDIANS

Introduction

Recovering Yamasee History

DENISE I. BOSSY

It began in the heart of Pocotaligo, an important Upper Yamasee town that had so often been the meeting place between the Yamasees and the British. But during the early morning hours of April 15, 1715, the circumstances were dire. Rather than negotiating trade prices or wartime alliances, the British were themselves the subject of discussion and dispute. A small group of British agents had intruded on what was already a tense dialogue among the Yamasees, who had come together to consider how to best handle the expanding British colony of South Carolina, especially its traders. The Yamasees understood that the escalating enslavement of their kin, theft of their lands and property, and abuse of their leaders and people by British traders was largely a result of their increasing indebtedness to the Carolinians. (Perhaps they realized that the British traders were also struggling with mounting debts, as merchants began calling in their loans, taking numerous traders to court.) And so the Yamasees considered a plan that the Lower Creeks had advocated at a separate meeting just a short time earlier—to pay down their debts despite shrinking opportunities for their most lucrative endeavors: slave raiding and deer hunting.[1]

But then the British agents arrived. Without invitation. They claimed they wanted peace, but in the dark hours after the official meeting adjourned, word arrived that one of the agents—John Wright— threatened to kill four of the Yamasee Indian headmen and "take all of the rest of them for Slaves."[2] This cut the Yamasees to the core. They had themselves been born out of the violence of slavery. In the early

1660s their ancestors fled their homelands in interior Georgia to escape slave raids led by the Westo Indians, who sold their captives to Virginian colonists. Dispersing to the coast, fragments of the Altamaha, Ocute, and Ichisi chiefdoms began to coalesce. They briefly settled in Santa Elena, but then another series of Westo slave raids prompted them to move south, into La Florida, where they hoped that old Indian friends and new Spanish allies might offer them safe harbor. From the 1660s through the 1680s the Yamasees established twelve identifiable settlements in La Florida, the majority in the Guale-Mocama region north and south of the present-day border between coastal Georgia and Florida. Two decades passed, decades during which the Westos continued to attack and enslave Indians, especially those living in Spanish mission provinces.[3]

By the early 1680s it was evident to many of the Yamasees that they were far too vulnerable in La Florida. Not only slave raids, but pirate attacks, Spanish labor demands, pressure by Franciscans to convert, and a clash or two with local Indian leaders, prompted the Yamasees to leave in a number of waves. Following them in this exodus were many of the Guales, who would become the primary inhabitants of the Yamasees' Upper Towns once in South Carolina. The first Yamasees to leave La Florida briefly settled along the Savannah River, but by 1684 they had moved north, returning to Santa Elena (Port Royal), where there was soon a new Scottish settlement called Stuarts Town. Their confederation at Port Royal was impressive, incorporating over a thousand Yamasees and Guales who came from the Savannah River, Guale-Mocama, Apalachicola, and Apalachee.[4]

As their numbers grew, the Yamasees also began to engage in slave raiding, with encouragement from the Scots and English. Some fifty Yamasees traveled back to La Florida in 1685, destroying a Franciscan mission and coming away with more than twenty Timucuas.[5] While the Yamasees were not indiscriminate slavers, and surely not all Yamasee men engaged in slave raiding, for the next thirty years the Yamasees were one of the most active slave raiding communities in the Southeast and sold many of their captives to the British, exchanging them for guns, knives, pots, needles, mirrors, rum, and other objects. The Yamasees kept some of these goods but used others to strengthen their alliances, funneling them into old and new gift exchange networks, thereby balancing the red paths of Indian slaving and warfare with white paths of diplomacy, kinship, and trade.[6] It is not yet possible to quantify how many of the fifty thousand southeastern Indians enslaved during this period were captured and sold to the Carolinians by the Yamasees. We do know that the Yamasees were part of the major slave raids that the British engaged in for reasons that were both geopolitical and economic, especially those led by James Moore into La Florida in 1702 and likely again in 1703–4 during Queen Anne's War. A contingent of Yamasees also joined Colonel John Barnwell on his campaign into North Carolina during the Tuscarora War over the winter of 1711–12. But Yamasees more often led their own slave raids, and from 1685 to roughly 1715 they embarked on numerous raids into La Florida and North Carolina. This dangerous commerce jeopardized the stability of the entire South, devastating countless Indian communities, normalizing unprecedented levels of violence, and serving as the avenue for the proliferation of the first region-wide epidemics.[7]

Increasingly a number of scholars have categorized the Yamasees as a "militaristic slaving society" along with other southeastern Indian communities such as the Westos, Creeks, and Chickasaws.[8] However, in type casting the Yamasees as slavers we risk overlooking the reality that even as some Yamasees assumed the role of slavers, they also remained vulnerable to enslavement. The Yamasees did not need to conjure up memories of Westo slave raids to realize the fragility of their own freedom, though understanding their experiences as the targets of slave raiders helps to explain why they turned to slave raiding. They had only to look around Port Royal and Goose Creek to see that many colonists, including the traders who had storehouses in Yamasee towns, also had Indian slaves on their plantations. John Wright, for example, owned numerous Indian slaves, including "Maria Yamasee" (perhaps her Spanish name indicated that Maria was a Guale Yamasee born in a Spanish mission in La Florida).[9] Much more than the lure of British goods, especially weapons, this was the reason for Yamasee involvement in the Indian slave trade. To protect their loved ones and their sovereignty, to attract new clans people, to survive the onslaught of colonialism, some of the Yamasees became slavers. But it was a costly endeavor. The Yamasees lost hundreds of their warriors to the violence of slave wars.[10] And even as they tried to direct slave raiding away from their communities and their allies, the Yamasees also lost family members to enslavement. After the fall of the Apalachee mission chain in 1704, the Yamasees had to travel ever farther in search of new captives.[11] As the number of captives they brought back to South Carolina shrank, so did the Yamasees' value to the British as free people. In the past the Yamasees had periodically complained about traders illegally enslaving their kin.[12] Those complaints grew far more common by the 1710s. Traders increasingly seized Yamasee family members, claiming them as a form of debt repayment.[13] While some were redeemed, there were other individual Yamasees who remained enslaved on plantations in South Carolina and beyond. And there were signs that the wholesale enslavement of Yamasee communities was on the horizon.[14] John Wright's threat was not empty.

While by no means the sole cause of the Yamasee War, Wright's tirade helped to ignite a war that very nearly destroyed South Carolina. Knowing the British well from years of trade, the Yamasees assembled at Pocotaligo did what seemed most logical to them and what their justice system demanded: they killed Wright and the other traders sent as agents (only two of whom managed to escape). Prepared to fight for their land, the Yamasees secured the main routes into their Upper and Lower towns and then turned to attack the colonial settlement at Port Royal that had increasingly posed a threat to their sovereignty and people. While they intended to stay in their homelands, a series of colonial counterattacks forced the Yamasees to flee southward. Dispersing in May 1715, several hundred Yamasees ultimately made their way to La Florida, where they were invited by the Spanish to settle in communities near St. Augustine.[15] Perhaps as many as eight hundred Yamasees did not go to St. Augustine but went inland, likely retreating first to Savano Town and then moving with the Lower Creeks when they returned to the Chattahoochee in early 1716.[16] For many of the Yamasees the war continued for decades. They periodically raided colonial settlements in and near their former South Carolina homelands. And the British embarked on a campaign to annihilate the Yamasees.[17]

The war that began in Pocotaligo spread quickly. Labeling this event "the Yamasee War" masks the participation of many other Indian communities in what was a pan-Indian war. It is true that the Yamasees engaged in the most sustained and direct fighting, living as they did on lands surrounded by colonial settlers who progressively pushed into their territory. They also held out against the British far longer than any other community. The Cherokees signed a peace treaty with the British in 1716 and the Creeks in 1717. But the Yamasees were far from alone in striking against the British. Most scholars believe that the war was largely decentralized. Indian towns and communities generally chose of their own accord whether or not to engage in violence against the British. At their discretion, too, they decided what form of violence to inflict. But there is evidence of some coordinated campaigns—especially those involving the Yamasees and Lower Creeks—and of widespread communication about the war along indigenous networks.

This pan-Indian war was, to a large extent, a retaliation against British traders. And this dimension of the war had the broadest level of support and spurred the most participation. Within weeks, Yamasees, Lower Creeks, Catawbas and other piedmont Indians, then Upper Creeks, Choctaws, Cherokees, and even Chickasaws collectively killed ninety of the one hundred British traders then in their towns. A smaller number of Indians also engaged in direct assaults on the colony, generally those who had the most intensive interactions with the British and lived fairly close to Carolina's settlements. Soon after the early campaign by the Yamasees (likely joined by some Lower Creeks), two regional coalitions of Indians emerged. Beginning in late May 1715, the "Northern Indians"—Catawbas, other piedmont Indians, and (early on) Cherokees—began to engage the British. When the South Carolinians mobilized a large force against these Northern Indians in July, a coalition of six to seven hundred "Southern Indians," consisting of Yamasees, Apalachees, Lower Creeks, Euchees, and Savannahs, marched over the now undefended southern route into the low country. Crossing over the Edisto River, they burned dozens of plantations and the Pon Pon bridge, a key link in the path between Charleston and Port Royal. By the end of the summer the Northern coalition was spent and expressed their interest in a rapprochement with the

British. For the Indians in the Southern coalition, peace was slower in coming if it came at all.[18]

The Yamasee War was a transformative event, as its Indian participants had intended. Almost an entire generation of British traders and several hundred colonists lost their lives. The commercial enslavement of Indians came to a fairly swift end, and as South Carolina tried to rebuild its Indian trade—now a trade predominantly in deerskins—colonial officials made a far more concerted effort to inhibit and curb trade abuses by (briefly) establishing a state monopoly to control the trade. But the unintended consequences of the war were tremendous. The Yamasees were forced to abandon their homelands. Though it took years, colonial settlers ultimately took over Yamasee lands in waves of rice plantations. The war accelerated the rise of the old South, as South Carolinians turned even more intensely to plantation agriculture and the African slave trade. Though Indians were no longer the target of intensive slaving, those enslaved before the Yamasee War remained in bondage. The war also prompted many southeastern Indians and the British to consolidate their geopolitical authority. For the Carolinians this entailed a revolt against their Proprietors and a turn to Crown rule. For the Creeks and Cherokees this meant developing even more powerful confederacies. An era of intensive imperial competition followed as Creeks, British, and Spanish all fought for control of the debatable land—the borderlands between South Carolina and La Florida. Often in the middle of this fight were the Yamasees. The Yamasee War had truly transformed the South.[19]

The Yamasee Indians are best known for the two events outlined here: their involvement in the Indian slave trade and the war that took their name. Over the last fifteen years the study of Indian slavery has emerged as one of the most productive fields in southern history, catalyzed by Alan Gallay's watershed study of the commercial Indian slave trade that engulfed the South between 1670 and 1715. In both Gallay's work and subsequent studies of Indian slavery, the Yamasees are consistently identified both as "South Carolina's closest allies" and as major suppliers of Indian captives for the commercial slave trade.[20] Indian slavery has also increasingly been recognized as a major cause of the Yamasee War, yet the war itself has not attracted the same level of scholarly interest. Since the 1928 publication of Verner Crane's *The Southern Frontier, 1670–1732*, there have been just two book-length scholarly studies of the war. Covering the same chronological scope as Crane's classic tome, historian Steven Oatis situated the war in a broader analysis of the complex cross-cultural relations of the early South, arguing that participants on both sides of this conflict were not united and offering a useful analysis of how different Indian communities determined the level and contours of their participation in the war. In a sensitive analysis of the war, historian William Ramsey put Indians and ethnohistorical methodology more squarely at the center of his study to understand better the "sparks" that ignited the war, the war itself, and its aftermath. Through a deep reconstruction of cross-cultural diplomacy, trade, and Indian networks, Ramsey made a compelling argument that the Yamasees, Lower Creeks, and other southeastern Indians were responding to economic stresses and a deterioration not just of trade relations but of political communication with South Carolina, as officials and traders neglected Indian diplomacy in the years leading up to the war, distracted by their own political factionalism.[21] Despite the merits of these works, the Yamasee War largely remains the purview of early southern archaeologists and historians, little known outside the region, while Indian slavery studies is quickly becoming a field of its own.[22] Still, with the exception of a master's thesis by David McKivergan, there are no published, book-length studies that focus on the Yamasee Indians at all.

Modern study of the Yamasees began in the late 1980s when archaeologist Chester DePratter began to work with two graduate students on Yamasee sites in South Carolina, launching the Yamasee Archaeological Project, which yielded important master's theses by William Green and David McKivergan. Collectively the work by DePratter, McKivergan, and Green represented the first attempt at comprehensive reconstruction of Yamasee ethnogenesis and their early migrations during the seventeenth century.[23] This work resulted in the reconstruction of Yamasee ancestral origins in interior Georgia, their migrations into La Florida and South Carolina, and most significant, the identification of over a dozen Yamasee sites in South Carolina and of a preliminary Yamasee archaeological signature. A mix of San Marcos/ Altamaha ceramics together with some Spanish and British goods, this signature reflects both Yamasee origins and their seventeenth-century migrations.[24] The number of Yamasee sites identified by archaeologists working in South Carolina has more than doubled since the 1980s. However, because much of that work has been the product of private economic development projects, reports are not always available for every site, and many collections in need of analysis are left waiting for future scholarly interest or funding.[25]

While ethnohistorians have yet to embark on an endeavor comparable to the Yamasee Archaeological Project, a number have helped to piece together more of the Yamasees' complex history. In their studies of Florida Indians, John Hann and John Worth have done much to advance our understanding of the Yamasees who lived in La Florida during the first Spanish period. Worth's essay in the *Handbook of North American Indians* remains one of the most significant studies of the Yamasees, particularly by identifying five distinct historical phases of their migration and coalescence between 1659 and 1763, a chronological structure that informs many of the essays in this anthology.[26] More recently ethnohistorians have begun to examine the indigenous networks that connected disparate Indian communities across the Native South, and this construct has proven extremely useful for advancing our understanding of the Yamasees because networks were so essential to their coalescences and migrations. In his study of the gift exchange networks that linked Native communities across the South, Joseph Hall offers a nuanced analysis of the relationship between the Yamasees and Lower Creeks during the decades prior to the Yamasee War. Alejandra Dubcovksy's incisive study of the indigenous information networks that shaped the South reveals that for many southeastern Indians, notably the Yamasees, network building—especially control over information—was essential to their political power as they tried to contain European colonial ambitions.[27]

In the past decade new archaeological work has emerged on Yamasee sites in Florida, especially under the stewardship of Carl Halbirt, St. Augustine's formidable city archaeologist. Marshaling crews of volunteers, Halbirt has excavated some of the major Yamasee sites that date from roughly 1717 to 1763 in St. Augustine: La Punta, Pocotalaca, and Nombre de Dios.[28] This work has been analyzed by a number of graduate students, leading to three master's theses focusing on La Punta and one on Pocotalaca. Additionally, a dissertation by Gifford Waters examines Indian mission communities in St. Augustine after the Yamasee War more broadly, including La Punta and Pocotalaca, where, he finds, Yamasees were able to retain their traditional identities to a greater extent than other Indians in this highly multi-ethnic and coalescent environment.[29] Still, much work remains to be done in Florida. Most notably, there has been virtually no archaeological analysis of late seventeenth- and early eighteenth-century Yamasee sites.[30]

Part of what has complicated study of the Yamasees is their mobility. With some notable exceptions, the Yamasees generally moved at least every twenty to thirty years during the first hundred years of their community history. And, with the exception of their time in South Carolina, the Yamasees usually lived in dispersed communities that could be hundreds of miles apart. Though this unusual strategy of dispersal was empowering, it also helps to explain their near invisibility in the scholarship. Their many and often simultaneous migrations have made understanding the Yamasees a real challenge. Yet their choices about where to settle also aid in their study, for the Yamasees often placed themselves at significant geopolitical crossroads, seeing opportunity there. The result is that the Yamasees appear at select moments in British, Spanish, and archaeological records. Recovering Yamasee history thus requires collaboration between historians and archaeologists across the Southeast, and this is the project that we embark upon together in this volume.

The contributors to the volume assembled from April 16 to 18, 2015, three hundred years after the start of the Yamasee War. Meeting in St. Augustine, we were just blocks away from sites where some Yamasee refugees established new towns after the war. Inspired but not constrained by the tercentenary, we set out to recover a richer history of the Yamasees before, during, and after the war. Collectively the essays in this first ever anthology on the Yamasees seek to answer elusive questions about Yamasee identity, Yamasee political and social networks, and the fate of the Yamasees after the Yamasee War. What makes this collection particularly important is that the contributors are archaeologists of South Carolina and Florida, and historians of the Native South, Spanish Florida, and British Carolina, coming together for the first time to answer these questions.

Our anthology covers crucial periods in Yamasee history: their coalescence in the seventeenth century; their several migrations in Georgia, Florida, and South Carolina during the seventeenth and eighteenth centuries; and their survival in the century after the Yamasee War. Collectively we examine Yamasees at the community, town, and individual level and reconstruct their many and complex social and political networks. In the process we have also developed new insights that are essential to understanding southeastern Indians. The Yamasees were at the center of events that reshaped the South, often situating themselves in contested borderlands, and also built connections to numerous Indian, European, and African communities. As a result, in reconstructing their experiences we also shed new light on the early South more broadly.

In part 1 of the book scholars examine "Yamasee Identity," especially by reconstructing the formative phase of Yamasee ethnogenesis: their initial coalescence along the Georgia coastline, early migrations into Spanish Florida, and their exodus to South Carolina. In chapter 1 historian Amy Bushnell offers a comprehensive historical overview of Yamasee migrations and their relationship with the Spanish of La Florida, focusing on the period from the 1660s to the 1710s. She also provides an illuminating analysis of Yamasee mentality. Arguing that the Yamasees were a freedom-loving people, Bushnell understands Yamasee geopolitical decisions as largely driven by their intent to remain free and independent. Having once been the victims of slave raids, the Yamasees sought to protect their independence at all costs. This entailed the freedom to live where and how they chose and to make and break alliances. Perhaps recognizing this, the British actively courted the Yamasees by professing to protect the "liberty of conscience" of their Indian allies. Their own role as slave raiders while living near the British from the 1680s to 1710s only further strengthened Yamasee resolve to protect their freedom, resolve that frustrated

Introduction   11

Spanish officials and missionaries who sought to bring the Yamasees into subjection.

In chapter 2 Keith Ashley also asks what it meant to be Yamasee and teases out answers from recent archaeological findings. Focusing on late seventeenth-century Yamasee settlements in peninsular Florida, Ashley suggests that Yamasee identity was largely geopolitical during this first stage of ethnogenesis. Ethnically diverse, geographically dispersed, and politically decentralized, the Yamasees of the 1660s–1680s were a "resistance movement" within the Spanish mission system, and attracted Indians who similarly sought to reject Catholicism and to assert their autonomy. But rather than withdraw or seclude themselves, the Yamasees developed their identity through and against their interactions with Indians and Europeans.

One of the issues that Ashley and other contributors in the volume tackle is the perplexing question of how to identify the Yamasees in the archaeological record. The problem is particularly acute in Florida because the Yamasees produced the same type of pottery as the Guales and Mocamas (San Marcos/Altamaha) and primarily occupied Guale and Mocama sites while living in La Florida, making it nearly impossible to discern specific Yamasee occupations within these sites. The answer, Ashley suggests, may be for Florida archaeologists to examine Yamasee sites to the south of the Guale-Mocama region, where indigenous communities produced St. Johns rather than San Marcos pottery. This research could lead to the identification of a specific Yamasee archaeological signature in La Florida.

While Florida archaeologists (and historians) have focused on mission Indians, almost completely ignoring early Yamasee sites, this is not true of South Carolina, and yet the same problem of how to identify an archaeological signature specific to the Yamasees apart from other San Marcos/Altamaha producers is also present in that field. Taking up this problem in chapter 3, Eric Poplin and Jon Marcoux trace changes in pottery—produced by women working within their own kin groups—to determine how the Yamasees' identity changed as they migrated from interior Georgia to the coast. What they find is that Yamasee potters adopted the San Marcos/Altamaha pottery forms and motifs of the Spanish mission Indians while living in Guale, likely in an effort to fit in with other Indians groups along the coast even as they rejected Spanish Catholicism. Once in South Carolina the Yamasees continued to produce San Marcos/Altamaha pottery but, Poplin and Marcoux suggest, there may be an identifiable regional variation. The Guales who settled into the Upper Yamasee towns seem to have continued to carve paddles with complex designs, while those Yamasees originally from interior Georgia who settled into the Lower Yamasee towns produced paddles with simple lines and then over-stamped to produce more complex designs. Taken together chapters 2 and 3 suggest that focusing on paddle stamping techniques may be one way to distinguish the pottery produced by interior Georgia Yamasees in sites across Florida as well as South Carolina. Southeastern archaeologists are currently in the midst of an important debate about the meaning of pottery styles. John Worth, in particular, argues that pottery styles tell us not who the potters were ethnically but rather with whom they interacted.[31] Shared technologies, styles, and motifs therefore could tell us a great deal about the connections that Yamasee women had with other Indian women in and beyond the Yamasee world.

Another distinct form of Yamasee identity production is also evident in Yamasee sites in South Carolina, one aimed at communicating Yamasee status and power to outsiders. Through their trade alliance with the British, the Yamasees were able to establishing a daunting reputation across the region as warriors and slave raiders. They not only accumulated an unusually large number of trade goods and firearms but also fashioned decorations out of their goods and booty, as Poplin and Marcoux demonstrate in their chapter. Yamasee warriors wore gun parts as gorgets (pendants), attached reckoning counters to their clothing, and slipped Catholic rings taken from captives onto their fingers. These displays were physical proof of Yamasee military success and power.

It is worth remembering that this posturing was not only functional but also necessary. Born out of the chaos of slave raids and other colonial stresses that were so severe that scholars increasingly describe the whole of the Southeast as a shatter zone during this period, the Yamasees survived by migrating, creating a portable culture and military reputation that attracted refugees.[32] But what were the effects of migration on their cultural practices? In chapter 4 archaeologist Alex Sweeney tackles the question of cultural change. Focusing on what scholars have long considered to be the primary town of the Lower Yamasees—Altamaha—he finds meaningful continuities between late Mississippian Oconee chiefdoms and the descendant community of Altamaha both in domestic and public spaces.[33] There were dramatic changes, to be sure. While living in South Carolina, the Yamasees became slave raiders and commercial hunters who focused far less on intensive agriculture. And colonization took a toll. Most notably, Yamasee family sizes progressively decreased, first as they moved to South Carolina and then again as they fled to St. Augustine during the Yamasee War. Yet in some of the most significant ways, the Altamaha Yamasees lived and died like their ancestors. They built and laid out their homes in much the same way and engaged in many of the same domestic practices. Perhaps most significant, the South Carolina Altamahas buried their dead as their ancestors had: within their houses, in semi-flexed or flexed positions with burial goods, all signs that they had largely rejected Christian conversion efforts.

Part of the Yamasees' success in weathering Westo slave raids, Spanish missionization, the commercial slave raid, and British expansionism, rested on their considerable ability to build networks with other Indians, especially the Guales and Apalachicolas (Lower Creeks), as well as enslaved Africans and (more selectively) with the Spanish and British. The Yamasees were skilled diplomats with a vast network of alliances that stretched across much of the Southeast. Part 2 of this book, "Yamasee Networks," examines the political and social networks that grounded the Yamasees and supported their mobility and survival.

In chapter 5, I focus on the lengthy trip made to England by a seventeen-year-old Yamasee "Prince," the only southeastern Indian dignitary to travel to England between 1672 and 1730 and one of the few to convert nominally to Anglicanism. The Prince sought to forge a new network for the Yamasees, especially with his own town of Euhaw, which had just recently joined the Yamasees in South Carolina after spending over a hundred years living in the Spanish mission province of Guale. To help his town negotiate its status within the Yamasee world, to gain new skills and connections for his future as the next mico (chief) of his town, and to strengthen the Yamasees' alliance with the British, the Prince traveled to the political and spiritual center of the British world. But metropole British missionaries sought to transform him into an agent of British imperialism, and British colonists enslaved the Prince's family during the Yamasee War even though his uncle (the mico of the Euhaws) did not join in the war and tried to maintain peace with the British. The Prince's voyage ultimately was a failure, but it reveals how the Euhaw Yamasees attempted to construct a new network through the practice of "spiritual diplomacy." While ethnohistorians working on Indian "conversion" in other regions have fruitfully unpacked this concept, revealing how many Indians translated Christian concepts into indigenous terms and appropriated these for their own purposes, the same cannot be said of La Florida and South Carolina. My essay provides a much-needed Yamasee perspective on religious encounters with the Spanish and British.

Even as the violence unleashed by European imperialism and slave regimes shattered the lives of the Prince's family and other Native communities across the Southeast, the Yamasees found new allies who had also suffered under South Carolina's oppressive regime: enslaved Africans. Chapter 6, by historian Jane Landers, demonstrates that Yamasee connections with Africans likely began in the late seventeenth century but became most meaningful and most evident during the Yamasee War, when many Africans joined Yamasee troops. Fighting the British in common, the Yamasees and Africans forged treaties between their communities and relocated together to St. Augustine after the war. Into the 1720s Yamasees and Africans continued to raid South Carolina with Spanish encouragement and (at times) assistance, liberating enslaved Africans on many of their raids. Careful not to generalize, Landers does point to other moments when particular Yamasees (especially Yfallaquisca) treated Africans as chattel. But for the most part, Yamasees guided enslaved Africans on their flight to St. Augustine, liberated enslaved people, and joined with escaped slaves on guerilla raids against the British, forging cultural and familial ties that lasted well beyond the eighteenth century.

While the Yamasee War facilitated the incorporation of Africans into Yamasee networks, it also led to the destruction of some of the

Yamasees' most crucial networks with some Lower Creek communities. The Yamasee War is the subject of historian Steven Hahn's work in chapter 7. Hahn focuses on a neglected legacy of the war: the long period of violence between the Yamasees and select Lower Creek factions, especially the Pon Pon Indians and the Yamacraws. This was a particularly personal brand of violence. The Yamasees and Lower Creeks were deeply connected by generations of kinship, friendship, and political alliance. But the war forced the Yamasees and Creeks to make hard choices. Even as the Yamasee raids against South Carolina nurtured their alliances with Africans and the Spanish, the British increasingly pressured the Creeks to distance themselves from this violence by moving against the Yamasees, especially after the British invaded St. Augustine to strike against the Yamasees in 1728. Not all Lower Creeks severed their network with the Yamasees living among them or in St. Augustine but, especially for those Lower Creek factions allied with the British, sustaining both networks became impossible and led to violence that lasted well into the 1740s. Hahn's work demonstrates the value of examining the war from Yamasee and Lower Creek perspectives. In so doing he fundamentally changes our understanding of the war's time line and reveals its lasting consequences for Yamasee and Lower Creek relationships.

In part 3 of the book, "Surviving the Yamasee War," archaeologists and historians come together to consider what happened to Yamasee communities after the Yamasee War, pushing back against narratives that interpret this period as one of simple decline for the Yamasees. As they abandoned South Carolina, the Yamasees fled to three major zones: St. Augustine, Apalachicola, and Apalachee. Here Yamasee communities survived by reviving, reconstructing, or building anew networks with the Spanish and those Lower Creek towns that were not part of the violence recounted by Hahn. In chapter 8 archaeologist and historian Amanda Hall explains how the Yamasees of Pocotalaca—the descendant community of the Upper Yamasee Town of Pocotaligo—were able to preserve their culture when they returned to La Florida by making themselves politically important to the Spanish. By serving as spies and military allies for the Spanish, the Pocotalacas carved out cultural space for themselves and were thereby able to maintain their lifeways and socioeconomic activities, from the foods they ate, to the pottery they produced, to their smoking and architectural practices. Over the decades the Pocotalacas weathered epidemics and numerous attacks by Creeks, Yuchis, and the British. Though their population declined and they became increasingly isolated from other Yamasee communities outside northeast Florida, the Pocotalacas nonetheless maintained their identity and political status. Even when compelled to aggregate with other mission Indians, Pocotalaca retained its former prominence. Even as he moved his people into Nombre de Dios in 1759, Pocotalaca's cacique Juan Sanchez assumed the leadership of this diverse community.

Emphasizing coalescence as one of the strategies pursued by the Yamasees during the diaspora that followed the Yamasee War, in chapter 9 archaeologist Andrea White examines the Yamasee town of La Punta in St. Augustine. Established shortly after the 1725 destruction of the Yamasee town of Candelaria de la Tamaja by Lower Creek Indians, La Punta was likely created by the survivors of Tamaja, who briefly relocated to Moze, incorporated the Apalachees living there, and then moved en masse to the southern outskirts of St. Augustine. Through a pattern of coalescence and local migration, the La Punta Yamasees endured this difficult period by periodically evacuating their town when attacked, relocating to the Castillo or elsewhere. This approach proved successful in two major ways. First, while the Indian population around St. Augustine declined markedly from the 1720s to the 1750s, the population of La Punta grew by incorporating other Indians and perhaps mestizos and Africans. Second, archaeological evidence reveals that La Punta's inhabitants—much like the Yamasees at Pocotalaca—were largely able to continue their traditional customs and lifeways. Only in the late 1750s did La Punta aggregate with one of the last two remaining Indian refugee towns in St. Augustine.

While the Yamasees at Pocotalaca and La Punta drew on traditional strategies to maintain their political and cultural autonomy as they negotiated their status within Spanish St. Augustine, other Indians survived by joining Spanish society and becoming vecinos (residents). In chapter 10 historian Susan Parker reconstructs the remarkable life of Cacique Jospogue to illustrate these two different paths as taken by the Guales. Jospogue remained in La Florida even as the majority of Guales—including much of his lineage—joined the Yamasees in their general exodus from Spanish Florida during the 1680s. While the Jospos who went to South Carolina established the Upper Yamasee town of Huspah, Cacique Jospogue became the cacique of those Guales who remained in La Florida. During the Yamasee War the Huspah "king" led his people from South Carolina back to La Florida, where they settled into a Yamasee mission community. Meanwhile, Cacique Jospogue began to lay the foundation for a different move: out of the world of mission villages and into Spanish St. Augustine. By securing a pension and mobilizing his baptismal connections, Jospogue was finally able to relocate his family into St. Augustine proper in the 1730s, where they lived on the appropriately named St. George Street—the street to San Jorge (Charleston)—and where they became part of a small group of long-term, elite mission Indians who joined Spanish society.

In the final essay archaeologist and ethnohistorian John Worth shifts our focus from St. Augustine to West Florida, which became an important resettlement zone for many Yamasees. Examining two Yamasee communities—Tamasle in Apalachee and Punta Rasa in Pensacola—Worth identifies persistence in Yamasee approaches to resettlement. Even as these Yamasees respectively left Lower Creek towns in the 1720s and St. Augustine in the 1740s—under mounting pressure and direct attacks by the British and Creeks—they nonetheless continued to seek out geopolitically strategic areas. Led by savvy caciques who, like the Yamasee Prince, were fluent in Spanish culture and language, these Yamasee bands positioned themselves as influential middlemen in the Spanish-Creek borderlands. By moving out of Lower Creek and Spanish towns and taking on the roles of intermediaries, they were largely able to avoid the violence that had plagued their communities in the previous decades. As a result, they also survived as Yamasee communities well beyond the eighteenth century. The Punta Rasa Yamasees left with the Spanish in 1763, settling in Vera Cruz, where their descendants likely remain today, and the Tamasle Yamasees became part of the Apalachicola band, who were granted their own separate reservation apart from the Seminoles in 1823.

As naturalist William Bartram traveled across Georgia and Florida in 1773 and 1774 he tripped across evidence of Yamasee history and survival. In a series of disjointed vignettes, Bartram described an alleged Yamasee graveyard; recounted a Creek legend of "incomparably beautiful" Yamasee women rumored to live in the Okefenokee swamp, where they were fiercely guarded by their husbands; and came face-to-face with Yamasee slaves whom the Alachua leader Cowkeeper had purportedly taken captive as a young man. With a local trader's help, Bartram was able to locate "a very ancient Chief" who could put some of the pieces together. Couching Yamasee history in terms that reinforced Creek alliance with the British and Creek geopolitical dominance, this chief explained that long ago the Creeks had "intirely conquered and extirpated" the Yamasees for their alliance with the Spanish, all "except a small remnant," whom they allowed to live among them.[34] Even on the eve of the American Revolution and with both Floridas in British hands, the Yamasees still symbolized a (failed) resistance movement against the British. To effect this reworking of historical memory, Bartram and his Creek informants had to forget that the Yamasees had been British (and Creek) allies for more than twenty years and to remember only that some Yamasees had allied with the Spanish after the Yamasee War. Even as Bartram came across living Yamasee people or stories of Yamasee survival, he constructed them as little more than remnants, slaves, ancients, or legends.

To be fair to Bartram, he has not been alone in struggling to make sense of Yamasee history. Outside of slave raiding or the Yamasee War, the Yamasees still appear only sporadically in studies of southern history and archaeology. Their culture and political structure, the complexities of their many migrations, their kinship networks, and their survival have remained largely mysterious to most scholars.

In this volume archaeologists and historians weave the fractured narratives of Yamasee experiences and ask probing questions about their mobility, identity, and networks in order to recover more fully the history of this important community.

One of the most important questions that we seek to answer is simply who the Yamasee were. It is a deceptively simple question. What it meant to be Yamasee and who the Yamasees were changed over the time period under study. Rather than their being a cohesive cultural, ethnic, or political group, our work demonstrates that the Yamasees engaged in numerous instances of coalescence, migration, and reformulation over the course of a full century and more. By analyzing what Yamasees understood as their identity through their political and social behaviors and choices, we identify three major patterns in what we might call Yamasee identity.

First, at the town and community level the Yamasees incorporated outsiders with remarkable frequency and success. This is perhaps most evident during their time in South Carolina, when hundreds of Guales and some Apalachicolas and Apalachees joined their nascent confederacy. But it also remained a vital strategy well beyond the Yamasee War in places like St. Augustine, where La Punta Yamasees were able to reverse demographic decline under severe stress by incorporating new people. To an unusual degree, the Yamasees also fostered political alliances with Africans, some of whom joined in the common fight against British exploitation, and some of whom became kin. As Guales, Africans, and others joined the Yamasees, they brought skills, knowledge, and practices that benefited the Yamasees as a whole. Many of the Guales who joined the Yamasees, for example, had long experience in spiritual diplomacy with the Spanish and had appropriated elements of the Spanish religious educational system. At least some of the enslaved Africans who allied with the Yamasees during the Yamasee War were highly skilled warriors, linguists, artisans, and agriculturalists. And yet the Yamasees did not enforce a singular cultural identity. This, in fact, was one of their greatest strengths.

Second, the Yamasees greatly valued networking. They were willing to aggregate, coalesce, and relocate to a degree that was unusual (though not unique) in the Native South. To balance their physical mobility and cultural diversity they embraced opportunities to build new networks with Indians, Europeans, and Africans. Evidence of these networks comes from both historical and archaeological sources. When Yamasees first established settlements in La Florida, Yamasee women began to produce the regional variant of pottery with remarkable speed. When they relocated to South Carolina, they retained this pottery style even as they accumulated an unprecedented quantity of British trade goods, including guns. Altamaha pottery and British goods were physical manifestations of the power of Yamasee networks. These connections proved useful to a point. But when they led to severe clashes over a host of issues ranging from conversion to debt to political independence, the Yamasees could and did break their alliances with the Spanish, British, and even the Lower Creeks.

Finally, Yamasees were especially active in using a variety of political mechanisms to build and preserve their sovereignty, and this was central to their political identity. Yamasees fervently and self-consciously protected their "freedom" and "liberty." Yamasee communities moved great distances when they felt that their ability to make decisions about their religion, political alliances, labor, lifestyle, and status as free people was threatened. The Yamasees actively constructed their identity in juxtaposition to other communities who wanted alliance to entail subjection, especially the Spanish and British. They valued freedom, sovereignty as they defined it, and were willing to change political course to protect this, from allying with the Spanish to becoming slave raiders, warring against the most powerful European colony in the Southeast, and making hard choices to adopt new political organizations and coalesce with new communities. It was their well-defined sense of what freedom meant that led them to see enslaved Africans as true allies. To preserve that sovereignty, the Yamasees also proved time and again that they were not risk adverse but were willing to move into contested geographical spaces and to reformulate their networks, families, and communities. The Yamasees were able to craft a cohesive identity that was flexible enough to accommodate this level of geopolitical and social change. The stories of Yamasees and Guales like Prince George, the Mico Huspah, Cacique Jospogue, Mico Yfallaquisca, and Mico Andrés Escudero demonstrate that Yamasees and their kin did not pursue one singular path.

Collectively we reveal how Yamasee individuals and communities took decisive action as they negotiated their way through the shockwaves caused by European colonization. Despite the considerable toll of the Yamasee War, its long legacy, and persistent borderlands violence, the Yamasees were able to sustain their identities and cultures on their own terms. As the following essays reveal, they were far more than the remnants described by Bartram and his Creek informants.

Introduction

The political decisions they made enabled them to define and protect daily life well beyond the Yamasee War. From Altamaha in South Carolina to Pocolataca in St. Augustine, the Yamasees maintained their cultural identity as expressed in their homes and graves through the second half of the eighteenth century. This is not to say that the Yamasees did not suffer tremendously. For, as these essays reveal, the cost of fighting for Yamasee sovereignty was tremendous.

Notes

Thank you to Michel-André Bossy, Alan Gallay, and Steve Hahn for their insightful comments on an earlier version of this chapter.

1. For an account of the war's start by Yamasee and Lower Creek representatives, translated by a Christian Guale and recorded by a Spanish scribe, see Autos y demas diligencias, May 28, 1715, enclosed in Governor Francisco Córcoles y Martínez to the King, January 25, 1716, Archivo General de Indias, Santo Domingo 843, Stetson Collection, St. Augustine Historical Society, Florida. For a British account see George Rodd, lettre à son employeur, May 8, 1715, CO 5/387, no. 1, Records of the Colonial Office, National Archives, London (hereafter cited as CO). For the best recent analyses of the Yamasee War see William L. Ramsey, *The Yamasee War: A Study of Culture, Economy, Conflict in the Colonial South* (Lincoln: University of Nebraska Press, 2008); Joseph M. Hall, *Zamumo's Gifts: Indian-European Exchange in the Colonial Southeast* (Philadelphia: University of Pennsylvania Press, 2009), 117–44; Steven J. Oatis, *A Colonial Complex: South Carolina's Frontiers in the Era of the Yamasee War, 1680–1730* (Lincoln: University of Nebraska Press, 2004), 112–39; Alan Gallay, *The Indian Slave Trade: The Rise of the English Empire in the American South, 1670–1717* (New Haven: Yale University Press, 2002), 315–45. On traders struggling with mounting debts see Denise I. Bossy, "Godin & Co.: Charleston Merchants and the Indian Trade, 1674–1715," *South Carolina Historical Magazine* 114 (April 2013): 96–131. By all accounts it was Brims, the head mico of Coweta, who was the author of this debt relief plan. Ramsey, *Yamasee War*, 76–77.

2. Huspaw King to Charles Craven, enclosed in Captain Jonathan St. Lo to Burchett, July 12, 1715, in Ramsey, *Yamasee War*, 228.

3. John E. Worth, "Yamasee," in *Handbook of North American Indians*, vol. 14, *Southeast*, ed. Raymond D. Fogelson (Washington DC: Smithsonian Institution Press, 2004), 245–53.

4. Caleb Westbrooke to Colonel John Godfrey, Deputy-Governor, February 21, 1685, CO 5/287/028.

5. Amy Bushnell, this volume.

6. On gift giving and network construction see Hall, *Zamumo's Gifts*.

7. On Yamasee slave raids see especially John E. Worth, "Razing Florida: The Indian Slave Trade and the Devastation of Spanish Florida, 1659–1715," in *Mapping the Mississippian Shatter Zone: The Colonial Slave Trade and Regional Instability in the American South* (Lincoln: University of Nebraska Press, 2009); David La Vere, *The Tuscarora War: Indians, Settlers, and the Fight for the Carolina Colonies* (Chapel Hill: University of North Carolina Press, 2013). On the role of the Indian slave trade in making possible the South's initial region-wide epidemics, beginning in 1692, see Paul Kelton, *Epidemics and Enslavement: Biological Catastrophe in the Native Southeast, 1492–1715* (Lincoln: University of Nebraska Press, 2007).

8. This is part of Robbie Ethridge's broader work on what she terms the Mississippian shatter zone. For an overview of both constructs and their derivations see Denise I. Bossy, "Shattering Together, Merging Apart: Colonialism, Violence, and the Remaking of the Native South," *William and Mary Quarterly* 71 (October 2014): 611–31.

9. For an analysis of Wright's Indian slaveholding see Bossy, "Godin & Co.," 129.

10. Francis le Jau to the Secretary of the Society for the Propagation of the Gospel, August 10, 1713, in *The Carolina Chronicle of Dr. Francis le Jau, 1706–1717*, ed. Frank J. Klingberg (Berkeley: University of California Press, 1955), 134–35.

11. Thomas Nairne to the Lords Proprietors of Carolina, July 10, 1708, CO 5/382/Part 1/008.

12. For example, in 1692 the mico of Altamaha complained to the South Carolina Grand Council that a trader had enslaved his son. Entry for August 11, 1692, in *Journal of the Grand Council of South Carolina, April 11, 1692–September 26, 1692*, ed. A. S. Salley (Columbia SC: State Company, 1907), 55.

13. For an example of Yamasees lodging complaints that traders had falsely enslaved their kin see Entry on July 28, 1711, *Journals of the Commissioners of the Indian Trade: September 20, 1710–August 29, 1718*, ed. W. L. McDowell Jr. (Columbia: South Carolina Archives Department, 1955), 11.

14. One sign that greatly worried the Yamasees was the census taken of their towns by the British in 1715 and their belief that the English had kidnapped and sold Indian children as slaves. Hall, *Zamumo's Gifts*, 122–24.

15. A 1717 census by the Spanish revealed three Yamasee towns: Our Lady of Candelaria de la Tamaja, Pocotalaca, and Pocosabo. John H. Hann, "St. Augustine's Fallout from the Yamasee War," *Florida Historical Quarterly* 68 (October 1989): 180–200.

16. Ramsey, *Yamasee War*, 117–19.

17. See, for example, Journal of the Upper House, June 14, 1722, CO 5/425/311, and June 21, 1722, CO 5/425/323.

18. Ramsey, *Yamasee War*, 101–58.

19. Gallay, *Indian Slave Trade*; Ramsey, *Yamasee War*; Steven C. Hahn, *The Invention of the Creek Nation, 1670–1763* (Lincoln: University of Nebraska Press, 2004).

20. For a recent historiographical overview of Indian slavery studies in the South see Denise I. Bossy, "The South's Other Slavery: Recent Research on Indian Slavery," *Native South* 9 (2016): 27–53.

21. Verner W. Crane, *The Southern Frontier, 1670–1732* (New York: G. E. Stechert and Company, 1928); Oatis, *A Colonial Complex*; Ramsey, *Yamasee War*.

22. More recently Larry Ivers has published a military history of the war that is limited almost entirely to British perspectives. While Ivers attempts to draw on recent ethnohistorical analyses to offer some sense of Indian motives and tactics—scholarship which he sometimes fails to cite—he nonetheless also engages in offensive typecasting of the Yamasees (and other southeastern Indians) as driven by a desire for "plunder," "revenge," and "martial glory" and as having little in terms of military strategy or tactics. For instance, in describing the first attack by the Yamasees on Port Royal he claims that the Yamasees were "operating without any tactical plan other than to burn plantation buildings, kill hogs and cattle, and kill or capture South Carolina families." See, for example, pp. 56, 58, 98, 99, and 135. Larry E. Ivers, *This Torrent of Indians: War on the Southern Frontier, 1715–1728* (Columbia: University of South Carolina Press, 2016).

23. This is not to suggest that they were the first to consider these questions. In 1920s John Swanton, a researcher for the Bureau of American Ethnology, attempted to piece together the long history of the Yamasees through the nineteenth century, suggesting that their origins lay in the Georgia hinterland, but he struggled to understand the relationship between the Yamasees and Guales. Historian Verner Crane offered a more nuanced analysis of Yamasee relation-

Introduction

ships with the Spanish, British, and Creeks but was not as interested in Yamasee origins. In 1940 Chapman Milling, a physician by trade, published a history of Carolina's Indians but could do little more than either Swanton or Crane to illuminate Yamasee origins. The most enlightening work on the Yamasees prior to the 1980s was produced by anthropologist James Covington, who wrote several articles touching on the Yamasees, including a particularly fine piece on those Yamasees who went to St. Augustine after the Yamasee War. John R. Swanton, *Early History of the Creek Indians and Their Neighbors* (1922; repr., Gainesville: University Press of Florida, 1988); Verner Crane, *The Southern Frontier, 1670–1732* (1928; repr., New York: W. W. Norton and Company, 1981); Chapman James Milling, *Red Carolinians* (1940; repr., Columbia: University of South Carolina Press, 1969); James W. Covington, "The Yamasee Indians in Florida: 1715–1763," *Florida Anthropologist* 23 (September 1970): 119–28.

24. Archaeologists working on Florida sites use the term San Marcos, while those working on South Carolina and Georgia sites use the term Altamaha to delineate the same ceramic type. For the etymologies of these terms see Chester B. DePratter, "Irene and Altamaha Ceramics from the Charlesfort/Santa Elena Site, Parris Island, South Carolina," in *From Santa Elena to St. Augustine: Indigenous Ceramic Variability (A.D. 1400–1700)*, ed. Kathleen Deagan and David Hurst Thomas, Anthropological Papers of the American Museum of Natural History, no. 90 (New York: American Museum of Natural History, 2009), 19–47. David Andrew McKivergan Jr., "Migration and Settlement among the Yamasee in South Carolina," MA thesis, University of South Carolina, 1991; William Green, *The Search for Altamaha: The Archaeology and Ethnohistory of an Early 18th Century Yamasee Indian Town*, Volumes in Historical Archaeology 21 (Columbia: University of South Carolina, Institute of Archaeology and Anthropology, 1992). Also see William Green, Chester B. DePratter, and Bobby Southerlin, "The Yamasee in South Carolina: Native American Adaptation and Interaction along the Carolina Frontier," in *Another's Country: Archaeological and Historical Perspectives on Cultural Interactions in the Southern Colonies*, ed. J. W. Joseph and Martha Zierden (Tuscaloosa: University of Alabama Press, 2002), especially 13–14.

25. Brockington and Associates has been the main cultural resources firm in this endeavor, especially Brockington archaeologists Eric Poplin, Alex Sweeney, and Bobby Southerlin.

26. The Yamasees figure to some degree in all of John Hann's book-length studies, including *Apalachee: The Land Between the Rivers* (Gainesville: University Press of Florida, 1988); *Missions to the Calusa* (Gainesville: University Press of Florida, 1991); and *The Native World Beyond Apalachee: West Florida and the Chattahoochee Valley* (Gainesville: University Press of Florida, 2006). John E. Worth, *The Struggle for the Georgia Coast* (1995; repr., Tuscaloosa: University of Alabama Press, 2007); Worth, "Yamasee," in *Handbook of North American Indians*.

27. Hall, *Zamumo's Gifts*. Alejandra Dubkovsky, *Informed Power: Communication in the Early American South* (Cambridge: Harvard University Press, 2016).

28. Carl D. Halbirt, "Back Under the Spanish Fold: 18th Century Yamasee Mission Sites in St. Augustine, Florida," paper presented at the Yamasee Indians: From Florida to South Carolina conference, St. Augustine, Florida, April 18, 2015.

29. Andrea P. White, "Living on the Periphery: A Study of an Eighteenth-Century Yamasee Mission Community in Colonial St. Augustine," MA thesis, College of William and Mary, 2002; Willet A. Boyer III, "Nuestra Senora del Rosario de La Punta: Lifeways of an Eighteenth-Century Colonial Spanish Refugee Mission Community, St. Augustine, Florida," MA thesis, University of Florida, 2005; Sarah Bennet, "Cultural Crossroads and Other Complexities: Examining Creolization at Nuestra Señora del Rosario de la Punta," MA thesis, University of West Florida, 2015; Amanda A. Hall, "San Antonio de Pocotalaca: An Eighteenth-Century Yamasee Indian Town in St. Augustine, Florida, 1716–1752," MA thesis, University of North Florida,

2016; Gifford J. Waters, "Maintenance and Change in 18th Century Mission Indian Identity: A Multi-Ethnic Contact Situation," PhD diss., University of Florida, 2005.

30. Rebecca Saunders is the exception to this, but her work has been hampered by the same issue of identification. In her work on Amelia Island, she initially identified the Santa María mission on Amelia Island as Yamasee, but John Worth has subsequently argued that the site is actually Mocama. Saunders, *Stability and Change in Guale Indian Pottery A.D. 1300–1702* (Tuscaloosa: University of Alabama Press, 2000). Rebecca Saunders, pers. comm., September 26, 2014.

31. John E. Worth, "What's in a Phase? Disentangling Communities of Practice from Communities of Identity in Southeastern North America," in *Forging Southeastern Identities: Social Archaeology, Ethnohistory, and Folklore of the Mississippian to Early Historic South*, ed. Gregory A. Waselkov and Marvin T. Smith (Tuscaloosa: The University of Alabama Press, 2017), 117–56.

32. On the shatter zone construct see Robbie Ethridge, *From Chicaza to Chickasaw: The European Invasion and the Transformation of the Mississippian World, 1540–1715* (Chapel Hill: University of North Carolina Press, 2010).

33. Chester DePratter has recently challenged the idea that the Yamasees had primary towns, a point that Sweeney acknowledges in his chapter in the present volume. Chester DePratter, "Yamasee Settlements in South Carolina: From Port Royal Sound to the Ashepoo and Combahee Rivers," paper presented at the Yamasee Indians: From Florida to South Carolina conference, St. Augustine, Florida, April 17, 2015.

34. Thomas P. Slaughter, ed., *William Bartram: Travels and Other Writings* (New York: Library of America, 1996), 129, 165, 46–47, 166, 522. The Yamasee graveyard was likely neither Yamasee nor a graveyard at all. Rather, it was probably a shell mound midden. See Gregory A. Waselkov and Kathryn E. Holland Braund, *William Bartram on the Southeastern Indians* (Lincoln: University of Nebraska Press, 1995), 421–22, note 36. That Bartram would rhetorically transform a shell mound into Yamasee "tumuli" strongly suggests, I believe, that he was already predisposed to see the Yamasees as extinct and as part of Florida's ancient past, rather than as a living people. He describes the Yamasees as "ancient" in several places. Slaughter, *Bartram,* 47, 183, 309.

ONE

Yamasee Identity

I

Living at Liberty
The Ungovernable Yamasees of Spanish Florida

AMY TURNER BUSHNELL

In January 1702 don Antonio Ponce de León, organist for the parish church of St. Augustine, forwarded to the Council of the Indies a three-year-old letter from an Apalachee chief to Charles II of Spain by the hand of St. Augustine's parish priest, Bachiller don Alonso de Leturiondo. Don Patricio de Hinachuba, *cacique* of Ivitachuco, wished to inform His Majesty that the *naturales* of Apalachee were forsaking their towns and moving to San Jorge (Charles Town) to "live at liberty."[1] Florida governor Laureano de Torres y Ayala had warned the same king late in 1697 about the "liberty of conscience" with which the English suborned his vassals.[2] By the time don Patricio's letter came before the Council in August 1702, the empire had been overtaken by events—the Spanish Habsburgs were out, the Bourbons were in, and the colonies of Carolina and La Florida would soon be at war—but the derogatory discourse of liberty was intact. In the opinion of Spanish authorities, civil and religious, Natives who lived at liberty lived without constraint or subjection, doing as they pleased, obeying the law of the flesh. Theirs was not the pardonable ignorance of *infieles* (heathen) but a conscious rejection of the law of God.[3] But the Yamasees did not regard themselves as either infieles or apostates. They had not come to La Florida to change their beliefs and habits but to continue living as they saw fit. By evading baptism they could escape a charge of apostasy, and by keeping their distance from the Republic of Indians they could preserve a measure of autonomy, avoiding labor drafts, military call-ups, and the production of an agricultural surplus subject to seizure when the maize in Spanish granaries ran low.[4]

The origins, mergings, and settlings of the Yamasee people are as intricate as a five-part fugue, and other scholars have dedicated themselves to unraveling and analyzing them. This chapter focuses instead on their mentality.[5] The Yamasees were a nation with an ethos of liberty that put them at odds with the Spanish ideal of "inviolable and blind obedience"[6] and could on occasion strain the norms of a southeastern town. Twice, under pressure, they took refuge in the provinces of La Florida, where the record is studded with examples of Yamasees speaking and acting for themselves, as resistant to Spanish authority as they were to authority in general. Such fragments allow us to glimpse the mindset of this self-governing people caught in a cycle of violence, for the Yamasees faced a painful choice: either they could flee from the militaristic slaving societies of their day, or they could join forces with arms dealers and slave buyers and become a slaving society themselves. In the Southeast of the late seventeenth and early eighteenth centuries, they did both.[7]

Since the 1560s Florida missionaries and royal officials had been describing the nature and behavior of Indians in language that scholars love to quote. In 1568 Father Juan Rogel, a Jesuit, despaired of converting the Oristas near Santa Elena, then the capital of La Florida, because they wandered scattered nine months of the year.[8] In a properly run *pueblo*, wrote Accountant Bartolomé de Argüelles in 1600, Indians were required to obtain their chief's license to be absent; otherwise, there was no way of knowing who was in town and who wasn't.[9] In 1602 Fray Francisco Pareja, a Franciscan, complained of the Timucuan Mocamos that the "bad and willful ones go inland to pueblos of infieles where they remain for a year or two without hearing Mass."[10] In 1605 Governor Pedro de Ybarra advised the Crown, and in 1612 the Franciscans affirmed, that people who lived in the woods "as free as deer" were never likely to be conquered "like those of New Spain," who had houses and properties to lose.[11] The same Franciscans went on to petition the king to send soldiers to help the chiefs of Apalachee subdue their disobedient vassals so that conversions could commence.[12] Yet governance was relatively light in Florida, an area of limited statehood.[13] The friars in chapter did not hesitate to remind Governor

Diego de Rebolledo that chiefs were not soldiers, obeying orders without question.[14]

The question about whether a "lord of the land" should behave like a Spaniard was still unsettled when the Chichimecos (Westos), equipped with firearms in Virginia, brought their brand of terror to the Southeast. After one of their bands raided the mission towns of Guale, north of Mocama on the Atlantic coast, Governor Alonso de Aranguiz y Cotes moved to secure the northeastern border, and in 1661 the mission town of Santa Catalina became the garrison town of Santa Catalina de la Frontera.[15] The Yamasees were forged in the Chichimeco crucible. According to historian Eric Bowne, they first appeared in the record in 1662 as a confederacy of refugee peoples largely drawn from the three chiefdoms of Altamaha, Ocute, and Ichisi, all part of an early mission frontier in what is now central Georgia.[16] Their name was still young in the documents when many of them appeared in Guale and Mocama, so many that they threatened to outnumber the existing inhabitants.[17] Spanish authorities made the refugees welcome and invited them to occupy abandoned mission sites, hoping to reinforce the colony's borders with "live missions" that would produce agricultural surpluses and field warriors.[18] The success of the plan hinged on whether the Yamasees would settle down, "reduce[d] beneath the bell of their *doctrinas* and the hand of their *doctrineros*," and produce food for themselves and others, as was the lot of peasants everywhere.[19] But the Yamasees entering the provinces of Florida knew their rights, including the right to refuse conversion, and as events would show, they also knew when to disregard orders and when to discard a connection. They were experts in what James C. Scott calls the "art of *not* being governed."[20]

Whatever their habits in their places of origin, in La Florida the Yamasees proved indifferent farmers, preferring to live off the land. According to an exasperated missionary, Fray Juan Miguel de Villarroel, charged with restoring an abandoned mission site, their *estilo antiguo* was to live like wild beasts. Never planting enough to carry themselves through the year, they ran short of maize and were forced to "go into the woods to maintain themselves on plants and roots," and knowing no better, they thought it "a good life."[21] To a Spaniard, wild food was famine food. According to parish priest Alonso de Leturiondo, some roots took eight days to process, a task so laborious that nobody would do it for money, which was why, when Governor Laureano de Torres y Ayala denied him maize during a food shortage, he had been forced to lock the doors of the church on St. Mark's Day and go on foot into the swamps with one slave, to dig roots for himself and his household.[22]

All Indians were believed to have inside knowledge about the properties of plants. During his *visita* (inspection) of Timucua in 1694–95, Joachin de Florencia gathered information about *curanderas* who were suspected of aborting pregnancies with medicines and herbs.[23] And the Guales who abandoned St. Catherines Island under fire in 1680 declared that rather than be forced to return, they would kill themselves with the poison of a vine.[24] The cacique of Salamototo, a town charged with operating a ferry across the St. Johns River, reported to Visitor Florencia that his people were in need and lived by gathering *frutos silvestres* (wild plant foods) like acorns, *ache*, and grapes in the woods of nearby *haciendas*. For two winters, he said, the ranch overseers had tried to stop them. Inasmuch as the fruits were "common to all" and the right to gather them was not extinguished when the land was sold, he asked that anyone who interfered with this right be fined fifty ducats.[25]

Yamasees were expert gatherers. When they were on the road, the hunters and warriors carried parched maize and the dried meat of deer, buffalos, and bears, but when their travel food ran out, they ate roots and *palmitos* (heart-of-palm).[26] Merenciana, the *cacica* of San Juan del Puerto and of all Mocama, upon hearing in 1681 that Yamasees were living on "her" islands, Santa María and San Pedro, demanded a portion of the "bear fat, deerskins, acorns, and palmetto berries" that the islands yielded. Instead, a delegation went to the *presidio* (garrison headquarters) to complain to Governor Juan Marquez Cabrera. Siding with the immigrants, the governor reminded the cacica that in Florida, where Christian Indians were exempt from the royal tribute, and infieles from laboring in the fields of the convents, the Yamasees were voluntarily participating in the labor draft.[27] They were also jockeying for the best town sites, and Captain Francisco Fuentes warned the governor not to let the chief of San Pedro take the land that had been promised to the Colones, a group from Escamaçu who had come under Chichimeco attack twice, if he wanted to make sure of them and the other Yamasees.[28]

In theory, any labor contributed by infieles was voluntary, for only the Republic of Indians was subject to the colonial labor draft that historians call the *repartimiento*. Each doctrinero kept a *padron* (census) of his parishioners who "complied with the church" by making their annual confession at their home parish during Lent.[29] These padrones were the basis for applying the labor levy evenly throughout the province, giving every male commoner an equal opportunity to be drafted. For many non-Christians, this was reason enough to keep doctrineros at arm's length. The Yamasees, however, entered the Florida economy as seasonal workers, hiring out as substitutes for the Guale labor levy.[30] According to ex-Governor Francisco de la Guerra y de la Vega, who had left Florida in 1671, barely a fifth of the laborers who came to St. Augustine from Guale were *not* infieles.[31] However, it was one thing to go work in St. Augustine with your friends for a couple of weeks a year, and another thing to be ordered there.

Marquez Cabrera had learned this the hard way. When he arrived at his post in 1680, he had arbitrarily extended the labor levy to the infiel Yamasees living in Guale and had confined a nameless, uncooperative cacique in the unfinished *castillo*.[32] A short time later, Yamasee chief Altamaha had left for the Savannah River, to keep open house for every Yamasee and Guale who bore a grudge against Spain.[33] Years later Fray Pedro de Luna would charge that it was Marquez Cabrera's abusive treatment of this one Yamasee cacique that had triggered the outmigration of the Yamasees from Guale to live among infieles and heretics, who had in turn incited the cacique and his vassals to make war on the province of Timucua.[34]

Under the policy of pacification, proposed as a way of ending conquests by the sword, the only acceptable way for the king of Spain to add to his realms in the Indies was for a "natural lord of the land" to request friars and submit to a conquest by the gospel. Some Yamasees and two or three other nations on the Gulf side of Florida had reportedly asked for friars as early as 1672.³⁵ An episcopal visit by the energetic don Gabriel Díaz Vara Calderón in 1675 had stimulated further requests; and in Spain the wheels had begun to turn to send a mission of Franciscans to Florida. But when the twenty-three fresh-faced missionaries arrived in 1679, unprepared to hear confessions in any Native language, Governor Pablo de Hita Salazar was at a loss to know where to station them without adding to the burden of veteran friars.³⁶ Fray Jacinto de Barreda agreed to take one of the interns if the governor would reassign Fray Bartolomé Quiñones from San Salvador de Mayaca to the band of Yamasees at the nearer site of [San Antonio de] Enacape. They had not asked for friars, nor did they show a disposition to join the company of the faithful, he allowed, but "they are like monkeys, and what they see done, they do."³⁷ Two years later there was still an excess of interns. Five chiefs of Apalachicola who had come all the way to St. Augustine to warn Hita Salazar's successor, Marquez Cabrera, that they exercised no control outside their towns and thus could not be expected to keep their vassals (wandering fugitive and lawless in the woods) from murdering outsiders, added firmly that they had never asked for friars and did not find themselves with that intention, but that if God ever wanted them to be Christians, they would let the governor know.³⁸

In 1677 Visitor Antonio de Argüelles had found the town of Santa María de los Yamasis on Amelia Island without a leader. Their cacique had resigned, they told Argüelles, because nobody would obey him.³⁹ It may have been this self-assured band of Yamasees who in 1681 moved from Santa María to the deserted missions of San Antonio de Enacape and San Salvador de Mayaca to butt heads with Franciscans. The aforementioned Fray Juan Miguel, trying to reopen the mission at Enacape, complained to the governor that ten of the men had gone missing, leaving him with barely five men to "make a place" and none to spare for the three Spanish ranchers who were pressing him for ranch hands. The doctrinero knew where the fugitives were and was ready to bring them back, with the aid of a cacique and a soldier. But Marquez Cabrera responded that Yamasees went wherever they pleased, and he only hoped that some of the absentees had headed to Santa Catalina, a "frontier with the enemy," whose provisions had been "the succour of this presidio."⁴⁰ Disappointingly, Santa Catalina remained uninhabited, but its fruit trees continued to produce in season for anyone to gather.⁴¹

A year later the news from Mayaca and Enacape was that Mayaca had lost its friar. With the assistance of Captain Domingo de Leturiondo, Defender of the Indians, caciques Francisco and Matheo of that town brought suit against Fray Bartolomé, who had not moved to Enacape after all, and charged him with having packed up their doctrina's sacred ornaments and two bells and taken them downstream to the ferry town of Salamototo. These items the king had "given to their town and no other," and they wanted them back. Their friar, they said, had taken it "ill that they let infieles come and mix with Christians," but "they could not dismiss them nor refuse to receive them, being one and alike their vassals." If they had no friar, they shrugged, they could always get another one.⁴²

Asked by the governor how many people were in the two doctrinas, the two royal officials of the treasury, Antonio Menéndez Marquez and Francisco de la Rocha, replied that no padron was on file for either one. Mayaca and Enacape were not true towns, they said, because the Yamasees did not farm; they just wandered about and ate roots, which was why they could not be reduced to live like Christians and were unable to keep a doctrinero. At the governor's request, the Franciscans submitted reports on the number of inhabitants in each place. In 1682 Mayaca, with a population of 79, had 21 women, 30 children, and 28 grown men, caciques included. Enacape's population had fallen to 21, with 5 women, 9 children, and 7 men, of whom one was blind and two were caciques exempt from manual labor.⁴³ Fray Juan Chrisóstomo, a friend of the friar who had carried off the bells, volunteered some years later that the Yamasees of Mayaca were an indomitable, unreasonable nation who would not settle down and plant and that Fray Bartolomé had made himself sick trying to chase them down.⁴⁴

For all their reluctance to reduce themselves to *pueblos en forma*, or towns with Spanish-style governments, the Yamasees could be counted on to remain connected to Spain as long as Spain remained a reliable source of trade goods, especially the guns, powder, and ammunition required to sustain the manly arts of hunting and war.[45] By the 1680s the Spanish had given up the idea of keeping guns out of the hands of Indian commoners and would have armed all their allies, had they been able.[46] On the subject of guns, the English expressed neither reservations nor compunction. As Governor James Colleton of Carolina observed to Governor Diego de Quiroga y Losada in 1688, he traded powder, guns, and shot "to all Indians indifferently."[47] Over the course of proxy raids and retaliations across the Florida-Carolina border, punctuated by heated exchanges between the colonies' governors, neither side raised the topic of gun control.

La Florida's governors, who held the rank of captain general and who had been in training since adolescence to exercise command, were forced to engage warriors and fill shortages in the ranks with mercenaries, or "men who come sold," until conversions advanced to the point that fighting men in the towns of Christians could be organized into militias under their caciques and *principales*.[48] These Native allies fought bravely and knew how to handle a weapon, but governors found them short on discipline and disposed to revert to customs that a Spaniard considered barbaric. For example, a warrior's way of advancing through the ranks to the rank of *tascaya* was to take scalps, worn on those solemn occasions when warriors painted their faces and danced, and this custom was difficult to eradicate. When Governor Joseph de Zúñiga y Cerda learned in 1701 that some of the Timucuas and Yguajas (the eighteenth-century term for Guales) on an expedition against the rebels of Mayaca (not the Yamasees, but later occupants) had taken scalps, he outlawed scalping on the spot, storming that the custom was "diabolical" and "abhorrent in the eyes of God" and that the Indians of Florida must find a different way to distinguish themselves than to murder stray people.[49]

Better, it seemed, to appropriate them. Militia Indians received their pay in the form of booty, and their leaders supervised the dividing of the spoils, with one exception: a warrior's captives were his to dispose of how he liked. Governor Torres y Ayala, in his orders to the four hundred Apalachees who were preparing to go against the four towns of Caveta, Casista, Oconi, and Tiquipache in order to recover forty-two Christians that the Apalachicolos had carried off in a raid on the town of San Carlos de los Chacatos in 1694, cautioned them to go and come in a body and not split up to go hunting in the woods. Like their enemies, the Apalachees hunted people; on this occasion, they managed to surprise one place and return with fifty captives. Torres y Ayala and other governors either saw nothing wrong with an Indian slave trade, or they tolerated the practice as too entrenched to combat, hoping only to contain the violence by putting revenge warfare to an ancient test. Before consenting to a campaign of retaliation, a *junta de guerra* (council of war) in St. Augustine established that the expedition would be a "just war," the only kind that legalized the sale of infiel captives, and these, the governor reminded the Crown, belonged by custom to the warrior who took them.[50]

Zúñiga y Cerda, the governor so scandalized by scalping, let slave-taking stand, going so far as to post on the *bujíos* (council houses) of the provinces in 1704 that whatever infieles "our Indians" captured were theirs to sell wherever they liked and that his deputy governors were not to intervene in the transaction, directly or indirectly.[51] Where Florida's Christian Indians were marketing their captives begs investigation. Certainly it was not something that governors disclosed, then or in association with earlier campaigns against infieles. The French were known to buy enslaved Indians, and in the late seventeenth century buccaneers were a presence in the Gulf; but then so were unlicensed Cuban vessels.

Altamaha and his vassals were not the only Yamasees who changed their minds about Florida and took the open road out of the provinces. In 1683 after the pirate known as the Sieur de Grammont raided the settlements north of St. Augustine, most of the Yamasees deserted Mocama, some to join Altamaha on the Savannah River and others to head to Apalachicola.[52] Alonso Solana's well-known map of that year shows towns of Christians and infieles that may already have been abandoned.[53]

When, in 1684, a shipload of Scots Covenanters landed at Port Royal, where Santa Elena had stood a century earlier, the new trading hub of Stuarts Town drew Yamasees like a magnet. After parleying with

William Dunlop, Altamaha sent the Scots forty warriors to help them erect beacons and prepared to move from the Savannah River to old Santa Elena. The Yamasees living in Guale came next, followed by the Guales of the northernmost doctrinas, to unite at Santa Elena under the Yamasee chief Niquisalla. Finally, a thousand Yamasees removed to Santa Elena from Apalachicola, and all that Governor Marquez Cabrera could think to do was to send Captain Antonio Matheos into Apalachicola to burn four empty towns—Coweta, Kasita, Tuskegee, and Kolomoki—that had broken ranks to trade with the enemy.

While the Scots had not brought enough firearms and cutlasses for everyone, the trader Caleb Westbrooke was able to equip a band of Altamaha's warriors. Niquisalla, with his ear to the ground, learned that they were on their way to Timucua and sent the Spanish a warning that arrived too late. According to Juan Rodríguez Tiznado, teniente of Timucua, writing on March 10, 1685, sixty enemies surprised Santa Catalina de Afuyca before dawn on what was probably March 7. The cacique and 16 men being away, they killed 18 people, captured 22 (two-thirds of them women), sacked the church and convent, and burned the town. By eight o'clock the attackers were ready to travel. They and their captives walked all that day and until the moon set that night. One of the two women who escaped in the dark and separately made their way home described their ordeal.[54]

She had recognized the raiders as Yamasees, although they claimed to be Movilas and Tiquipaches. Half of them had guns of varying length tucked into their sashes; the rest carried bows and round shields. They urged their captives, burdened with plunder, to walk with a will, for they were on their way to Tama and great dancing, and from there they would go on to San Jorge, where the English would receive them and clothe them. They warned their captives that if they did not keep up they would be killed, and they did kill and scalp one woman who was unable to complete the 14 leagues that they traveled on foot the first day—a good 36 miles.[55] If the raiders were indeed heading to Charles Town, they were intercepted at the Savannah River, where the Scots' leader, Henry Erskine Lord Cardross, bought their plunder and prisoners. Nicolás, a twenty-one-year-old Christian Yamasee from Sápala who had gone north with some other Yamasees to see San Jorge, testified that in Santa Elena he heard that the Yamasees of Santa Elena and Cosapue had brought in 25 Timucuas, 22 of them women. How many had been captured in Afuyca and how many during a later raid on the Timucuan town of Santa Cruz de Tarihica he did not know.[56]

Later that year a Native of Santa Cruz de Sabacola living in Apalachee told Fray Juan Mercado that Englishmen were building a bujío at Sabacola—at least they looked English to him, being small, white, and "short like Spaniards."[57] Now that the rivers and paths to the interior had been thrown open by emissaries such as Dr. John Henry Woodward, the Indian trade was falling into English hands, and change was in the air.[58] From Apalachee two Christian Yamasees traveled north to the province of Apalachicola to spy on the interlopers. One of them, staying at a "house of Yamasees" two leagues outside Coweta, heard that an Englishman with a band of Yamasees had arrived in the town of Apalachicola and decided to see for himself. He hid his *conga* (blanket) and his quiver of arrows, and with a *gamuza* (deerskin) thrown over his shoulder to pass as an Apalachicolo, he set out. On the way he met twenty Yamasee sentinels with firearms, who told him that they were watching the roads in case of an Apalachee attack. They and their companions stood out with their new weapons and clothes. The 45 men of the band had, among them, 25 guns and 30 pistols, and each of them sported a *machete*, a *sombrero*, and a *justacor* (lined coat).[59] A warrior could now dress as well as a chief. The one who had led the raid on Afuyca told the spy that the captured boys had been divided among "the valiant" and the women given to the English, all but one, who had died of *pesadumbre* (sorrow), refusing to eat.[60]

The Sieur de Grammont returned to raid Mocama and Guale in 1686, but this time a corsair hunter was trailing him. Alejandro Thomás de León, out of Havana, paused in St. Augustine to pick up reinforcements of men and ships and resumed the pursuit with three galliots, a hundred men from the city's two militia units, Spanish and mulatto, and fifty Indians. De León engaged and defeated Grammont, and then, staying within the letter of the law, burned an empty Stuarts Town, on the Florida side of the line set by treaty in 1670. But when he went on to attack San Jorge's outlying plantations and steal eleven enslaved Africans, he crossed the line from privateer to pirate.

The hurricane that killed de León, riding out the storm aboard his flagship, left the *floridanos* with two galliots to carry them home and the Indians without transport. Five men said to be "*pláticos*" (knowledgeable) about Guale Province stole a canoe and were on their way home when a boatload of five Englishmen came out of the mouth of a river and captured them. Managing to free themselves during the night, they killed four of the Englishmen with their own guns and four days later reappeared in Florida with their boat and a haul of 180 deerskins and 200 furs. In honor of their exploit, Marquez Cabrera granted them the prize and exempted them from the labor obligations of commoners, a sign that they were Christian. The Crown responded with a *cédula* commending the governor and consenting for him to favor the five in ways "proper to their estate and to Indians."[61] Status and caste would continue inviolate.

Punishing the Yamasees in league with Stuarts Town was unfinished business, so Marquez Cabrera sent Captain Francisco Fuentes north with a galliot and three *piraguas*, forty soldiers, and one hundred Indians (none of them Guales), to "dislodge" the Yamasees and apostate Guales populating the sea islands around Santa Elena.[62] Although Governor Colleton would later charge that the expedition came in peacetime "to the frontiers" of his government, "sacking, destroying, killing, and carrying off people," all that Fuentes managed to accomplish was to drive the Yamasees across the line into Carolina, where, with Stuarts Town a thing of the past, they would have headed anyway.[63]

When Governor Quiroga y Losada took over in 1687 and became aware of Florida's contracted sphere of influence and the Guale *despoblado* (vacant quarter), he sent Fray Simón de Salas up to contact the Yamasee and Guale defectors "wandering in the woods like *bárbaros*" and offer them a pardon. In his letter of introduction, he asked Governor Colleton to "tell the Indians of this obedience who find themselves in those parts to return to their places, or at least to prohibit them from molesting their countrymen," and the English from inciting them.[64] Colleton responded that the Yamasees were beyond his control: "I cannot gratify the Rev. Father in sending to you . . . the Yamases, who take no notice of our government. Now they are confederated with a larger nation, . . . it is impossible for me to send them back without making war upon them, which I must not do without my King's order. Nor did I think it good the father should go in person lest he should come by some misfortune amongst those barbarous people, whom with all my heart I wish were home with you."[65] Despite Colleton's efforts to keep Fray Simón and the Yamasees apart, news of the friar's presence in the city reached them, and a cacique appeared to tell him that they would be at Santa Catalina when the figs were ripe, if anyone wanted to know—an overture that Governor Quiroga y Losada received with relief.[66] But the Yamasees did not elect to repopulate St. Catherines Island, which remained a no-man's land. And although 225 Guales and Yamasees were living in a combined refugee pueblo near St. Augustine by 1689, there were too few of them to help the Spanish recover their lost province, had they been so inclined.[67]

While the Yamasees had a common language, a common name, and by 1695 two capitals—Pocotaligo for the Upper Yamasees, and Altamaha Town for the Lower—they lacked the will and the means to act in concert that characterized a European nation, the absence of which gave flexibility to an Indian one.[68] During the War of the League of Augsburg (1689–97), while Spain and England were at peace, many Yamasees remained at war. Jointly, Yamasees and Uchises (Lower Creeks) attacked the Timucuan mission town of San Juan de Guacara on August 30, 1691, killing many people and taking others captive.[69] A 1694 raid on San Carlos de los Chacatos provoked the Apalachees into retaliating, and the next year, after a threatening letter from Carolina governor Joseph Blake, Governor Torres y Ayala listed his own government's losses in people and money and demanded that Blake return all the king of Spain's vassals: the Yamasees and Guales taken by pirates to San Jorge and from thence sold to the Windward Isles, the Guale defectors, and the Yamasees born and raised in Guale. They might not be Christians, but they were birthright vassals.[70]

A handful of Yamasees, possibly intermarried, remained with the Guales on the islands of Santa María and San Pedro, but judging from the complaints registered during Juan de Pueyo's 1695 *Visita* of Guale and Mocama, they too were preparing to move on. Fray Pedro de la Lastra, *doctrinero* of the towns of Santa Clara de Tupiqui and

San Felipe, sent a Yamasee named Juan Lorenzo to the house of Lastra's syndic in St. Augustine to pick up some things from "his situado," a Franciscan's vow of poverty requiring that his stipend be paid in kind.⁷¹ The items were not ready, and after waiting around for several days and running out of food, Juan Lorenzo started home. On the road he met Fray Pedro and the teniente of Guale, Ensign Diego de Jaén. The friar berated him, and the teniente threatened to put him in the stocks overnight, whip him in the morning, and send him back to the presidio "at his own cost." The next morning, Tupiqui awoke to find one of its canoes missing and with it Juan Lorenzo, his wife and son, and three other residents.⁷²

This defection left them with only one Yamasee in all of their places, the Guale *micos* (chiefs) admitted to Pueyo, and he was ready with a complaint of his own. Santiago, the sole Yamasee at Santa María, headquarters of the relocated Guale garrison, often went fishing in order to feed his four small children and give something to the "soldiers' house." (In matrilineal Guale, a man with four children might still be the Last of the Yamasees.) One day, when he had invited a cacique to eat with him and was cooking a large fish on a grill out of doors, a soldier walking by helped himself to a piece of it. A short time later the teniente sent for the rest of the fish to feed the servants at the garrison, leaving Santiago with nothing to put before his guest.⁷³

Late the following year, a party of twenty-four English and African castaways under Spanish escort came to these same towns to purchase provisions and hire canoes and rowers for a journey through the former province of Guale and up to Charles Town. In his account of their travels, *God's Protecting Providence*, the Quaker Jonathan Dickinson observed that "the Carolina Indians called the Yammasees, which are related to these Indians [of Santa María] were here about a month since trading for deerskins," and noted that the friar of the place had made the journey to Charles Town himself a few years before. The former province of Guale was a wasteland; it had plenty of deer and feral pigs, but few hunters, who avoided the party of sixty persons in seven large canoes. However, Dickinson recounted, at "the place called St. Catalena" they met a "a canoe of Carolina Indians being a man his wife and children having his dogs and other hunting implements for to lie out this winter season," who for a consideration agreed to carry his and the Spanish captain's letters to the governor of Carolina, lest the arrival of the small armada should trigger an alarm.[74] Yamasees were in a position to act as go-betweens.

In a pensive Memorial to the Crown, written in 1700 while he was in Spain, Father Alonso de Leturiondo asked himself why the English got along so well with Indians and concluded that it was because they did not try to make them live "beneath the bell" in law and righteousness, but let them do as they pleased, and also because the English brought them firearms, ammunition, glass beads, knives, hatchets, iron tools, and woolen blankets in exchange for such commodities as deerskins, bearskins, buffalo hides, otter and beaver pelts, and Indian children.[75] On the existence of a trade in enslaved children, the priest did not comment.

Spain's abrupt switch from a Habsburg to a Bourbon monarchy and the ensuing War of the Spanish Succession (1701–14) made its holdings fair game to the enemies of France. In North America, where its English name was Queen Anne's War, the war opened in 1702 with an attack on St. Augustine. Colonel James Moore Sr. left Charles Town with an amphibious army: three hundred Carolinians and two hundred Indians went with him in the supply boats, and "a multitude" of Indian and Black auxiliaries with Colonel Robert Daniel, who stopped in Mocama to destroy the little mission towns in his path. Moore and Daniel were Goose Creek men, a Barbadian faction notorious in Carolina for their dealings with pirates and slave raiders.[76]

While St. Augustine readied its defenses, a Yamasee named Juan Lorenzo, well armed for a Christian and accompanied by a girl and a woman with an infant, appeared to seek shelter in the castillo. It was a grave mistake, for Juan Lorenzo had a record: he had twice been confined in the same castillo for "murders and other offenses" and had just returned from serving a sentence in Havana. Suspecting him of coming to plant a bomb or foment an insurrection, Zúñiga y Cerda had him apprehended and questioned. Being an *indio ladino* who could pass as Spanish, he withstood the torture, reported the governor, but the girl confessed to something or other, and there the story ends, with unanswered questions. If this was the same Juan Lorenzo who had absconded with a canoe in 1695, he had squeezed a lifetime of crime into seven short years.[77]

Unable to take the castillo, Moore burned St. Augustine and retired. His invasion of Apalachee Province the next year at the head of an army of fifty Englishmen and a thousand Creeks and Yamasees was more successful, and he returned to Carolina at the head of a column of captives from the four towns that had surrendered unconditionally and subjects from the three towns that had agreed to relocate.[78] The invasion netted 4,000 enslaved Apalachees and a subject population of 600, resettled to serve as burdeners in the Indian trade, which would not make the shift to packhorses until after the Yamasee War.[79]

The depopulating of Apalachee did not bring an end to the raids. In 1705 Teniente Andrés García, stationed at San Francisco with a handful of soldiers, informed the governor that an Indian from the Timucuan town of San Pedro [de Potohiriba] had shown up with a good *escopeta* (gun), his face painted in stripes, pendants hanging from his ears, and his hair cropped *a lo infiel*, all of which signified that he must be guiding a band of Yamasees.[80] The trader Thomas Nairne described to the Lord Palatine of Carolina a Yamasee raid far into southern Florida that he had accompanied in 1708. Any scruples of Nairne's about man-stealing he had long since rationalized, and he commented only that "The good prices The English Traders gives them for slaves Encourages them to this trade Extremely and some men think it both serves to Lessen their number before the French can arm them and it is a more Effectual way of Civilizing and Instructing, Then all the Efforts used by the French Missionaries."[81] For Nairne, Spanish missionaries were a thing of the past, best forgotten.

In 1715 the Yamasees of Pocotaligo attacked a party of Indian traders visiting their town, in the opening salvo of what has come to be known as the Yamasee War. Despite the initial violence to the trade network, attributable to retribution, this was not a war of extermination, argues Max Edelson, but the deliberate targeting of Carolina's edges and southern coastal frontier, particularly the area between the Savannah and Edisto rivers, a region Carolina planters and their slaves would not resettle until the 1740s. In future the colony's growth would be more regular, its frontiers more defensible, and its Indian trade less predatory.[82]

The Yamasees who in 1715, "hated by all nations," took refuge in what remained of Spanish Florida must have thought that they had nowhere else to go, but the Spanish were pleased to have them change sides, no questions asked.[83] In 1716 Philip V almost tripled the Indian fund to accommodate their needs, and two years later, Interim Governor Juan de Ayala y Escobar built a fort at San Marcos de Apalachee to serve as a trading post for them and others of Spain's allies.[84] But security was an illusion, for the Yamasees had not made peace but were sallying from their strongholds to mount raids on the English and their allies, and Carolina, ignoring the Creek policy of neutrality, insisted that its trading partners show good faith by making war on them. The "Long Yamasee War," as Steven Hahn calls it, "did not so much conclude" as "gradually burn out following the War of Jenkins' Ear."[85]

Meanwhile, incidents in the boundary zone were reflected in the Spanish record. In 1723 word came to Diego Peña, in charge of the fort at San Marcos, that a band of Uchises and Englishmen were coming to "wipe out the verb Yamas." The English did not materialize, but Uchises and Talapuses killed and scalped two women in Apalachicola, then headed toward the Yamasee pueblos in Apalachee. Chislacaliche, cacique of the pueblo whose name he bore, swore to Peña that he would defend his pueblo to the death, but after reconsidering, returned to the fort to demand "the rest of the clothing." When Peña said no, that he and the other cacique, Tamasle, had already had half of it, Chislacaliche threatened darkly to seize it "on the road," which Peña told him he would do at his peril.[86] Under the terms of the colonial contract that had evolved in Florida during the seventeenth century, a cacique in league with the Spanish could expect a yearly issue of European clothing and other symbols of authority, paid for by the *gasto de indios* in St. Augustine's annual situado.[87] By importing large quantities of trade goods, the British had upset this arrangement, through which scarcity gave added value. It was in this same year, 1723, that the governor of Carolina reportedly paid a barrel of rum, a gun with plenty of ammunition, and clothing piled high enough to reach a man's shoulders for a single important captive.[88]

On the east coast, four Yamasee chiefs announced to Governor Antonio de Benavides in 1724 that they were in no position to defend their pueblos, having gone nine years without new guns.[89] A year and a half passed, then a band of three hundred Uchises surprised the pueblos in the vicinity of St. Augustine, with many casualties. A priest saying Mass on All Saints Day at the Yamasee pueblo of Thama had to flee with his chalice in a canoe. Governor Benavides called on all the pueblos to move within cannon range of the castillo, and many did, ready to rush inside the walls and afraid to hoe their fields or gather firewood. The Thama survivors joined the Apalachees at the pueblo of Mose, which was not yet identified with fugitive slaves.[90] Twenty-three *vecinos* (Spanish householders) signed a letter entreating the Crown to let them send their wives and children to Havana.[91] Bowing to pressure, the governor sued for peace, and a delegation of Uchises duly arrived in St. Augustine to sit in the great hall of government and smoke the *cachimbo* (peace pipe). They had a proposition to make. If the Spanish would supply them with guns, ammunition, and other goods, they would stop trading with the English. This, the governor promised to do, trusting in the Crown's support, but the peace did not hold.[92]

In 1728, allegedly to expose the futility of Spanish sanctuary and to punish the Yamasees and fugitive slaves who with Spanish backing had been mounting raids on the Carolina perimeter, an expedition of three hundred Englishmen and one hundred Indians under Colonel John Palmer assaulted the unfortified pueblos near St. Augustine, concentrating on Nombre de Dios Macariz. For three days the attackers pillaged and burned, killing thirty Yamasees and taking fifteen prisoners, without one soldier's being dispatched from the castillo to their aid.[93] One might think that this would mark the end of the Spanish-Yamasee alliance, but as John Hann has shown, if some Yamasees abandoned St. Augustine or Apalachee, others stood ready to take their place.[94]

In 1740 Governor Manuel de Montiano received an extraordinary letter from "Cesar Augusto, Yamas Chalaque, king of the Indians," on

Living at Liberty   45

his way to St. Augustine with General James Oglethorpe. The king of the Indians had seven things to say to His Lordship:

1. I have news that vs (*Vuestra Señoría*) has Indian prisoners.

2. No one can resist the valor of my warriors; they have captured a Spaniard.

3. My clemency is as great as the valor of my warriors.

4. I have granted life to a Spaniard named Francisco García, of the horses of don Pedro.

5. If vs burns an Indian, I will burn all of your men that I capture. . . .

6. I will never leave your people until I kill them all, excepting the women. . . .

7. Your men will know me by the design on my skin.

Whoever penned this letter in Spanish, perhaps cavalryman García himself, carefully copied the tattoo design onto it. What the Yamasee-Cherokee chief was proposing was not a prisoner exchange, but a moratorium on prisoner burning. In a cover letter, Oglethorpe endorsed his proposal and suggested that, as men of honor, he and Montiano agree to observe the European rules of war and refrain from shedding Christian blood. He had, he said, prevented his allies from burning the prisoners they had taken at Pupo and Picolata, small forts across from each other on the St. Johns. Montiano's sputtering response to Cesar Augusto and Oglethorpe was that the Spanish and their allies would never burn a prisoner, not if he were the most evil man in the world.[95] He did not remind them that in 1711, during the Tuscarora War, Colonel James Moore's son and namesake had burned to death several hundred people trapped inside a fort.[96]

Three years later, when the War of Jenkins' Ear was over, Governor Montiano asked the Crown to reestablish a trading post on the Gulf for the Uchises, who wanted pistols and guns. In their fourteen towns, he said, were many Yamasee and Apalachee Christians, living like infieles for lack of contact with Spaniards.[97] Apalachee's trading post was duly rebuilt and fortified, but the monopoly Royal Company of Havana whose business it was to keep the post in goods proved unable to supply the soldiers stationed there, let alone stock a store.⁹⁸ In 1747 the Uchises of Apalachee broke with their allies, the Talapuses and Chalaques, and sent a crier on horseback to the Yamasees, demanding that they join the Uchises in making war. Resisting the order to mobilize, the Yamasees prepared to be refugees yet again. Most of them headed with their families to Pensacola, but "Pancho el Jamais" sent word to Captain Isidoro de León at the trading post that the rest were bringing their families to the post by canoe to be supported until they could become self-sustaining. In a letter reporting developments to the Crown, Montiano calculated that feeding the refugees and making peace with the Uchises would cost the Viceroy of New Spain no less than twelve thousand pesos.⁹⁹ As expected, the Uchises sent Montiano two embassies of peace and the plume of a white heron, inviting him to forget the past and "provide them with arms, munitions, clothing, and other things of their use, in exchange for skins of deer and other animals," and reminding him that they had "solicited many times" for the Spanish to open this commerce, "for Indians must go where they can find what they need."¹⁰⁰

In the post-mission eighteenth century, troops stationed in Spanish Florida had a low opinion of infieles, Yamasees included. Pedro Sánchez Griñán reported in 1756 that the "Llamases" and other nations of the interior were tall and *morenos* (dark-skinned); they dressed in skins and painted their faces and bodies. They had their plantings, but neglected them to hunt and make war. They were drunken and cruel, and they fought from ambush, never "*a pecho descubierto*" (out in the open, literally "bare-chested").¹⁰¹ For an officer used to men trained by musket drills and close order marching to fight like automatons, the Indian way of fighting was undisciplined and unsporting.¹⁰² Yet John Worth's research on the Yamasees of western Florida shows that those who took refuge in Apalachee and Pensacola after the Yamasee War, by acting as intermediaries between the Spanish and the Lower Creeks, found a niche in the eighteenth-century Southeast and were able to maintain their autonomy.¹⁰³

To summarize, the Yamasee confederation emerged in the early 1660s as a consequence of the Chichimeco invasion. From the speed with which the component societies coalesced around their new identity, it was clear that the confederated Yamasees were prepared to move in new directions, form new alliances, and assume new roles, yet they were flexible only to a point. The Spanish could give them refuge but could not change them into what they were not. From the relative security of the colony's ecumene of mission provinces, the Yamasees watched while Carolina made use of the Chichimecos, then turned on them. They watched while English traders overran the Spanish sphere of influence and pirates wreaked havoc on both coasts.[104] When it became clear that England was going to win the arms race, the pragmatic Yamasees changed sides, taking with them many of their Christian friends and relatives. For thirty years they would remain in the English orbit, some in Apalachicola and others closer to Charles Town, filling Carolina's demand for Indian slaves by raiding deeper and deeper into Florida. When in 1715 their relationship with the English soured, and like the Chichimecos they came out on the losing side of a war, the old men remembered the provinces that they had helped to depopulate, and the Yamasees moved back, some to Apalachee and Pensacola, and others to pueblos outside St. Augustine. Again, the Spanish welcomed them and tried to supply them with the trade goods that had long since become necessities.

Did Florida's two waves of Yamasee refugees ever intend to join the Republic of Indians, trade only with Spaniards, and restrict their fighting to just wars? Not according to the evidence. Individual Indians might accept baptism, but the nation as a whole resisted reduction, and the default term for them continued to be "infiel." On principle, Yamasees resisted subjugation to authorities of any kind, whether they were missionaries, officers, governors, caciques and cacicas, or Goose Creek traders. In Spanish terms, they were by nature ungovernable, yet in the post–Yamasee War period they and the Spanish came to an understanding, and in the interstices of the Spanish-English, Spanish-Creek borderlands, the Yamasees lived at liberty.

Notes

1. Letter from Cacique don Patricio Jinachuba to Ensign don Antonio Ponce de León, from Hivitachuco, April 10, 1699, Archivo General de Indias, Seville, ramo Gobierno: Santo Domingo, legajo 863, número 22 (hereafter cited as SD), enclosed with don Antonio Ponce de

León, from Havana, January 29, 1702, SD 863/43 (unless otherwise noted, the address of origin in St. Augustine and the addressee is the Crown), received at the Council of the Indies on August 7, 1702, from the hand of Bachiller don Alonso de Leturiondo and considered by the Council on August 11, 1702. For details on these *floridanos* see Amy Turner Bushnell, "Patricio de Hinachuba: Defender of the Word of God, the Crown of the King, and the Little Children of Ivitachuco," *American Indian Culture and Research Journal* 3 (July 1979): 1–21; Amy Turner Bushnell, *The King's Coffer: Proprietors of the Spanish Florida Treasury, 1565–1702* (Gainesville: University Presses of Florida, 1981), 40, 45; and John H. Hann, trans. and ed., "Translation of Alonso de Leturiondo's Memorial to the King of Spain [1700]," *Florida Archaeology* 2 (1986): 165–225.

2. Gov. Laureano Torres y Ayala to the Crown, from St. Augustine, February 7, 1697, SD 839/134.

3. Friars in chapter, depositions, May 19–30, 1681, in Auto on the abuses of Gov. Marques Cabrera, May 30, 1681, SD 226; Fray Domingo de Ojeda to the Crown, February 20, 1687, SD 864/4.

4. Amy Turner Bushnell, *Situado and Sabana: Spain's Support System for the Presidio and Mission Provinces of Florida*, American Museum of Natural History, Anthropological Papers, no. 74 (Athens GA: Distributed by University of Georgia Press, 1994), 148–60.

5. "Yamasee" is an umbrella term for the societies that shared a language and customs and that federated in the 1660s under pressure by the Chichimecos (Westos), an Iroquoian group with firearms who sold their captives in Virginia. See Eric E. Bowne, *The Westos: Slave Traders of the Early Colonial South* (Tuscaloosa: University of Alabama Press, 2005), and John E. Worth, *The Struggle for the Georgia Coast: An Eighteenth-Century Spanish Retrospective on Guale and Mocama*, American Museum of Natural History, Anthropological Papers, no. 75 (Athens GA: Distributed by University of Georgia Press, 1995).

6. Gov. Manuel de Montiano to the Crown, May 28, 1738, SD 844/55.

7. On the "militaristic slaving society," see Robbie Ethridge, *From Chicaza to Chickasaw: The European Invasion and the Transformation of the Mississippian World, 1540–1715* (Chapel Hill: University of North Carolina Press, 2010), 89–115.

8. Juan Rogel, from Havana, to Pedro Menéndez de Avilés, December 9, 1570, in Eugenio Ruidíaz y Caravia, *La Florida: Su conquista y colonización por Pedro Menéndez de Avilés* (Madrid, 1893–1894), II: 301–8.

9. Bartolomé de Argüelles to the Crown, February 20, 1600, SD 229/32. Three quarters of a century later another Argüelles protested that the Indians of Guale traveled freely from town to town without permission. See Antonio de Argüelles, *Visita* of the Province of Guale and Mocama, 1677–1678, in the *Residencia* of Gov. Pablo de Hita Salazar, [1681], Archivo General de Indias, Seville, ramo Escribanía de Cámara, legajo 156B (hereafter cited as EC).

10. Fray Francisco Pareja, Declaration, n.d., in Franciscan depositions on St. Augustine and Florida, September 14–16, 1602, SD 235/10. Five years later the Mocamos were still reluctant to reduce themselves to "regular towns" and continued to "wander off to their relatives." See Fray Alonso de Peñaranda and Fray Francisco Pareja to the Crown, November 20, 1607, SD 224/84.

11. Gov. Pedro de Ybarra to Fray Benito Blasco, December 7, 1605, SD 232; Franciscans in chapter to the Crown, October 16, 1612, SD 232/61.

12. Franciscans in chapter to the Crown, October 16, 1612, SD 232/61. The Spanish coopted the chiefs and governed through them. See Amy Turner Bushnell, "Ruling the Republic of Indians in Seventeenth-Century Florida," in *Powhatan's Mantle: Indians in the Colonial Southeast*, ed. Gregory A. Waselkov, Peter H. Wood, and Tom Hatley, 2nd ed. (Lincoln: University of Nebraska Press, 2006), 195–213.

13. "Governance in Areas of Limited Statehood," Collaborative Research Center 700, Freie Universität Berlin, http://www.sfb-governance.de/en/index.html.

Living at Liberty 49

14. Franciscans in chapter to the Crown, September 10, 1657, SD 235.

15. Worth, *Struggle for the Georgia Coast*, 15–20.

16. Eric E. Bowne, "'Caryinge aways their Corne and Children': The Effects of Westo Slave Raids on the Indians of the Lower South," in *Mapping the Mississippian Shatter Zone: The Colonial Indian Slave Trade and Regional Instability in the American South*, ed. Robbie Ethridge and Sheri M. Shuck-Hall (Lincoln: University of Nebraska Press, 2009), 106–9.

17. Bushnell, *Situado and Sabana*, 144–45.

18. For "live missions" see Bushnell, *Situado and Sabana*, 142–44. On the first wave of Yamasee migrations into Spanish Florida see Keith Ashley, "Yamasee Migrations into the Mocama and Timucua Mission Provinces of Florida," this volume.

19. Amy Turner Bushnell, "The Sacramental Imperative: Catholic Ritual and Indian Sedentism in the Provinces of Florida," in *Columbian Consequences*, vol. 2: *Archaeology and History of the Spanish Borderlands East*, ed. David Hurst Thomas (Washington DC: Smithsonian Institution Press, 1990), 475–90, quote on 486.

20. James C. Scott, *The Art of Not Being Governed: An Anarchist History of Upland Southeast Asia* (New Haven: Yale University Press, 2009).

21. Franciscans in chapter to Gov. Juan Marquez Cabrera, May 19–30, 1681, in Auto on Gov. Marquez Cabrera, May 30, 1681, SD 226.

22. Santos de las Heras and don Joseph de Prado to the Crown, August 24, 1653, SD 229/III; Alonso de Leturiondo to the Crown, April 29, 1697, SD 235/143.

23. Joachín de Florencia, Visita of the Provinces of Apalache and Timucua, 1694–1695, in the Residencia of Gov. Laureano de Torres y Ayala [1699?], EC 157A, cuaderno 1, folios 33–205.

24. Worth, *Struggle for the Georgia Coast*, 30–33.

25. Florencia, Visita of Apalache and Timucua, 1694–1695.

26. Michael C. Scardaville, ed., and Jesús María Belmonte, trans., "Florida in the Late First Spanish Period: The 1756 [Pedro Sánchez] Griñán Report," *El Escribano* 16 (1979): 1–24.

27. Worth, *Struggle for the Georgia Coast*, 35, 70.

28. Captain Francisco de Fuentes, from Sápala, to Gov. Marquez Cabrera, February 7, 1681, SD 226; Worth, *Struggle for the Georgia Coast*, 19, 28, 31, 59.

29. Bushnell, *Situado and Sabana*, 34–35, 70–71, 121–22.

30. Bushnell, "Ruling the Republic of Indians."

31. Robert Allen Matter, *Pre-Seminole Florida: Spanish Soldiers, Friars, and Indian Missions, 1513–1763* (New York: Garland Publishing, 1990), 149, 157n43.

32. Gov. Marquez Cabrera to the friar of Enacape [Fray Juan Miguel de Villarroel], June 22, 1681, in Auto on the conversions at San Salvador de Mayaca and San Antonio de Enacape, 1681–1682, Enclosure B in Gov. Marquez Cabrera to the Crown, October 7, 1682, SD 226/95.

33. Bushnell, *Situado and Sabana*, 165–67; Worth, *Struggle for the Georgia Coast*, 43, 45, 167, 168.

34. Inquisitor Fray Pedro de Luna, Informe on Gov. Marquez Cabrera [March 29, 1688?], SD 864/9.

35. Domingo de Leturiondo, from Madrid, to the Crown, December 30, 1672, SD 848/11.

36. Gov. Pablo de Hita Salazar to the Crown, October 31, 1679, enclosed with Gov. Hita Salazar, February 26, 1680, SD 226.

37. Gov. Pablo de Hita Salazar to Fray Jacinto de Barreda, October 31, 1679, and Fray Jacinto de Barreda to Gov. Hita Salazar, n.d., in Gov. Hita Salazar to the Crown, February 26, 1680, SD 226.

38. Declaration by five caciques from Apalachicola, September 20, 1681, Enclosure A in Gov. Marquez Cabrera to the Crown, October 7, 1682, SD 226/95.

39. Argüelles, Visita of Guale and Mocama, 1677–1678.

40. Fray Juan Miguel de Villarroel, from San Antonio [de Enacape], to the Governor [Marquez Cabrera], June 21, 1681, and Gov. Marquez Cabrera to Fray Juan Miguel de Villarroel [at San Antonio de Enacape], June 22, 1681, in Auto on the conversions at Mayaca and Enacape, 1681–1682.

41. Gov. Diego de Quiroga y Losada to the Crown, April 1, 1688, SD 839/119.

42. Petition on behalf of Francisco and Matheo, caciques of Mayaca, by Domingo de Leturiondo, Defender of the Indians, to Gov. Marquez Cabrera, [April 1682?], in Auto on the conversions at Mayaca and Enacape, 1681–1682.

43. Antonio Menéndez Marquez and Francisco de la Rocha to the Crown, n.d. [before March 11, 1682], Fray Bartolomé de Quiñones, Relation of San Salvador de Mayaca, March 11, 1682, and Fray Juan Miguel de Villarroel, Relation of San Antonio [de Enacape], April 12, 1682, in Auto on the conversions at Mayaca and Enacape, 1681–1682.

44. Fray Juan Chrisóstomo, Declaration, in Auto on the Ecclesiastical Visita of Lic. Juan Ferro Machado, March 29, 1688, SD 864/10B.

45. Amy Turner Bushnell, "'These people are not conquered like those of New Spain': Florida's Reciprocal Colonial Compact," *Florida Historical Quarterly* 92, no. 3 (Winter 2014): 524–53.

46. Crown to Gov. Marquez Cabrera, Cédula on the firearms, March 22, 1685, SD 852/34.

47. Governor of Carolina [James Colleton] to Gov. Quiroga y Losada, April 1, 1688, SD 839.

48. Gov. Marquez Cabrera to Teniente Antonio Matheos, Apalachee, December 5, 1685, in Gov. Marquez Cabrera to the Crown, March 19, 1686, SD 839/82.

49. Gov. Joseph de Zúñiga y Cerda, Orders on scalptaking, March 14, 1701, in the Residencia of Gov. Joseph de Zúñiga y Cerda [1706?], SD 858/B-252.

50. Junta de Guerra, St. Augustine, November 3, 1694, and Gov. Torres y Ayala, Orders to Teniente Jacinto Roque Pérez, Apalachee, November 4, 1694, in Gov. Torres y Ayala to the Crown, March 11, 1695, SD 839/130A.

51. Gov. Zúñiga y Cerda, Orders to post on the bujíos, n.d. [after March 30, 1704], in the Residencia of Gov. Zúñiga y Cerda [1706?], SD 858/B-260.

52. Except where otherwise noted, the next few pages are taken from Bushnell, *Situado and Sabana*, chapters 15, 16, and 18.

53. Alonso Solana, Mapa de la Ysla de la Florida [1683], printed without attribution in Verne E. Chatelain, *The Defenses of Spanish Florida, 1565 to 1763*, Publication 511 (Washington DC: Carnegie Institute of Washington, 1941), map 7.

54. Juan Rodriguez Tiznado, teniente of Timucua, from Santa Fé [to Gov. Marquez Cabrera], March 10, 1685, in Auto on [Santa Catalina de] Afuyca, March 10–22, 1685, SD 839/82.

55. Juan Rodriguez Tiznado [to Gov. Marquez Cabrera]. The league originated as the distance that could be covered in an hour on foot; the Spanish *legua común* was 2.6 miles.

56. Gov. Marquez Cabrera to the Crown, December 29, 1685, SD 839/82.

57. Fray Juan Mercado, from Santa Cruz [de Sabacola], to Teniente Antonio Matheos, San Luis [de Apalachee], November 27, 1685, enclosed with Antonio Matheos to Gov. Marquez Cabrera, November 27, 1685, in Gov. Marquez Cabrera to the Viceroy of New Spain, March 19, 1686, SD 839/100B.

58. Eric E. Bowne, "Dr. Henry Woodward's Role in Early Carolina Indian Relations," in *Creating and Contesting Carolina: Proprietary Era Histories*, ed. Michelle LeMaster and Bradford J. Wood (Columbia: University of South Carolina Press, 2013), 73–93; Bushnell, *Situado and Sabana*, 136, 138, 142, 147, 166–68.

59. The Yamasees' hats were not the picturesque *sombreros* of Mexican *charro* outfits but the serviceable felt hats manufactured in England from beaver furs traded by Indians to the Hudson's Bay Company. In the Southeast, well-dressed Spaniards and Hispanized chiefs wore this

Living at Liberty 51

same hat, exported in large quantities to Spain and Brazil. See Ann M. Carlos and Frank D. Lewis, *Commerce by a Frozen Sea: Native Americans and the North American Fur Trade* (Philadelphia: University of Pennsylvania Press, 2010). The *justacor*, or *justacor de picote*, was a coat faced in a contrasting color, with oversize cuffs.

60. Teniente Antonio Mateos [from Apalachee], to Gov. Marquez Cabrera, March 14, 1686, in Gov. Marquez Cabrera to the Crown, March 19, 1686, SD 839/82.

61. Gov. Marquez Cabrera to the Crown, September 8, 1686, SD 839/130; Crown, Cédula to Gov. Marquez Cabrera, September 2, 1687, in Gov. Laureano de Torres y Ayala to the Crown, March 11, 1695, SD 839/130A.

62. Gov. Marquez Cabrera to the Crown, February 8, 1687, SD 840/112.

63. Gov. Diego Coleton [James Colleton] of Carolina to Gov. Diego de Quiroga y Losada, August 12, 1687, SD 839/116.

64. Gov. Quiroga y Losada to Gov. Coleton of Carolina, November 12, 1687, SD 839/116.

65. Gov. Colleton of Carolina to Gov. Quiroga y Losada, n.d., in Gov. Quiroga y Losada to the Crown, April 1, 1688, SD 839/119.

66. Gov. Quiroga y Losada to the Crown, April 1, 1688, SD 839/119.

67. Kathleen A. Deagan, "Accommodation and Resistance: The Process and Impact of Spanish Colonization in the Southeast," in *Columbian Consequences*, vol. 2: *Archaeology and History of the Spanish Borderlands East*, ed. David Hurst Thomas (Washington DC: Smithsonian Institution Press, 1990), 297–314.

68. On the two capitals see Alexander Y. Sweeney, "Cultural Continuity and Change," this volume.

69. John H. Hann, *A History of the Timucua Indians and Missions* (Gainesville: University Press of Florida, 1996), 265–66.

70. Junta de Guerra de Indias, [Spain], [to Gov. Quiroga y Losada], August 7, 1693, SD 6/89; John H. Hann, *Apalachee: The Land Between the Rivers* (Gainesville: University Presses of Florida, 1988), 48–49; Gov. Joseph Blake of Carolina [to the governor of Florida], January 24, 1695, SD 839/130; Gov. Torres y Ayala to the governor of Carolina [Joseph Blake], March 3, 1695, SD 839/130.

71. On the stipends, rations, and allowances of Florida Franciscans see Bushnell, *Situado and Sabana*, 52–59.

72. Juan de Pueyo, Visita of the Provinces of Guale and Mocama, 1695, in the Residencia of Gov. Laureano de Torres y Ayala [1699?], EC 157A, cuaderno 1, folios 109–40.

73. Juan de Pueyo, Visita of the Provinces of Guale and Mocama.

74. Evangeline Walker Andrews and Charles McLean Andrews, eds., *Jonathan Dickinson's Journal or, God's Protecting Providence* [1696–97] (Stuart FL: Valentine's Bookstore, 1975), 68–71.

75. John H. Hann, trans. and ed., "Translation of Alonso de Leturiondo's Memorial to the King of Spain, [1700]," *Florida Archaeology* 2 (1986): 165–225, citing 175. See Bushnell, *Situado and Sabana*, 169.

76. Gov. Zúñiga y Cerda to the Crown, January 3, 1703, in the Residencia of Gov. Zúñiga y Cerda [1706?], SD 858/B-135; Bushnell, *Situado and Sabana*, 190; Charles W. Arnade, *The Siege of St. Augustine in 1702* (Gainesville: University of Florida Press, 1959).

77. Gov. Zúñiga y Cerda, December 14, 1702, in the Residencia of Gov. Zúñiga y Cerda, SD 858/ B-113.

78. Paul E. Hoffman, *Florida's Frontiers* (Bloomington: Indiana University Press, 2002), 178–79. For details on this invasion and its aftermath see Mark F. Boyd (trans. and ed.) with Hale G. Smith and John W. Griffin, *Here They Once Stood: The Tragic End of the Apalachee Missions* (Gainesville: University of Florida Press, 1951), and Bushnell, "Patricio de Hinachuba."

79. Ramsey, *Yamasee War*, 110–11, 192–94.

80. Andrés García, from San Francisco, to Governor [Zúñiga y Cerda], June 17, 1705, in the Residencia of Gov. Zúñiga y Cerda, SD 858/4–104. For more on the mop-up raids see Amy Turner Bushnell, "The Menéndez Marquez Cattle Barony at La Chua and the Determinants of Economic Expansion in Seventeenth-Century Florida," *Florida Historical Quarterly* 56 (1978): 407–31, and Bushnell, "Patricio de Hinachuba."

81. Thomas Nairne, Report to the Lord [Palatine], n.p., July 10, 1708, in *Records in the British Public Records Office Relating to South Carolina*, 5 vols., ed. Alexander S. Salley (Columbia SC), 5: 196–97.

82. S. Max Edelson, "Defining Carolina: Cartography and Colonization in the North American Southeast, 1657–1733," in LeMaster and Wood, eds., *Creating and Contesting Carolina*, 27–48.

83. Fray Joseph Bullones, from Havana, to don Gerónimo Valdés, Bishop of Cuba, August 13, 1728, SD 865; Consejo de Indias, Consulta on the Yamasees, January 8, 1716, SD 833.

84. Bushnell, *Situado and Sabana*, 195–96. See also Amy Turner Bushnell, "'Gastos de Indios': The Crown and the Chiefdom-Presidio Compact in Florida," in *El Gran Norte Mexicano: Indios, misioneros y pobladores entre el mito y la historia*, coord. Salvador Bernabéu Albert (Sevilla: Consejo Superior de Investigaciones Científicas, 2009), 137–63.

85. Steven C. Hahn, "The Long Yamasee War," and John E. Worth, "The Yamasee in West Florida," this volume.

86. Diego Peña, from San Marcos de Apalachee, to Gov. Antonio de Benavides, August 6, 1723, enclosed with the Marqués de Casafuerte, Viceroy of New Spain, to the Crown, August 7, 1724, SD 842/76. Uchises was the Spanish term for Lower Creeks during this era. See Worth, "The Yamasee in West Florida," this volume.

87. Bushnell, "'These people are not conquered like those of New Spain.'"

88. Diego Peña, from San Marcos de Apalachee, to Gov. Benavides, August 6, 1723, enclosed with the Viceroy of New Spain to the Crown, August 7, 1724, SD 842/76.

89. Declaration of four Yamasee caciques to Gov. Benavides, May 20, 1724, enclosed with Gov. Benavides to the Crown, June 16, 1725, SD 842/79.

90. Fray Joseph Bullones, from Havana, to don Gerónimo Valdés, Bishop of Cuba, August 13, 1728, SD 865.

91. Twenty-three vecinos of St. Augustine to the Crown, November 14, 1725, SD 842/88.

92. Parley with the Uchises of Caveta, February 5, 1726, enclosed with Gov. Benavides to the Crown, February 24, 1726, SD 842/92.

93. Fray Joseph Bullones, from Havana, to don Gerónimo Valdés, Bishop of Cuba, August 13, 1728, SD 865.

94. John H. Hann, "St. Augustine's Fallout from the Yamasee War," *Florida Historical Quarterly* 68, no. 2 (1989): 180–200.

95. Cesar Augusto, Yamas Chalaque, king of the Indians, to the Governor of San Agustín, June 20, 1740; James Ogletorpe and Vicente Pierse, from the British Camp in Florida, to the Governor, Bishop and Concejo of Florida, June 20, 1740 (old style); Gov. Montiano to Cesar Augusto, Yamas Chalaque, king of the Indians, n.d. [July 2, 1740]; and Gov. Montiano to General James Ogletorpe and Comandante Vicente Pierse, July 2, 1740, signed by the governor, the Bishop of Tricale, the royal officials, and the captains. Copies of all four letters were enclosed with Gov. Montiano to the Crown, August 9, 1740, SD 845/8. In *Struggle for the Georgia Coast*, 210, Worth identifies Chalaque with Cherokee.

96. Michelle LeMaster and Bradford J. Wood, "Introduction: Creating and Contesting Carolina," in LeMaster and Wood, eds., *Creating and Contesting Carolina*, 1–23. In her chapter "War,

Masculinity, and Alliances on the Carolina," 164–85 in the same volume, LeMaster discusses the inability of the Carolinians to control their Indian allies.

97. Gov. Montiano to the Crown, March 15, 1743, SD 848.

98. Don Juan Isidoro de León, from San Marcos de Apalachee, to Gov. Montiano, February 21, 1746, enclosed with Gov. Montiano to don Fernando Treviño, March 14, 1746, SD 845/62.

99. Captain Ysidoro de León, from Apalachee, to Gov. Montiano, June 26, 1747, enclosed with Gov. Montiano to the Crown, August 3, 1747, SD 845/65.

100. Gov. Montiano to the Crown, March 15, 1748, SD 845/66.

101. Scardaville and Belmonte, "The 1756 Griñán Report" (see note 26 to the present chapter).

102. Patrick M. Malone, *The Skulking Way of War: Technology and Tactics among the New England Indians* (Lanham MD: Madison Books, 1991).

103. Worth, "The Yamasee in West Florida," this volume.

104. Amy Turner Bushnell, "How to Fight a Pirate: Provincials, Royalists, and the Raiding of San Marcos," in *Pirates, Jack Tar, and Memory: New Directions in American Maritime History*, ed. Paul A. Gilje and William Pencak (Mystic CT: Mystic Seaport, 2007), 11–25.

2

Yamasee Migrations into the Mocama and Timucua Mission Provinces of Florida, 1667–1683
An Archaeological Perspective

KEITH ASHLEY

A round 1667, less than a decade after their emerging coalescence along the northern periphery of Spanish La Florida, several refugee communities retreated into the Guale and Mocama mission provinces under mounting attacks by Chichimeco Indian slave raiders. Spanish officials allowed these immigrant Yamasee to settle at abandoned mission *doctrina* and *visita* locations on Atlantic coastal barrier islands. In present-day Florida, they initially reoccupied settlements formerly inhabited by Mocama on Amelia Island and, by 1679, also had repopulated Timucua missions along the middle St. Johns River, north (Anacape) and south (Mayaca) of Lake George. No Yamasee settlements appeared in the St. Augustine vicinity during this initial wave of refugees into Spanish Florida. Though not missionized at this time, the Yamasee were expected to provide tribute and laborers to local chiefs and the Spanish colony, respectively. By 1683 most of these towns were again emptied as the Yamasee evacuated Florida and fled north to English Carolina.

Archaeological evidence of this first phase of Yamasee occupation in Florida (ca. 1667–83) is limited, as few sites of this era have been excavated or even systematically sampled. Moreover, early Yamasee sites on Amelia Island that have been tested also were occupied earlier by mission period Mocama and later by Guale immigrants—all three of whom manufactured San Marcos/Altamaha pottery—making it difficult to identify distinct Yamasee occupational components. This chapter reviews the first Florida phase of Yamasee history and discusses what is currently known about the distribution of early Yama-

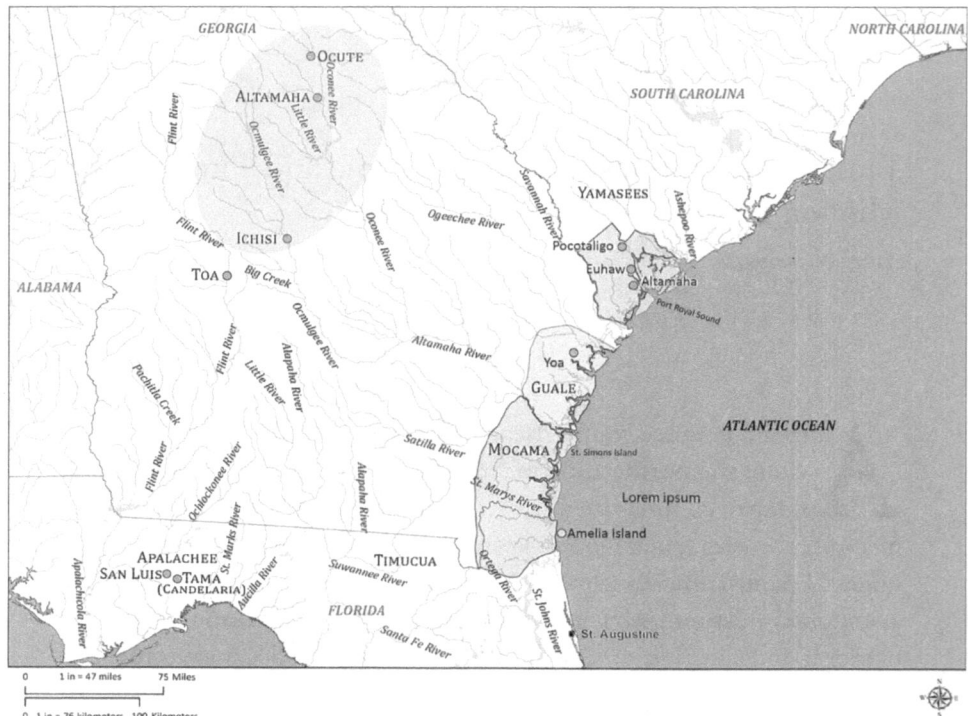

MAP 1. The colonial Southeast. Map by David W. Wilson, Center for Instruction and Research Technology, University of North Florida.

see sites in peninsular Florida, with the hope of creating a springboard for future research.

Yamasee Origins and First Occupation of Florida

The Yamasee are a Native American group not often identified with Florida. In part, I suspect this is because Yamasee occupations there were brief, episodic, localized, and restricted to the late seventeenth and eighteenth centuries. Moreover, their identity has been often blanketed beneath a mission Indian cover or falsely equated or combined with that of the Guale Indians. But this veil is being lifted by recent scholarship, revealing a lengthier and more widespread Yamasee presence in Florida.[1] Entanglements in European rivalries and internecine slave raids that ranged across the lower Southeast framed Yamasee history.

A willingness to move long distances and shift European allegiances enabled them to adapt to their turbulent surroundings. As a result, a tradition of resistance was forged among a growing amalgam of interior and coastal Native refugees whose collective identity as Yamasee was eventually borne out of the devastating circumstances wrought by European colonization.[2]

One hundred and fifty years before the term "Yamasis" appeared in Spanish letters dating to 1663, antecedent groups were apparently living in villages and farmsteads associated with the Mississippian chiefdoms of Altamaha, Ocute, and Ichisi along the Oconee and Ocmulgee river drainages of the interior Georgia piedmont.[3] By the early seventeenth century, mound building had ceased and the interior river valleys were undergoing demographic collapse.[4] What remained of a once densely populated region were scattered remnants of disease-damaged chiefdoms that by the mid-seventeenth century became easy targets for roving Chichimeco slave raiders outfitted by Virginia traders.

Rather than succumb to these increasing attacks, piedmont groups fled their ancestral homeland between 1659 and 1663. Around this time Spanish documents report "Yamasis" living in at least five settlements "six, eight, four, three, two, and more days distant by road from these provinces [of Escamaçu and Guale along the Atlantic coast]."[5] Current evidence suggests a location inland from the mouth of the Savannah River between the Guale mission province and Chichimeco villages along the middle Savannah River.[6] These refugee communities, which apparently possessed ancestral town names but bore little resemblance to their chiefdom progenitors, came to form the core of an ever-expanding mélange of Native groups eventually known to Europeans as Yamasee.

The South Carolina–Georgia border, however, proved only a temporary haven for the fledgling Yamasee towns. By 1667 a new round of attacks by Chichimeco slavers forced them south into the coastal mission provinces of Guale and Mocama, where they concentrated their communities on St. Simons Island, Georgia, and Amelia Island, Florida, respectively.[7] Town leaders gained settlement lands and refugee status through a formal request to the colonial Spanish governor and the verbal consent of the appropriate provincial chief.[8] Yamasee arrival filled several empty mission town sites, bolstered the rapidly dwindling coastal mission Indian population, and provided a new pool of laborers and warriors for the Guale and Mocama provinces. Though these people were not subject to direct missionization, friars appeared confident the refugees and migrants would someday heed the calling of the lord through interactions with nearby Christian Indians.[9] But their optimism would be dashed, as the number of Christianity-resisting Yamasee continued to grow throughout their nearly two-decade-long tenure in Spanish Florida.

To ensure Spanish protection from the Carolina colony and their Indian allies, Yamasee men contributed to the yearly mission labor draft (*repartimiento*), often being the leading supplier of workers from the northern mission provinces during their first decade in Spanish Florida.[10] However, documented complaints about absentee and runaway Yamasee laborers in St. Augustine suggest that the immigrants' support may not always have lived up to Spanish expectations.[11] Moreover, the second half of the seventeenth century witnessed a loosened Spanish strategy toward Native labor, whereby officials attempted to recruit or entice Indian cooperation through payment of some form. Other than rendering obedience to the Spanish Crown, the labor draft was the only official requirement of the Yamasee because "as pagans they were not to work in the mission fields."[12]

Yamasee tribute to mission chiefs was deemed voluntary, although noncompliance or at least an unwillingness to contribute led to cases of friction between Christian leaders and more traditional communities situated in their territory. In one instance the cacica of San Juan del Puerto in 1681 demanded payment from Yamasee on Amelia Island in the form of "bear fat, deerskins, acorns, and palmetto berries," but the governor intervened and exempted the island's Yamasee "who were to be protected and treated with charity."[13]

The indigenous Mocama occupied four mission settlements along the Atlantic coast in the decades prior to Yamasee incursions into La Florida. From north to south, these were San Buenaventura de Guadalquini at the south end of St. Simons Island and San Pedro de Mocama on Cumberland Island in Georgia, and Santa María de Sena on Amelia Island and San Juan del Puerto on Fort George Island in

Florida.[14] Around each friar-occupied mission community (*doctrina*) was a small outlying cluster of Native villages or *visitas* that fell under the spiritual guidance of the neighboring mission friar.[15] In time, continuing population loss within the mission provinces due to epidemics and emigration led the Spanish to coordinate the relocation of *visita* communities to nearby *doctrinas*, a process known as *congregación*. The formal combining of mission settlements (*reducción*) among the Mocama began around 1655, with the transfer of the entire San Pedro population to Santa María, and they all moved to San Juan in 1665. Therefore, at the dawn of Yamasee arrival in the Mocama province, only the region's northernmost (San Buenaventura) and southernmost (San Juan) missions were still in existence.

The relocation of four Yamasee towns to Amelia Island (Santa María) in 1667 helped partly fill a gap in the Mocama mission chain. Placed at the northern end of the island was an unnamed Yamasee town followed by Ocotoque one league to the south, La Tama another two leagues to the south, and Santa María one-half league farther south. Two more Yamasee settlements relocated to the Mocama province in 1680. One community took over the former mission of San Pedro de Mocama and the other settled to the north, both on Cumberland Island. In 1675 the four towns on Amelia Island had a total population of 190, with each town possessing between 40 and 60 residents.[16] In 1678 "the caciques and leading men and heirs" of the island's Yamasee communities convened for an official visitation by Antonio de Argüelles in the council house at Santa María.[17] Appointed by the governor of Spanish Florida, Argüelles visited the missions of the Guale and Mocama provinces to gather demographic information and intelligence on the current state of affairs within these Spanish-allied settlements.

By the time of the next census in 1681, only one Amelia Island town was home to Yamasee, and that was Santa María with a population of 101.[18] Although Santa María's population apparently increased by about 40 percent from 1675 to 1681, the overall number of Yamasee on the island during this same time dropped by nearly 50 percent. It appears that residents of some of the three abandoned villages on Amelia Island relocated to Santa María, while others may have emigrated to new Yamasee settlements that existed on Cumberland Island between ca. 1680 and 1683.[19] Others may even have headed south to the reestablished missions of San Antonio de Anacape and San Salvador de Mayaca along the middle St. Johns River, as discussed later in this chapter.

The Amelia Island towns were not the only Yamasee communities in Florida during the first wave of Yamasee immigration. Some groups fled farther south and inland from the Atlantic seaboard, establishing a settlement in Timucua at San Antonio de Anacape and another in Mayaca at San Salvador de Mayaca along the middle St. Johns River. When the Yamasee arrived in 1679, both missions were vacant and likely had been for years. The two were on a 1655 mission list but neither appeared on two 1675 registries.[20] A 1680 document listed the two as "new conversions" and identified their residents as Yamasee, intimating "that most or all of the mission's earlier populations had disappeared."[21]

Unlike in the Amelia Island towns, missionaries arrived in Anacape and Mayaca to resurrect mission life among these refugee communities. Although the Florida governor appears to have been under the impression that the Yamasee there had requested a friar, such a claim is refuted by later inquiries.[22] Mission documents indicate that by 1682 residents included both baptized Christian and unconverted Indians. Anacape had a population of 21, while Mayaca had 69 residents.[23] Both, however, had recently experienced defections, with some members moving to Yamasee settlements on the coastal islands. The previous year Fray Juan Miguel de Villarroel of Anacape had requested Governor Juan Márquez Cabrera to retrieve the fugitives and return them to his mission, to which the governor responded that it would be "a mistake to try to force *infieles* to live anywhere they did not want to."[24] Moreover, the governor expressed the belief that being content in their place of residence might foster conversion, although his real motive for keeping them on the coast may have been the need for military protection against English attack from the north.[25]

But success at conversion appears to have been more apparent than real, as rumor had it that the Yamasee at Anacape were "not disposed to join the assembly of the faithful."[26] Moreover, the fatigued and perhaps disillusioned friar (Bartolomé de Quiñones) deserted his Mayaca mission in 1681 and, in the process, removed many of the church possessions to the Timucuan mission of Salamototo farther north along the St. Johns River.[27] His rationale for leaving apparently was predicated on the Yamasees' disinterest in farming combined with their seasonal subsistence cycle that took them deep into the woods, where they lived as roaming foragers, only using mission towns as temporary base camps.[28] Apparently, owing to the erratic supply of provisions from St. Augustine, Fray Quiñones was often forced to rely heavily on the Native fare of plants and roots, causing him to become sick. This itinerant lifestyle, which allowed Natives to avoid the labor draft, was a frequent criticism of the Indians of southern Florida, bemoaned by both Spanish government and religious officials.[29]

By 1683 many Yamasee were on the move again, as their settlements throughout La Florida were abandoned amid turmoil brought on by French pirate raids and English-sponsored slave-catching expeditions. In addition to these external circumstances, internal factors apparently were at play. As Yamasee numbers increased, their participation in the labor draft appeared to wane even as threats of severe punishment were issued for noncompliance.[30] In 1695 a Christian Yamasee named Santiago, who resided at the Guale mission of Santa María on Amelia Island and claimed to be the last of his people living in the Mocama province, wrote of the abuses inflicted on him at the hands of Spanish soldiers and implied that such treatment may have been why many Yamasee had earlier "all gone to the English."[31] These factors seemed to have fostered a growing dissatisfaction among the Yamasee with Spanish governance of La Florida.

The Yamasees' destination this time was the Port Royal region of South Carolina, where they hoped a change in colonial allegiance would inspire protection and an upper hand in trade relations with the fledgling Carolina colony.[32] The defection was massive and widespread, affecting Yamasee in the provinces of Guale, Mocama, and Apalachee, as towns evacuated Spanish Florida in waves between 1683 and 1685. The Mayaca and Anacape missions survived until the first decade of the eighteenth century, although it is unclear if Yamasees were part of these missions following the exodus of Florida by their coastal-dwelling counterparts. Did those living along the St. Johns

River choose to leave with their brethren or did they stay in the lake- and marsh-dominated environs of the middle St. Johns? John Hann suggests that "some, if not all of the 104" non-Mayaca recorded on the 1692 census for Salvador de Mayaca were Yamasee, but concedes that this is not known for certain.[33]

For three decades the Yamasee confederation in South Carolina grew, as Upper and Lower Yamasee towns became staunch English allies.[34] By 1715, however, relations between the two had turned sour, and the Yamasee undertook a second retreat deep into La Florida, where they would establish themselves in or near mission communities around St. Augustine and in Spanish West Florida.[35] Ironically, these are the same Natives who over the past two decades had "played prominent roles in the destruction of the Florida missions."[36]

Assessing the First Yamasee Phase in Florida

What can we glean from the Spanish documents about the Yamasee during their first phase of occupation in Florida? First, the Yamasee were not a unified social or ethnic group at that time. Instead they were a decentralized series of towns derived from separate precontact chiefdoms. Some of these communities appear to have carried their ancestral names with them, including Altamaha (La Tama) and Ocotoque (possibly Ocute).[37] Moreover, documents indicate that Chachises (Ichisi) were living adjacent to San Phelipe on northern Cumberland Island in 1681.[38] Early on, only a small number of immigrant towns in the mission provinces bore a Yamasee cultural affiliation in Spanish documents, while others frequently carried the generic label of "pagan" or "infidels."[39] In time, Yamasee became the term of convenience by which Spanish and English officials referred to them as a collective whole.

When a small handful of ethnically varied refugee communities first received admittance into Spanish Florida in the late 1660s, their population numbered only in the hundreds. Based on the Pedro de Arcos population figures of 1675, these groups accounted for about seven hundred Natives inhabiting the provinces of Guale, Mocama, and Apalachee.[40] This same census outlines an immigrant population that outnumbered baptized Indians in the Atlantic coastal provinces.

The total number of less than one thousand pales in comparison to counts given by Scottish settlers and Indian traders residing in Stuarts Town (Carolina), who in 1685 reported "a thousand or more Yamasee are coming down daily."[41] The context of this comment clearly illuminates the multiethnic composition of the term Yamasee by this time, also including Lower Creeks, Guale defectors, and other fugitive mission Indians. Thus, during their first Florida phase of occupation, the Yamasee were neither geographically consolidated nor ethnically exclusive.

While the colonial setting of the Southeast wreaked havoc on indigenous populations, it also created a context for the genesis of new ethnic groups through the syncretism of formerly distinct entities. A blending of ethnically different people against a backdrop fraught with sweeping social, political, and epidemiological uncertainties eventually gave birth to a Yamasee identity. This process of ethnogenesis resulted in an eventual conscious recognition, by insiders and outsiders, of a new cultural (ethnic) group identity different from its ancestral roots.[42] In other words, the cultures did not just blend but actively forged a new identity and developed new practices. In the Southeast, while migrant and remnant groups did in time cultivate a self-identified Yamasee tribal identity, this recognized transformation had yet to crystalize prior to their departure from Spanish Florida for English Carolina in the early 1680s.[43]

Spanish documents are rather mute with respect to early Yamasee sociopolitical organization. Political affiliation and loyalty of the La Florida refugees appeared tethered first to their town, which served as a primary source of identity. Early towns may have been somewhat homogeneous in internal composition, but combined they were heterogeneous and consisted of "a remarkable variety of diverse aboriginal towns."[44] Political and economic decisions arose at the town level in council houses where titular chiefs apparently held positions subordinate to councils or other collective forms of leadership and wielded little authority over lands or vassals.[45] This is evident in one of the few documentary references to Yamasee politics in which the cacique at Santa María, during a 1678 visitation to Amelia Island, stated that "his vassals did not obey him and that for this reason he was resigning from the chieftainsip."⁴⁶ Though open to interpretation, this statement intimates that Spanish officials imposed the term *cacique* on Yamasee town leaders for diplomatic purposes, meaning that individuals actually held minimal political authority in their communities. Similarly, so-called chiefs at Anacape and Mayaca seem to have had little control over their fellow villagers.[47]

Towns, portable and each loosely allied with the Spanish colonial system, operated independently, and responses to all circumstances were not necessarily uniform. Although there is no evidence for any sort of overarching political apparatus or leadership structure, some form of intercommunity connections likely existed between them. These may have included new institutions and ideologies that eventually brought together varied Native interests, agendas, and worldviews. Conceivably, a shared sense of resistance to relations of dominance imposed by the new world order of the colonial Southeast precipitated the formation of integrative, collective, and consensual governance among the Yamasee. The process of town adoption was additive as new groups were absorbed into the ongoing process of becoming something consciously oppositional to Europeans and affiliated mission Indians. Both the Spanish and English may have contributed to the emergence of a Yamasee identity by treating all Indian towns outside the mission system in similar ways and with the same expectations.

Because the Yamasee were not a coherent social or ethnic group in Florida during their first phase of occupation, historian Bradley Schrager has described these "people-in-formation" as a "resistance movement" embedded squarely within the Spanish mission provinces of Guale, Mocama, Timucua, and Apalachee.[48] While perhaps not a movement per se, the Yamasee did manifest a persisting tradition of resistance that sought survival and autonomy on their own terms. From the moment they first arrived along the Atlantic Coast of Spanish Florida, these immigrants were blatantly disinterested in Christianity. Not only did they refuse baptism, but towns avoided building churches and raising wooden crosses for all to see. These constructed features were the most public form of signaling affiliation with the Spanish colonial world, and their absence in Yamasee towns made a strong and unequivocal statement of resistance. This nonconformity appears to have attracted Indians within and along the fringes of La Florida who were dissatisfied with mission life but seemingly allowed entry to help reinforce Spanish defenses against the English. Upon acceptance into the Spanish fold, refugees complied to the least extent possible. Most of their resistance appears to have been nonviolent and likely manifested through routine (and perhaps unconscious) daily actions aimed at asserting distinction and autonomy. But violence was not outside their arsenal of civil resistance, as demonstrated by the Yamasees' fierce raiding of Spanish missions shortly after relocating to Carolina and taking up with the British in the mid-1680s.

In looking back on their history, one finds that the Yamasee have the markings of a persistent tradition of resistance "made and reproduced through egalitarian social relations, mobility, and an ongoing process of separation."[49] In his overview of the Yamasee, archaeologist John E. Worth notes that they maintained "a distinctive identity as a group regardless of geographic location and neighboring groups," migrated "huge distances to suit immediate political expediency," and seemingly had a "new and more egalitarian and fluid social formation" compared to ancestral times.[50] These general features are among the parallels found "in the structures and actions of resistant traditions" as each works "to create identities that are deliberately oppositional to the conditions of oppression they experienced."[51] Asserting difference in these cases is an ongoing process through social interactions, not geographic isolation. Even on the occasions when the Yamasee decided to vote with their feet, their intent involved relationships with new allies, not spatial seclusion. Thus the Yamasee created and reproduced their social identity through ongoing encounters with neighboring Natives and Europeans as they moved across the colonial Southeast landscape. A shared interest in and commitment to resisting Christianity and Spanish rule provided empowerment and partly underwrote their broadly egalitarian or at least nominal hierarchical political structure during their first phase of occupation in Florida. With this historical overview in place, let us now explore what current archaeology has to say about early Yamasee occupations in peninsular Florida.

Yamasee Archaeology in Peninsular Florida (excluding St. Augustine)

At present, only one archaeological project in Florida outside the city of St. Augustine has targeted a Yamasee settlement as a focus of research and excavation, and this site's Yamasee component is currently under revaluation (discussed later). This does not mean that archaeological sites containing evidence of Yamasee occupation have not been documented or even sampled by archaeologists. But this lack of attention does mean that we know virtually nothing archaeologically about the layout of early Yamasee villages or details of subsistence and daily life during the late seventeenth century. I believe the same is true for the Georgia coast. Despite this dearth of archaeological data, I propose that viable candidates exist for the location of most early Yamasee villages in Florida based on previous surface collections or field testing designed to elucidate other occupational components.

The signature archaeological correlate of Yamasee sites is a grit-tempered ware known as San Marcos in Florida and Altamaha in Georgia.[52] San Marcos assemblages include vessels that are undecorated, incised, check stamped, curvilinear stamped, and most commonly stamped with a line blocked design that in fragments resembles simple stamping. A minor but consistent part of the assemblage is red-filmed wares, most of which are plates or other European vessel forms referred to by archaeologists as colonowares.[53] Unfortunately, seventeenth-century Guale and Mocama potters along the Atlantic coast made and used the same San Marcos pottery types as the Yamasee.[54] Confounding this situation is the fact that some Yamasee towns in Florida were occupied earlier by Mocama and/or later by relocated Guale, all of whom manufactured San Marcos wares. And therein lies the rub—how do we distinguish late seventeenth-century Yamasee, Guale, and Mocama occupations at sequentially occupied sites when they all produced the same pottery?[55]

The reason for its widespread acceptance during the 1600s is unclear, although Worth attributes the homogenization of Native-made pottery along the Atlantic coast (i.e., San Marcos/Altamaha style zone) to communities of practice in which potters routinely interacted with one another, thereby learning and performing the same preparation, manufacturing, and firing techniques. In other words, frequent movements and interactions among female potters through the coastal mission system created pottery learning networks that crosscut villages so that "groups with different political, ethnic, linguistic, and religious identities [e.g., Yamasee, Guale, Mocama] could produce essentially the same inventory of ceramic types and series [e.g., San Marcos/Altamaha]."[56] Worth distinguishes between communities of practice and communities of identity; the latter is a social network of common group affiliation based on ethnicity, language, politics, religion, kinship, etc.[57]

But beneath this gloss of homogeneity likely lie subtle ceramic attribute distinctions (microstyle) that point to the existence of communities of potters at a smaller spatial scale of more frequent household interaction. As highlighted by Poplin and Marcoux in chapter 3, archaeologists working on Yamasee sites in South Carolina suggest that late Yamasee San Marcos/Altamaha assemblages are marked by a dominance of plain and relatively high percentages of check stamped pottery.[58] Poplin and Marcoux also propose that overstamping is more common in South Carolina assemblages than those from Mocama and Guale mission sites. Others have proposed that Mocama and Guale San Marcos/Altamaha assemblages show an increase in the ratio of stamped to plain pottery through time.[59] It is unclear if both of these observations hold for early Yamasee sites, and testing these proposals is difficult at this time due to the mixed nature of the existing San Marcos/Altamaha ceramic assemblages. Provided tight temporal controls are in place, detailed technological ceramic attribute analysis could help identify slight variations that might indicate smaller interacting communities of practice. With these ceramic issues in mind, I now examine the known archaeological record of northern peninsular Florida to highlight the possible location of early Yamasee sites.

Mocama Province, Amelia Island

In the early 1950s an unsystematic surface survey of selected areas of Amelia Island by Ripley Bullen and John Griffin resulted in the recording of forty-six archaeological sites. Of these, nine produced varying

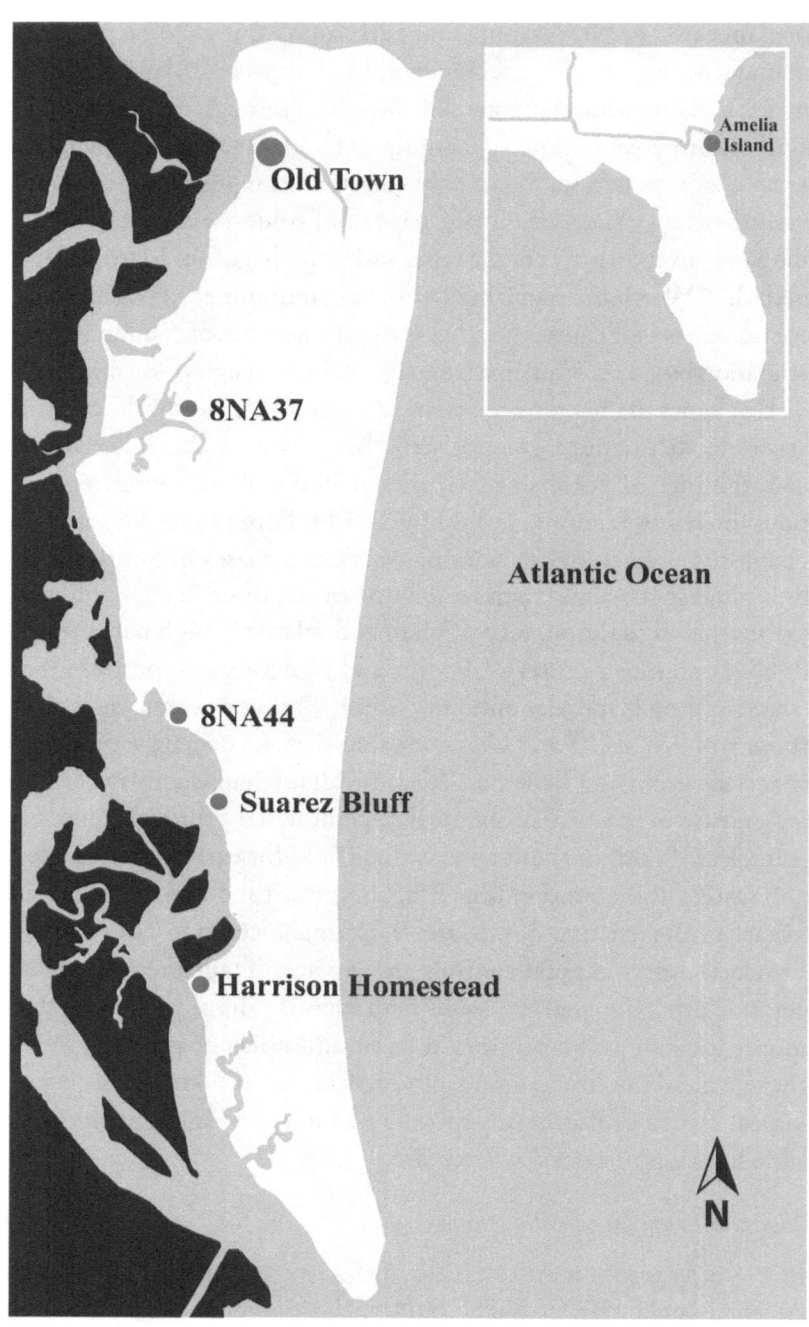

MAP 2. Yamasee sites, Amelia Island, Florida. Map by Keith Ashley.

quantities of San Marcos pottery. All are along the western side of the island, with four located in or around Old Town at its northern tip, one along Jackson Creek, two in the Suarez Bluff–Amelia City vicinity, and two at the island's southern end near Harrison Creek. For the most part then, San Marcos wares were confined to four distinct locations on the island, which Bullen and Griffin equated with the four Yamasee settlements mentioned in a 1675 census document by Pedro de Arcos.[60] From north to south the connections made were Old Town (8NA9) to the unnamed Yamasee village, Peterson Creek (8NA37) to Ocotoque, Amelia City–Suarez Bluff (8NA15 and NA44) to La Tama, and Harrison Homestead (8NA41) to Santa María. Of these, only the most northern and southern sites have received any archaeological attention since Bullen and Griffin's survey.[61]

To the north, Old Town has been the scene of limited archaeological testing and monitoring projects.[62] Both Mocama-made San Pedro and San Marcos pottery have been recovered, although no unequivocal mission period features or distinct precincts have been reported. San Marcos wares are most concentrated at or near the Plaza Lot in Old Town along the bluff overlooking the Amelia River to the east. At this location, more than one thousand San Marcos sherds were recovered in the 1950s, most of which were taken from units associated with the excavation of the early nineteenth-century Spanish Fort San Carlos.[63] Smaller amounts of San Marcos pottery have been collected from the adjacent lower beach area and from a few locations within a kilometer of the Plaza Lot. Relying on ceramics found in the Old Town vicinity, it is conceivable that in addition to the unnamed Yamasee settlement mentioned in the Arcos document, the earlier indigenous Mocama *visita* of Santo Domingo de Napoyca and the relocated Guale mission community of Santa Clara de Tupiqui (1684–1702) were also located in the Old Town area.

To date, the largest collection of San Marcos pottery from Amelia Island comes from the Harrison Homestead site (8NA41). This multicomponent site is the irrefutable location of Mission Santa Catalina de Guale (1683–1702), owing to the identification of the mission's core area and the recovery of the mission seal.[64] The site was tested by

Deagan and Hemmings in the early 1970s and excavated by the University of Florida in the late 1980s.[65] Broad-scale excavations exposed the mission compound of Santa Catalina, which included a church, cemetery, and *convento*. Forty meters to the south, excavations partly exposed shell footers associated with a second mission church, heavily damaged by tidal erosion. At this location excavations revealed more than one hundred burials beneath an intact section of a clay church floor. Originally interpreted as the Yamasee church of Santa María, it now appears that this church was instead associated with the earlier Mocama *visita* or *doctrina* of Santa María de Sena.[66] At present no documentary evidence exists suggesting that the Spanish-labeled "pagan" Yamasee on Amelia Island had churches or missionaries.

At the time of excavation the Mocama Santa María was thought to have been positioned on either northern Amelia Island or perhaps the mainland near the St. Marys River.[67] John Worth was the first to place Santa María de Sena along Harrison Creek and propose that once the Yamasee community relocated there around 1667, their community assumed the earlier place name of Santa María.[68] In the wake of this reinterpretation, only two intrusive, flexed burials placed under the church floor at Santa María are now deemed Yamasee.[69] These two individuals were both robust males aged approximately 26 and 40.[70] Two additional intrusive burials are extended and oriented in the same direction as those below the northern church, suggesting these two interments are affiliated with the later Santa Catalina de Guale mission. The approximately one hundred remaining burials beneath the Santa María church floor then are likely Mocama.

What was once thought to be a rather straightforward interpretation at the Harrison Homestead site has become somewhat problematic. Triple occupation of the site by sequential Mocama, Yamasee, and Guale populations is complicated by the fact that all three groups made and used San Marcos/Altamaha pottery during the late seventeenth century. Instead of containing evidence of Guale and Yamasee mission compounds, the site exhibits loci that relate to Guale and earlier Mocama missions activities with a Yamasee occupation thrown in between. Clearly, the site's complex archaeological record needs to be reexamined in light of this new evidence.

Timucua Province and Mayaca

Moving south to the middle St. Johns River, what about the two Yamasee communities established among the Timucua and Mayaca? Anacape, the more northern of the two, appears to have been located at the Mt. Royal (8PU35) archaeological site. Excavations there by the State of Florida in the mid-1980s and early 1990s were performed within proposed residential roads and selected house lots prior to subdivision development.[71] The artifact assemblage generated by these projects is composed of a large collection of Native and historic-era artifacts, the latter of which date to the Spanish mission and later British periods. Postcontact indigenous St. Johns pottery, Spanish majolica and olive jar fragments, glass trade beads, and religious-related artifacts appear to be associated with the first phase of mission occupation by indigenous Timucua (ca. 1587–1655), confirming John Goggin's earlier suspicion that Mt. Royal is the site of the Timucuan Mission of San Antonio de Anacape.[72]

State excavations also produced a handful of San Marcos sherds and their place of recovery suggests that the later Anacape community inhabited by Yamasees extends outside the area examined by the state survey on private lots in the southeastern part of the site.[73] It is worth noting that John Goggin surface collected more than sixty San Marcos sherds from the Mt. Royal site between 1951 and 1956, although exactly where within the site these were found is unknown.[74] To date, no state-reported archaeological sites near Mt. Royal have yielded San Marcos wares, but other than sand burial mounds, the area immediately north of Lake George has been the scene of minimal archaeological attention in the past century or so.

The great unknown for the location of Yamasee sites in peninsular Florida is the Mayaca region south of Lake George. Currently no San Marcos pottery has been reported for sites along this part of the St. Johns drainage. Several sand mounds have yielded historic artifacts in Native contexts, including Thursby and Raulerson mounds, but most of these finds are modified pieces of precious metal that likely date to the late sixteenth century.[75] Located in the middle of the river channel, Hontoon Island has yielded postcontact-dated

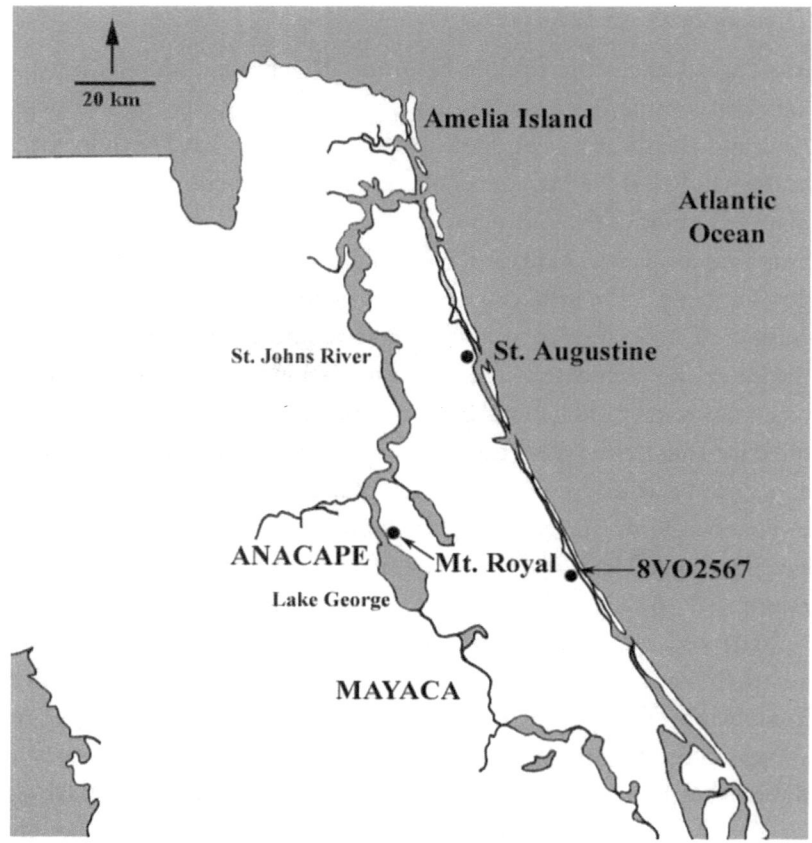

MAP 3. Yamasee regions along St. Johns River. Map by Keith Ashley.

maize fragments, although Barbara Purdy insists that "Hontoon Island was not occupied during the mission period."[76] Moreover, recent survey and testing by the University of Florida also failed to find any evidence of colonial period Native occupations on the island.[77] But the riverbanks opposite the island cannot be ruled out at this time as possible locations for mission-related communities. Going back to the documentary record and the complaints of the friar stationed at San Salvador, if the early Yamasee were following a seasonal foraging routine, then their sites likely consist of small encampments with light artifact scatters, perhaps tied to a larger base camp or mission community.

TABLE 1. San Marcos series pottery from the Riverbend site

	count	percent	percent (excluding unidentified)
Plain	23	22.8	26.4
Complicated stamped	10	9.9	11.5
Simple/cross simple stamped	39	38.6	44.8
Red filmed	15	14.9	17.2
Unidentified stamped	6	5.9	
Unidentified	8	7.9	
Total	101	100	99.9

Atlantic Coast South of St. Augustine

Before concluding, I would like to draw attention to what appears to be an anomaly in the distribution of San Marcos pottery that implicates the Riverbend site (8VO2567) in Volusia County (see table 1).[78] Situated along the west bank of the Tomoka River, this colonial period site lies less than four miles inland from the Atlantic Ocean. Lake George is approximately 26 miles due west and St. Augustine is about 40 miles to the northwest following the Atlantic coastline. Archaeological testing of the site in 1989 yielded 101 San Marcos and red filmed sherds.

Of note is the absence of San Marcos Check Stamped sherds, although a few of the red film fragments displayed check stamping. In addition, five majolica plate fragments were recovered, including Puebla Polychrome and San Agustin Blue on White; the presence of the latter majolica type points to a post-1700 date of occupation. Charred corn cobs from colonial contexts were radiocarbon dated to the late seventeenth or early eighteenth century.

I am aware of no unequivocal documentary evidence that places Guale or early Yamasee immigrants in this part of coastal Florida. Historic Florida Indians referred to as Los Costas were in the general area, or perhaps a little farther south, but they are not known to have produced San Marcos pottery. However, in a 1734 letter to the Spanish Crown, Fray Joseph Ramos Escudero writes of the Yamasees' 1715 exodus from Carolina, the governor's approval of their move to

Spanish Florida, and the establishment of their "towns at a distance of ten and twelve leagues from the said city [of St. Augustine]."[79] This distance would put the relocated settlements in the vicinity of the Riverbend site, although we must keep in mind that Escudero's letter was written nineteen years after the fact. In 1728 Fray Joseph de Bullones wrote that the Yamasee community of Pocotalaca had been located six leagues south of St. Augustine in an area known as Las Rosas.[80] This distance places the Yamasee about 20 miles north of the Riverbend site.

An alternative scenario for the Riverbend site is that it is related to one of the two settlements established in the aftermath of the 1697 uprising by Indians in Mayaca. Afafa was reported to have been located two days from Mayaca, and the other village, Las Cofas, was two days from Afafa.[81] These settlements may have held remnant Yamasee populations associated with Anacape and Mayaca. Little is known about the exact locations and durations of these two settlements, so it is unknown whether either was occupied into the early 1700s. Additional archaeological and archival research are needed to determined exactly when the Riverbend site was occupied and by whom.

In conclusion, the Yamasee for too long have been a neglected or at least underpursued topic of research in Spanish Florida studies, often taking a back seat to mission Indians. Their fascinating history, which witnessed the loss and uprooting of previous cultures and the creation of something new, played out against a turbulent backdrop of European and Native alliances and rivalries. While some strides have been made in building a foundation for future Yamasee research in northern peninsular Florida, we have only scratched the surface. I hope this volume sparks more interest in Yamasee archaeology and leads to new rounds of broad-scale excavations and detailed analyses. We still need to contend with how to identify Yamasee components at sites also occupied, either earlier or later, by Guale and Mocama, all of whom manufactured San Marcos pottery. Future investigations at Mt. Royal and in the Mayaca area, which lack Mocama and Guale occupations, might help to identify details of early Yamasee ceramic assemblages that distinguish them from Guale and Mocama. The Riverbend site in Volusia County is also an excellent candidate for additional research. At a more theoretical level, a critical examination of the Yamasee through combined efforts of archaeology and ethnohistory holds the potential to elucidate conditions and processes in which ethnic groups are created and how they endure within a broader milieu of sweeping change and discontinuity.

Notes

1. Yamasees were in northeastern Florida in 1667–83 and returned to St. Augustine and West Florida during the period 1715–63. Some even remained after the Spanish evacuated Florida in 1763, living with Creeks, Seminoles, and Cherokees. See Amanda Hall, "The Persistence of Yamasee Power and Identity at San Antonio de Pocotalaca, 1716–1752," this volume; Andre White, "Refuge with the Spanish," this volume; John E. Worth, "The Yamasee in West Florida," this volume.

2. Recently historians and archaeologists have addressed the coalescence of Native groups in the aftermath of European contact through the concept of a shatter zone. See Robin Beck, *Chiefdoms, Collapse, and Coalescence in the Early American South* (Cambridge: Cambridge University Press, 2013); Robbie Ethridge and Sheri M. Shuck-Hall, eds., *Mapping the Mississippian Shatter Zone: The Colonial Indian Slave Trade and Regional Instability in the American South* (Lincoln: University of Nebraska Press, 2009).

3. John E. Worth, "Yamasee," in *Handbook of North American Indians*, vol. 14: *Southeast*, ed. R. D. Fogelson (Washington DC: Smithsonian Institution Press, 2004), 245; John E. Worth, *The Struggle for the Georgia Coast* (1995; repr., Tuscaloosa: University of Alabama Press, 2007), 20.

4. Mark Williams and Gary Shapiro, "Mississippian Political Dynamics in the Oconee Valley," in *Political Structure and Change in the Prehistoric Southeastern United States*, ed. John F. Scarry (Gainesville: University Press of Florida, 1996), 128–49; Stephen A. Kowalewski and James W. Hatch, "The Sixteenth-Century Expansion of Settlement in the Upper Oconee Watershed, Georgia," *Southeastern Archaeology* 10 (1991): 1–17.

5. Frays Carlos de Anguiano and Juan Bauptista Compana, April 1663, Archivo General de Indias, Santo Domingo, 2584, translated in Worth, *Struggle for the Georgia Coast*, 92.

6. Worth, "Yamasee," 249; Worth, *Struggle for the Georgia Coast*, 19–20.

7. Worth, *Struggle for the Georgia Coast*, 20.

8. Antonio de Argüelles Order 7, August 18, 1667, in Worth, *Struggle for the Georgia Coast*, 76.

9. Amy T. Bushnell, *Situado and Sabana: Spain's Support System for the Presidio and Mission Provinces of Florida*, Anthropological Papers of the American Museum of Natural History, no. 74 (Athens GA: Distributed by University of Georgia Press, 1994), 165.

10. Spain's vulnerability along its northern edge likely contributed to their willingness to allow Native groups to move into La Florida, hoping the refugees would strengthen their first line of defense against the expanding English Carolina colony. See Worth, *Struggle for the Georgia Coast*, 92. For an overview of the *repartimiento* system see Bushnell, *Situado and Sabana*, 121–23.

11. Argüelles Order 7, August 18, 1667, and Argüelles Order 8, April 27, 1668, in Worth, *Struggle for the Georgia Coast*, 76–78.

12. Worth, *Struggle for the Georgia Coast*, 35.

13. Worth, *Struggle for the Georgia Coast*, 35.

14. John H. Hann, *A History of the Timucua Indians and Missions* (Gainesville: University Press of Florida, 1996), 18; Jerald Milanich, *Laboring in the Fields of the Lord: Spanish Missions and Southeastern Indians* (Washington DC: Smithsonian Institution Press, 1999), 47, 115; Worth, *Struggle for the Georgia Coast*, 12.

15. Keith Ashley, "Distribution of Contact and Early Mission Period Sites in the Mocama Province," *Florida Anthropologist* 67 (2014): 152–53.

16. The Pedro de Arcos census is translated in Mark F. Boyd, "Enumeration of Florida Spanish Missions in 1675 With Translations of Documents," *Florida Historical Quarterly* 27 (1948): 183.

17. Antonio de Argüelles [Visitation of the Place of Santa María de los Yamases], translated in John H. Hann, *Visitations and Revolts in Florida, 1656–1695*, Florida Archaeology 7 (Tallahassee: Florida Bureau of Archaeological Research, 1993), 93.

18. Worth, *Struggle for the Georgia Coast*, 34.

19. Worth, "Yamasee," 247.

20. John H. Hann, "The Mayaca and Jororo and Missions to Them," in *The Spanish Missions of La Florida*, ed. Bonnie G. McEwan (Gainesville: University Press of Florida, 1993), 122.

21. Hann, "The Mayaca and Jororo and Missions to Them," 122.

22. Hann, "The Mayaca and Jororo and Missions to Them," 122.

23. Hann, "The Mayaca and Jororo and Missions to Them," 121–22. The majority of the inhabitants of both San Antonio de Anacape and San Salvador de Mayaca were Yamasee. See John H. Hann, *Indians of Central and South Florida, 1513–1763* (Gainesville: University Press of Florida, 2003), 92.

24. Bushnell, *Situado and Sabana*, 165.

25. Bushnell, *Situado and Sabana*, 165.

26. John H. Hann, "Summary Guide to Spanish Florida Missions and Visitas with Churches in the Sixteenth and Seventeenth Centuries," *Americas* 46 (1990): 417–513, see 504–5.

27. Hann, "The Mayaca and Jororo and Missions to Them," 123–24.

28. Amy T. Bushnell, "The Sacramental Imperative: Catholic Ritual and Indian Sedentism in the Provinces of Florida," in *Columbian Consequences*, vol. 2, ed. David H. Thomas (Washington DC: Smithsonian Institution Press, 1990), 482; and Hann, "The Mayaca and Jororo and Missions to Them," 123–24.

29. Bushnell, "The Sacramental Imperative," 480–81. See Amy T. Bushnell, "Living at Liberty," this volume, for a discussion on the ungovernable nature of the Yamasee.

30. Worth, *Struggle for the Georgia Coast*, 77.

31. John H. Hann, "Twilight of the Mocamo and Guale Aborigines as Portrayed in the 1695 Spanish Visitation," *Florida Historical Quarterly* 66 (1987): 22–23.

32. Worth, *Struggle for the Georgia Coast*, 37.

33. Hann, "The Mayaca and Jororo and Missions to Them," 125.

34. William G. Green, Chester B. DePratter, and Bobby Southerlin, "The Yamasee in South Carolina: Native American Adaptation and Interaction along the Carolina Frontier," in *Another's Country: Archaeological and Historical Perspectives on Cultural Interactions in the Southern Colonies*, ed. J. W. Joseph and Martha Zierden (Tuscaloosa: University of Alabama Press, 2002), 13.

35. See Hall, "Persistence of Yamasee Power and Identity"; White, "Refuge with the Spanish"; Worth, "Yamasee."

36. John H. Hann, "St. Augustine's Fallout from the Yamasee War," *Florida Historical Quarterly* 68 (1989): 186.

37. Worth, "Yamasee," 247.

38. Hann, *Visitations and Revolts in Florida*, 124.

39. In 1675 Pedro de Arcos notes that in the mission province of Apalachee, "there are La Tama and Yamases all of one Nation" living in the newly established mission of Candelaria. See Boyd, "Enumeration of Florida Spanish Missions," 185.

40. This total combines Yamasee and all other towns deemed "pagan" by the Spanish. See Boyd "Enumeration of Florida Spanish Missions," 183.

41. Calendar of State Papers, America and the West Indies, February 21, 1685, in Bradley Scott Schrager, "Yamasee Indians and the Challenge of Spanish and English Colonialism in the North American Southeast, 1660–1715," PhD diss., Northwestern University, 2001, 64.

42. Norman E. Whitten Jr., "Ethnogenesis," in *The Encyclopedia of Cultural Anthropology*, ed. D. Levinson and M. Ember (New York: Henry Holt, 1996), 407.

43. Worth, *Struggle for the Georgia Coast*, 20, suggests that Yamasee existence came about in the early 1660s. Although Schrager, "Yamasee Indians and the Challenge of Spanish and English Colonialism," 13, 67, acknowledges Yamasee origins in the 1660s, he maintains that "the move from Florida to Carolina, from Spanish to English alliance, stands as the defining moment when 'yamasi' as a category gained powerful meaning." While Yamasee tribal ethnicity had not been formed during the early years in Spanish Florida, it is important to note that Mocama and Guale tribal ethnicity had not been lost at this time, despite being part of the mission system.

44. Worth, *Struggle for the Georgia Coast*, 20.

45. Worth, "Yamasee," 250.

46. Argüelles, in Hann, *Visitations and Revolts in Florida*, 93.

47. Bushnell, "The Sacramental Imperative," 481–82; Hann, *Indians of Central and South Florida*, 71.

48. Schrager, "Yamasee Indians and the Challenge of Spanish and English Colonialism," 67, 74, 113.

49. Kenneth Sassaman, "Hunter Gatherers and Traditions of Resistance," in *The Archaeology of Traditions: Agency and History Before and After Columbus*, ed. Timothy R. Pauketat (Gainesville: University Press of Florida, 2001), 227,

50. Worth, *Struggle for the Georgia Coast*, 249, 250.

51. Sassaman, "Hunter Gatherers and Traditions of Resistance," 219–20.

52. Kathleen A. Deagan, "St. Augustine and the Mission Frontier," in *The Spanish Missions of La Florida*, ed. Bonnie G. McEwan (Gainesville: University Press of Florida, 1993), 95; John S. Otto and Russell L. Lewis Jr., "A Formal and Functional Analysis of San Marcos Pottery from Site SA 16–23 St. Augustine Florida," *Bureau of Historic Sites and Properties Bulletin* 4 (1974): 97. Rebecca Saunders, *Stability and Change in Guale Indian Pottery, 1300–1702* (Tuscaloosa: University of Alabama Press, 2000), 248.

53. Vicki L. Rolland and Keith H. Ashley, "Beneath the Bell: A Study of Mission Period Colonoware from Three Spanish Missions in Northeastern Florida," *Florida Anthropologist* 53 (2000): 36–61; Richard H. Vernon and Ann S. Cordell, "A Distribution and Technological Study of Apalachee Colono-Ware from San Luis de Talimali," in *The Spanish Missions of La Florida*, ed. Bonnie G. McEwan (Gainesville: University Press of Florida, 1993), 418–33.

54. San Marcos/Altamaha pottery appears to be rooted in the precontact Irene and Lamar ceramic traditions of coastal and interior Georgia, respectively. See various articles in Kathleen Deagan and David Hurst Thomas, eds., *From Santa Elena to St. Augustine: Indigenous Ceramic Variability (A.D. 1400–1700)*, Anthropological Papers of the American Museum of Natural History, no. 90 (New York: American Museum of Natural History, 2009).

55. Rebecca Saunders, "Pottery and Ethnicity: Yamasee Ceramics in Florida during the Mission Period," paper presented at the 57th annual Southeastern Archaeological Conference, Macon, Georgia, November 8–11, 2000, 1.

56. John E. Worth, "Materialized Landscapes of Practice: Exploring Native American Ceramic Variability in the Historic-Era Southeastern United States," paper presented at the 81st meeting of the Society of American Archaeology, Orlando Florida, April 9, 2016, 3. This argument is based on the concept of "community of practice," which entails the active learning of a craft among practitioners that leads to the formation of a group affiliation based on a shared history of practice.

57. See Suzanne L. Eckert, *Pottery and Practice: The Expression of Identity at Pottery Mound and Hummingbird Pueblo* (Albuquerque: University of New Mexico Press, 2008), for a case study.

58. William G. Green, *The Search for Altamaha: The Archaeology and Ethnohistory of An Early Eighteenth Century Yamasee Indian Town*, Volumes in Historical Archaeology 21 (Columbia: South Carolina Institute of Archaeology and Anthropology, University of South Carolina, 1992), 96; Gifford J. Waters, "Aboriginal Ceramics at Three 18th-Century Mission Sites in St. Augustine, Florida," in *From Santa Elena to St. Augustine: Indigenous Ceramic Variability (A.D. 1400–1700)*, ed. Kathleen Deagan and David Hurst Thomas, Anthropological Papers of the American Museum of Natural History, no. 90 (New York: American Museum of Natural History, 2009), 173.

59. Keith Ashley, Vicki Rolland, and Robert L. Thunen, "Missions San Buenaventura and Santa Cruz de Guadalquini: Retreat from the Georgia Coast," in *Life Among the Tides: Recent Archaeology on the Georgia Bight*, ed. Victor Thompson and David Hurst Thomas, Anthropological Papers of the American Museum of Natural History, no. 98 (New York: American Museum of Natural History, 2013), 417.

60. Ripley P. Bullen and John W. Griffin, "An Archaeological Survey of Amelia Island, Florida," *Florida Anthropologist* 5 (1952): 59–60; Boyd, "Enumeration of Florida Spanish Missions," 183.

61. Other sites reported to have yielded small amounts of San Marcos on Amelia Island are 8NA11–12 in the vicinity of Old Town; 8 NA24 southwest of Old Town along the west side of Clark Creek; and 8NA30 near Harrison Homestead. See Bullen and Griffin, "An Archaeological Survey of Amelia Island," 42.

62. John W. Griffin and Robert H. Steinbach, "Archeological Survey of Old Town Fernandina: A Study of the Archeological Resources in Old Town and Recommendations for Their Preservation," report on file with the Florida Division of Historical Resources (Tallahassee, 1991); Greg C. Smith, "Archaeological Monitoring in Old Town (8NA238) Fernandina Beach, Nassau County, Florida," report on file with the Florida Division of Historical Resources (Tallahassee, 1998); Hale G. Smith and Ripley P. Bullen, *Fort San Carlos*, Notes in Anthropology 14 (Tallahassee: Florida State University, 1971).

63. Bullen and Griffin, "An Archaeological Survey of Amelia Island," 42; Smith and Bullen, *Fort San Carlos*, 65. According to the excavators of Fort San Carlos, "It now appears that most of the aboriginal materials were brought into the area when the earthworks were built. . . . However, there were various areas where undisturbed aboriginal campsites occurred as evidenced by fireplaces in which San Marcos Complicated Stamped and earlier types were found." See Smith and Bullen, *Fort San Carlos*, 34.

64. The seal, which was pressed onto wax to send official documents from the mission through the colonial bureaucracy, portrays the Christian martyr St. Catherine of Alexandria. See Saunders, *Stability and Change in Guale Indian Pottery*, 140.

65. Thomas Hemmings and Kathleen Deagan, *Excavations on Amelia Island in Northeast Florida*, Contributions of the Florida State Museum 18 (Gainesville: University of Florida, 1973); Rebecca Saunders, "Architecture of the Missions Santa María and Santa Catalina de Amelia,"

in *The Spanish Missions of La Florida*, ed. Bonnie G. McEwan (Gainesville: University Press of Florida, 1993), 35–61; Saunders, "*Stability and Change in Guale Indian Pottery.*"

66. Saunders, "*Stability and Change in Guale Indian Pottery*," 8–10; Worth, *Struggle for the Georgia Coast*, 11, 20, 28, 197.

67. Amy T. Bushnell, *Santa María in the Written Record*, Florida State Museum Department of Anthropology Miscellaneous Project Report 21 (Gainesville: University of Florida, 1986); Milanich, *Laboring in the Fields of the Lord*, 115. Hann, "Summary Guide to Spanish Florida Missions and Visitas," 453–54.

68. Worth, *Struggle for the Georgia Coast*, 10–12, 20, 28, 30.

69. Saunders, "Pottery and Ethnicity," 6; Christopher M. Stowjanowski, *Mission Cemeteries, Mission Peoples* (Gainesville: University Press of Florida, 2013), 213, 218, 241, 243.

70. Clark S. Larsen, "On the Frontier of Contact: Mission Bioarchaeology in La Florida," in *The Spanish Missions of La Florida*, ed. Bonnie G. McEwan (Gainesville: University Press of Florida, 1993), 322–56, 329.

71. Calvin B. Johns and Louis Tesar, "1983–1995 Survey, Salvage and Mitigation of Archaeological Resources within the Mount Royal Site (8PU35) Village Area, Putnam County, Florida," report on file with the Florida Division of Historical Resources (Tallahassee, 2001).

72. John W. Goggin, *Space and Time Perspective in Northern St. Johns Archaeology, Florida*, Yale University Publications in Anthropology 47 (New Haven: Yale University Press, 1952), 25.

73. Jones and Tesar, "1983–1995 Survey, Salvage and Mitigation," 264, 269.

74. Keith H. Ashley, "Archaeological Overview of Mt. Royal," *Florida Anthropologist* 58 (2005): 273.

75. Jeffrey M. Mitchem, "Florida Indians after A.D. 1492: The Question of Archaeological Evidence for Antillean-Florida Migrations," *American Anthropologist* 91 (1990): 762–65.

76. Barbara A. Purdy, "American Indians after A.D. 1492, Reply to Jeffrey, M. Mitchem," *American Anthropologist* 91 (1990): 765. Purdy's assertion does contradict reports by residents of nearby Deland, who claim that a mission bell was recovered on Hontoon Island in the 1920s. See Ryan J. Wheeler and Christine L. Newman, "An Assessment of Cultural Resources at the Lake George State Forest Including Mount Taylor and the Bluffton Site," report on file with the Florida Division of Historical Resources (Tallahassee, 1997), 2.

77. Asa Randall, pers. comm., 2015.

78. Michael Russo, Janice R. Ballo, Robert J. Austin, Lee Newsom, Sylvia Scudder, and Vicki Rolland, "Phase II Archaeological Excavations at the Riverbend Site (8VO2567), Volusia County, Florida," report on file with the Florida Division of Historical Resources (Tallahassee, 1989).

79. John R. Swanton, *Early History of the Creek Indians and Their Neighbors*, Bureau of American Ethnology Bulletin 73 (Washington DC: Smithsonian Institution, 1922), 102; Kathleen Deagan, *Spanish St. Augustine: The Archaeology of a Colonial Creole Community* (New York: Academic Press, 1983), 32.

80. Translation in John H. Hann, *Missions to the Calusa* (Gainesville: University of Florida Press, 1991), 378. In 1725 the Yamasee village of Pocotalaca at Las Rosas de Ayamón was purported to have been located about sixteen miles south of St. Augustine or two or three miles south of Matanzas Inlet. See Susan R. Parker, "The Second Century of Settlement in Spanish St. Augustine," PhD diss., University of Florida, 1999, 48.

81. Afafa was located twenty leagues south of St. Augustine on the St. Johns River. Hann, "Summary Guide to Spanish Florida Missions and Visitas," 509; Hann, *Indians of Central and South Florida*, 96.

3

Yamasee Material Culture and Identity
Altamaha/San Marcos Ceramics in Seventeenth- and Eighteenth-Century Yamasee Indian Settlements, Georgia and South Carolina

ERIC C. POPLIN AND JON BERNARD MARCOUX

The Yamasee Confederacy became one of the most powerful and wealthiest Native groups in the Southeast during the late seventeenth and early eighteenth centuries through their military and economic alliance with the Carolina colony. Pressures associated with an expanding European presence in North America and colonial efforts to create and obtain wealth through trade with the Natives prompted the migration to the coast of La Florida and the subsequent move north into Carolina of the interior people who became the Yamasee. But the newcomers and the events and processes associated with European colonization did not push or drive the Yamasee solely. The Yamasee made decisions as they attempted to control their fate and to influence the trajectory of not only their own interactions but also those of their neighbors with the European newcomers.

Parties of the Yamasee Confederacy ranged from the Mississippi River to the Atlantic coast and from the Ohio River to South Florida seeking deerskins and Indian slaves to feed the markets of Carolina from 1683 to 1715. Though able to exert their presence and power over such a large area, they remained a small group in toto, with their strength tied tightly to their Carolina alliance and the access it provided to firearms and other essentials. For such a small number of people to wield this much influence required outward expressions that conveyed their identity to all and reflected the power they possessed.

Thus the Yamasee Indians of Carolina attempted to create an identity that conveyed their role and importance in the social networks and power structures of the colonial Southeast. Recent research on the identity of communities notes two salient aspects that apply in most, if not all, cases.[1] First, identity expresses sameness and difference; it distinguishes members of the group/community (*us*) from non-members (*them*), binding community members and separating the community from its neighbors. Second, identity is expressed through actions tied to specific decisions by community members to express their collective identity.[2] These aspects apply both to the individual Yamasee settlements noted in the historic record and to the collective of these settlements as the Yamasee Confederacy established itself as a larger community of allied settlements. Conscious decisions by members of the Yamasee settlements should be reflected in their material culture and how they used items during their daily activities. This chapter explores elements of Yamasee material culture that reflect their efforts to develop, maintain, and communicate their identity.

Recent study of Yamasee Confederacy settlements in South Carolina, now archaeological sites, provides the most detailed glimpses of how the Yamasee adapted themselves to the fluid social environment of the colonial Southeast. Detailed analyses of Yamasee material culture, the items they made, acquired, and used during their daily activities, suggest efforts to characterize and distinguish themselves among the other Native groups of the Southeast. While many of the goods the Yamasee acquired from Europeans are identical to those acquired by other groups, their particular and unusual adaptations of these items demonstrate an effort to display their wealth and power during their time in Carolina.

Examples of this effort include the preponderance of European manufactured goods at their sites compared to the sites of indigenous Natives of coastal South Carolina and the alternate uses of numerous European-manufactured items. The former reflects how quickly the Yamasee established themselves as the principal middlemen in the Carolina deerskin and slave trade, and their willingness to assist Carolina in its military actions against the Spanish and hostile Native groups. This rapid and close association gave the Yamasee Confederacy a direct conduit to the supply of European goods and ready access to a valuable commodity (Indian slaves) that allowed them to grab a larger share of these goods than their neighbors. The latter reflects a deeper social function and conveys more than just their wealth. Two groups of

European-manufactured items are consistently recovered from Yamasee settlements in South Carolina. These are adornments (e.g., glass beads; brass rings, tinkers, and bells; and silver jewelry and bells) and weapons and munitions (e.g., lead shot, gun flints, and gun parts). Historical documentation notes that they also received iron tools, brass and iron cooking vessels, European ceramics, and commodities in glass bottles (particularly spirits), but these are found in much lower frequencies or not at all. Some of the known but missing trade goods occur in burials; others were less likely to be discarded due to their usefulness and strength, and likely were carried away when the Yamasee left Carolina.

However, adornments and weapons are the most common European goods recovered from Yamasee sites in South Carolina. And many functional items were modified to serve as adornments after their original function was lost. We do not know if the Yamasee adopted this practice (projecting wealth and power and their identity through adornments) after arriving in Carolina or if it was a part of their culture before arriving on the coast. Unfortunately, there has been insufficient study of Yamasee, Guale, and Mocama sites in Georgia and Florida to address the development and evolution of this trait.

One element of material culture present in all coastal Yamasee settlements during the seventeenth and eighteenth centuries that has received varying levels of analysis to date is Altamaha/San Marcos series pottery. Elements of this ceramic series so closely tied to the Natives associated with the Spanish colonial presence in La Florida, including the interior Yamasee after they arrived on the coast, can provide additional insight into Yamasee efforts to create and maintain an identity among all of the Native American groups vying for influence and power in the colonial Southeast. Before examining recent research of Altamaha/San Marcos pottery, a brief summary of the social and political organization and development of the Yamasee is in order to provide a framework for analyzing some of the differences between Yamasee communities as reflected in Altamaha/San Marcos pottery.

Yamasee Social and Political Organization

At least three small, closely associated communities of Muskogean-speaking people in the interior of Georgia became the Yamasee when they decided to move to the coast of La Florida in the 1650s. These communities or towns (Altamaha, Ocute, and Ichisi) would remain the central settlements of the descendants of the former interior people throughout the seventeenth and eighteenth centuries. Ever-increasing pressure from slave-raiding Native groups associated with English traders from Virginia prompted the Yamasee move to the coast. Groups like the Westo (thought to be the Iroquoian-speaking Erie who fled south to avoid annihilation or assimilation by the Haudenosaunee), also called the Chichimeco by the coastal peoples, moved into empty spaces along the central Savannah River and began raiding into the interior of Georgia for captives. Unable to defend themselves successfully from these raiders, the Yamasee decided to move to the coast and seek the protection of Spanish colonists.

Once in La Florida, they moved several times in an effort to accommodate the Spanish and to create a more favorable setting for their future development. These moves were more a decision by the Yamasee than the Spanish, since colonial records indicate a frustration on the part of the colonial government, which wanted to affix the Yamasee to a particular location. Disaffection with Spanish colonial practices and continued slave raids prompted the Yamasee to move north into Carolina soon after the establishment of the English settlement at Charles Towne. Once in South Carolina, the Yamasee organized into two major groups—the Lower Yamasee (interior Georgia people from the former towns of Altamaha, Ichisi, Ocute, and later Toa who lived at Altamaha, Chechessee, Okatee, and Euhaw towns in South Carolina) and the Upper Yamasee (Guale, Mocama, and other Georgia/Florida groups who lived in the towns of Pocotaligo, Tomatley, Pocosabo, Huspah, Sadketche, and Tulafina in South Carolina). The coastal peoples followed the Lower Yamasee into Carolina for the same reasons the latter left La Florida—better protection from slave raiders, closer access to European-manufactured goods (particularly firearms), and less intrusion by colonial administrations. The upper and lower distinction, basically an ethnic divide within the confederacy, would remain in place until the Yamasee fled back to La Florida during the Yamasee War.

Each Yamasee town appears to have been an independent community. Town members made decisions based on their needs and desires, with some consideration of the needs of the other members of the confederation. A principal town was associated with both the Upper and Lower Yamasee—Pocotaligo and Altamaha, respectively—although the strength of this hierarchical arrangement appears substantially less than what likely existed among Mississippian societies prior to the European arrival in the Southeast. Next we examine the results of recent research to seek differences within the Altamaha/San Marcos pottery series that may reflect the ethnic divisions within the Yamasee Confederacy in South Carolina and possibly distinguish the interior people from the coastal peoples of La Florida.

Altamaha/San Marcos Pottery—the Hallmark of Colonial Natives in La Florida

All the Native people who lived along the coasts of Florida and Georgia during the sixteenth, seventeenth, and eighteenth centuries manufactured and used Altamaha/San Marcos series pottery. Derived from the Late Mississippian Lamar ceramic tradition, Altamaha/San Marcos differed from its progenitor in the variety of vessel forms. Old forms were dropped and new forms were added, resulting in an overall reduction in the diversity of forms. Additionally, the most frequent decorative motifs were simplified, altered, or abandoned. The Mississippian ceramic tradition from which Lamar and Altamaha/San Marcos derived originally developed in central Georgia during the later centuries of the first millennium C.E. Mississippians carved elaborate designs into wooden paddles and then impressed them onto pottery vessels prior to firing. Initially, these designs combined straight lines forming triangles, diamonds, and nested squares, but curving designs replaced these rectilinear motifs by the second millennium C.E., and their use spread across much of the southeast Atlantic seaboard. In the coastal regions of what are now Georgia, South Carolina, and northern Florida, the fylfot cross (four arms radiating out from a central element with recurving termini) eventually dominated these curvilinear designs. Individual elements of the cross, particularly the arms that form P- or 9-shapes, occurred with great frequency also. And they were central elements of the incised decorations that mark the

Lamar tradition during the final centuries of Mississippian ceramic manufacture in the Southeast.[3]

Sometime during the early sixteenth century the people living along the coasts of Georgia and northern Florida began to make Altamaha/San Marcos series pottery.[4] As already noted, both vessel forms and decorative techniques and motifs changed. The coastal peoples manufactured a much simpler repertoire of vessels than their Mississippian forebears. European-made ceramic and metal vessels replaced some of the abandoned forms, but others were merely dropped. Presumably the coastal Indians no longer practiced specific activities associated with these forms, eliminating the need for them.

While the fylfot cross dominated the Late Mississippian Irene/Savannah series of the Georgia and Florida coasts, this motif evolved into the most common stamped motif of the Altamaha/San Marcos series: the line block stamp. Archaeologists believe that the fylfot cross dominated the Late Mississippian ceramic traditions of the region due to its association or its expression of the sun deity that figures prominently in Muskogean cosmology. The central element of the cross (often a circle or raised dot inside a square of lines) is the sun; the four arms of the cross, composed of multiple lines radiating out from each side of the central square, represent the rays of sunlight. The four sides or arms represent the four principal directions of the compass, a concept that continues to influence Muskogean social organization strongly. All communities are organized around a square plaza with each side associated with specific gender or age groups and moieties within the group. Thus, while Altamaha/San Marcos potters abandoned the cross itself, they retained the central square with radiating and perpendicular lines, presumably the most powerful elements for defining Muskogean identity, as the line block motif.[5]

Once on the coast, the interior Yamasee quickly adopted the Altamaha/San Marcos ceramics of their neighbors, making vessels in the ubiquitous coastal Mission forms and adapting decorative motifs from both the Lamar ceramic traditions of their interior Georgia homeland and the newly emerged Altamaha/San Marcos tradition of the coast. At this time we assume that they continued their Lamar ceramic traditions while living in the interior, despite intermittent contacts with

Spanish explorers and persecution from the slave-raiders during the mid-seventeenth century. There is even some limited information to suggest that groups along the Oconee River gave up paddle-stamped surface treatments by this time. If so, the interior Yamasee would have had to relearn this element of ceramic manufacture when they began making Altamaha/San Marcos pottery.[6]

The rapid transition from the manufacture of traditional Lamar ceramic forms and decorations to Altamaha/San Marcos forms and decorations is not entirely unexpected. Archaeologist Rebecca Saunders noted a rapid change from Irene and Savannah to the Altamaha/San Marcos ceramic series during the late sixteenth century at most sites analyzed in her extensive study of Guale pottery on the Georgia and Florida coasts.[7] Jon Marcoux and colleagues note a similar shift in decorative techniques in Ashley pottery around Charleston Harbor during the same time period.[8] We assume that the rapid adoption of Altamaha/San Marcos pottery reflects a decision by the interior Yamasee to fit in among their new neighbors on the coast, although they never really accepted the Spanish efforts to bring them into the fold of Christianity and the Spanish mission-settlement colonization process. Similarly, we assume that the interior Yamasee possessed a desire to create and maintain their group identity within the changing social and economic milieu of the southern Atlantic seaboard of the seventeenth and early eighteenth centuries. This desire prompted them to adopt a new ceramic tradition, albeit with a few retained elements of their ancestral one. Ultimately, this would both integrate and distinguish them among the coastal Guale and Mocama.

In South Carolina the Yamasee (who came to include Guale and other Georgia and Florida coastal groups who moved north with them) were the only Native Americans making Altamaha/San Marcos pottery in the seventeenth and eighteenth centuries. Late Lamar (Irene series) ceramics continued to be made in the Port Royal area during the sixteenth century, with Ashley series wares appearing around Charleston Harbor at this time.[9] Excavations at a late sixteenth–early seventeenth century household on Daniel Island in Charleston Harbor indicate that some Altamaha/San Marcos influence (vessel forms and stamped line block motifs) reached this far north prior to the arrival of the Yamasee but that Lamar (Irene) traditions were still predominant.[10] Insufficient research has been conducted on contemporary sites in the Port Royal area, but Native American ceramics from Santa Elena–Charlesfort remain very similar to the late Lamar (Irene) wares of the terminal Mississippian traditions of the region.[11]

Expressions of Yamasee Identity in Altamaha/San Marcos Pottery

Despite the widespread similarity of Altamaha/San Marcos series pottery along the Southeast coast, are there differences in the Altamaha/San Marcos ceramics produced by the Yamasee that reflect their migrations and organization and that helped to maintain their identity? That is, did Yamasee-related Altamaha/San Marcos ceramics change through time as the interior Yamasee arrived on the coast, moved to Carolina, merged with the Guale and other coastal groups, and eventually moved back to Florida? It should be noted that pottery was manufactured by women among the Native American groups of the Southeast. Thus traits that emphasize aspects of group cosmology, like fylfot cross or line block stamp motifs, serve to reinforce the group identity within individual households. With most pottery vessels used within a single household within a single village or town, children within the household were the community members who would daily observe the decorative motifs and other morphological attributes that help to define identity. This is one mechanism through which one generation passed information to the next that helped to maintain culture and create identity. Pottery reinforced identity within the group more than separating one group from another, in most instances.

We should note that there have been no successful efforts to date that separate the newly arrived interior Yamasee from their coastal Guale and Mocama neighbors of the 1660s–1680s on the Georgia and Florida coasts. Ashley (this volume) describes the sites that likely contain the Yamasee occupations of this period. He notes rightly that archaeologists have yet to identify cultural material correlates within the ceramic assemblages from these sites that serve to separate the Yamasee from their coastal precursors or those who settled on the same sites after the Yamasee departure. We do not know if this is impossible since no researcher has focused on this particular aspect of Altamaha/San Marcos pottery to date.

A rapid and dramatic shift from complicated stamped wares (both curvilinear and rectilinear motifs) to rectilinear and simple stamped motifs has been documented in late sixteenth to early seventeenth-century Ashley ceramics.[12] Comparisons of Ashley assemblages with Altamaha/San Marcos ceramics from two Yamasee Confederacy households at Altamaha Town in South Carolina demonstrate that the eighteenth-century Yamasee Confederacy assemblages correlate well with Ashley ones from the mid-seventeenth century in terms of the frequencies of complicated and simple stamped decorations.[13] Similar changes also occur in Cherokee pottery in western North Carolina and eastern Tennessee during the mid-seventeenth century.[14] The relationship of these similar changes in numerous ceramic traditions in the Southeast is a topic worthy of additional research beyond the scope of our discussion here.

Similar changes in paddle stamped decorations are documented in recent examinations of Altamaha/San Marcos pottery assemblages from seventeenth-century Guale sites on the Georgia coast (Fort King George and Sapelo Island) that predate the Yamasee/Guale/Mocama move north; from five households at the Lower Yamasee town of Altamaha; and from the Upper Yamasee towns of Pocotaligo and Huspah (all in South Carolina). Shifts from curvilinear stamped motifs to rectilinear and simple stamped motifs appear to reflect time. Earlier Georgia assemblages have slightly higher frequencies of curvilinear stamped decorations, while later South Carolina assemblages have higher frequencies of simple stamped decorations.[15]

Another difference noted among all of the surface treatments included in the analysis is the higher incidence of check stamping among the Guale-Mocama assemblages from the Georgia coast when compared to the Yamasee Confederacy assemblages from South Carolina, with one exception. The pottery collection from Pocotaligo Town also has a high incidence of check stamped decorations, albeit diamond-shaped checks rather than the square checks seen in the collections from the Fort King George Site and Sapelo Island. Pocotaligo Town was the principal seat of the Upper Yamasee, who were predominantly

Guale-Mocama immigrants to Carolina. Perhaps this decoration is an indicator of the coastal groups compared to the interior groups, but we do not have sufficient information from other Guale and Mocama sites at this time to make this assertion with any degree of certainty. However, it does reflect a decision by the pottery makers at Pocotaligo to create a fairly specialized surface treatment that served to distinguish them from the other Yamasee Confederacy communities in South Carolina.[16] Presumably this helped define an identity for Pocotaligo residents among their Yamasee neighbors and other Native groups.

A more striking difference is the increased frequency of over-stamped expressions of the line block motif at most of the South Carolina sites. Four of five households sampled at Altamaha Town all displayed nearly equal relative frequencies of paddle stamped and over-stamped line block motifs (paddle stamped = 42–51.7 percent; over-stamped = 48.3–58 percent). One Altamaha household, the Huspah Town assemblage, and the Fort King George assemblage display substantially higher relative frequencies of paddle stamped line block motifs (77.2–80.8 percent) and concomitant reduced frequencies of over-stamped line block motifs (19.2–22.8 percent). Statistical comparisons demonstrate that these differences are significant.[17]

While we expected a difference between the Georgia and South Carolina assemblages, we did not expect the observed similarities between the one Altamaha Town household and the Huspah Town assemblage and the Fort King George collections. Originally we hypothesized the expected difference to reflect time devoted to the carving of paddles.[18] Through time, Altamaha/San Marcos pottery makers had less time to spend creating the paddles, since they were engaged in new or different suites of activities after the coming of European colonists, or there was a loss of knowledge and skill retained in the populations who survived the diseases and conflicts that marked the early centuries of European exploration and settlement. Obviously more time is needed to create a paddle that has the complete line block motif carved upon it than is needed to carve straight lines into a paddle that is then manipulated during the stamping process to create the desired decoration. Since two of the five later South Carolina sites do not conform to the expected distributions, another factor may have influenced when one approach was used rather than the other. Perhaps the higher frequency of over-stamped motifs among the South Carolina sites reflects more about the past traditions of the potters than about the time devoted to carving paddles. If, as noted, the interior Yamasee communities had abandoned paddle stamped pottery decorations prior to their arrival on the coast, then the female group members may have lacked the knowledge and skill necessary to carve complete motifs into their paddles. This may be one attribute of Altamaha/San Marcos pottery that can serve to distinguish these interior peoples from the coastal Guale and Mocama once the interior Yamasee moved to the coast. The analysis of many more samples of Altamaha/San Marcos pottery from sites in Florida and Georgia will be necessary to determine if this truly is a hallmark of the interior Georgia Yamasee.[19]

Thus detailed analyses of Altamaha/San Marcos pottery offers some evidence of decisions made by the female members of Yamasee communities to maintain group identity through the repeated presentation of symbolic decorative motifs within individual households. We also observed differences in the frequencies of specific decorative types (primarily check stamped) that may serve to distinguish the ethnic divisions that we know existed among the Yamasee Confederacy in South Carolina. Also, there appears to be a difference in the mode of creating line block motifs (complex carved paddle stamped vs. simple carved paddle over-stamped) that may reflect the ethnic differences between the interior Georgia people who moved to the coast of La Florida and became the first Yamasee and the coastal Guale and Mocama who would become members of the Yamasee Confederacy during the last decade of the seventeenth century and the first decade of the eighteenth century.

Outward Expressions of Yamasee Identity

With pottery providing an internal or nurturing medium for intergenerational continuity and reinforced group identity, then other forms of material culture should reflect efforts to project or establish one's identity to others outside the group. As noted, two groups of European manufactured items are present at South Carolina Yamasee Confederacy sites: adornments and firearms. The principal adornment item is glass beads. Small glass beads are found throughout almost all southeastern Native American sites occupied during the colonial period. There is some thought that glass beads provided abstract expression of cosmological constructs present throughout much of the Southeast if they are a corollary for freshwater pearls.[20] Southeastern Indians routinely attached beads to articles of clothing or accoutrements as well as wearing them in strands as bracelets and necklaces. Since these items are fairly ubiquitous during the seventeenth and eighteenth centuries with all Native groups, we have difficulty determining how the Yamasee might have used beads to distinguish themselves. Undoubtedly the number of beads available to members of the Yamasee Confederacy was greater than for their neighbors, since they were the ones bringing in the majority of the Indian slaves and deerskins to the Carolina traders. The number of beads on Yamasee clothing and outer apparel would have been a sign of their power and wealth. They may also have created specific patterns of beads or colors that served to identify them among others. Nineteenth-century Plains Indians certainly had distinctive patterns of beadwork among different major groups or tribes.[21]

The presence of firearms also was a projection of power and wealth and easily distinguished members of the Yamasee Confederacy from the Indians allied to the Spanish in La Florida. The Spanish determination to not arm their Native allies proved decisive in the competition between Carolina and La Florida for control of the Southeast Indian trade. The Natives wanted guns, and those people with guns preyed upon the unarmed with little or no restraint.

Other markers of identity found at many Yamasee Confederacy sites in South Carolina include the use of broken items or pieces of larger tools (like firearms) as adornments. Many items of European manufacture recovered from Altamaha Town (the principal Carolina settlement of the Lower Yamasee) were modified, probably after the original use was not practical or desired, to create adornments.[22] Indians perforated gun parts to allow fragments or broken elements of these most valuable tools to be worn as pendants or gorgets. They pierced a reckoning counter, normally used by the Indian traders to tally items during exchanges, to permit its attachment to clothing or jewelry. Archaeologists recovered brass finger rings, traditionally given by monastic missionaries to Native apostates, from both Altamaha and Chechessee towns. Yamasee raiders either took these adornments from Christian captives who were then sold as slaves to the Carolina traders or they belonged to Christian individuals who lived at these Yamasee Confederacy settlements. If the latter, the rings may have been the property of female captives who were forcibly married into the Yamasee Confederacy community, since the interior or Lower Yamasee strongly resisted Spanish proselytization while in La Florida. The wearing of adornments, especially by Yamasee Confederacy men during slave raids and military actions, would display their wealth to their prey and enemies.

Yamasee Confederacy raiders likely accoutered themselves in other ways to convey a sense of ferocity and power. Recent research suggests that the Catawba, who eventually replaced the Yamasee Confederacy as the principal military allies of the Carolinas, adorned themselves to that end.[23] The Catawba gained the reputation of fierce and able warriors who promoted fear among their opponents, which would lower their antagonists' morale and enhance the possibility of Catawba victory. It is likely that the Yamasee Confederacy did the same, especially given its military prowess and slaving predominance during the early eighteenth century, despite its relatively small population when compared to the many Native groups the Yamasee routinely raided.

All of these outward expressions of wealth, ferocity, and strength conveyed the power and identity of the Yamasee Confederacy as its members interacted with other Native groups and the European colonists of the Southeast. These presentations were conscious decisions by members of the group to express their identity and project their role in the economic and social network of the region. Undoubtedly, there were other actions (manners of bearing, patterns of speech, rituals of interaction) that also reinforced and maintained this identity. Unfortunately, these actions are not reflected in the material culture, or not as clearly as those described earlier. We must rely on historical narratives for descriptions of these actions. Yamasee Confederacy efforts to create an identity and a prized role were very successful, as measured by the wealth the members amassed and their success at reducing if not eliminating the Indian allies of the Spanish in La

Florida. The fear that prevailed throughout the Carolina backcountry and the sporadic appearance of Yamasee Indians in the Port Royal area up through the 1760s attest to their success as well.

Summary and Avenues for Future Research

The interpretations of items of material culture from Yamasee Confederacy settlements in South Carolina presented here appear to be indicators of identity that the interior Yamasee and their coastal compatriots used to define themselves within their family groups and towns and within the larger social setting of the colonial Southeast. Differences in modes of application of line block motifs appear to distinguish the Yamasee from the interior of Georgia from the Guale and Mocama who became part of the Yamasee Confederacy in South Carolina. Firearms and adornments appear to express the identity and role of members of the Yamasee Confederacy as they raided their neighbors and interacted with the European colonists of Carolina and La Florida. Undoubtedly these efforts helped the Yamasee to survive and to wield great power in the region during the 1690s–1710s.

Unfortunately, there has been little detailed analysis of Yamasee occupations in Florida and Georgia that predate and postdate the South Carolina settlements (see Ashley, this volume). Thus we do not know if the interior Yamasee used the same artifacts or similar artifacts to distinguish themselves from their neighbors prior to their arrival in Carolina or if they continued these efforts after their return to Florida. Future detailed analyses of settlements in Florida and Georgia occupied before and after the Yamasee immigration into and emigration out of Carolina will provide the necessary comparisons for interpretation. Also, we may be able to discern changes in Altamaha/San Marcos pottery that reflect its evolution during the sixteenth, seventeenth, and early eighteenth centuries. Saunders employed the widths of lands and grooves in paddle stamped designs to distinguish Altamaha/San Marcos pottery from earlier Mississippian Savannah/Irene ceramic series (the lands and grooves are wider in Altamaha/San Marcos, creating larger or bolder motifs).[24] Similar changes mark the development of the Ashley series around Charleston Harbor.[25] If there is a continuum of increasingly wider lands and grooves, we may be able to place specific collections within a decade or two of manufacture. This would help tremendously in determining how the Yamasee, Guale, Mocama, and other groups who eventually lived along the coast of La Florida and made Altamaha/San Marcos pottery interacted.

All of these expressions hint at the adaptability and conscious efforts of the interior Yamasee and other coastal groups to create a niche within the dynamic social and economic environment of the southeast Atlantic coast in the seventeenth and early eighteenth centuries. The interior Yamasee were not overwhelmed by their first encounters with newcomers from across the sea or from other parts of North America. They attempted to establish themselves among the many groups of the coast and control their lives and interactions to their advantage. They adapted local ceramic traditions while maintaining or creating their own expressions of the tradition. They decorated their pottery and themselves in such a way that they were easily distinguished from their neighbors. They initiated and maintained political alliances that helped preserve their identity. The initiation of the Yamasee War in 1715 attempted to maintain or reinforce their role in the region and their control over themselves and their neighbors, despite its contrary outcome.

Notes

1. Robert Boyd and Peter J. Richerson, "The Evolution of Ethnic Markers," *Cultural Anthropology* 2 (1987): 65–79; Bruce Lincoln, *Discourse and the Construction of Society: Comparative Studies of Myth, Ritual, and Classification* (New York: Oxford University Press, 1989); Eugene E. Roosens, *Creating Ethnicity: The Process of Ethnogenesis* (London: Sage, 1989).

2. Michelle Callon, "Some Elements of a Sociology of Translation: Domestication of the Scallops and the Fishermen of Saint Brieuc Bay," in *Power, Action and Belief: A New Sociology of Knowledge?*, ed. J. Law, 196–233 (London: Routledge and Kegan Paul 1986); Bruno Latour, "Technology Is Society Made Durable," in *A Sociology of Monsters: Essays on Power, Technology and Domination*, ed. J. Law, 103–31 (London: Routledge, 1991); Bruno Latour, "Where Are the Missing Masses? Sociology of a Few Mundane Artefacts," in *Shaping Technology, Building Society: Studies in Sociotechnical Change*, ed. W. Bijker and J. Law, 225–58 (Cambridge MA: MIT Press, 1992); Bruno Latour, "On Recalling ANT," in *Actor Network and After*, ed. J. Law and J. Hassard, 15–25 (Oxford: Blackwell and the Sociological Review, 1999); Bruno Latour, *Reassembling the Social: An Introduction to Actor-Network-Theory* (Oxford: Oxford University Press, 2005); John Law, "After ANT: Topology, Naming and Complexity," in *Actor Network and After*, ed. J. Law and J. Hassard, 1–14 (Oxford: Blackwell and the Sociological Review, 1999); Frank A. Salamone and Charles H. Swanson, "Identity and Ethnicity: Ethnic Groups and Interactions in a Multiethnic Society," *Ethnic Groups* 2 (1979): 167–83.

3. Rebecca Saunders, *Stability and Change in Guale Indian Pottery: AD 1300–1702* (Tuscaloosa: University of Alabama Press, 2000).

4. Saunders, *Stability and Change.*

5. Saunders, *Stability and Change.*

6. Mark Williams, director, Lamar Institute, University of Georgia, pers. comm., November 2013.

7. Saunders, *Stability and Change.*

8. Jon Bernard Marcoux, Brent Lansdell, and Eric C. Poplin, "Revisiting the Ashley-Series: A Qualitative Analysis of a Contact-period Household Ceramic Assemblage," *South Carolina Antiquities* 43 (2011).

9. Chester DePratter, pers. comm., 2014; Stanley South, "The Indian Pottery Taxonomy of the South Carolina Coast," *University of South Carolina South Carolina Institute of Archaeology and Anthropology Notebook* 5 (1973): 54–57. Stanley South, *Archaeological Pathways to Historic Site Development* (New York: Kluwer Academic–Plenum, 2002).

10. Brent Lansdell, Jon Bernard Marcoux, and Eric C. Poplin, Data Recovery at 38BK1633: A Contact-Era Household on Daniel Island, Berkeley County, South Carolina (draft) (Charleston, South Carolina: Daniel Island Company, 2008); Marcoux, Lansdell and Poplin, "Revisiting the Ashley-Series."

11. Chester DePratter, pers. comm.

12. Marcoux, Lansdell, and Poplin, "Revisiting the Ashley-Series."

13. Eric C. Poplin and Jon Bernard Marcoux, "Transformation of Native Populations in 17th Century Carolina: Exploring Stylistic Changes in Ashley Series Pottery," paper presented at the 46th annual conference of the Society for Historical Archaeology, Leicester, England, January 9–12, 2013.

14. Brett H. Riggs and Christopher B. Rodning, "Cherokee Ceramic Traditions of Southwestern North Carolina, ca. A.D. 1400–2002: A Preface to 'The Last of the Iroquois Potters,'" *North Carolina Archaeology* 51 (2002): 34–54; Christopher B. Rodning, "The Cherokee Town at Coweeta Creek," PhD diss., University of North Carolina, 2004; Christopher B. Rodning, "Temporal Variation in Qualla Pottery at Coweeta Creek," *North Carolina Archaeology* 57 (2008): 1–49.

15. Eric C. Poplin and Jon Bernard Marcoux, "Altamaha Ceramics in the 17th and 18th Centuries: Comparing Yamasee Indian Occupations in Coastal Georgia and Coastal South Carolina," paper presented at The Yamasee Indians: From Florida to South Carolina conference, St. Augustine, Florida, April 16–18, 2015.

16. Poplin and Marcoux, "Altamaha Ceramics."

17. Poplin and Marcoux, "Altamaha Ceramics."

18. Poplin and Marcoux, "Altamaha Ceramics"; Saunders, *Stability and Change.*

19. Idiosyncratic behavior also can influence these frequencies. Perhaps the single Altamaha household that produced higher frequencies of paddle stamped line block decorations was occupied by an artisan who took the time to create complex carved paddles. Or the woman of that household was not of the same lineage as her neighbors. We do not know if there was frequent movement of females or males between the Yamasee towns in South Carolina or earlier communities in Georgia and Florida. If so, a Guale or Mocama woman may have become the bride of a Yamasee male who lived in Altamaha Town with the rest of his kin. We assume that all of these groups traced descent through their mothers, but we do not know if there were prescribed residential dictates when members of one group/town/moiety married into another group/town/moiety.

20. See Sudha A. Shah, "Pearls and the Lady of Cofitachequi," paper presented at the 74th Annual Conference of the Society for American Archaeology, Atlanta, Georgia, April 22–26, 2009, for the meaning of pearls as gifts to Hernan de Soto when he visited Cofitachequi in April 1540.

21. John C. Ewers, "A Half Century of Change in the Study of Plains Indian Art and Material Culture," *Papers in Anthropology* 24 (1983): 97–112; Michael H. Logan and Douglas A. Schmittou, "With Pride They Made These: Tribal Styles in Plains Indian Art," *Frank H. McClung Museum Occasional Paper* 12 (1995); Howard D. Rodee, "The Stylistic Development of Plains Indian Painting and Its Relationship to Ledger Drawings," *Plains Anthropologist* (1965) 10: 218–32; Douglas A. Schmittou, "A Stylistic Analysis of the White Swan Robe: Crow Representation and Applied Art as Ethnic Markers," MA thesis, University of Tennessee.

22. Alex Y. Sweeney and Eric C. Poplin, "Perspectives on Yamasee Life: Excavations at Altamaha Town," paper presented at the 8th Biennial Conference of the Society of Early Americanists, Savannah, Georgia, February 28–March 2, 2013, and at the 59th annual meeting of the American Society for Ethnohistory, New Orleans, Louisiana, September 11–14, 2013.

23. Mark R. Plane, "Catawba Ethnicity: Identity and Adaptation on the English Colonial Landscape," *North Carolina Archaeology* 53 (2004): 60–79.

24. Saunders, *Stability and Change*.

25. James Nyman, "The Ashley Series as Native American Persistence: Lowcountry Indians in the Period of European Expansion," MA thesis, University of South Carolina, 2011.

4

Cultural Continuity and Change
Archaeological Research at Yamasee Primary Towns in South Carolina

ALEXANDER Y. SWEENEY

Archaeologists examining indigenous cultures in contact with European colonizing entities have documented processes of culture change for over half a century. Contact period studies allow archaeologists to observe the adoption of new suites of material culture as well as the continuity of certain other cultural traditions for Native communities in contact settings. However, to document the processes of cultural change fully, researchers need to incorporate the complexities of a culture's migration and ethnogenesis. The multiethnic, confederated Yamasee Indians are an excellent case study in the effects of migration on ethnogenesis and the influences of cultural contact on material and ideological expressions in daily life. This study explores how particular aspects of Yamasee culture with regard to domestic and spiritual spheres remained broadly similar to practices initiated by their Late Mississippian ancestors, while their economic sphere was altered through their sustained interactions with British colonists. These ancestral traditions of the Yamasee are reflected in their construction of houses, use of domestic spaces, community settlement patterning, burial practices, and other spiritual beliefs. The retention of these descendant traditions persisted despite dramatic changes to their economy, which incorporated slaving and commercial deerskin trading with a de-emphasis on intensive agricultural practices, and despite missionizing attempts from neighboring Christian colonists.

Between 1695 and 1715 the Yamasee of coastal South Carolina lived within two distinct groups or divisions, the Upper and Lower Yamasee. Each of these groups contained a primary town that served as a political capital; Pocotaligo served as the Upper Yamasee capital, while Altamaha Town was the capital of the Lower Yamasee. Archaeological and archival research from these towns has provided data regarding Yamasee material culture, settlement patterning, activities, and burial customs. From this body of data we can gain insight into Yamasee lifeways and illustrate that, despite numerous migration episodes over time, the addition of new group members, and pressures exerted by Spanish and British colonial entities, the Yamasee were able to retain a variety of their traditional cultural practices. This retention of cultural practices is further explored throughout this chapter as I provide a cultural and historical context for the Yamasee in Carolina. Specifically, I compare archaeological and historical data pertaining to Yamasee houses, communities, activity areas, burials, religious practices, and slaving enterprises.

The Yamasee and Their British Colonial Neighbors

The two Yamasee primary towns were approximately 15.5 miles apart and separated largely by the Broad River. The general locations of the Upper and Lower Yamasee groups flanked the English settlements of Beaufort and Port Royal to the northwest and southwest.

The available datasets for this investigation are derived from both archival documentation and archaeological excavations. British colonial documents provide accounts of tumultuous trade relations between the Yamasee and the Indian traders from Charleston and Beaufort.[1] Pocotaligo, and its chief, King Lewis, are mentioned more frequently in the *Journals of the Commissioners of the Indian Trade* and other archival documents than are Altamaha Town and its leader. In contrast to this, substantially more archaeological data are available for Altamaha Town than for Pocotaligo. Despite differing amounts and types of available data on these two Yamasee primary towns, we are still able to reconstruct their traditional cultural practices and to situate them within the historical context of their interactions with British colonists.

Archival documentation provides the best evidence for attempts to understand the sociopolitical structure of the Yamasee in Carolina. When, in 1712, the Commissioners of the Indian Trade sent the Indian Agent John Wright and the Yamasee Commissioner Thomas Nairne

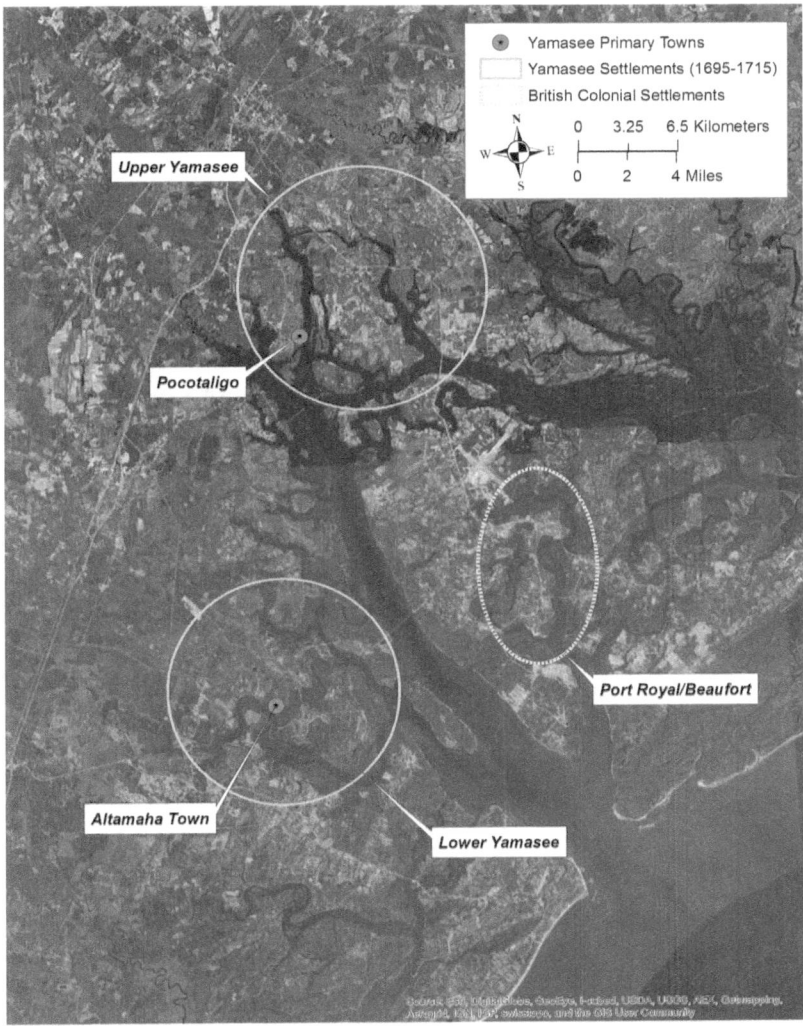

MAP 4. Location of the Upper and Lower Yamasee in South Carolina. By Alexander Y. Sweeney.

to address the Yamasees, they ordered Wright to assemble the Upper Yamasees at Pocotaligo and the Lower Yamasees at Altamaha Town. The objectives of these meetings were to solidify the Yamasee and British colonial alliance by proclaiming the British colonial government's concern for Yamasee welfare, to confirm the Yamasee rights to settle undisturbed within the designated Indian lands, and for Indian trade agents to hear Yamasee complaints and settle trading disputes.[2] The location of each meeting suggests that at least in the eyes of the commissioners, some political structure was in place distinguishing Pocotaligo and Altamaha as primary towns to the other eight secondary Yamasee towns (Huspah, Pocosabo, Sadketche, Tomatley, Tulafina, Chechessee, Euhaw, and Okatee). However, as noted by Chester DePratter, archival records hinting at a political structure that distinguished paramount and secondary towns are quite limited; therefore, the specific relationship between Yamasee primary towns and their associated secondary towns is rather unclear in terms of their sociopolitical structure.[3] The designation of these primary towns as political capitals for both the Upper and Lower Yamasee may have been a construct of British colonial and Western political ideology and may not actually have represented the true political relationship between these Yamasee towns at the local level.

British colonial documents also indicate that the British colonists may have overestimated or misunderstood the political power and influences that chiefs held over the members of their community. With regard to warfare, historical documents indicate that Yamasee chiefs maintained a strong military leadership role over their Yamasee soldiers. In 1687 Chief Altamaha, despite the wishes of some fellow Yamasee soldiers and Captain William Dunlop's English soldiers, successfully halted a retaliatory attack against the Spanish on Amelia Island for the destruction of Stuarts Town.[4] With regard to political influences, both Chief Altamaha and King Lewis appear to have retained at least a diplomatic role as a recognized representative for their respective groups, since they reported numerous complaints of various trader abuses on behalf of the members of their communities. However, a 1713 order in the Indian trade journals implied that the Yamasee leaders also held fiscal accountability over individual community members. This particular order stated that traders could only engage and trade with individuals who had the consent of their town's leader. The order also contained a clause that charged each town's leader as responsible for paying the debts of consenting members who became insolvent, refused to repay their debts, or ran away.[5] The fol-

Cultural Continuity and Change   103

lowing year, in 1714, King Lewis of Pocotaligo complained that a trader unreasonably charged him with a debt, perhaps evidence that traders had already begun to capitalize on the commissioners' orders.[6] This presumed fiscal responsibility may reflect a one-sided view that many British colonists had when judging the interactions between Yamasee leaders and the greater population of their community.

This misunderstood British colonial view of chiefly power and responsibility may have extended beyond fiscal responsibility as British colonists likely sought paramount leaders to make binding decisions on behalf of their communities or polities, even if these chiefs did not hold these powers. An entry in the *Journals of the Commissioners of the Indian Trade* dated July 9, 1712, stated that the Indian trader agents were to "acquaint [themselves] with [Indian] Custom, Usage, [etc.], giving the King and Head Men Advice in Relation to managing their People to better to keep them in Subjection, and with Example and Arguments drawn from a Parallel with our Government, and always as much as in you layes, keep in Favor with the Chief Men, advising and assisting them to maintain the Authority given to them by this Government.[7] This suggests that the British colonial government wanted the Yamasee chiefs to have the ability to govern over their communities with authority similar to that held by the British colonial political leaders over other British colonists, even if this chiefly authority was not inherently in place for the Yamasee chiefs.

It appears that the Upper and Lower divisions of the Yamasee in South Carolina may have been based on differential patterns of ethnicity related to distinct cultural origins. Numerous researchers (including Chester DePratter, William Green, John Hann, and John Worth) have traced the cultural origins of the Yamasee towns in the Port Royal region of South Carolina from 1695 to 1715 to Spanish Florida and earlier sixteenth- and seventeenth-century Indian provinces in the interior of Georgia.[8]

The Upper Yamasee capital of Pocotaligo, along with three other Upper Yamasee towns (Huspah, Sadketche, and Tulafina), can be traced to Spanish Florida along the Georgia coast. Pocotaligo originated from the Yamasee settlement of Ocotonico located in St. Simons Island, which contained the largest population of non-Christian Indians (n

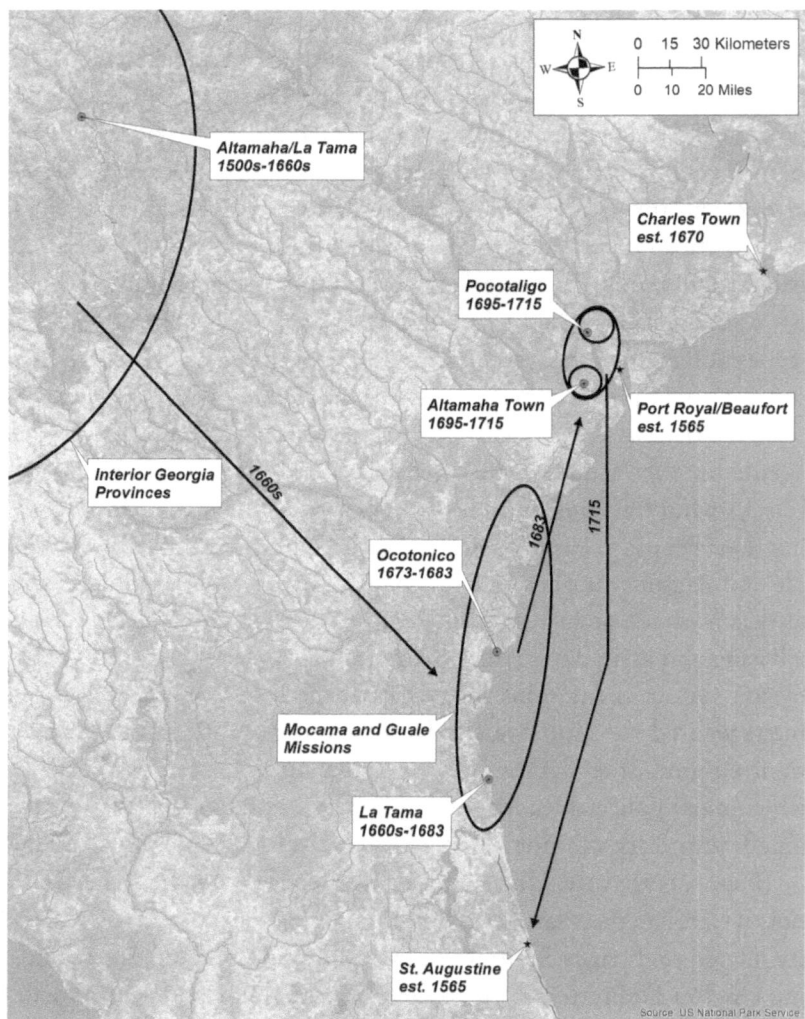

MAP 5. General location of Yamasee migrations from the 1660s to 1715. By Alexander Y. Sweeney.

= 160) in the region.⁹ The Lower Yamasee town of Altamaha can also be traced to Spanish Florida to the south of Ocotonico, at the settlement of La Tama on Amelia Island. Altamaha, along with the three other Lower Yamasee towns of Chechessee, Euhaw, and Okatee, can be traced even further back to the Late Mississippian Period interior

Indian provinces located in the Oconee River Valley.[10] In the following discussion, archaeological data provide support for the persistence of many cultural traditions that descended from these distinct origins.

Houses and Community

Yamasee houses and communities in South Carolina provide some of the best archaeological examples of their cultural resilience and ties to ancestral lifeways. While archival documentation of these patterns is sorely lacking, recent archaeological excavations have provided us with household and community information that is not otherwise available. At Pocotaligo one household was inferred based on the spatial distribution of recovered artifacts.[11] This distribution was identified by examining the locations of San Marcos/Altamaha series ceramics and shell fragments that were recovered from shovel tests excavated at five-meter intervals. The inferred location of the household contained the highest concentrations of San Marcos/Altamaha ceramics and was devoid of shell. This is distinct from the remaining concentrations of San Marcos/Altamaha ceramics at Pocotaligo that also happened to contain shell fragments; these particular areas were interpreted as areas of refuse disposal.

The Altamaha Town excavations identified the earliest well-defined examples of Yamasee houses in South Carolina. Similar spatial distributions of cultural materials to those identified at Pocotaligo were also recognized from data found at Altamaha Town. Subsequent and larger excavations within the locations of these distributions at Altamaha Town confirmed that these patterns are related to Yamasee households and outdoor activity areas. A total of six similarly shaped circular structures were identified, containing interior posts that were remnants of either sleeping platforms or wall partitions (fig. 1). Storage pits filled with San Marcos/Altamaha pottery vessels and trade items were identified within one of the houses. Five of the excavated Yamasee houses also contained human burials just inside the exterior walls of the house. One house contained two burials; the remaining four houses with burials each contained only one.

The cultural origins of Altamaha Town can be traced to the Late Mississippian Period in interior Georgia, in the vicinity of the Oconee

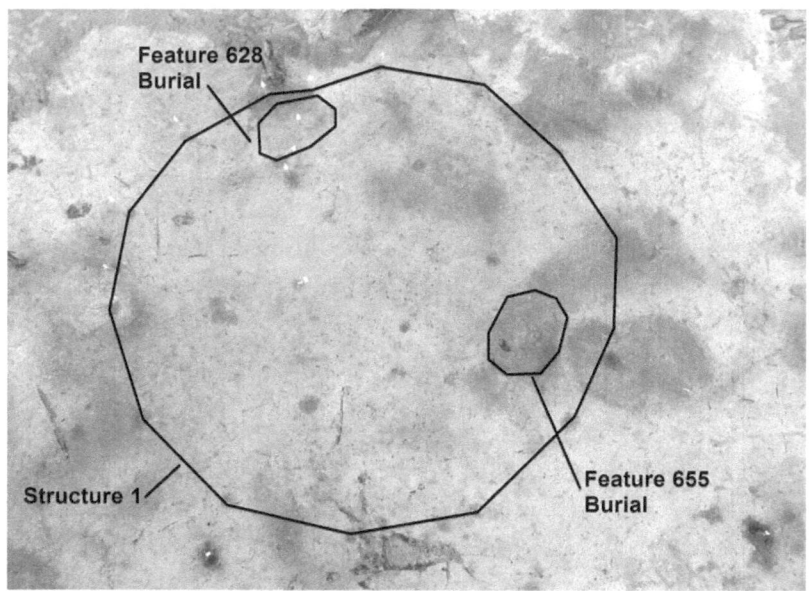

FIG. 1. View of Yamasee house (Structure 1) from Altamaha Town. By Alexander Y. Sweeney.

River Valley. Research conducted by James Hatch provides data on Late Mississippian houses located in this region; these data are valuable for comparing the Yamasee houses from Altamaha Town to the location and temporal association of their presumed ancestors.[12] The identified Yamasee structures from Altamaha Town appear to be similar in multiple respects to the round Late Mississippian houses in the Oconee River Valley.

Aside from their identical shape, both groups of houses contained interior support posts, storage pits, and human burials. One observable difference between the two datasets is that the Late Mississippian Oconee River Valley houses are slightly larger, ranging from 8 to 10.5 meters in diameter, compared to the Yamasee house that ranged from 6.4 to 8.1 meters in diameter. The largest Yamasee house is approximately the same size as the smallest Late Mississippian houses reported by Hatch from the Oconee River Valley.[13] The overall similarities between the Yamasee buildings and these Late Missis-

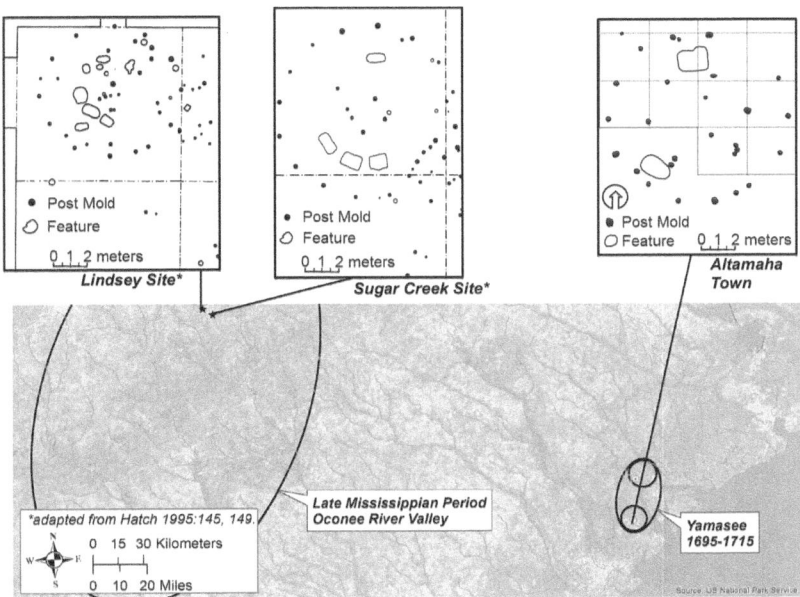

MAP 6. General location and sketch plan view of late Mississippian and Yamasee houses. By Alexander Y. Sweeney.

sippian Period buildings from the Oconee River Valley suggest that despite multiple migrations and repeated interactions with Europeans and several other Indian groups, Yamasee houses can be seen to reflect descendant cultural traditions over a period spanning several hundred years.[14]

Archaeological excavations and archival research conducted by Andrea White at the Yamasee settlement of La Punta in St. Augustine further demonstrate this descendant cultural tradition of domestic spaces.[15] La Punta, which was a mission settlement occupied by refugee Yamasee from Carolina sometime between the late 1720s to the 1750s, also contained three (likely noncontemporaneous) circular structures interpreted by White as Yamasee houses. On average, these houses at La Punta have a diameter of approximately six meters, which is slightly smaller than the houses from Altamaha Town (6.4 to 8.1 meters) and the Oconee River Valley (8.0 to 10.5 meters).[16] Not only are the similar Yamasee houses identified at La Punta an example of cultural continuity in Yamasee architecture; they also demonstrate that the descendant cultural tradition for houses endures over time, space, and within different cultural contexts including Spanish mission communities.

Ethnographic studies have been applied by southeastern archaeologists in an attempt to estimate household size. Casselberry's formula estimates that the number of individuals within a given household is equal to approximately one-sixth of the calculated floor area of a domestic structure.[17] Using this formula, Altamaha Town structures may have been designed to accommodate six to nine individual household members, with the average household size large enough to accommodate about seven individuals. This is similar to Jon Marcoux's calculation for Mississippian houses from eastern Tennessee, which projected an average of seven individuals per Mississippian household.[18] Unfortunately, specific data regarding floor area are not available for the Late Mississippian Oconee River Valley, making a direct comparison of household size between the two related groups difficult at present. However, if we calculate the area based on the circumference reported by Hatch (assuming that these are perfectly circular structures), we can at least attempt to make inferences regarding household sizes over time (table 2).[19] Using the assumptions outlined, it would appear that Late Mississippian houses from the Oconee River Valley could accommodate between eight and fourteen individual household members. Likewise, if we apply the same calculation to houses identified by White, the average household at La Punta contained approximately five individual members.[20] Hence, over time and multiple migration episodes, it appears that the Yamasee houses decreased in size as people moved from the Oconee River Valley to Altamaha Town and from Altamaha Town to St. Augustine. If the estimates for household sizes as calculated using Casselberry's formula are valid, then we can infer that this decrease in household size is a reflection of an appreciable decrease in population with regard to size of extended families.[21]

Yamasee communities also appear to retain similar aspects of their ancestral cultural traditions. Approximately one-third of Altamaha Town has been excavated; the remaining two-thirds of the site are located on a preserve protected from future development. The houses

TABLE 2. Calculated household sizes (after Casselberry 1974)

houses	calculated floor space (square meters)	estimated household size (rounded)
Altamaha Town		
Structure 1	41.686	7
Structure 2	39.844	7
Structure 3	35.592	6
Structure 4	51.771	9
Structure 5	46.428	8
Structure 6	39.117	7
Late Mississippian*		
Minimum	50.24	8
Maximum	86.54625	14
La Punta**	28.26	5

Sources: Basis derived from Samuel E. Casselberry, "Further Refinement of Formulae for Determining Population from Floor Area," *World Archaeology* 6 (1974): 117–22. *Data from James W. Hatch, "Lamar Period Upland Farmsteads of Oconee River Valley, Georgia," in *Mississippian Communities and Households*, ed. Daniel Rogers and Bruce D. Smith (Tuscaloosa: University of Alabama Press, 1995), 135–55. **Data from Andrea P. White, "Living on the Periphery: A Study of an Eighteenth-Century Yamasee Mission Community in Colonial St. Augustin," MA thesis, College of William and Mary, Williamsburg, 2002.

within the excavated portion of Altamaha were spaced approximately 60–100 meters apart; the exception to this is the one area containing two houses spaced only a few meters apart (these two particular house locations may not be contemporaneous and actually represent separate periods of occupation). This spatial patterning of houses is consistent with findings of previous researchers who have described Yamasee settlements and communities as non-nucleated.[22] If we presume that the spatial patterning of houses across the preservation area of the site is consistent with the excavated area, then we can project that another twelve Yamasee houses are located to the west, for a total of eighteen houses within all of Altamaha Town.

Archival evidence indicates that the Yamasee capitals of Altamaha and Pocotaligo also contained council houses. The Indian trade journals mention these council houses at both Altamaha and Pocotaligo,

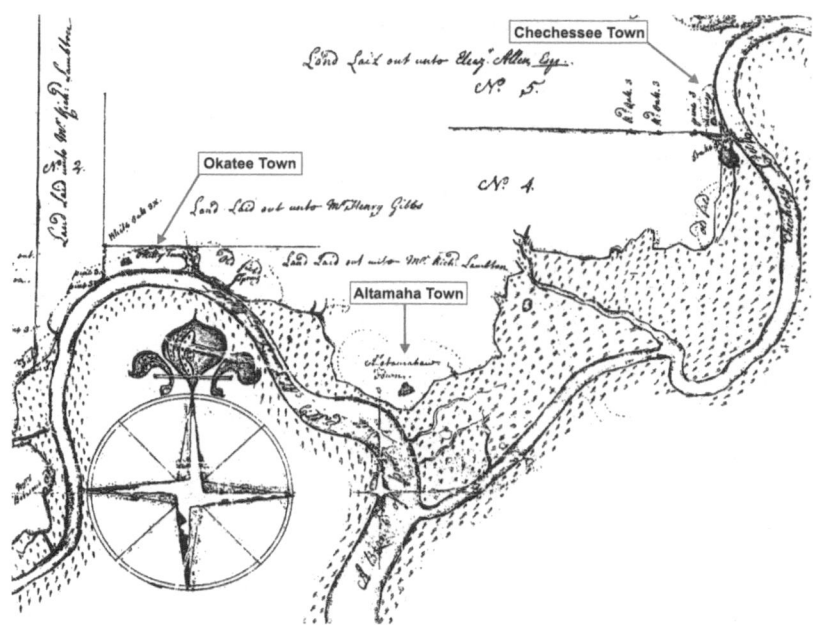

MAP 7. Location of Lower Yamasee settlements of Altamaha Town, Chechessee Town, and Okatee Town, ca. 1732. By Carol Poplin.

which may have been the locations for diplomatic meetings between different Yamasee Indians and Indian trade agents. A portion of a 1732 plat of the area, which depicts the location of Altamaha Town as flanked by the Yamasee towns of Chechessee Town to the east and Okatee Town to the west, shows a larger structure within each town that may have represented its council house (map 7). A round council house, which could have also served as the chief's residence, may have been centrally located within Altamaha Town. Since no evidence for a council house was identified through the excavations, it is possible that the council house/chief residence is actually located to the west on the preservation portion of the site. A comparison between the location of the council house on the 1732 plat and the site map for Altamaha Town indicates that the council house/chief residence was likely near, and quite possibly on top of, a prehistoric earthen mound on the preservation area of the site. Chiefly and noble residences were often constructed on these earthen mounds in Missis-

Cultural Continuity and Change   111

sippian communities.[23] The location of Chief Altamaha's residence atop the mound at Altamaha Town would be another example of the Yamasee continuing the descendant cultural traditions of their Late Mississippian ancestors.

If the preservation area of Altamaha Town does contain an additional twelve houses in addition to a council house/chief residence, then an estimated nineteen residences would be located across the entire settlement. If these residences contained the same average number of calculated individuals per household found on the excavated portion of the site (which is seven), then we can estimate that the entire town may have contained a population of approximately 133 individuals. The 1715 Barnwell census of the Yamasee just before the start of the Yamasee War enumerated a total of 1,220 Yamasee men, women, and children within the ten towns. If we make the assumption that each town contains approximately the same number of individuals, then based on the previously mentioned calculations for Altamaha Town, there should have been a total of approximately 1,330 Yamasee individuals in Carolina; which is approximately 110 members higher than the number of Yamasee tallied in 1715 census. However, if we assume that the capitals of the Upper and Lower Yamasee, Pocotaligo and Altamaha had similar populations (n = 133) that were higher than in the remaining eight secondary towns, then, using the number of quantified Yamasee from the Barnwell census, each of the remaining eight secondary towns would have had a lower average of approximately 119 individuals. As noted by Chester DePratter, there is little available archival evidence to support clear political distinctions between the Yamasee capitals and secondary towns.[24] Based on the latter calculated population sizes presented here, this could suggest that another distinction between primary and secondary Yamasee towns could be a slightly increased population at the Yamasee capitals. Future excavations at secondary Yamasee towns may provide data that can be compared to the Altamaha Town excavations as well as the 1715 census. These comparisons may eventually allow for refined estimates of populations at Yamasee settlements. Further explorations of the sociopolitical relationships between primary and secondary towns would also benefit from ancillary archaeological evidence.

Activity Areas

As discussed earlier, houses reflected a descendant tradition practiced by the Yamasee that traces back several hundred years to their Late Mississippian ancestry to the west in the Oconee River Valley. A comparison of activity areas between Late Mississippian and Yamasee yard areas also reveals similarities. Hatch reported that smudge pits, trash pits, and animal hide processing racks were found in nearby yard areas outside Late Mississippian houses.[25] In addition, outdoor hearths and storage pits were identified in the Oconee River Valley. The appearance of similar activity area features between the Yamasee in Carolina and the Late Mississippian Oconee River Valley further illustrates the descendant tradition for the Yamasee, extending beyond their persistence in architectural choices, to include continuity in many of their traditional domestic activities.

The Altamaha Town excavations also recovered information on the yard areas located outside the defined Yamasee houses. Cultural features were identified within these yards that suggest defined activity areas that were a part of everyday Yamasee domestic life. The activity areas varied in their distance from their associated house and tended to be located approximately 2.5 to 12.5 meters outside the houses. Several of the yards contained additional arrangements of post holes, which likely are the remnants of screens or racks. These screens or racks were likely used for processing animal hides and fish through drying and smoking.[26]

Smudge pits, which are small pits filled with the remnants of charcoal and other burned materials, were identified between 1.0 and 6.5 meters from the Yamasee houses at Altamaha Town. Smudge pits were used by Indians to produce dense smoke, which could be useful for smoking hides and repelling insects and other pests. The smudge pits located at greater distances from the houses and found in association with the animal processing screens or racks, were likely used for hide smoking activities. The smudge pits located close to the Yamasee houses that were not found in association with animal processing racks may have been used for repelling insects.

Additional features such as trash pits, linear trenches, and various

Cultural Continuity and Change   113

piles of shell were also identified in the activity areas outside the Yamasee houses. The linear trenches are fairly shallow in depth and may have been associated with farming activities for small household garden plots. Trash pits located in the activity areas were filled with substantial amounts of animal bones, broken pottery vessels, and a bone point used for fishing. The shell piles were filled primarily with oyster shells that were collected from nearby streams. These shell piles are suggestive of Yamasee cooking and feasting activities.

The animal hide processing screens and the smudge pits associated with hide smoking activities are indicative of both the persistence of Yamasee hunting and Yamasee participation in the commercialized deerskin trade with their neighboring and allied English colonists. The deerskin trade to Great Britain was one of the economic foundations of the Yamasee alliance with the British colonists. As British colonial demands for deerskins increased, the Yamasee responded by increasing their hunting of wild deer to acquire more European manufactured goods over time, resulting in an eventual severe depletion of the deer population. This depletion, along with other factors such as unethical trading practices, increased the Yamasee debt to the Indian traders.[27] As a symbol of the centrality of deerskins to this relationship, beginning in 1693 all Indians allied to the English were required to provide deerskins annually to the British colonial government.[28]

However, given that the Yamasee engaged in and thrived through the deerskin trade with their allied British colonial trading partners, it is possible that this specific economic exchange and enterprise, which was likely not as intensive for their Late Mississippian ancestors, may have had some effect on animal hide processing. This exchange with British colonial traders transformed a routine domestic process into an intensive economic enterprise, which would have altered the scale of animal hide processing vastly. A logical methodology to explore this would be a more detailed comparative activity-area study between the Oconee River Valley and later Yamasee households to infer further what effects this enterprise of processing deerskins for market would have had on this traditional activity. This could be explored through comparing the spatial patterning, frequencies, and adaptive technologies of animal hide processing. For the Yamasee at Altamaha Town, the recovery of glass hide-scraping tools that were knapped from rum bottles acquired through trade points to their willingness to incorporate new suites of material culture into their traditional daily lives.

Burials

The persistence of the Yamasee practicing descendant cultural traditions from their ancestral ties to the Late Mississippian Oconee River Valley also extends well beyond the architectural and domestic spheres outlined and includes mortuary customs and spiritual beliefs. The retention of these customs and beliefs is best illustrated through the comparison of burials over time and space. The excavations at Altamaha Town provided us with the first Yamasee burials recorded in South Carolina. Five of the six graves identified were located in the western portion of their associated house; the sixth grave was located in the northern side of the one particular house that contained two graves. One specific Yamasee grave contained an individual buried in a semi-flexed position, wrapped in cane matting with blue glass seed beads around the neck and wrists (fig. 2). This woven mat was folded or wrapped around the individual, and iron nails identified in the burial suggest that they were used to close and pin the mat in place. Other artifacts that were identified within Yamasee graves include San Marcos/Altamaha pottery vessels, kaolin pipes, rum bottles, and an iron sickle or scythe.

The practice of burying individuals within houses seems to reflect the traditional burial customs of the Yamasee and to reference the cultural traditions of their ancestors. Common traits between Yamasee burials and Late Mississippian burials include location, interment position, and ideologically charged mortuary objects of similar themes. Hatch indicated that Late Mississippian burials from the Oconee River Valley were also located within houses, almost always contained only a single individual, and individuals were typically buried in a flexed or semi-flexed position.[29] These are the very same burial traits observed for the Yamasee several hundred years later in South Carolina. An emic interpretation for the semi-flexed positioning of the interred within both the Yamasee and Late Mississippian burials has been suggested by Chief Se'khu of the Yamassee Nation of South

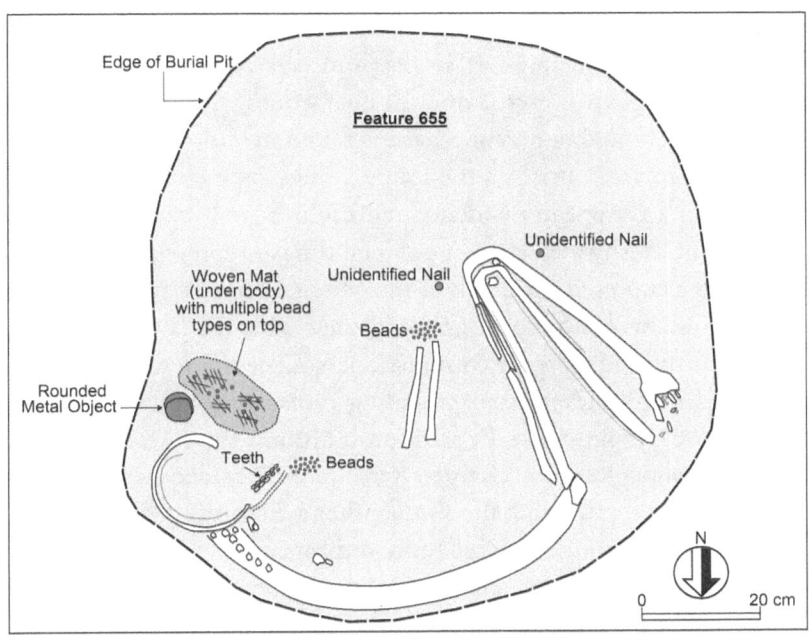

FIG. 2. Plan view of semi-flexed burial from Altamaha Town. By Allison Wind.

Carolina. Semi-flexed burials placed on their sides resemble the fetal position, and individuals are positioned to return to the world as they came into the world.[30]

Also of interest is the comparison of mortuary objects identified in the Late Mississippian burials to those found in Yamasee burials at Altamaha Town. Hatch reported that ceramic vessels were the most common Late Mississippian mortuary objects, along with "columella shell bead necklaces, freshwater clam 'spoons,' chunky stones, a monolithic ax effigy pipe, and a piece of faceted graphite."[31] The Yamasee mortuary objects are strikingly similarly themed items, with one notable exception; they are not all items of Native American manufacture. Only the San Marcos/Altamaha pottery appears to be manufactured by the Yamasee; everything else included in these burials was acquired through trade.

The Late Mississippian columella shell beads were very likely exotic items from coastal areas that were imported through trade with other indigenous groups to the interior. The Yamasee counterparts to this funerary jewelry, the blue seed beads from Altamaha Town, were also trade items but were acquired through interactions with European trading partners. Smoking paraphernalia is found in both Late Mississippian and Yamasee burials; a monolithic effigy pipe in the precontact burials and a European manufactured kaolin pipe in the postcontact burials. The freshwater clam spoon could have represented a vessel, similar to a cup used for drink in the Mississippian burials. Yamasee burials contained rum bottles, incongruous with the laws of the day, given that the Indian trade commissioners made numerous efforts to prohibit Indian traders from providing rum to the Indians through any means. Despite these English prohibitions, the rum bottle vessels became ideologically charged items to be included within burial interments. It appears that the similar-themed mortuary objects from Late Mississippian to Yamasee times indicate a shared tradition continuing throughout time and space through processes of migration. Even though the specific items may be different, they are substituted with an available, contemporary, surrogate item that can convey the same symbolic meaning.

The location and positioning of burials for the Yamasee and their ancestors in the Late Mississippian Oconee River Valley are not similar to burials found in the missionized context of coastal Georgia. Burials of "Christianized" Guale Indians in Spanish missions in both Florida and Georgia are within defined cemeteries or beneath the floor of the mission church, with the individuals extended and lying on their backs. However, many of the mortuary objects from Spanish mission contexts do appear to share some similarities with the mortuary objects recovered from the Yamasee and Late Mississippian burial contexts.[32]

Some of the items from burials at the Spanish mission Santa Catalina de Guale on St. Catherines Island, Georgia included glass beads, shell beads, bone beads, shell earrings, medallions, crosses, Majolica plates, cups, and pitchers, a chunky stone, and a projectile point base.[33] The majolica plates may be substitutes in the Spanish mission burials for locally Indian-produced ceramic vessels found in the Yamasee and Late Mississippian burials. The increased quantities of personal adornments with Christian iconography, such as the medallions and crosses, along with the absence of any tobacco-related artifacts, are differences within the Spanish mission Guale mortuary objects. There has been some debate as to whether Franciscan priests allowed the Guale to include available religious items as substitutes for more traditional Guale burial goods, as opposed to whether the Guale added available mortuary items at the final stages of burial without the knowledge of Franciscan priests.[34] Despite these differing attempts to explain whether Franciscan priests approved (or were even aware) of the inclusion of mortuary objects, the inclusion of any mortuary object goods is arguably a trait similar to more traditional Late Mississippian burial practices.[35]

Carl Halbirt also provides data for several Yamasee burials identified in association with a Franciscan mission church at the Yamasee settlement of La Punta in St. Augustine that was occupied from the late 1720s to the 1750s.[36] Similar to the Guale burials identified at Santa Catalina de Guale on St. Catherines Island, all of the single interment burials identified within the La Punta mission church were located underneath the church floor with individuals interred fully extended and lying on their backs. However, unlike the Guale burials from underneath the St. Catherines Island church floor, no mortuary objects were identified within the burials inside the La Punta mission church. Halbirt notes that one burial located outside the church, which was also fully extended with the individual lying on the back, did contain a greenstone celt/axe and a shell bead necklace.

Mortuary practices in general may be more of a reflection of the wider community, and the beliefs of those who buried the deceased, than they are a reflection of the individuals who are interred.[37] Looking at the burials for the Late Mississippian Period, the Guale in Spanish Florida, the Yamasee in Carolina, and the Yamasee in St. Augustine, it would appear that the burial location and positioning of the individual is dependent on the context and the environment of the community. Postcontact, some Indians were found to have Christianized burial traits in Spanish mission contexts when constrained by the spiritual leadership and rule of the Franciscan priests, only to return to their traditional burial customs when removed from the Spanish mission context. The influence of Christianity may have been adopted as a matter of convenience or acceptance within the specific mission environment (as seen among the Guale on St. Catherines Island and the Yamasee in St. Augustine). With regard to the positioning of burials, Franciscans may have retained enough control and power to influence the burial customs of the Native groups directly. Alternatively, the Yamasee and Guale within mission contexts may have adapted or accommodated the parameters of their social environment by willingly conforming to a more Christianized burial pattern. Nonetheless, there does appear to be a strong correlation between certain Yamasee burial traits (location, individual positioning, and mortuary objects) and the contexts of their specific settlement patterning.

Christianity

Seventeenth-century Spanish documents have referred to the Yamasee as pagans and heathens, thereby suggesting that any effect of Spanish missionization on the Yamasee religious beliefs was minimal. It is difficult to assess the lasting effects and influences, if any, that the Spanish mission system may have had on the Yamasee, or even on the missionized Guale. When the Yamasee and the Guale abandoned coastal Georgia and Florida and migrated into Carolina in 1683 (as outlined in detail by Keith Ashley in this volume), both groups became collectively known as the Yamasee, a combination of "Christianized" and non-Christianized people.[38] Unfortunately, it is not possible to determine the specific demographic breakdown of Yamasee and former Guale living in particular Yamasee towns in Carolina. Arguably, based on evidence seen in the Altamaha Town burials, it does not appear that the influence of Christianity was long-lasting.

Pocotaligo's chief is referred to as King Lewis in British colonial documents. The European name Lewis suggests that perhaps he was baptized by the Spanish. Meanwhile, the chief of Altamaha Town, sometimes referred to as King or Chief Altamaha in British colonial documents, likely was neither Christian nor baptized.[39] If chiefs retained a strong influence over the community members whom they governed, then perhaps this chiefly influence extended beyond political influence, toward ideology and religion as well.

Archival documents suggest that the British colonists also attempted to bring Christianity to Yamasee in Carolina. Between 1710 and 1711, schoolmaster Ross Reynolds of St. Bartholomew's Parish (modern-day Colleton County) provided education in language and religion to young Yamasee. The letter discussing this account also makes some reference to the inconvenient distance from Reynolds's school to the Yamasee towns, which suggests reasons as to why the educational services of Reynolds to the Yamasee did not last beyond 1711.[40] According to other archival documents, Reynolds denied ever teaching any Indian children and admitted only to teaching three métis children whose mothers were Indians and whose fathers were traders.[41] It is unknown if these three métis children had Yamasee mothers.

Additional archival documentation suggests that attempts by Carolina clergy to bring Christianity to the Yamasee ultimately failed. This was likely due to a combination of a lack of desire from many Yamasee to adopt and embrace Christianity fully and a lack of dedication by the clergy to carry out any Yamasee conversion. Reverend Samuel Thomas's attempt to convert the Yamasee in the first decade of the eighteenth century failed before it even started, given his refusal to follow church orders and settle among the Yamasee. In a 1706 letter of excuses by Thomas to his superiors that explains his failures to convert the Yamasee, Thomas stated that despite the Yamasee being a civilized group that could be receptive to Christianity, they seemed to have no time for or interest in converting to Christianity. Thomas also cites concerns for his personal safety living on the frontier of Carolina and suggests that language barriers were thwarting his attempts at Yamasee conversion. Of interest regarding the language barrier issue, Thomas stated that attempts to translate the Lord's Prayer into the Yamasee language were frustrating, as they did not have suitable translations for portions of the prayer. "Our Father which art in heaven" became "Our father who art atop" and "Thy Kingdom come" translated to "thy great town come."[42] These translations appear to be literal translations of the words of the prayer into the closest relevant meaning to the Yamasee. According to Thomas, this translation appears to miss much of the symbolic meaning of the prayer. As demonstrated further by Denise Bossy in this volume, Yamasee conversion to Christianity was a selective process that at times may have been more likely politically and not ideologically charged.[43] Furthermore, Jane Landers in this volume uses the phrase "nominally converted" to refer to those Yamasee and others who may have been baptized yet adopted only limited elements of Christianity into their daily lives, without undergoing a wholesale transformation of their traditional spirituality.[44]

Evidence for Christian religious items was also identified among the trade goods recovered in activity areas at Altamaha Town. Two Franciscan rings were recovered from the yard areas of two different houses. Rings similar to these were often given to converted Indians by Franciscan missionaries in the seventeenth century. However, within the context of Altamaha, the rings may have been loot taken from converted Indians to the south who were victims of Yamasee slave raiding. Alternatively, the rings may have been acquired earlier (in the mid- to late seventeenth century) by the Yamasee and Guale while living among the Spanish in coastal Georgia and Florida. If these rings were plunder recovered from raiding converted Indians, then this would substantiate a remark from Thomas Nairne describing slaving raids, stating that they had been fighting to bring Christianized people to "downright barbarity and heathenism."[45] Nonetheless, it is likely that these rings no longer retained any of their original religious implications within the early eighteenth-century Altamaha Town settlement.

Slaving

Slaving upon other Indian groups became paramount in the bond and alliance between the Yamasee and the British colonists in Charleston. It was common for the Yamasee and other Indians to conduct slave raids armed with firearms and accompanied by British colonial trade agents and soldiers. In July 1711 King Lewis of Pocotaligo stated to the Commissioners of Indian Trade that he did not want to be accompanied by traders or other British colonists during slave raids against other indigenous groups. This request was granted by the Board, unless they were given specific orders from the government to accompany the raiders. A few days later, the commissioners also declared in their articles to the Indian traders that all slaves and goods acquired through raids had to be retained in each Yamasee town for at least three days before they could be traded to the Indian traders.[46] These two details in the journal suggest that the Yamasee needed some distancing between

Cultural Continuity and Change

themselves and the Indian traders during and immediately after raids, possibly due to unfair trading practices or unequal shares and claims on plundered slaves and goods acquired through the raids.

Archaeological evidence for Yamasee slaving into Spanish Florida, aside from recovered firearms-related artifacts such as musket balls and gun flints, and the previously mentioned Franciscan rings, includes the recovery of a heavily sooted St. Johns ceramic bowl from Altamaha Town.[47] This vessel is distinctive due to its chalky paste made from clays taken from freshwater sources that contain sponge spicules. The freshwater sponge spicules used to make the paste of this vessel are only found along coastal areas of Florida, and not in South Carolina. Only two Native groups were still making St. Johns pottery into the early eighteenth century, the Ais from the central portion of eastern Florida between Cape Canaveral and the St. Lucie Inlet, and the Christianized Timucuas living in Spanish mission settlements between St. Augustine and Amelia Island.[48]

Archival documents indicate that the Ais were raided and enslaved by the Yamasee sometime between 1704 and 1711 (map 8). The southern portion of Nairne's 1711 map of South Carolina documents Yamasee slaving forays by showing a location just north of the Ais Territory indicating the canoe landing of the Yamasee along the St. Johns River: "Here the Car[o]lina Indians leave th[eir] Canoes when they go to war against the Floridians." Nairne also outlined the locations of several villages belonging to the Floridians; one cluster of villages is located within the general territory of the Ais. This St. Johns vessel, recovered from Altamaha Town, may have been acquired during the raiding of the Ais and could have been used as a container to transport plundered goods from the Ais back to Carolina.

During Queen Anne's War (1702–13), the frontier between the English Province of Carolina and Spanish Florida became one of the theaters of violent conflict. Much of this conflict came in the form of indigenous slave raiding. Yamasee slaving raids against the Timucuas, who had been Christianized by the Franciscans, are also well documented in the historical records. The Timucuas were attacked and raided by joint Indian and British colonial forces in 1702. Carolina Governor James Moore organized approximately a thousand troops

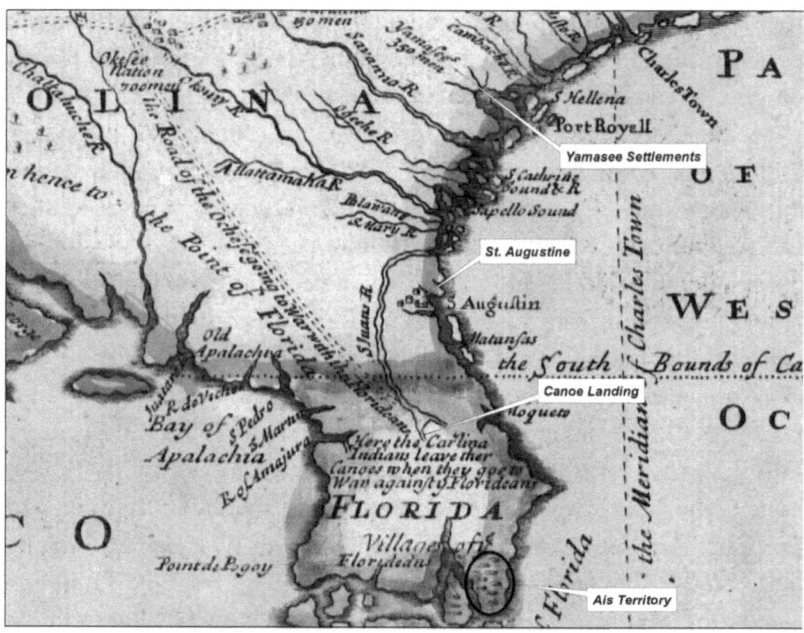

MAP 8. Location of Ais territory and Yamasee canoe landing for slaving into Florida depicted on a portion of Thomas Nairne's 1711 map. By Alexander Y. Sweeney.

consisting of British colonial soldiers, Yamasee, and Creeks. This force landed on the northern end of Amelia Island and raided to the south into St. Augustine.[49] Following a lengthy three-month siege at the Castillo de San Marcos in St. Augustine, Moore's forces retreated with more than five hundred captive Timucuas.[50]

Yamasee participation in the slave trade became a prominent economic endeavor that was encouraged through their contact and interactions with British colonials. Although there is also evidence for warfare among Native groups during the Late Mississippian period, the scale of Native violence expanded later during periods of alliance with British colonials. As documented in the *Journals of the Commissioners of the Indian Trade*, British colonial-allied Indians were offered a bounty of five pounds for each Christian slave captured through warfare.[51] The payment for Christianized Indians would have incentivized Yamasee warfare against the Spanish-allied Natives, weakening Carolina's primary British colonial adversary. The British colonial practice of subcontracting warfare among Native groups in Carolina not only created new slaves; it also eased British colonial expansion by removing indigenous groups from their land.[52]

Slaving and colonial-client warfare are perhaps the most dramatic and fundamental changes to the worldview of the Yamasee and all contemporary Native groups. Slaving, along with European demands for fur and hides, intensively increased competition among Native groups. The introduction of firearms into the Native toolkit also created a dependency on British colonial entities to access new commodities that Natives could not produce themselves, including gun parts and powder.[53] As this dependency grew over time, Native groups developed new specializations and altered their self-sufficient subsistence practices.[54] Sedentary intensive farmers who had been part-time hunters were rapidly transformed into commercial hunters and mercenaries after initial contact with European colonizing forces.[55] This is a significant shift from subsistence strategies practiced since at least the Late Mississippian period.

Archaeologists examining cultures in contact often emphasize acculturation and the processes of historical continuity and cultural change. Historical continuities as well as disjunctures are evidenced in architecture and in suites of artifacts from both domestic and mortuary contexts at two Yamasee capital towns from seventeenth-century Carolina. The genealogies of the classes of artifacts recovered at Pocotaligo and Altamaha Town point to some degree of material acculturation with the incorporation of firearms, rum, and other Euro-manufactured goods.[56] Additionally, we may be seeing the rejection of certain material and even ideological aspects of British colonial influence and oversight. The process of acculturation for the Yamasee in Carolina appears to be differentially expressed when examining their routine domestic lives and spirituality compared to their economy.

The domestic and spiritual spheres of Yamasee lifeways appear to remain fairly constant, and many traditions apparently were retained from Late Mississippian ancestors. Most notably, Yamasee methods of house construction, and the design of domestic spaces, are reflective of

Late Mississippian traditions known from interior Georgia. One difference among the houses over time is a slight reduction in floor space, which may indicate a decrease in household size. Late Mississippian and Yamasee houses outside direct European contexts also both contain single interment burials. The positioning of burial interments and the inclusion of mortuary items appear to be consistent between the Yamasee in Carolina and their Late Mississippian ancestors. The inclusion of any European items within burials exhibits adaptability by the Yamasee to substitute available exotic goods for traditional (and possibly unavailable) Native manufactured items; these exotic goods may have retained spiritual meanings similar to those of the Native items they replaced in burials. Notably, attempts for conversions to Christianity by Carolina clergy appear to have largely failed. Limited research at La Punta suggests that Yamasee burial positioning in this Spanish mission settlement may have conformed to Catholic standards, suggesting that those Yamasees living within Spanish mission communities after the Yamasee War might have been more willing to alter their burial practices.

The economic sphere of Yamasee lifeways provides more dramatic examples of cultural change. Both slaving and intensive commercial deerskin trading were economic endeavors that expanded through Yamasee alliances with British colonists. In engaging in these commercial enterprises, the Yamasee altered traditional modes of livelihood. The adoption of items such as firearms created both dependency on their British colonial trading partners for related equipment and skill specializations for Native warfare.[57] Intensive agricultural practices witnessed during the preceding Mississippian periods likely declined, as more emphasis was placed on engaging in these relatively new economic endeavors.

As demonstrated throughout this chapter, multiple continuities as well as changes are evident in various aspects of Yamasee culture. Elsewhere in this volume, researchers use other lines of material evidence to address cultural continuities and changes before and after the Yamasee migration to Carolina.[58] In the preceding chapter of this volume, Poplin and Marcoux demonstrate how interpretations of material culture can be correlated to fluctuating Yamasee identities.[59] Future documentation of Yamasee cultural changes can compare additional aspects of their lifeways, including diet, other classes of material culture, and settlement patterns from their Late Mississippian ancestral homelands in the Oconee River Valley, to their initial migrations into Spanish Florida mission systems in the 1660s, to their settlements in British colonial Carolina, and finally their return to Spanish Florida after the Yamasee War in 1715. A detailed comparative study of these contexts will allow for enhanced documentation of indigenous responses to British colonization throughout time and space.

Notes

1. Alan Gallay, *The Indian Slave Trade: The Rise of the English Empire in the American South, 1670–1717* (New Haven: Yale University Press, 2002), 241–56, emphasizes this factionalism between Indian traders.

2. William L. McDowell Jr., ed., *Journals of the Commissioners of the Indian Trade: September 20, 1710–August 29, 1718* (Columbia: South Carolina Archives Department, 1955), 30–31; hereafter cited as JCIT.

3. Chester B. DePratter, "The Yamasee Settlements in South Carolina: From Port Royal to the Ashepoo and Combahee Rivers," paper presented at the Yamasee Indians: From Florida to South Carolina conference, St. Augustine, Florida, 2015.

4. William Dunlop, "Capt. Dunlop's Voyage to the Southward, 1687," *South Carolina Historical and Genealogical Magazine* 30 (1929): 133.

5. McDowell, JCIT, 33–34.

6. McDowell, JCIT, 58.

7. McDowell, JCIT, 32.

8. Chester B. DePratter and William Green, "Origins of the Yamasee," paper presented at the Southeastern Archaeological Conference, Mobile, Alabama, 1990; William Green, *The Search for Altamaha: The Archaeology and Ethnohistory of an Early 18th Century Yamasee Indian Town*, Volumes in Historical Archaeology 21 (Columbia: South Carolina Institute of Archaeology and Anthropology, University of South Carolina, 1992); John H. Hann, "Summary Guide to Spanish Florida Missions and Visitas with Churches in the Sixteenth and Seventeenth Centuries," *Americas* 46, no. 4 (1990): 417–513 (repr., Oceanside CA: Academy of American Franciscan History, 1990); John E. Worth, *The Struggle for the Georgia Coast: An Eighteenth Century Retrospective on Guale and Mocama*, Anthropological Papers of the American Museum of Natural History, no. 75 (Athens GA: Distributed by University of Georgia Press, 1995).

9. Worth, *Struggle for the Georgia Coast*, 28–29.

10. DePratter and Green, "Origins of the Yamasee"; Green, *Search for Altamaha*; Hann, *Summary Guide*; Worth, *Struggle for the Georgia Coast*.

11. Alexander Y. Sweeney, "Investigating Yamasee Identity: Archaeological Research at Pocotaligo," MA thesis, University of South Carolina, Columbia, 2003.

12. James W. Hatch, "Lamar Period Upland Farmsteads of Oconee River Valley, Georgia," in *Mississippian Communities and Households*, ed. Daniel Rogers and Bruce D. Smith (Tuscaloosa: University of Alabama Press, 1995), 135–55.

13. Hatch, "Lamar Period Upland Farmsteads," 135–55.

14. Alexander Y. Sweeney, "The Archaeology of Indian Slavers and Colonial Allies: Excavations at the Yamasee Capital of Altamaha Town," paper presented at the Society for Historical Archaeology Annual Conference, Toronto, Ontario, Canada, 2009.

15. Andrea P. White, "Living on the Periphery: A Study of an Eighteenth-Century Yamasee Mission Community in Colonial St. Augustine," MA thesis, College of William and Mary, Williamsburg, 2002; Andrea P. White, "Refuge among the Spanish," this volume.

16. White, "Living on the Periphery."

17. Samuel E. Casselberry, "Further Refinement of Formulae for Determining Population from Floor Area," *World Archaeology* 6 (1974): 117–22.

18. Jon Bernard Marcoux, "Cherokee Households and Communities in the English Contact Period, A.D. 1670–1740," PhD diss., University of North Carolina, Chapel Hill, 2008.

19. Hatch, "Lamar Period Upland Farmsteads," 135–55.

20. White, "Living on the Periphery," and "Refuge among the Spanish."

21. Casselberry, "Further Refinement of Formulae," 117–22.

22. Chester B. DePratter, "National Register of Historic Places Form," U.S. Department of the Interior, National Park Service, 1994; William Green, Chester B. DePratter, and Bobby Southerlin, "The Yamasee in South Carolina: Native American Adaptation and Interaction Along the Carolina Frontier," in *Another's Country: Archaeological and Historical Perspectives on Cultural Interactions in the Southern Colonies*, ed. J. W. Joseph and Martha Zierden (Tuscaloosa: University of Alabama Press, 2002), 13–29; Bobby Southerlin, *Archaeological Testing at the Cedar Point Development Tract, Beaufort County, South Carolina*, prepared for Chechesee Land and Timber, Okatie, South Carolina, 2000.

23. As shown in Alexander Y. Sweeney and Eric C. Poplin, "The Yamasee Indians of Early Carolina," in *South Carolina's Hidden Heritage: The Archaeology of the Palmetto State*, ed. Adam King (Columbia: University of South Carolina Press, 2016), 62–81; Kent Flannery and Joyce Marcus, *The Creation of Inequality: How Our Prehistoric Ancestors Set the Stage for Monarchy, Slavery, and Empire* (Cambridge: Harvard University Press, 2012), 305–6, 311; Owen Lindauer and John H. Blitz, "Higher Ground: The Archaeology of North American Platform Mounds," *Journal of Archaeological Research*, 5, no. 2 (1997): 169–207.

24. DePratter, "The Yamasee Settlements in South Carolina."

25. Hatch, "Lamar Period Upland Farmsteads," 148.

26. Sweeney, "Archaeology of Indian Slavers."

27. Sweeney, "Archaeology of Indian Slavers," 68–73.

28. Green, *Search for Altamaha*, 71.

29. Hatch, "Lamar Period Upland Farmsteads," 148–52.

30. Chief Se'khu of the Yamassee Nation of South Carolina, pers. comm., 2015.

31. Hatch, "Lamar Period Upland Farmsteads," 148–52.

32. Bonnie G. McEwan, "The Spiritual Conquest of La Florida," *American Anthropologist* 103, no. 3 (2001): 633–44; Elliot H. Blair, "The Distribution and Dating of Beads from St. Catherines Island," in *The Beads of St. Catherines Island*, Anthropological Papers of the American Museum of Natural History, no. 89 (New York: American Museum of Natural History, 2009) 125–66.

33. Blair, "The Distribution and Dating of Beads."

34. McEwan, "The Spiritual Conquest of La Florida," 633–44; Elliot H. Blair, "The Role of Beads from St. Catherines Island," in *The Beads of St. Catherines Island*, 167–78; John E. Worth, "Spanish Missions and the Persistence of Chiefly Power," in *The Transformation of the Southeastern Indians, 1540–1760*, ed. R. Ethridge and C. Hudson (Jackson: University Press of Mississippi, 2002).

35. Lauren Winkler, "The Social Structuring of Stress in Contact-Era Spanish Florida: A Bioarchaeological Case Study from Santa Catalina de Guale, St. Catherines Island, Georgia," MA thesis, Ohio State University, Columbus, 2011.

36. Carl Halbirt, "Back Under the Spanish Fold: 18th Century Yamasee Mission Sites in St. Augustine, Florida," paper presented at the Yamasee Indians: From Florida to South Carolina conference, St. Augustine, Florida, 2015; Carl Halbirt, email message to author, June 18, 2015.

37. Alice Stevenson, "Introduction: The Materiality of Burial Practices," *Archaeological Review from Cambridge*, 22 (2007): 1–5.

38. Keith Ashley, "Yamasee Migrations into the Mocama and Timucua Provinces of Florida, 1667–1683," this volume.

39. Sweeney, "Investigating Yamasee Identity"; Alexander Y. Sweeney "Identifying Pocotaligo, and Upper Yamasee Town in Jasper County, South Carolina," paper presented at the Annual Meeting of the Southeastern Archaeological Conference, Columbia, South Carolina, 2005.

40. Frank J. Klingberg, "Early Attempts at Indian Education in South Carolina: A Documentary," *South Carolina Historical Magazine* 61, no. 1 (1960): 5–6.

41. Frank J. Klingberg, *Carolina Chronicle: The Papers of Commissary Gideon Johnston* (Berkley: University of California Press, 1946), 108–9.

42. Reverend Samuel Thomas, "Documents Concerning Reverend Samuel Thomas," *South Carolina Historical and Genealogical Magazine* 5 (1904): 21–55.

43. Denise Bossy, "Spiritual Diplomacy," this volume.

44. Jane Landers, "Yamasee-African Ties in Carolina and Florida," this volume.

45. Thomas Nairne, "Letter from Thomas Nairne to Doctor Marston," Society for the Propagation of the Gospel in Foreign Part, Papers, Manuscript Division, Library of Congress, Washington DC, 1705; Gallay, *The Indian Slave Trade*, 230.

46. McDowell, JCIT, 12.

47. Sweeney and Poplin, "Yamasee Indians of Early Carolina."

48. John Worth, pers. comm., 2006; Gifford Waters, pers. comm., 2015.

49. John T. Lanning, *The Spanish Missions of Florida* (Chapel Hill: University of North Carolina Press, 1935), 186, 227–28; Jerald T. Milanich, *The Timucuan* (Oxford: Blackwell Publishers, 1996), 208.

50. Lanning, *The Spanish Missions*, 228; John H. Hann, *A History of the Timucua Indians and Missions*, Florida Museum of Natural History, Ripley P. Bullen Series (Gainesville: University Press of Florida, 1996); John E. Worth, *The Timucuan Chiefdoms of Spanish Florida*, vol. 2: *Resistance and Destruction* (Gainesville: University Press of Florida, 1998).

51. McDowell, JCIT, 33, 36.

52. Gary B. Nash, *Red, White, and Black: The Peoples of Early America* (Englewood Cliffs NJ: Prentice Hall, 1977), 117.

53. John E. Worth, "Reign of Terror: The Indian Slave Trade and the Devastation of Spanish Florida, 1659–1715," paper presented at the Southeastern Archaeological Conference, Biloxi, 2002.

54. Eric R. Wolf, *Europe and the People Without History* (Berkeley: University of California Press, 1982), 161.

55. Worth, "Reign of Terror."

56. Chris Gosden, "What Do Objects Want?" *Journal of Archaeological Method and Theory* 12, no. 3 (2005): 193–211.

57. Wolf, *Europe and the People Without History*; Worth, "Reign of Terror."

58. Ashley, "Yamasee Migrations"; Eric C. Poplin and Jon Marcoux, "Yamasee Material Culture and Identity," this volume; Amanda Hall, "The Persistence of Yamasee Power and Identity at San Antonio de Pocotalaca, 1716–1752," this volume; and White, "Living on the Periphery."

59. Poplin and Marcoux, "Yamasee Material Culture and Identity."

TWO

Yamasee Networks

5

Spiritual Diplomacy
Reinterpreting the Yamasee Prince's Eighteenth-Century Voyage to England

DENISE I. BOSSY

In 1713 a Yamasee Indian "Prince" traveled from Charleston to London, where he was schooled in Anglican principles, reading, writing, and arithmetic.[1] His voyage has become the stuff of historiographical legend, culminating as it did with his 1715 baptism in the Royal Chapel at Somerset House and presentation to King George I. To the Anglican missionary society that funded the Prince's twenty-one-month trip and sponsored his education in England, he represented the great potential of British missionaries and schoolteachers to convert, civilize, and thereby conquer Indians. This Society for the Propagation of the Gospel (SPG), which had been founded in 1701 to send missionaries and schoolteachers to America, expected that the baptism of one southeastern Indian Prince would lead to many conversions and would politically knit the Yamasees to the fragile British Empire in the South, while also enlarging the kingdom of God.[2] Yet the Prince's case remains a rare instance of Indian "conversion" to Anglican Christianity, and this essay interrogates what that conversion meant to the Yamasees. Historian Frank Klingberg, who first reconstructed the story in 1962, considered it a sad symbol of the general decline of southern Indian peoples and cultures.[3] Indeed, shortly after returning to South Carolina in 1715, the Prince disappeared from Charleston, leaving no further traces in the British archival record. Moreover, by the 1740s the British and their Creek allies had greatly weakened the Yamasees after years of mutual borderlands violence and warfare, as Steve Hahn demonstrates in this volume. Over the past fifty years historians have echoed Klingberg's narrative of the Prince.

Little effort has been made to understand who he was, why the Yamasees sent him to London, and how they understood his trip and his engagement with Christianity.[4]

To reconstruct the Yamasee Prince's narrative from a Yamasee perspective, we begin where the story actually started: with the decision by a Yamasee matrilineal clan and community to send the seventeen-year-old nephew of their *mico* (chief) to London. The narrative then becomes less about Indian acculturation or decline and more about Yamasee practices of pursuing political and religious alliances with Europeans, a practice we could call spiritual diplomacy.[5] Because southeastern Indians understood political and spiritual power as symbiotic, they expected that political encounters and alliances might include ceremonies and exchanges that were imbued with spiritual import. Furthermore, they actively sought opportunities to gain access to sacred and political knowledge, practices, connections, and technology. Although European missionaries hoped and even expected that Indians who accepted baptism would renounce their prior spiritual beliefs, they were usually sorely disappointed. Yamasee and other southeastern Indians interpreted Christian rituals, symbols, and words through their own cultural frameworks and for their own reasons. As was the case with the Yamasee Prince, many adopted and shed aspects of Christianity to fit their particular political and spiritual needs. This article examines the Prince's voyage to England in 1713 and his consent to be baptized by the SPG in 1715 as an extension of the protocols of spiritual diplomacy practiced by southeastern Indians.

The Prince was from Euhaw, a crucial point that Klingberg and subsequent scholars have failed to recognize.[6] The Euhaws—or Yoas as the Spanish called them—had engaged in spiritual diplomacy with Spanish Franciscans in Guale for over a hundred years when they moved to South Carolina to join the Yamasee confederacy in 1703, just ten years before the Prince's trip. The Euhaws applied their practices of spiritual diplomacy to their new alliance with the British in part because of their long experience with the Spanish. But above all the Euhaws were seeking to establish their place in the Yamasee world by making a spiritually and politically significant connection that would benefit the confederacy. The Euhaws selected the Prince for that overseas mission because he was being groomed for a position of political power within his community. They hoped that this future leader would gain invaluable new cultural skills and connections in England, which would help the Euhaws negotiate a changing world order. Told in this way, the Prince's story opens a larger window into how the Euhaws, Guales, and Yamasees responded to the geopolitical instabilities of the seventeenth and eighteenth centuries and the importance they placed on building networks and educating young leaders who could help to stabilize their communities. This story also offers a rare glimpse into the process of Yamasee confederation, following the Euhaws as they made their way from La Florida to Port Royal and settled in the very heart of the Yamasee world.[7]

The Euhaw-Yamasees and Spiritual Diplomacy

Aside from the Prince, no other southeastern Indian dignitary traveled to England between 1672 and 1730.[8] A surviving document from an SPG missionary describes the Prince as the son of the "head man of the hewaas" (Euhaws)—which Klingberg inadvertently transcribed as Newaas in 1956, a small but consequential error.[9] The SPG missionary may also have erred in calling the Prince the son of the Euhaw headman, a common mistake among British men who struggled to understand Indian family structure. Most southeastern Indians practiced political and familial matrilineal descent, whereby a mico's heirs were the children of his eldest sister, generally his nephews. Uncles, not biological fathers, commonly assumed the main paternal obligations for their sisters' sons.[10] In 1692, for example, the mico of Altamaha (the head town of the Lower Yamasees) applied to the Grand Council of South Carolina to have a boy liberated from a trader. The council described him as "an Indian boy yt: *he calls his Sonn.*" This phrasing intimates that the council members recognized but didn't fully comprehend the paternal relationship between the mico of Altamaha and a boy who was more likely his nephew than his son. Identifying this cultural confusion, the Altamaha mico perhaps used the English label "son" for a boy who was his nephew.[11] The Prince could have been the mico's beloved son (*usinjulo*), a position of political and spiritual importance.[12] But it is more likely that he was the mico's nephew and heir.

In either case, the Euhaws brought with them to Port Royal more than a hundred years' worth of experience in spiritual diplomacy with the Spanish. That expertise predisposed them to use conversion and other rituals to solidify diplomatic, spiritual, and economic ties with Christians.[13] By contrast, many of the Yamasees whom they joined in South Carolina had rejected spiritual diplomacy with the Spanish, particularly conversion to Spanish Catholicism. The earliest evidence of Euhaw spiritual diplomacy dates from the late sixteenth century. The Euhaws were most likely Guales, though some scholars believe they may have been descendants of the Toa chiefdom from interior Georgia who moved from the Flint River region to the Georgia coast around this time.[14] By 1597 the Yoas were officially counted by the Spanish as belonging to the mission region of Guale. The Yoas and many other Guales deepened their religious and political affiliation with the Spanish over the course of the seventeenth century. In 1605 the Spanish Franciscans established a *visita* at Yoa, which indicates that the mico had nominally converted to Catholicism by accepting baptism and instruction.[15] Surviving slave raids, depopulation from epidemic diseases and flight, and even pirate attacks, the Yoas remained in northeastern Florida.

In contrast, many of the Oconee-Ocmulgee Indians—who would become the core of the Yamasees in the mid-seventeenth century—spent only twenty years living in Spanish missions (1660s–1680s). They considered political integration into the Spanish mission system but resisted conversion to Catholicism and ultimately rejected Spanish alliance on a number of different occasions. In the late 1650s or early 1660s, roughly fifty-five years after Yoa (Euhaw) began to engage formally in spiritual diplomacy with the Spanish, Altamaha, Ocute, and Ichisi were pushed out of interior Georgia by Westo slave raids. Fleeing to the coast, they initially sought an alliance with Indians in the Santa Elena region and moved into Spanish territory only when the Westos began to attack their new settlements just a few years later. Relations with the Spanish were fraught with tension, and the Yamasees largely refused to engage in spiritual diplomacy with them, preferring to cultivate alliances with other southeastern Indian communities. This was part of a broader strategy employed by the Yamasees. Through their

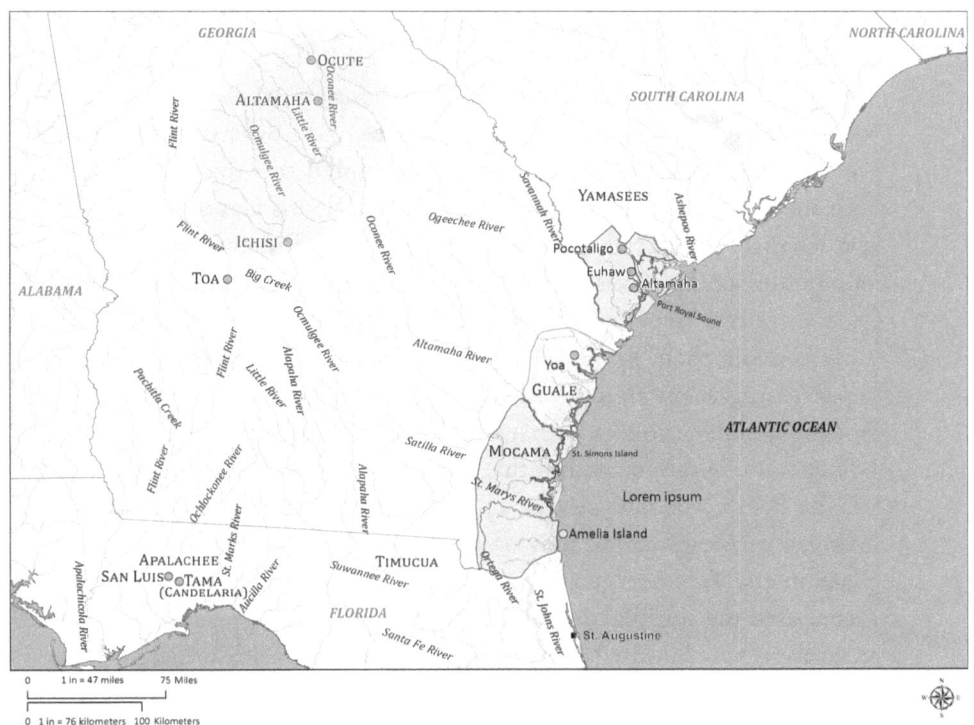

MAP 9. Euhaw and Yamasee worlds. Map by David W. Wilson, Center for Instruction and Research Technology, University of North Florida.

seventeenth-century migrations the Yamasees established ties with the Guales, Mocamas, Apalachees, Timucuas, and Apalachicolas. A third series of slave raids by the Westos and their allies in 1680 and pirate attacks in 1683 and 1684 convinced most Yamasees and many Guales that Spanish alliance was worthless. Led by the mico of Altamaha, they moved back to Santa Elena (renamed Port Royal by the English), where there was soon a new Scottish settlement associated with South Carolina. Altamaha's people were quickly joined there by hundreds—perhaps thousands—of other Yamasee and Guale Indians. The Guale Indians, like the Euhaws, had lived in Spanish missions and had converted in large numbers since the late sixteenth century but now they severed their ties with the Spanish and joined the growing Yamasee confederacy.[16]

Even as most of the Yamasees and Guales deserted the Spanish missions in the 1680s, the Euhaws remained in La Florida. In 1702 they probably lived in one of the three missions on Amelia Island that were destroyed by invading English, Yamasee, and Lower Creek forces in November of that year. This attack prompted the Yoa Indians to join the Yamasees then living in Port Royal, South Carolina, where the English would call them the Euhaws.[17] The Euhaws had maintained their connections with other Yamasee and Guale communities in the midst of separate migrations, as demonstrated by their decision to rejoin them in 1703. Though empowering in one sense, these separate migrations and the complexities of Yamasee ethnogenesis in South Carolina also meant that the Euhaw Prince's uncle-father had to negotiate his status within the Yamasee confederacy. As newcomers the Prince's people were in a precarious position. Having left the Spanish mission system, they now acutely needed to establish their place in the Yamasee geopolitical world. The Prince and his uncle-father used the spiritual diplomacy that their chiefly lineage had practiced for over a hundred years with the Spanish of La Florida.

When the Euhaws joined the Yamasee confederacy, it was divided into two town groupings, which the British called the Upper and Lower towns and which fell largely along ethnic lines. The Lower towns were primarily occupied by Oconee-Ocmulgee people and the Upper towns by Guales.[18] Each region seems to have been under the influence of a head town. There stood the main council house, the seat of government and center of spiritual and ceremonial power. The Prince's uncle-father was the mico of a secondary town and, as such, fell under the influence of the head town's mico. Evidence that the Prince's uncle-father consulted with the head town mico on issues of foreign policy comes from the Prince's trip to England, a matter of both local and confederacy-wide importance for the Yamasees. SPG records demonstrate that the Prince's uncle-father and the head town mico joined in asking the most powerful SPG missionary in South Carolina to take the Prince to England. Upon their arrival in London, this missionary commissary, Gideon Johnston, explained to his superiors that "he brought over with him from South Carolina a Young Man whose father is one of the Chief among the Yamousea Indians,

And at whose Request together with the Emperour of the Yamousea Indians, he was sent over to be Instructed in the Christian Religion, and Manners of the English Nation."[19]

The titles invoked in this passage signal the relationship between the Euhaws and the head town. The Prince's uncle-father was "one of the Chief[s]," and the other mico was the "Emperour." During this period the British frequently used the term *emperor* to describe chiefs who had extensive influence over a number of towns beyond their own (or whom they hoped would try to exert this kind of influence if given the title).[20] It is likely that the "Emperour" to whom Johnston referred was the mico of Altamaha, since Euhaw was probably one of three Lower Yamasee towns whose head town was Altamaha.[21] It is also likely that Altamaha was the white head town of a Yamasee confederacy that included Upper and Lower towns. As the white head town, Altamaha would be responsible for promoting peaceful alliances with outsiders, which explains the role of the "Emperour" in the Prince's mission. Similarly, the Prince's uncle-father was probably the Euhaw peace chief. Many southeastern Indian communities adhered to such a dual moiety system, where specific towns and chiefs were responsible for diplomacy in times of peace and others for war.[22]

The Euhaw and Altamaha micos chose to send the Prince to England in 1713 to open a new path of spiritual and political power. In an atmosphere of escalating tension with the Carolinians, the Euhaws tried to apply the practices they had already used with the Spanish in La Florida: establishing an alliance by traveling to a politically important capital and promoting the public conversion of an elite representative. For the Prince and the Euhaws this conversion likely did not signify a profound change in the Prince's faith, as the British and Spanish before them wished, but rather the Prince's success in fostering a new political connection to the British.

The Yamasees lived next to a growing colonial community of British traders and planters on the southeastern border of South Carolina, and their relations with the British rapidly deteriorated in the first decade of the eighteenth century. They suffered from a litany of colonial abuses. British men killed and enslaved Yamasee people, stole their land and property, and assaulted and physically abused Yamasee people, including women and children, some from politically powerful clans.[23] In 1711 representatives from the Prince's own town appeared before the South Carolina Board of Indian Commissioners to request the return of two women and one child recently kidnapped and enslaved by British traders and the removal of six British colonists who had illegally settled on Yamasee lands.[24] According to Yamasee and southeastern Indian laws more generally, the enslavement and murder of loved ones and the theft of lands were criminal acts that—when committed by outsiders like the British—were punishable by war.[25] Instead, by sending his seventeen-year-old nephew across the Atlantic Ocean, the Euhaw mico volunteered, it seems, to engage in spiritual diplomacy on behalf of the Euhaws and the Yamasees more generally to stop the violence.

The Politics of the Euhaw Prince's Conversion

Now that we understand the motives and expectations of the Prince's family and town in sending a representative to England, we can ask why their choice fell on the Prince. If not already a political adviser, the Prince was in all likelihood being groomed to assume a prominent role in his community. It was fitting to send such a rising leader as an emissary into the new state of affairs, a world in which daily interactions between the British and Yamasee were becoming more common. As the paramount cacique of the Calusas explained to a Spanish Jesuit missionary, a chief's ability to govern his people rested on his own knowledge of spiritual and political affairs.[26]

By journeying to England the Prince would acquire new spiritual and political connections and invaluable practical skills in English culture, including exposure to sacred rituals and stories, literacy, and mathematics. The Prince traveled first to London, not just the center of the British Empire but also the headquarters of the SPG (which is still at Lambeth Palace today, as it was in the eighteenth century). His voyage gave him direct access to the fountainhead of British political and spiritual power. No other elite Yamasee or southeastern Indian could make the same claim.

To be sure, elite youth from other southeastern Indian groups left their natal communities to serve as ambassadors. Previous scholars have stressed how southeastern Indian women married to British traders

Spiritual Diplomacy

promoted cross-cultural alliances. Some attention has also been paid to the role of *fanni micos*, high-status men adopted by a clan or community to represent their interests. Indian women and fanni micos similarly enabled southeastern Indian communities to integrate foreign men into their communities by establishing fictive kinship ties.[27] Though largely overlooked by scholars, younger Indian men from elite clans, particularly the nephews and sons of micos, performed analogous mediating functions. The settings differed, however: it was mostly within their natal communities that Indian women and fanni micos spoke on behalf of their fictive kin, whereas the Euhaw Prince and other young male ambassadors journeyed to diplomatic meetings in foreign centers, such as Charleston and St. Augustine. They often traveled in peace parties headed by micos and their advisers, and in some cases these young men were the primary diplomats.[28] In 1666, for example, the mico of Santa Elena (Port Royal) appointed his nephew—described as "a proper young fellowe" who was the mico's "Sister's sonne"—to travel with the English captain Robert Sandford. Since the Santa Elena region was where Yamasee ethnogenesis began in the 1660s, this exchange illustrates diplomatic protocols in which the Yamasees also participated.[29] External politics was, in short, a family affair.

Though invisible in the archival record, the Euhaw Prince's matrilineal clan—not just his uncle-father—must have played an important role in his appointment as ambassador to the English. Fictive kinship ties probably bound the Prince's family with the British missionary who assumed responsibility for the Prince, Gideon Johnston, although he never described the particular ceremonies connected to the Prince's departure from his natal community. We don't know whether gifts were given or exchanged, or whether the length of the Prince's voyage was a subject of negotiation, as it was in other instances. But we might conjecture that the Euhaws engaged in the protocols of kinship diplomacy common to other southeastern Indians from the same region.

Soon after the Euhaws migrated to South Carolina in 1703, the SPG began to receive requests from the Yamasees for missionaries to convert their children. John Norris believed that there was interest among the Yamasees in having their children educated in reading and writing, if only they had a school nearby, for they "admire, that we make paper speak (as they term it) and are very sensible & apprehensive of what they are instructed in."[30] Writing to his SPG superiors in London in 1708, Francis le Jau related that the "Yamoussees have sent for a Clergyman to baptize their Children."[31] In 1709 the SPG responded by ordering three hundred copies of the New Testament for the Yamasees in Spanish.[32] Their earlier exposure to Spanish Catholicism made the Yamasees the primary target of SPG missionary acculturation programs in early South Carolina. The British colonial trader Thomas Nairne remarked that "it [is] easier for us to undertake propagating the Christian faith among them, than tis for the Northern Colonies besides that their Language is micht with abundance of Spannish words perticularly those pertaining to Religion." The Yamasees—especially the Guales among the Yamasees—were already familiar with Christian concepts; this, the SPG believed, would make them easier to convert. Anglican missionaries would ensure that these Catholic Indians did not revert "from something of Christianity to downe right Barbarity & Heathenism."[33]

Yamasee parents, however, proved largely unwilling to send their children to English-run schools in Charleston, London, and elsewhere. Five years before the Euhaw Prince's trip, Francis le Jau, an SPG missionary, complained that Indian parents in the South would not "part with their Children tho' they lead miserable poor lives."[34] British missionaries across the region echoed his complaint during the eighteenth century. Although some Yamasees asked SPG missionaries to educate their children, they wanted that process to happen in their own communities and in accordance with their parenting practices. Their behavior was shaped by their experiences in La Florida. Spanish officials had a long history of extorting and even seizing children from elite Indian families as the price of alliance. Spanish friars had learned the hard way that the most effective way to promote the conversion of Indian children was to educate them in their own communities.[35]

The SPG's failures in converting southern Indians can be ascribed partly to systemic problems within the SPG, as many scholars have pointed out.[36] Yet one must not underestimate the deep cultural differences in educational and parenting practices that prompted so many

Indians to reject SPG efforts to convert and educate their children. Displaying some awareness of that, a number of the SPG's field missionaries working in South Carolina proposed modeling themselves on the Spanish: they recommended learning Indian languages, translating catechisms and Bibles into those languages, and establishing churches and schools within Indian communities aimed specifically at children and youths.[37]

Many of the SPG metropole leaders, however, found the option of schooling Indian children in English far preferable to the converse option of immersing young missionaries in Indian languages. Deeming it unfeasible and undesirable for missionaries and schoolteachers to adopt Native languages, they proposed that Indian children be placed in an English-language learning environment where the SPG could control both the curriculum and the cultural climate. This was precisely the program in which the Prince was placed.[38] He was expected to adjust to the demands of a culturally foreign educational system.

The SPG rightly interpreted the Euhaws' decision in 1713 to send an elite youth to England for Christian education as a breakthrough. Though the SPG was deeply interested in converting Yamasees, their efforts were frustrated by their own missionaries, deteriorating political relations, and most important, Yamasee resistance. Still, the Euhaw Prince's voyage to England was not an instance in which Yamasee parents simply acquiesced to the SPG by sending a child to the English for conversion and education. Rather, he was a young adult and a representative of a chiefly lineage, and his voyage was part of a spiritual and political strategy to educate a rising leader and to promote new spiritual and political connections. By the early eighteenth century not only young Indian men, but also colonial youths in South Carolina, took on more responsibilities that involved such travel abroad.[39] It would have been hard even for the British to construct the Prince as a child in terms of his years. Yet, as we will see, the SPG struggled to come to terms with his status as a diplomat.

Reinterpreting the Euhaw-Yamasee Prince's Voyage to England

For generations the micos of Euhaw had been able to preserve their power and lineage in La Florida through spiritual diplomacy. Indian elites who chose to ally themselves with the Spanish and to convert to Catholicism understood this as a political and spiritual act of self-empowerment rather than the first step in a slippery slope of assimilation. Rather than agreeing to a project of acculturation, the Prince was engaging in the political and spiritual practice of his ancestors. As the nephew of a cacique who lived in a Spanish mission, the Yamasee Prince undoubtedly had been baptized a Catholic. We can also assume that he had spent time in a Spanish school before he arrived in Carolina at the age of seven (he was born around 1696). He was probably fluent in Spanish as well as his own Muskogean language, and it is likely that he could already read and write. Knowing one western European language undoubtedly made the process of studying a related language easier.[40] The Prince also understood the politics surrounding his Catholicism and its Anglican opponent. He knew the implicit political alliances and the power that they brought to his lineage, and he saw the practical and spiritual significance of his education in rival European languages and rites.

Yet what is most clear about the Prince's voyage is that the Yamasees and British had divergent expectations. Over the course of his time in England, the Prince jockeyed with the SPG to fulfill the diplomatic and spiritual dimensions of his visit. Most tellingly, when he reflected on his experiences in London, the Prince was subtly critical. Upon his return to Charleston, he wrote a letter to the society that ostensibly thanked it but in fact quietly criticized his schooling. The Prince had learned the English language and culture well enough to understand the importance of writing such a letter and the rhetorical deference that the occasion required. But he nonetheless characterized his trip as a disappointment when he said, "I hope I learn better than when I was in school."

Like the Euhaws, the SPG had spiritual and political motives in directing and funding the Prince's education. The society expected that the Euhaw Prince would assimilate spiritually and culturally to Anglican Christianity, however, and would be converted to its political agendas. By having the Prince "cloath'd and sent to School" on its account, the SPG believed that he would not only learn religion, literature, and English culture but also be "dispos'd to a Love of the *English Nation.*" He would then return to his natal community "to help sup-

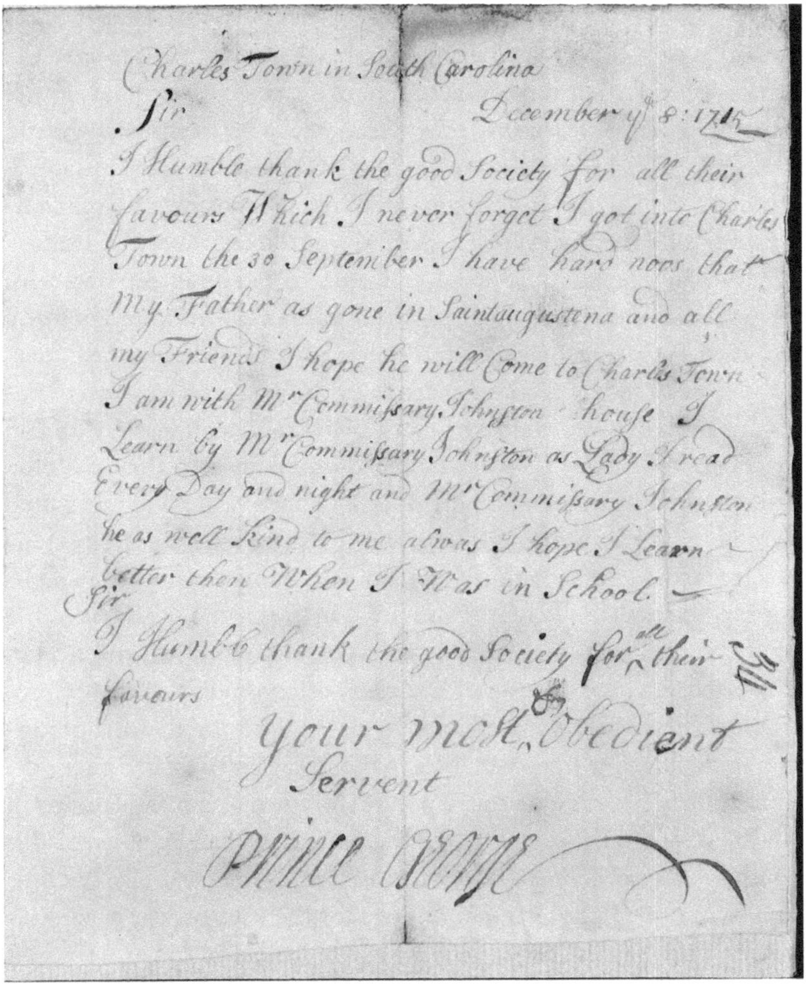
Charles Town in South Carolina
Sir December ye 8:1715
I Humble thank the good Society for all their favours Which I never forget I got into Charles Town the 30 September I have hard noos that My Father as gone in Saintaugustena and all my Friends I hope he will Come to Charles Town I am with Mr Commissary Johnston house I Learn by Mr Commissary Johnston as Lady I read Every Day and night and Mr Commissary Johnston he as well kind to me alwas I hope I Learn better then When I Was in School
Sir
I Humble thank the good Society for all their favours
Your most Obedient Servent
Prince George

FIG. 3. The Euhaw Prince's letter to the Society for the Propagation of the Gospel, 1715. Courtesy of the United Society for the Propagation of the Gospel and the Bodleian Library of African and Commonwealth Studies at Rhodes House, Oxford, England.

port the *British* Interest, and promote the Christian Religion."[41] The SPG hoped that the Prince would become an Indian missionary who would shepherd his people's wholesale conversion and promote British imperialism in the South.

But how do we unearth the Prince's reactions to his experiences in England? Aside from the single letter that he penned in 1715, the Prince left no other written accounts. Nonetheless, there is another way to recover echoes of his efforts to assert his own agenda while in London and his responses to the SPG's program of religious acculturation. The key lies in focusing on Gideon Johnston, the missionary who took the Prince to England. Over the course of the Prince's twenty-one months in England, Johnston voiced disagreements with the SPG leadership over the Prince's education, clothing, and political activities. Johnston's behavior and statements intimate that he understood himself to be functioning as the Prince's guardian, a form of fictive kinship that resonated with both British and southeastern Indian practices. Whenever possible, South Carolinians sent their children abroad for educational and networking opportunities and appointed guardians to care for them in their stead. These guardians also became advocates for children within their families, negotiating and even arguing with parents while representing the interests and opinions of the children. Similarly, in southeastern Indian communities adopted kin advocated for the interests of the clans or communities they represented. On at least two occasions, Johnston used the rhetoric of kinship to describe his responsibilities to the Prince, vowing to care for the Euhaw Prince as his own son. Upon their return to South Carolina in 1715, he wrote to the SPG, saying, "the same care shall be taken of this Youth in all respects with my own Children, as long as I live."[42] Johnston expressed strong paternal feelings for the young man, who—it is worth noting—was about the same age as his eldest son.

Just as some colonial and southeastern Indian children and youths learned to leverage their guardians to advocate for their interests with their parents, the Euhaw Prince also seems to have expressed his wishes to the SPG through Johnston. It seems likely, then, that Johnston's disagreements with the SPG—of which scholars have taken no note—reflected the Prince's own expectations for his trip, his reactions to his experiences in England, and his effort to exert some measure of control over the direction of his mission.[43] With this in mind, we turn to a more nuanced reading of the Prince's mission to England. This new narrative reveals the Prince's feelings of cultural alienation, loneliness,

Spiritual Diplomacy

and frustration with the SPG (which proved unwilling or uninterested in promoting the political dimensions of his voyage) and the Prince's own efforts to persuade the SPG to follow southeastern Indian protocols of spiritual diplomacy.

Because Johnston had failed to seek permission from his superiors to take the Prince to England or to leave his post in South Carolina, the SPG leadership was surprised by their arrival in late May 1713. The Prince was motivated to travel to England by a concern for the well-being of his family and community. For Johnston immediate family matters seem to have been paramount in his decision to return to London; he was suffering from illness and debt, had financial matters to take care of in Ireland, and wanted to tend to his sons' education. But he was also very eager to prove his worth to the SPG and to promote the status of the society and the colony in the British Empire and the eyes of God. Because it believed that the Prince had the potential to foster its religious goals, the SPG somewhat reluctantly decided to pay for his schooling, room and board, and clothing.[44]

The Prince stayed with his guardian, Johnston, in London for roughly a month. They lodged in a widow's home on the Strand in Exeter Exchange court, a shopping mall constructed in the late seventeenth century. It was a bustling sort of place, filled with shops and offices. The Prince's first month in London was a busy one. Shortly after he arrived, an enormous thanksgiving parade was held in the streets of London to celebrate Queen Anne's signing of the Treaty of Utrecht. Both houses of Parliament marched directly past the Prince's lodgings on the Strand as they made their way to St. Paul's Cathedral. Among the audience members were close to four thousand boys and girls enrolled in the charity schools run by the Society for the Promotion of Christian Knowledge (SPCK), the sister organization of the SPG, which established charity schools and libraries in England aimed at educating the English poor in reading, writing, and, most important, Church catechism. Lined up in eight tidy rows on platforms, the children sang two hymns honoring Queen Anne for close to three hours.[45]

In late July the Prince began his formal education, enrolling in the Chigwell Grammar School in Essex. There he joined Gideon Johnston's two sons, who already attended Chigwell, the elder, James, since 1710. Pupils enrolled at the age of ten or eleven to be educated in Greek and Latin, with the expectation that they would attend university by seventeen or eighteen years of age. The sons of clergymen and a few young men of note, including William Penn, attended the school. The Prince made the ten-mile trip from London to Chigwell by stagecoach. Like Johnston's sons, the Prince boarded at Chigwell, returning to Johnston only during the rare holiday. This reflected the British ideal that teachers, tutors, or masters outside the home best imparted education and skills. Though travel and long periods of separation from their natal home were crucial components of education for British and South Carolina colonial children, this was rarely the case for southeastern Indian children. With few good schools in South Carolina, wealthy British parents frequently sent their children abroad for schooling and experience, believing this practice ensured that their children received the best education possible while developing networks that would later prove instrumental to their family businesses.[46]

In stark contrast, in the Native Southeast the extended maternal family educated boys and girls as part of a distinct form of parenting that focused on homeschooling. Maternal uncles instructed their nephews in hunting, martial arts, and politicking; mothers and maternal aunts instructed girls in agriculture, domestic arts, and family governance.[47] When the Prince wrote his letter to the SPG in 1715, he implicitly contrasted his experiences in the English educational system with southeastern Indian practices. Once back in Charleston, Gideon and his wife, Henrietta Johnston, would decide—we could conjecture in consultation with the Prince, who was nineteen years old at the time—to assume responsibility for the Prince's further education. After being shuffled between a series of five different schools and tutors in the greater London area for close to two years, the Prince preferred this approach, a point he made clear in his letter to the SPG.

In addition to the isolation of boarding school, the Prince also experienced other dramatic changes in his educational experience at Chigwell. The rhythm of the Prince's daily life was dramatically altered. School days were long. Awakened by the Chigwell church bells that rang at 6:00 a.m., students arrived at school by 8:00 in the summer and 9:00 in the winter months; they did not return to their lodgings until 5:00

or 6:00 at night.⁴⁸ Most shocking to him was undoubtedly the use of physical violence by the schoolmaster. In both English schools and families, male authority figures were charged with preserving social (and by extension political) order and empowered to use corporal punishment when necessary. Students at schools were beaten with fists, open hands, whips, and even chains. Chigwell's school charter ordered that schoolmasters "chastise [students] severely for three vices, Lyeing, swearing, and filthye speaking." Even more ominous for the Prince was the rule that "for the speaking of English in the latine Schoole the Schollers be corrected by the Ferula." We can speculate that perhaps the headmaster showed the Prince some leniency on this count and did not beat him with a rod for speaking in English rather than Latin.

In any case, it is difficult to imagine the Prince acquiescing without objection to this type of treatment, which contradicted southeastern Indian educational practices and would especially not be tolerated by a mico's son or nephew. It is true that the Prince had been exposed to Catholicism early in his childhood and perhaps had witnessed the violence that missionaries and soldiers sometimes used to keep converts in line. But since the age of seven the Prince had lived in a largely Yamasee world where parents were starkly less authoritarian and where education was far more child-directed. One observer of southeastern Indian parenting explained that "the adults love their children so much that they speak no harsh words to them, but let them have their own way, and parental authority is unknown among them."⁴⁹

Chigwell was particularly renowned for the emphasis placed on Anglican education. Founded circa 1629 by the archbishop of York, Samuel Harsnett, it attracted the sons of clergymen in no small part because the SPG often paid for their tuition. Students were instructed in obedience and respect for the authority of their parents, schoolmasters, and God. Harsnett believed that discipline, manners, and religious education were more important than book learning, and he enjoined schoolmasters to "bring up their scholars in the fear of God and reverence to all men, that they teach them obedience to their parents, observance to their betters, gentleness and ingenuity in all their carriages."⁵⁰ Coming from a world in which the young were encouraged to play and self-correct and where disagreements were valued as part of politicking, the Prince must have found the emphasis on deference to authority and conformity challenging.

Chigwell students spent Saturday afternoons in catechism based on the Book of Common Prayer, and on Sundays they marched in two rows to church, where they sat in pews especially reserved for them. They were to be a model for others to observe. There was little free time, but once a week students engaged in athletic play for one hour. It is likely that the Prince would have demonstrated significant ability in many of the English games played at Chigwell, which included archery, running, throwing handballs, football, stoolball, and darts. Southeastern Indian communities placed great emphasis on the physical prowess of their boys; they proved their worth through success in hunting and warfare, which required skill in martial arts and great physical stamina and strength. Young men honed their skills by playing stickball (the ancestor of modern lacrosse) and chunkey, which involved throwing a pole as close as possible to a rolling stone disc as it came to a stop.[51]

Despite significant cultural differences in educational practices, the Prince initially seems to have adjusted reasonably well to life at Chigwell. Less than two weeks after his arrival, Headmaster Peter (Pierre) Noblet reported that the Prince was "blessed with a perfect health, and learns english apace, as well as French."[52] Noblet had served as the headmaster of Chigwell's Grammar School for roughly nine years before the Prince's arrival. He was a Huguenot refugee and had clearly added French to the school's language offerings. As a Dissenter who shared the Prince's experiences as a refugee, Noblet may have treated him with some patience. But we are left to wonder how Noblet accommodated the cultural gulf separating the two of them. Though the Prince's language skills are important to note, perhaps even more significant is that he was healthy. Remarkably, the Prince never suffered from any recorded illnesses during his time in England, although he would later become depressed when separated from Johnston and his sons.

The Prince remained at Chigwell for approximately nine months, but for a six-week interlude from November to December, during which he returned to Johnston in London. It was unusual for students to absent themselves from school for so long, and Johnston expressed concerns about this. But the Prince needed clothing suitable for both the climate and culture of Chigwell, and it took some negotiating to persuade the SPG to supply the needed funds. That December, with the Prince still at his lodgings, Johnston informed the society that he was moving his sons from Chigwell to a less expensive school in Leytonstone that was run by John Hewitt. Johnston requested permission to move the Prince as well, hoping to keep the young men together.[53] But the society clearly turned him down: the Prince returned to Chigwell. There he remained until June 1714, when he returned again to Johnston in London, who, apparently without consulting the SPG, decided to enroll the Prince in a charity school for seven weeks, probably to keep him close by.[54]

By this stage the Prince was homesick, having been away from his natal community for over a year. His profound sense of loneliness must have been accentuated by his repeated separation not just from Gideon Johnston but also from Johnston's two sons. In August 1714 Johnston had to spend several days persuading the Prince to remain in England at all. A month earlier the Prince had been scheduled to go back to South Carolina, but Johnston convinced him to delay another few months, promising that he would (finally) secure him a visit with the king and then accompany him back to South Carolina.[55]

Since his arrival in 1713, the Prince had asked to meet first Queen Anne (1707–14) and then her successor, King George I (1714–27), and had repeatedly requested more clothing. But the SPG leadership proved reluctant to introduce the Prince to high society or to dress him as a royal figure. Here we see two significant sources of tension between the SPG and Johnston; and remembering that Johnston was acting as the Prince's advocate, we can also see glimmers of the Prince's own expectations. Johnston expressed his expectation that once the Prince learned "to speak English a little more plainly," he should not only be introduced to high society but also would "often" wait on people of "Quality," including "her Majesty."[56] Though the Prince seems to have valued his education, he was above all trying to establish a political and spiritual relationship with the British Crown. He understood that to do so, he needed to look the part.

And so, early in the Prince's trip (probably in the fall of 1713), Johnston had requested that the society purchase clothing that would reflect the Prince's status. Anticipating that there would be a "whole debate" about whether the Prince's clothing should be "plain and Cheap" or "a little better than ordinary," Johnston advocated the latter. Though undoubtedly well versed in the political debates over men's clothing in England, Johnston also clearly understood and articulated the Prince's own views on the subject. The Glorious Revolution (1688) had ushered in a new era of fashion in England, one in which elite men largely eschewed the perceived frivolity and effeminacy of French fashion in favor of clothing that reflected proper masculine moral character: the modest three-piece suit.[57] Still, while keeping the fashion of their everyday clothing simple, elite men still marked their status by having that clothing made of the finest cloth with expert tailoring. They also continued to use more elaborate dress when the occasion called for it. Johnston understood the politics of clothing in England and was therefore asking the SPG to signify the Prince's status and its intention to have him introduced to high society through clothing that was "a bit better than ordinary."

But Johnston also understood the politics of clothing in southeastern Indian societies and explained that "the Indians in Generall are most affected with that kind of garb, which is gawdy and makes the finest shew." Even a simple suit made of fine cloth was not likely to impress them: "the Difference that is Between a fine and ordinary Suit of Cloathes, is so inconsiderable in their opinion." We can almost imagine the Prince urging Johnston to explain this to the society. His uncle-father had undoubtedly been the recipient of some elaborate clothing from the Spanish in La Florida, where governors frequently gave Indian elites the "gawdy" clothing that the English now disdained. The Spanish had followed Indian protocols when they bestowed gifts on Indian caciques and cacicas, at great expense to the Spanish Crown. While the particular goods were new, their symbolic currency was not. Just as they had been before contact with Europeans, such rare items were potent spiritual as well as political embodiments of chiefly power, symbolizing the expansive reach of the cacique or cacica's spiritual and political influence and connections. Indian leaders most visibly

Spiritual Diplomacy   151

displayed those connections and the power they wrought by wearing European clothing. Once in London, the Euhaw Prince pushed the SPG on a number of different occasions to engage in this form of gift giving. The Prince clearly wanted clothing that would communicate his elite status to his two audiences, not just the English but also (and perhaps more important) the Yamasees. Johnston and the Prince were not alone in thinking that his clothing needed to be impressive: Abel Kettleby, South Carolina's agent in London, gave the Prince a "handsome Cloacke and a Gun."[58]

For both Johnston and Kettleby a warm reception among London's powerful elite could not only raise their own status but also promote the colony's in the process; to the Prince this was an essential component of his spiritual diplomacy. It was the reason he had come to England. He sought to promote and empower the Euhaws and Yamasees. Johnston therefore requested that the SPG outfit the Prince with a "decent set of cloathes" as well as "3 or 4 Holland Shirts for one without the other will be very odd, and ridiculous." The society disagreed, authorizing Johnston to order only a simple "loose coat." Yet Johnston—usually a deferential man when it came to his superiors—disobeyed and had the tailor make breeches to match the coat, and he ordered a hat. He also purchased a pair of gloves and shoes, six shirts and matching muslin cravats.[59]

In August 1714, while Johnston tried to persuade the Prince to extend his stay in London, both diplomacy and clothing again proved to be key issues. The Prince consented to the extension largely because Johnston promised the Prince that he would finally meet the king. This was, in Johnston's words, "no small inducement to him to resolve to stay." Johnston also agreed to send the Prince's uncle-father gifts of a gun and pair of stockings, for which the society paid.[60] Though small when compared to the array of gifts the Spanish frequently gave to Indian micos, these were powerfully symbolic gifts, and the distance they had to travel from London to Port Royal increased their spiritual and political currency multifold. The Spanish had long limited the giving or sale of guns to Indians in La Florida, providing them only when absolutely necessary. Though other Yamasees who had lived in South Carolina since the 1680s were accustomed to receiving guns, the Prince's uncle-father probably still understood this as a special sort of gift that spoke of not just violence but power. The stockings were a particularly interesting selection: few micos would have received such a gift. Just as the Prince's clothing communicated his status to both English and Indian audiences, so too would his uncle-father's stockings.

This negotiation between the Prince and Johnston over the Prince's desire to return to Euhaw is revealing, demonstrating on the one hand the extent to which Johnston was willing to enter into a relationship that more closely approximated Indian negotiation practices and, on the other hand, the Prince's insistence that he was a diplomat who needed to be dressed and treated as such. Just a month later Johnston reported that the Prince was also asking for a new jacket, breeches, and a hat, "all of which he greatly wants." The society finally gave in.[61] Still, it made him wait to meet the king.

The SPG's priority was to transform the Prince into a missionary, rather than to introduce him to British royalty for a vaster purpose. His status as a prince was important, in the SPG's view, not because it would gain him credibility with British elites but because it meant that he had spiritual and political influence over his own people and could therefore more easily shepherd their conversions. Moreover, the SPG hoped that if it succeeded in converting the Prince, other Indian nations would (finally) send their youth and children to the society for Christian education. This could be a turning point for the society. While believing that younger children were easier to assimilate, the SPG also recognized the opportunity to create Indian missionaries out of youths and adults who could more immediately get to work. On this point, a particularly apt illustration is to be gleaned from Bishop White Kennett, an Oxford-educated Anglican minister who was a founding member of the SPCK and SPG and one of the most vocal proponents of both charity schools and Indian missions. In his *Commonplace Book* (ca. 1710) Kennett offered the sixth-century conversion of the Anglo-Saxons as a model for missionary work among American Indians: "It was [Pope] Gregorie's counsel to further the conversion of ye Saxons here by buying up Eng. Children & youths of 17 or 19 years, that they might be educated in God's services."[62] Just as Pope Gregory I had proposed, the Yamasee Prince was seventeen when he

Spiritual Diplomacy

first arrived in London and nineteen when he was baptized. This must have struck Kennett as fortuitous if not providential.

But after the Prince had spent a year in England, the SPG decided that putting him in mainstream schools had not proven effective. It was particularly disappointed by his lack of progress "in ye knowledge of Christianity," and it therefore moved him to a tutor who was also a minister. Under the Reverend Mr. Macbeth's tutelage, the society reported, the Prince made great advances within the short space of two months. Though we do not know how closely Headmaster Noblet had adhered to the grammar school curriculum at Chigwell, it is apparent that Macbeth scaled back the Prince's secular education. His bill to the SPG for a copybook, ciphering (math) book, and primer indicate that the Prince was still at a very early level in his education. Macbeth taught the Prince some of the fundamental elements of math and handwriting, as the SPG had instructed its schoolmasters to do in 1706 when preparing their students for employment. Macbeth also followed the "ordinary road" in his approach to the Prince's religious education, teaching him the fundamentals of reading so that he could then advance to more complex Christian texts. The primer he purchased for the Prince was elementary; it covered the alphabet, syllables, a few tables of words, and it contained fairly little explicit religious content. The Prince would have moved on to increasingly difficult texts: Psalter, Gospels, Book of Common Prayer, and finally the Old Testament. But Macbeth was abruptly called away from his post, so the Prince was moved to yet another tutor, Mr. Brooks, who oversaw his studies during his final seven months in London, from October 1714 to May 1715. Brooks, like Macbeth, concentrated on the Prince's religious education. It appears he may in fact have skipped a few steps, speeding the Prince through to the Bible more quickly than was normally the case.[63]

Despite (or perhaps because of) its ambitions for the Prince, the SPG kept him virtually hidden from both British elites and the public throughout his trip. That contrasts sharply with the experiences of the other elite North American Indians who were brought to London both before and after the Prince's voyage. In those cases their British sponsors generally engaged in significant publicity campaigns. A small group of New York–based men had brought four Iroquois "kings" to London just three years before the Prince's own visit. Hoping to raise political support for an invasion of Canada, they enlisted four Indian men who were not in fact Iroquois sachems, dressed them in elaborate costumes, arranged numerous meetings with powerful political elites, and displayed them to the public. Their visit ignited what one scholar describes as a "flurry of printing"; the Iroquois' every move was recounted in newspapers, broadsides, pamphlets, essays, ballads, verses, and engravings. Among their more important political occasions, the kings famously exchanged gifts with Queen Anne, met several times with the Board of Trade, dined with the Lords Commissioners of the Admiralty, and sailed with the commander on the flagship of the Royal Fleet. Followed by crowds when out in public, the Iroquois attended the theater a number of times, and in one instance their seats were moved onstage to satisfy a rambunctious crowd clamoring for a better view. The SPG not only knew of the visit, but also met the Iroquois kings, agreed to their request for missionaries, and gave each of them a Bible and Book of Common Prayer. Images of the so-called Iroquois "kings" were so popular that the Prince must have seen them and in them learned lessons about how to communicate his status to the British through his clothing and how other Indian diplomats had been feted.[64]

The SPG was strangely silent when it came to the Euhaw Prince, however. Despite the length of his trip, the English press seems to have taken no notice of the Prince's presence. He apparently did not attend the theater, or visit hospitals, or dine with religious or secular leaders, as had the Iroquois and other elite Indians before them. More strangely yet, although the SPG's affiliates included the most powerful Anglican bishops in England, there is no evidence that the Prince spent any meaningful time with those spiritual leaders. Nor are there any surviving images of the Prince. The SPG hired no artist to paint the Prince's portrait. It is possible that Henrietta Johnston—Gideon's wife and the first pastelist in South Carolina—drew his portrait in South Carolina. But if she did, it has not survived. Though Queen Anne had paid one hundred pounds to John Vereslt for portraits of the four Iroquois kings, the SPG spent less than eighty-eight pounds for the Prince's entire twenty-one-month trip; a little over a quarter of this budget went toward the Prince's education.⁶⁵ Perhaps it is not too much to say that the SPG kept the Prince hidden away. But why? In him they had a legitimate "prince" rather than the trumped-up Iroquois kings. There was no need to embellish his political power. Perhaps they were worried that their experiment might fail or that he might be corrupted if put on display, his focus distracted from the more important and pressing work of conversion and assimilation? We are left to wonder what this means.

Not until March 3, 1715, did the Prince finally meet the king of England. The bishop of London deemed the Prince's religious education sufficient and baptized him George on the Sunday before Ash Wednesday. Much as his people had in La Florida, the Euhaw Prince probably understood his conversion to Anglican Christianity in 1715 as a way to build a new strand in the web of spiritual and political alliances that empowered his chiefly lineage. In La Florida many but certainly not all caciques and cacicas who initiated an alliance with the Spanish converted to Catholicism, but in so doing they transformed what Catholicism meant, selectively adopting, rejecting, and translating practices and ideologies into their own constructs. After his baptism in 1715 the Euhaw Prince was presented to his namesake, King George I, later the same day. Still, hardly anyone noticed. A single paragraph in the *Post Boy* described the baptism but failed even to mention the Prince's meeting with the king. Though the SPG itself would later mark this as an important event in its accounts of the society's history, the Prince left England much as he came, without fanfare.⁶⁶

For the Prince, the Euhaws, and the Yamasees more generally, this experiment in spiritual diplomacy was ultimately an abject failure. Hampered by severe differences in educational practices and the SPG's disinclination to let him meet royal and secular political leaders, the Prince found his trip alienating, lonely, and disappointing. The SPG paid schoolmasters and tutors to instruct the seventeen-year-old Prince in the rudimentary skills an English child would have acquired at a much younger age. Completely unfamiliar with his Muskogean language, the Prince's instructors used teaching materials and practices developed for

English children. Most important, though the Prince and his guardian, Gideon Johnston, expected that he would meet British nobility and be dressed accordingly, the society balked at providing him with clothing that befitted his status and at promoting the diplomatic component of his mission. It was precisely the society's inflexibility in these matters that explains the Prince's assessment of his experiences as a failure, despite the society's claims that the Prince's conversion was a success.

The Prince's trip was also a failure on a larger scale. We might speculate that his long absence from Carolina did not ease Yamasee anxieties about their worsening relations with the British. After a three-month voyage that Johnston described as sickly and "tedious," the pair arrived in Charleston in September 1715 to discover that the colony was engulfed in the first pan-Indian war in the region.[67] The Yamasee War had started that April in Pocotaligo, the head town of the Upper Yamasees, and led to the exodus of the Yamasees from South Carolina. Among the refugees were the Prince's uncle-father, family, and people.

When he learned of his nephew-son's return, the Euhaw mico looked for a way to get back to Charleston without being killed. Within three months, the Euhaw mico had moved his community from St. Augustine north to "an Island between Port Royal and St Augustines" in the hope of reuniting with him. But in the spring the mico and his family were captured by British colonists and sold into slavery, sharing the same fate as tens of thousands of other southeastern Indians before and during the war. Johnston described the Prince as "extremely sunk and dejected."[68]

The enslavement of the Prince's uncle-father and his family was fraught with irony. The Euhaw mico had resisted joining the Yamasees in the war against the British and had instead attempted to continue to pursue a path of peace. When the Prince first returned to Charleston, Johnston incorrectly reported that his uncle-father had been killed "by the Indians for not Joyning with them in the war against us." Though wrong about the mico's death, Johnston was right about his reluctance to break his alliance with the British. It is not clear whether the Euhaw mico was motivated solely by his concern for the Prince's welfare or was also attempting to honor his son's political commitment as ambassador to the British. His actions mirror a 1708 description of the duties of a *fanni mico*, who was to "devert the Warriors from any designe against

Spiritual Diplomacy

the people they protect . . . and if after all, are unable to oppose the stream, are to send the people private intelligence to provide for their own safety." The Prince's uncle-father had done just that. Not only had he refused to join the war but also, as Johnston sadly noted, he had actually intended to show the colonial forces the way to surprise the Yamasees and Creeks.[69] But in the midst of this war, in some respects echoing Puritan treatment of Praying Indians during Metacom's War in New England, Carolina colonists seemed able to construe a Yamasee mico only as an enemy, despite his nephew's conversion to Anglicanism and his own continued efforts at preserving their spiritual alliance.

What became of the Euhaw Prince? Within the space of a single month, he lost first his Euhaw uncle-father and then his fictive British kin. On April 23, 1716, Johnston drowned in a boating accident off the Charleston coast as he tried to sail back to England.[70] Unfortunately, we know no more about the Prince's fate. He may have fled to Indian allies, seeking refuge in a Lower Creek town, or he may have joined the several hundred other Yamasees who returned to St. Augustine and continued to pursue a path of spiritual diplomacy with the Spanish. Perhaps he became a mico in his own right, taking up his uncle-father's mantle.[71]

Notes

A longer version of this essay was previously published as Denise I. Bossy, "Spiritual Diplomacy, the Yamasees, and the Society for the Propagation of the Gospel: Reinterpreting Prince George's Eighteenth-Century Voyage to England," *Early American Studies: An Interdisciplinary Journal* 12 (Spring 2014): 366–401.

1. The young man's Yamasee names are lost to us.

2. Rowan Strong, *Anglicanism and the British Empire, c. 1700–1850* (New York: Oxford University Press, 2007), 60–65; Edward E. Andrews, "Prodigal Sons: Indigenous Missionaries in the British Atlantic World, 1640–1780," PhD diss., University of New Hampshire, 2009, ch. 2.

3. Frank J. Klingberg, "The Mystery of the Lost Yamasee Prince," *South Carolina Historical Magazine* 63 (January 1962): 18–32.

4. For example, S. Charles Bolton, *Southern Anglicanism: The Church of England in Colonial South Carolina* (Westport CT: Greenwood Press, 1982), 102–8, and Alden T. Vaughan, *Transatlantic Encounters: American Indians in Britain, 1500–1776* (New York: Cambridge University Press, 2006), 133–35. For a critique see Margaret Szasz, *Indian Education in the American Colonies, 1607–1783* (1988; repr., Lincoln: University of Nebraska Press, 2007), 143–44.

5. *Mico* means chief in Muskogee, the language likely spoken by both the Yamasees and Guales who joined them. John Worth, "Guale" and "Yamasee," in *Handbook of North American Indians*, vol. 14: *Southeast*, ed. Raymond D. Fogelson (Washington DC: Smithsonian Institution Press, 2004), 238, 245.

6. Francis le Jau to the Secretary, March 19, 1716, Letterbook B4, #58, United Society for the Propagation of the Gospel Archives, Rhodes House, Oxford University, England (hereafter cited as USPG); Francis le Jau, *The Carolina Chronicle of Dr. Francis le Jau, 1706–1717*, ed. Frank J. Klingberg (Berkeley: University of California Press, 1956), 175.

7. Joseph M. Hall Jr., *Zamumo's Gifts: Indian-European Exchange in the Colonial Southeast* (Philadelphia: University of Pennsylvania Press, 2009); Steven C. Hahn, *The Invention of the Creek Nation, 1670–1763* (Lincoln: University of Nebraska Press, 2004); Joshua Piker, *Okfuskee: A Creek Indian Town in Colonial America* (Cambridge: Harvard University Press, 2004).

8. Vaughan, *Transatlantic Encounters*, 104–64. There were southeastern Indians in England, but they were not diplomats. For example, "Advertisement respecting a Canibal Indian or Man Eater who was taken in a skirmish near South Carolina, likewise an Indian woman, a princess of that country" (London, 1710?), British Library, London.

9. Francis le Jau to the Secretary, March 19, 1716, Letterbook B4, #58, USPG.

10. Thomas Nairne, *Nairne's Muskhogean Journals: The 1708 Expedition to the Mississippi River*, ed. Alexander Moore (Jackson: University of Mississippi Press, 1988), 33.

11. August 11, 1692, in A. S. Salley, ed., *Journal of the Grand Council of South Carolina, April 11, 1692–September 26, 1692* (Columbia: State Company, 1907), 55, emphasis added. This confusion persisted well into the 1740s. Michelle LeMaster, *Brothers Born of One Mother: British-Native American Relations in the Colonial Southeast* (Charlottesville: University of Virginia Press, 2012), 26.

12. John H. Hann, *Apalachee: The Land between the Rivers* (Gainesville: University Press of Florida, 1988), 104–5.

13. John E. Worth, *The Struggle for the Georgia Coast* (1995; repr., Tuscaloosa: University of Alabama Press, 2007), 51; William Green, *The Search for Altamaha: The Archaeology and Ethnohistory of an Early 18th Century Indian Town* (Columbia: South Carolina Institute of Archaeology and Anthropology, 1992), 9.

14. Green, *The Search for Altamaha*, 9. An alternative theory is that Euhaws were originally Guale. Worth, "Yamasee," 248.

15. Letter from Gonzalo Méndez de Canzo, February 23, 1598, in *Murder and Martyrdom in Spanish Florida: Don Juan and the Guale Uprising of 1597*, ed. J. Michael Francis and Kathleen M. Kole (New York: American Museum of Natural History, 2011), 98; "Relacion del Viage que Hizo el Senor Pedro de Ibarra, Gobernadors y Capitan General de Florida, a Visitar los Pueblos Indios de las Provincias de San Pedro y Guale, Noviembre y Diciembre de 1604," in *Documentos Históricos de la Florida y la Luisiana, siglos XVI al XVIII*, ed. Manuel Serrano y Sanz (Madrid: Biblioteca de los Americanistas, 1912), 187; John Worth, "Late Spanish Military Expeditions in the Interior Southeast, 1597–1628," in *The Forgotten Centuries: Indians and Europeans in the American South, 1521–1704*, ed. Charles Hudson and Carmen Chaves Tesser (Athens: University of Georgia Press, 1994), 104–22; Hann, *Apalachee*, 33.

16. Joseph Hall, "Anxious Alliances," in *Indian Slavery in Colonial America*, ed. Alan Gallay (Lincoln: University of Nebraska Press, 2009), 163; David McKivergan, "Migration and Settlement among the Yamasee in South Carolina," PhD diss., University of Maine, Orono, 1989, 219–20; Worth, *Struggle for the Georgia Coast*, 24–30, 35. Worth suggests that Yoa—and the Upper Yamasee Guale towns—may have been rebel towns from the Guale Revolt. Worth, "Yamasee," 245–53. More recent work demonstrates that Yoa played a limited role in the revolt and was quick to reconcile with the Spanish. Francis and Kole, *Murder and Martyrdom in Spanish Florida*, 97–98, 136–38.

17. A. S. Salley Jr., ed., *Journals of the Commons House of Assembly for 1703* (Columbia: Historical Commission of South Carolina, 1934), 48; Jerald Milanich, "Gone but Never Forgotten: Mis-

Spiritual Diplomacy 159

sion Santa Catalina on Amelia Island and the 1702 Raid," *El Escribano* 39 (2002): 1–15; Steven J. Oatis, *A Colonial Complex: South Carolina's Frontiers in the Era of the Yamasee War, 1680–1730* (Lincoln: University of Nebraska Press, 2004), 47–48; Hahn, *The Invention of the Creek Nation*, 62–63.

18. July 9, 1712, *Journals of the Commissioners of the Indian Trade: September 20, 1710–August 29, 1718*, ed. W. L. McDowell Jr. (Columbia: South Carolina Archives Department, 1955), 30–31; hereafter cited as JCIT.

19. June 19, 1713, Journal of the SPG, 2:297, USPG Archives, Rhodes House, Oxford University.

20. Nancy Shoemaker, *A Strange Likeness: Becoming Red and White in Eighteenth-Century North America* (New York: Oxford University Press, 2004), 43.

21. In other documents the Prince's uncle-father was alternately described as a "sachem" and "chief"; "chief" in Abstract of Proceedings printed with St. George Ashe, *A Sermon Preached before the Incorporated Society for the Propagation of the Gospel in Foreign Parts; at their Anniversary Meeting in the Parish-Church of St. Mary-le-Bow; On Friday the 18th of February, 1714* (London: Joseph Downing, 1715), 48; "sachem" in *An Abstract of the Proceedings of the Society for the Propagation of the Gospel in Foreign Parts, In the Year of our Lord 1715* (London: Joseph Downing, 1716), 29. See also William Green, Chester B. DePratter, and Bobby Southerlin, "The Yamasee in South Carolina: Native American Adaptation and Interaction along the Carolina Frontier," in *Another's Country: Archaeological and Historical Perspectives on Cultural Interactions in the Southern Colonies*, ed. J. W. Joseph and Martha Zierden (Tuscaloosa: University of Alabama Press, 2002), 15–18. Worth suggests that Euhaw was an Upper Yamasee town; Worth, "Yamasee," 248. But it seems more likely that Pocotaligo—where the Yamasees began their war with South Carolina in 1715—was a red head town and therefore would not have been involved in the Prince's diplomatic voyage.

22. A letter written by Francis le Jau intimates that the Prince's uncle-father was a peace chief, describing him as an "old man." Le Jau to the Secretary, March 19, 1716, Letterbook B4, #58, USPG Archives; J. Leitch Wright, *Creeks and Seminoles: The Destruction and Regeneration of the Muscogulge People* (Lincoln: University of Nebraska Press, 1987), 14–17.

23. Beginning in 1710 these complaints were recorded in the *Journal of the Commissioners of the Indian Trade*; see JCIT, 11, 37. For an analysis of these crimes from Native perspectives, see William L. Ramsey, *The Yamasee War: A Study of Culture, Economy, and Conflict in the Colonial South* (Lincoln: University of Nebraska Press, 2008), ch. 1.

24. July 28, 1711, JCIT, 11.

25. Denise I. Bossy, "Indian Slavery in Southeastern Indian and British Societies, 1670–1730," in *Indian Slavery in Colonial America*, ed. Alan Gallay (Lincoln: University of Nebraska Press, 2009), 210–11.

26. Father Juan Rogel to Uncle-father Jerónimo Ruiz del Portillo, April 25, 1568, in John H. Hann, ed. and trans., *Missions to the Calusa* (Gainesville: University Press of Florida, 1991), 248.

27. On relationships between Indian women and British traders, see LeMaster, *Brothers Born of One Mother*, 149–84; Theda Perdue, *Cherokee Women: Gender and Culture Change, 1700–1835* (Lincoln: University of Nebraska Press, 1998), 81–83; and Andrew Frank, *Creeks and Southerners: Biculturalism on the Early American Frontier* (Lincoln: University of Nebraska Press, 2005), 14–21. Non-elite families also engaged in cross-cultural relationships. For fanni micos see Nairne, *Nairne's Muskhogean Journals*, 40; Patricia Galloway, "'The Chief Who Is Your Uncle-father': Choctaw and French Views of the Diplomatic Relation," in *Powhatan's Mantle: Indians and the Colonial Southeast*, ed. Gregory A. Waselkov, Peter H. Wood, and Tom Hatley, rev. ed. (Lincoln: University of Nebraska Press, 2006), 340–70; Hahn, *Invention of the Creek Nation*, 21; Piker, *Okfuskee*, 22–23.

28. For other examples of young men functioning as diplomats, see John E. Worth, *Timucuan Chiefdoms of Spanish Florida*, 2 vols. (Gainesville: University Press of Florida, 1998), 1:55–56, 65; John Juricek, *Colonial Georgia and the Creeks: Anglo-Indian Diplomacy on the Southern Frontier, 1733–1763* (Gainesville: University Press of Florida, 2010), 57; Robbie Ethridge, *From Chicaza to Chickasaw: The European Invasion and the Transformation of the Mississippian World, 1540–1715* (Chapel Hill: University of North Carolina Press, 2010), 188–89.

29. Robert Sandford, "Relation of a Voyage on the Coast of the Province of Carolina, 1666," in *Narratives of Early Carolina, 1650–1708*, ed. Alexander S. Salley Jr. (New York: Charles Scribner's Sons, 1911), 104.

30. John Norris to Secretary, March 20, 1711, SPG Papers in the Lambeth Palace Library, 8:118, Lambeth Palace, London.

31. Francis le Jau to Secretary, March 13, 1708, in le Jau, *Carolina Chronicle*, 37.

32. Board Minutes, January 17, 1709, SPG Papers in Lambeth Palace Library, 2:1; Petition of Sebastian van der Eycken to the Society, n.d., SPG Papers in the Lambeth Palace Library, 8:245.

33. Thomas Nairne to Doctor Marston, St. Helena, August 20, 1705, SPG Papers in Lambeth Palace Library, 17:89–90.

34. Le Jau to the Secretary, September 15, 1708, in le Jau, *Carolina Chronicle*, 41.

35. Amy Turner Bushnell, *Situado and Sabana: Spain's Support System for the Presidio and Mission Provinces of Florida*, Anthropological Papers of the American Museum of Natural History, no. 74 (Athens GA: Distributed by University of Georgia Press, 1994), 105; "Relatio Anonym de Visitatione quam Petrus Mendendez Hispali Missionariis Floridae Fecit," in *Monumenta Antiquae Floridae, 1566–1572*, ed. Felix Zubillaga (Rome: Apud "Monumenta Hisorica Soc. Iesu," 1946), 217; Report of Governor Gonzalo Méndez de Canzo, July 1, 1598, in Francis and Kole, *Murder and Martyrdom in Spanish Florida*, 105. A number of leading SPG deans and bishops opposed using force, including Thomas Bray. Samuel Clyde McCulloch, *A Plea for Further Missionary Activity in Colonial America: Dr. Thomas Bray's Missionalia* (Austin TX: Historical Magazine of the Protestant Episcopal Church, 1946), 10; Gabriel Díaz Vara Calderón, *A Seventeenth Century Letter of Gabriel Díaz Vara Calderón, Bishop of Cuba*, trans. Lucy Wenhold (Washington DC: Smithsonian Institution Press, 1936), 14.

36. Laura M. Stevens, *The Poor Indians: British Missionaries, Native Americans, and Colonial Sensibility* (Philadelphia: University of Pennsylvania Press, 2004), ch. 4.

37. Le Jau to Secretary, March 22 and August 5, 1709, in le Jau, *Carolina Chronicle*, 54, 57–58.

38. Bishop White Kennett's Collections, volume 98, Lansdowne MSS 1032, f. 37, British Library, London.

39. Darcy R. Fryer, "'Improved' and 'Very Promising Children': Growing Up Rich in Eighteenth-Century South Carolina," in *Children in Colonial America*, ed. James Marten (New York: New York University Press, 2007), 107.

40. John Worth, "Spanish Missions and the Persistence of Chiefly Power," in *The Transformation of the Southeastern Indians, 1540–1760*, ed. Robbie Ethridge and Charles Hudson (Jackson: University Press of Mississippi, 2002), 39–64; Amy Turner Bushnell, "Ruling 'the Republic of Indians' in Seventeenth-Century Florida," in Waselkov, Wood, and Hatley, *Powhatan's Mantle*, 195–214; James Noblet to Gideon Johnston, August 11, 1713, Letterbook C7, #31, USPG Archives.

41. Prince George to the Society, Charles Town, S.C., December 8, 1715, Letterbook B4, #97, USPG Archives; "An Abstract of the Most material Proceedings and Occurrences within the last Years Endeavours of The Society for the Propagation of the Gospel in Foreign Parts, from Friday the 20th of February 1712 to Friday the 19th of February 1713," 46, Lambeth Palace Library.

42. September 30, 1715, Letterbook B, #28, USPG Archives.

Spiritual Diplomacy

43. Fryer, "'Improved' and 'Very Promising Children,'" 110–12.

44. Robert Johnston to the Secretary, June 2, 1713, Letterbook C, #30, USPG Archives. October 30, 1713, Journal of the SPG, 2:334; Memorial of Gideon Johnston to the Society, [October (?) 1713], Letterbook C7, #36, USPG Archives. Klingberg dates the letter to June, but I suspect it was written in the fall, given the location of the Memorial in the collection, the weather to which Johnston refers, and subsequent letters from Johnston and the society about the Prince's clothing that are dated December. See particularly Johnston to Secretary, December 19, 1715, Letterbook 5, # 37, USPG Archives. June 3 and July 17, 1713, Journal of the SPG, 2:295, 300.

45. J. H. Cardwell, *The Story of a Charity School: Two Centuries of Popular Education in Soho, 1699–1899* (London: Truslove, Hanson, and Comba, 1899), 53–57.

46. The Prince enrolled July 30, 1713; Johnston to Secretary, December 18, 1713, Letterbook C7, #42, USPG Archives; Fryer, "'Improved' and 'Very Promising Children,'" 105.

47. John Lawson, *A New Voyage to Carolina* (Chapel Hill: University of North Carolina Press, 1967), 210, 211, 245.

48. Godfrey Stott, *History of Chigwell School* (Ipswich, England: W. S. Cowell, 1960), 46.

49. Carole Shammas, *A History of Household Government in America* (Charlottesville: University of Virginia Press, 2002), 24–52; Cardwell, *The Story of a Charity School*, 15–16; "Chigwell Ordinances, April 13, 1629," in Stott, *Chigwell School*, 157–58; Philipp Georg Friedrich von Reck, *Von Reck's Voyage: Drawings and Journal of Philip Georg Friedrich von Reck*, ed. Kristian Hvidt (Savannah GA: Beehive Press, 1980), 48.

50. The bishop of London and the SPG paid for Johnston's sons to attend Chigwell. Johnston to Secretary, July 5, 1710, in Frank J. Klingberg, ed., *Carolina Chronicle: The Papers of Commissary Gideon Johnston, 1707–1716* (Berkeley: University of California Press, 1946), 62; Memorial of Gideon Johnston; October 30, 1713, Journal of the SPG, 2:333, quoted in Stott, *Chigwell School*, 21.

51. Stott, *Chigwell School*, 156; Charles Hudson, *The Southeastern Indians* (Knoxville: University of Tennessee Press, 1976), 221–22, 235–27.

52. Noblet to Johnston, August 11, 1713, Letterbook C7, #31, USPG Archives.

53. Johnston, on the other hand, was very ill during much of their time in England. Robert Johnston to the Society, June 1713, Letterbook C7, #30, USPG Archives; Gideon Johnston to Mr. Taylour, December 14, 1713, Letterbook C7, #339, USPG Archives. Chigwell students were given only twenty-five days off per year. Stott, *Chigwell School*, 157; Johnston to Society, December 18, 1713, Letterbook C7, #42, USPG Archives; Noblet to Johnston, August 11, 1713, Letterbook C7, #31, USPG Archives; Margaret Simons Middleton, *Henrietta Johnston of Charles Town, South Carolina: America's First Pastelist* (Columbia: University of South Carolina Press, 1966), 29.

54. Klingberg makes no mention of this charity school. Johnston to the Secretary, November 19, 1714, Letterbook C7, #51, USPG Archives. Of the charity schools in James Parish, it is most likely that Johnston sent the Prince to St. Martin's-in-the-Fields, which was nearer to his lodgings and was founded by Archbishop of Canterbury Thomas Tenison, president of the SPG from 1701 to 1715. "Historical Notes on Westminster Schools," (Westminster City Archives), 23, http://www3.westminster.gov.uk/docstores/publications_store/archives/schools.pdf.

55. Johnston to Secretary, July 16, 1714, Letterbook C7, # 44, USPG Archives; Johnston to Secretary, August 20, 1714, Letterbook A9, #22.

56. Memorial of Gideon Johnston.

57. David Kuchta, *The Three-Piece Suit and Modern Masculinity: England, 1550–1850* (Berkeley: University of California Press, 2002), 91–132.

58. For the best studies of this process, see Worth, *Timucuan Chiefdoms*, 1:35–43, and Hall, *Zamumo's Gifts*, 33–54. Memorial of Gideon Johnston. Kettleby was the colony's first perma-

nent agent. "An Act for Appointing an Agent to Solicit and Transact the Publick Affairs of This Province in the Kingdom of Great Britain, Dec. 18, 1714," *The Statutes at Large of South Carolina*, vol. 2: *1682–1716*, ed. Thomas Cooper (Columbia SC: Printed by A. S. Johnson, 1837), 628–29.

59. Johnston to Secretary, December 14, 1713, Letterbook C7, #39, USPG Archives; "The Taylor's Bill for the Indian Prince," Letterbook C7, #41, USPG Archives; "Mr. Johnston's Account of the charge necessary of the Cloths for ye Indian Youth," Letterbook C7, #37, USPG Archives.

60. Johnston to Secretary, July 16, 1714, Letterbook C7, #44, USPG Archives; Johnston to Secretary, August 20, 1714, Letterbook A9, #22, USPG Archives; "Society's Disbursements for the Prince, October 1713 to June 1715," Letterbook C7, #29, USPG Archives.

61. Johnston to Secretary, September 17, 1714, Letterbook A9, #24, USPG Archives; "Society's Disbursements for the Prince, October 1713 to June 1715."

62. Bishop White Kennett's Collections, vol. 78, Lansdowne MSS 1012, 148lh.

63. August 20, 1714, Journal of the SPG, 3:395; Mr. Macbeth's "Bill of Disbursement for the Indian Youth" Letterbook C7, #50, USPG Archives; "Society's Disbursements for the Prince, October 1713 to June 1715"; E. Jennifer Monaghan, *Learning to Read and Write in Colonial America* (Amherst: University of Massachusetts Press, 2005), 13, 143–65; William Brooks, bill for "The Indian Prince of Catalina," Letterbook C7, #27, USPG Archives.

64. Eric Hinderaker, "The 'Four Indian Kings' and the Imaginative Construction of the First British Empire," *William and Mary Quarterly* 53 (July 1996): 487–526.

65. "Society's Disbursements for the Prince, October 1713 to June 1715."

66. David J. Silverman, "Indians, Missionaries, and Religious Translation: Creating Wampanoag Christianity in Seventeenth-Century Martha's Vineyard," *William and Mary Quarterly* 62 (April 2005): 141–74. Archaeologists point to the persistence of burial practices and Indian council houses in nominally converted mission communities. Kathleen Deagan, "Native American Resistance to Spanish Presence in Hispaniola and La Florida, ca. 1492–1650," in *Enduring Conquests: Rethinking the Archaeology of Resistance to Spanish Colonialism in the Americas*, ed. Matthew Liebmann and Melissa S. Murphy (Santa Fe: School for Advanced Research Press, 2010), 52–53; Father Juan Rogel to Father Jerónimo Ruiz del Portillo, April 25, 1568, in Hann, *Missions to the Calusa*, 247; *London Post Boy*, March 10–March 12, 1715; Charles Frederick Pascoe, *Two Hundred Years of the S.P.G.*, vol. 1 (London: At the Society's Office, 1901), 17.

67. Johnston to Secretary, September 30, 1715, Letterbook B, #28, UPSG Archives.

68. Francis le Jau to Secretary, March 19, 1716, Letterbook B4, #58, UPSG Archives; Johnston to Secretary, April 4, 1716, Letterbook B4, #62, UPSG Archives. For more on the enslavement of the Euhaw mico see March 27, 1716, Commons House Journals, No. 5: 1716–1721, South Carolina Department of Archives and History, Columbia, 62. The Speaker of the House ordered the Public Receiver to "ship off the Euhaw king" to Barbados "by the first opportunity."

69. Nairne, *Nairne's Muskhogean Journals*, 40; Johnston to Secretary, February 28, 1716, postscript to January 27, 1716, Letterbook B, #21, UPSG Archives.

70. Clergy of South Carolina to John Robinson, Lord Bishop of London, May 31, 1716, in Klingberg, *Carolina Chronicle: The Papers of Commissary Gideon Johnston*, 167–69.

71. Hann believes that Euhaw (Yoa) Indians could have been the "Oapa" Indians listed in the census of the ten Indian settlements near St. Augustine taken by Joseph Primo de Rivera in 1717. If this is the case, then perhaps the Prince was one of the four "Oapa" men listed as "Christians" and "vassals" of Pocotalaca, whose cacique was Yfallaquisca. John H. Hann, "St. Augustine's Fallout from the Yamasee War," *Florida Historical Quarterly* 68, no. 2 (1989): 186.

6

Yamasee-African Ties in Carolina and Florida

JANE LANDERS

This essay examines the relations Yamasee Indians formed with enslaved Africans in early Carolina, their alliance in the Yamasee War that erupted in 1715, and their subsequent ties in Spanish Florida. English narratives and scholarship about the Yamasee War pay little attention, if any, to Africans in this history.[1] Africans were still relatively few in number in Carolina, and English proprietors, traders, and missionaries were naturally more focused on indigenous geopolitics. The Spanish, however, were long used to reporting on indigenous and African groups in their colonies and produced much more detailed records on each, of both a secular and religious nature. During decades of English oppression in Carolina abused Yamasee and enslaved Africans found common cause, and finally in 1715 they rose together in revolt. When their uprising ultimately failed, they fled southward to seek promised sanctuary in Florida and to become part of the Spanish community.

Spanish officials in St. Augustine considered the Yamasee returning converts and allies and allotted lands on the city's periphery on which the Yamasee chiefs formed new villages. Despite a 1693 order requiring Florida's governors to shelter runaway slaves from Carolina seeking the "True Faith," however, African veterans of the Yamasee War allies had a different outcome. "Heathens" among the Yamasee retained some Africans as their own slaves until Spanish officials purchased them, incorporated them into Black militia units, and deployed them alongside Indian counterparts on repeated guerrilla raids against Carolina. In 1738 the Yamasee Chief Jospo (as he was known in Spanish records) joined in the still enslaved Africans' legal efforts to secure a long sought freedom, which the Spanish Crown ultimately confirmed.[2]

Other scholars in this volume provide important new information on the earliest origins of the Yamasee and their amalgamated nature, the indigenous politics of the Southeast in which they were embroiled, and their initial conversion to Catholicism. Drawing on a variety of sources from colonial Carolina and Spanish Florida, I focus instead on the little known African engagement with the Yamasee and the implications for both groups. Africans proved valuable allies to the Yamasee during their war and their southward flight to Spanish sanctuary. Once reaching Florida, wartime alliances seem to have fractured, with Christian Yamasee remaining loyal to the African warriors who aided them, and non-Christian Yamasee (infidels, in Spanish terminology) treating them as disposable property, much as the English had.

The Yamasee first begin to appear in European records in the mid-seventeenth century, and scholars theorize they were remnants of earlier groups displaced multiple times across the Southeast by Chichimeco/Westo slave raiders, armed by Virginia traders.[3] In 1670 English planter-proprietors from Barbados launched the new colony of Carolina in Yamasee lands still claimed by Spain, "but 10 days journey" from St. Augustine, further destabilizing the geopolitics of the Southeast. The region's diverse Indian nations were soon swept into a terrible international contest that would ruin most of them.[4]

Although the 1670 Treaty of Madrid recognized England's settlements in Carolina and promised peace, Spanish settlers in St. Augustine were threatened by Protestant competitors on their borders and repeatedly tried to eliminate them. In 1670 Governor Guerra y Vega launched the first failed attempt against Carolina, and in 1676 Florida's royal treasurer, Don Juan Menéndez Márquez, commanded a small flotilla of three ships and fourteen *piraguas* in another abortive attempt to eject the "usurpers." That expedition, which probably included both Africans and Indians, was undone by a storm.[5] Thereafter more than a century of conflict ensued over the "debatable lands."[6] Anglo-Spanish hostilities triggered waves of migration, raids, and counter-raids that engulfed indigenous groups and African slaves alike in imperial contests for control of the Southeast.

Free and enslaved Africans had formed part of every Spanish exploration of the Southeast and also helped build Spain's earliest Atlantic coast settlements of St. Augustine and Santa Elena.[7] Carolina's earliest settlers also brought small numbers of enslaved Africans with them from Barbados to begin the hard work of clearing forests and building a new settlement. Over the next years the English colonists periodically imported more "seasoned" slaves from their sugar colonies of Barbados and Jamaica. As their counterparts in Virginia were also doing, Carolina settlers enslaved local Indians as well. But the increasing demand for labor proved greater than local indigenous supply, and in 1674 the Lords Proprietors of Carolina ordered Andrew Percival to "begin a Trade with the Spaniards for Negroes." No evidence survives that this plan was ever realized.[8]

Given their early numeric weakness, both the English and the Spaniards meanwhile used Indian and African surrogates to do much of their fighting on this unstable Atlantic frontier.[9] This, of course, was standard practice for Spanish colonizers. In 1681 Florida's governor, Juan Márquez Cabrera, followed the lead of short-handed governors across the Spanish Atlantic and created a new *pardo* (mulatto) and *moreno* (Black) militia in St. Augustine. A 1683 roster of the forty-two men and six officers who composed this unit offer little more than names. Two members are known from other sources. The negro Juan Merino, an ironsmith from Havana sentenced to exile in Florida for some unstated crime, later became free and served as second lieutenant in the Black militia. Merino owned an ironsmithing shop and repaired weaponry for the military. Christin de Tapia, a mulatto storeowner in St. Augustine involved in a trial of indigenous counterfeiters, was a corporal in the unit. They and the other Black militia members swore before God and the cross their willingness to serve the king. While their pledge may have been formulaic, it was also an effort to confirm their status as members of the religious and civil community and as vassals of a king from whom they might expect protection or patronage in exchange for armed service.[10] These Black militiamen and their successors proved an important asset for Florida's governors, who benefited from their linguistic and cultural abilities, their knowledge of the frontier, and their military skills.

In 1684 Scottish settlers established Stuarts Town, closer still to St. Augustine, and shortly afterward its founder, Lord Cardross (Henry Erskine), wrote to the Lords Proprietors in London, "Wee thought fitt to acquaint you that yesterday some more of the nation of the Yamasees arrived at St. Helena to settle with those of their nation formerly settled there having come from about St. Augustine." This report speaks to the historic geopolitical mobility of the Yamasee as they attempted to navigate between contending European powers.[11]

As Amy Bushnell describes in this volume, the newly settled Yamasee wasted no time in launching a series of attacks on the Spanish missions. In March 1685 they hit the Timucuan village of Santa Catalina de Afuyca, killing eighteen mission residents and taking twenty-five others as slaves back to Carolina. As an added insult, the former converts also sacked the mission's church.[12] Attacks, rebellions, and shifting alliances continued.[13]

The following August Governor Juan Márquez Cabrera retaliated for the Yamasee attack on Santa Catalina de Afuyca by sending a Spanish raiding party of fifty-three unnamed Indians and members of St. Augustine's Black militia to attack Carolina settlements.[14] At Governor Joseph Morton's plantation on Edisto Island they recovered the mission ornaments stolen by the Yamasee the previous year and seized "money and plate and eleven slaves to the value of £1500" before turning southward to burn down the Scottish settlement of Stuarts Town on their way home to St. Augustine. It is tempting to wonder if some among the Black and Indian militias might actually have known the enslaved they "liberated" on Edisto.[15] As noted, the repeated crosscurrents of raids and migrations past Edisto and across the Southeast acquainted many Blacks and Indians alike with the routes to St. Augustine as well as with the enmity existing between the English and Spanish colonies.[16] Africans enslaved in Carolina also learned, perhaps from St. Augustine's Black militia raiders, that Spanish religious and legal systems offered a path to freedom.

Such valuable information could also have come from the twenty-three Black and mulatto "prizes" sold in Charleston by the French pirate Sieur Nicolas de Grammont following his spectacular 1683 raid on the Spanish ports of Vera Cruz and Campeche. Grammont's multiracial crew included a Black corsair, Diego, and a mulatto named Thomas who served as a translator during Diego's interrogation by Governor Juan Márquez Cabrera. Diego and Thomas were the only two from Gammont's crew to survive several days of pitched battles against the Spaniards.[17] They, too, would have understood that freedom was possible among the Spanish. Carolina's "charter generation" of slaves was thus perhaps as diverse as the confederated Yamasees. It did not take long for those Africans ensnared in English chattel slavery to attempt to reach that freedom. And their numbers were growing.

Carolina's earliest settlers brought only small numbers of enslaved Africans from Barbados to begin the hard work of clearing forests and building housing and could not afford to let this policy go unchallenged. Although the Trans-Atlantic Slave Voyages Database lists no voyages from Africa to the North American mainland for the years 1670–1720, reports from Carolina indicate a larger volume of Africans imported into Carolina than earlier supposed. Carolina planters initiated a direct trade with Africa as early as 1697, when Barbadian merchant George Peters sent slaves to Charles Town on his ship *Turtle*, but naval officials there seized them before they could be sold because the captain was a "Scots man borne."[18] In 1699 English traders established Fort James in the Gambia River as their headquarters and Captain W. Rhett brought slaves directly from Guinea to Charles Town aboard the *Providence*.[19] The same year Edward Randolph reported to the Board of Trade and Plantations that there were only 1,100 families in the province and that there were "four negroes to one white man."[20] Over the next years Carolinians also imported more "seasoned" slaves from their sugar colonies of Barbados and Jamaica, Martinique, and Guadeloupe as well as from Madeira, where the Carolinians regularly traded.[21]

Many of the newly imported Africans were destined for work in the dense pine forests and swamps of Carolina, where, encouraged by British bounties on tar, pitch, rosin, and turpentine, settlers early established critical timber and naval stores industries.[22] As Peter H. Wood has shown, early Carolina's "Black pioneers" also became "Cattle-hunters" in the Carolina forests. Africans came to know the Carolina landscape by serving as "path-finders" and linguists for Indian traders. All these occupations allowed even recently imported Africans a certain amount of autonomy and mobility as well as access to Native peoples and their knowledge of the geopolitics of the region.[23]

In 1687 eight Black men and two women, one nursing a baby girl, stole a canoe and fled southward from Carolina to St. Augustine. On reaching the Spanish capital they requested baptism into the "True Faith."[24] Given the multicultural nature of the Gambia region, early missionary reports of Portuguese-speaking slaves in Carolina, and the 1683 arrival of enslaved Blacks from Vera Cruz, it is quite possible that some of the runaways reaching Florida had already been exposed to Roman Catholicism.[25] This group then may have known of the protections and opportunities the Catholic Church offered, possibly even manipulating confessional politics to their own advantage in making a shared request for religious sanctuary.[26] As required of a good Christian ruler, Governor Diego de Quiroga y Losada saw to the African runaways' Catholic instruction, baptism, and marriage and refused to return them to Captain William Dunlop, the Indian trader who arrived from Carolina to recover them the following year.[27]

Spanish officials reported additional groups of Carolina fugitives arriving in St. Augustine in 1688, 1689, and 1690. Carolina's governor, James Colleton, complained that slaves ran "dayly to your towns." Unsure about how to handle the refugees, St. Augustine's officials repeatedly solicited Spain for guidance and finally, on November 7, 1693, Charles II issued a royal proclamation "giving liberty to all . . . the men as well as the women . . . so that by their example and by my liberality others will do the same."[28]

English colonists still trying to stabilize Carolina could not afford to allow this policy to stand unchallenged. With the outbreak of the War of Spanish Succession, or Queen Anne's War, as it is known in English records (1702–13), Governor James Moore organized a combined force of about 1,000 men, including 600 Yamasee and Lower Creek (Uchise) warriors to wage war against the Spaniards. In September 1702 Governor Moore and Colonel Robert Daniel launched a combined naval and land attack on St. Augustine. Governor José de Zúñiga y Cerda (1699–1706) gathered his multiracial subjects into the Castillo de San Marcos during the fifty-two-day siege, and when support finally arrived from Cuba, Governor Moore burned the town and withdrew. But Moore's raid did produce results; he returned to Carolina with approximately 500 enslaved Timucuas gathered along the coast.[29] Altamaha and other Yamasee chiefs involved in Moore's raid later complained that Carolina trader John Cochran stole their plunder from St. Augustine, and the Commons House of Assembly ordered that they be given powder and shot in compensation.[30]

Although he failed to take St. Augustine, Governor Moore launched repeated raids on the Spanish colony. By 1705 Moore's forces had destroyed thirty-two Native towns, and Florida's new governor, Francisco de Córcoles y Martínez, gathered his remaining 401 indigenous subjects into six new towns: Nuestra Señora de Rosario (Apalachees), Nombre de Dios, Tolomato, Santa María, San Francisco Potano, and Costa (said to be a town of infidels).[31] Spanish accounts from the Archive of the Indies, which may have been inflated, record that thousands of Florida Indians were slaughtered and thousands more became slaves in Carolina or the Caribbean. English sources, which probably sought to minimize the carnage and the profits in their missives to the proprietors in London, put the number of killed and enslaved in the hundreds.[32]

In retaliation for these English raids, French allies joined Governor Francisco de Córcoles y Martínez's triracial forces in a counter-attack on Charles Town in August 1706. An English account of the event noted: "In 1706 the Spaniards at St. Augustine joined the French from Martinico in making up a fleet of ten Sail, with eight hundred Men, Whites, Mustees and Negroes, and two hundred Indians, to invade this province." This reference to mustees again recognizes the Indian-African intermixture common in Spanish worlds. Despite some initial success, this retaliatory expedition failed, but once again Blacks and Indians in Carolina would have learned more about the multiracial military of Spanish Florida, and the Anglo-Spanish enmity that offered them an alternative alliance.[33]

Spanish accounts state that Carolina raiders had been incorporating Blacks into their largely Indian forces for some time, but during the course of the War of Spanish Succession, Carolina officials created a militia of 950 "freemen," each of whom was to present for service "one able slave armed with gun or lance."[34] By 1709 Governor Edward Randolph reported to the Board of Trade that there were "four negroes to one white man" in Carolina.[35] This points again to large numbers of enslaved men in the colony, despite their invisibility in the Trans-Atlantic Slave Voyages Database.[36] Unlike the Spanish, however, the Carolinians did not offer freedom for military service or create a militia of free Black men. The newly armed, but still enslaved, Black men Carolina officials sent into service against St. Augustine's Black and Indian militias would surely have recognized the differences between Spanish and Anglo slave systems and that Spanish Florida offered them a refuge. It is tempting to wonder if any of those men later fought in the Yamasee War and subsequently fled to Spanish Florida.

Many studies of the Yamasee War have blamed that conflict on Carolina's Indian traders who exploited the local indigenous groups, enmeshing them in ruinous debt. But the Yamasee had many other complaints as well. The *Journals of the Commissioners of the Indian Trade* reported that in 1711 a number of traders, including Thomas Jones, John Whitehead, Joseph Bryan, Robert Steale, John Palmer, and Barnaby Bull, were all settled in Yamasee lands.[37] The Yamasee filed repeated complaints against these traders with the Carolina Commissioners of Indian Trade but usually to no avail. They charged that John Wright, the Indian agent posted at the paramount Upper Yamasee village of Pocotaligo forced them to carry burdens, demanded that they build a house for him next to that of the council house, and debauched their young girls.[38] "Lewis King of yr Pocotalligo Town," who Alexander Sweeney theorizes may once have been baptized as Luis, also complained against traders Cornelius MacKarty (sic) and Samuel Hilden for "stripping and beating Wiggasay and Haclantoosa, two of his people att one of their playes."[39] The Carolina Commissioners of Indian Trade finally convicted trader John Fraser of misconduct at Pocotaligo for having violently beaten the Tomatly king, but still trader abuses continued. The "Altamahaw King" and several of his warriors complained that trader Alexander Nichols "lately beat a Woman that he kept as his wife so that she Dyed and the child within her . . . he also beat "the Chasee King's Wife who is very ill & another Woman being King Altimahaws Sister." The Yamasee threatened to leave their towns if Nichols were not punished, which led commissioners to issue a warrant for his arrest. But attempts by authorities to try to curb the worst of these abuses were largely ineffective, and the traders lived almost as rulers in their host towns.[40] In an oft-cited complaint the Huspah king reported to Governor Charles Craven: "Mr. Wright said that the white men would come and . . . [fetch] the Yamasees in one night, and that they would hang four of their head men and take all the rest of them for Slaves, and that he would send them all off the Country."[41]

While English traders were abusing and alienating the Yamasee, Governor Francisco de Córcoles y Martínez (1706–16) was gifting delegations of Yamasee in St. Augustine and attempting to win back Spain's former allies. Traders living in Yamasee villages noted the visits of the caciques to St. Augustine and the gifts with which they returned.[42] The same traders also lost some of their own slaves to the Spanish sanctuary of St. Augustine. Indian traders Joshua Bryan and William Bray, like William Dunlop before them, tracked their runaway slaves to St. Augustine, but Spanish officials refused to hand them over.[43]

Black slaves continued to run from Carolina, and it was possible they were treated even more brutally by these traders than were the Yamasee. After an alleged slave conspiracy in 1711, Carolinians enacted a harsh new slave code in 1712 that permitted planters to punish slaves using mutilations like castration and amputation, and also execution. Reverend Francis Le Jau, who was sent to Carolina by the Society for the Propagation of the Gospel in Foreign Parts in 1701, documented the abuse from which slaves ran, horrified at some of the tortures and mutilations he witnessed and protested. He reported that one slave from Martinique launched an abortive rebellion and was executed, while others sought divine protection and remedy. Le Jau noted that some of the slaves could read and that one had reputedly received a book from an angel's hand, had heard voices and seen fires and predicted "there would be a dismal time and the moon would be turned into blood."[44]

On April 14, 1715, that slave prophet's dire prediction seemed to come true. In an effort to resolve long simmering tensions and hostilities with their Yamasee trading partners, Carolina's Indian commissioners sent a delegation to Pocotaligo. Among them were the traders William Bray, who had tracked some of his runaway slaves to St. Augustine earlier in the year; Thomas Nairne, Samuel Warner, and John Cochran; and John Wright, against whom the Yamasee had filed numerous complaints. The Yamasee at Pocotaligo received the traders and even feasted with them the night before, but on Good Friday, they launched a well-coordinated attack against their English oppressors. Painted in red and black stripes (for war and death), the Yamasee and other Indians who joined the war killed ninety English traders over the course of the war, including traders John Wright, John Ruffy, and John Cochran, and they tortured Thomas Nairne for three days, burning lightwood splinters under his skin until he expired.[45]

Upon hearing of the massacre at Pocotaligo, Governor Craven sent Colonel John Barnwell and Captain Robert Mackey by water to retaliate. Within a week Governor Craven and a hastily raised force that included 400 Black slaves battled an estimated 500 Yamasee engaged in a "hot engagement" at Sadketche town. After heavy fighting Sadketche's war captain, Yfallaquisca, and the Yamasee dispersed into the nearby swamps.[46] Soon after, another group of Yamasee attacked a small garrison of about twenty Carolinians, killing all but one. Captain George Chicken pursued this group and killed several. In late July 1715 the Yamasee launched another offensive, proving as Steven Hahn argues that this long war was not over. An estimated five hundred attacked St. Paul's parish, burning some twenty plantations. They also attacked Reverend William Treadwell Bull's parsonage, where they broke the church windows and tore the lining off the pews. These actions by the Yamasee might have been a repudiation of the evangelization efforts of the Society for the Propagation of the Gospel in Foreign Parts, one of their few advocates. But the Yamasee also killed cattle and horses they might have used, which is reminiscent of the millenarian Pueblo Revolt some years earlier, when rebels also sought to erase all evidence of the oppressors.[47] Like Reverend Francis Le Jau, Reverend Bull regarded the Yamasee War as God's punishment for the traders' abuse of the impoverished Yamasee and for the planters' equally horrific abuse of their African slaves.

Recognizing the chance for their own liberation, enslaved Africans living nearby joined in the Yamasee uprising. Unwilling to recognize such agency, Carolinians reported that their slaves had been "taken."[48] Initially it seemed they might succeed in eliminating the English colony. After military reinforcements from Virginia and North Carolina helped turn the tide for the embattled Carolinians, the Yamasees sought refuge among the very Spaniards they had once harried. Yamasee Chiefs Jospo (Huspah) and Yfallaquisca (Perro Bravo) and their African allies fled southward together to Spanish Florida, where they hoped to claim the religious sanctuary others had earlier received. The Reverend Francis Le Jau's letter of October 5, 1715, to the Society for the Propagation of the Gospel in Foreign Parts, reported that the father of the famed Yamasee Prince George, about whom Denise Bossy writes, was by that time safe in St. Augustine.[49]

Apparently not recognizing the irony, the Carolinians complained, "Their refusal to Deliver up these slaves has encouraged a great many more lately to run away to that Place, and what is still more Barbrous in ye Spaniards is, that they Suffer ye Yamasees to keep Divers of our white Women & Children as Slaves amongst them of which we have certain intelligence of captive hence by Hugh Brian, confirmed by ye Master of a New York Sloop, who actually saw none but two Children whom ye Spaniards have Got, in order to make good Christians as they call their Proselytes."[50] Perhaps in retaliation for the repeated enslavement of Yamasee women and children Chief Jospogue had captured Brian, the son of Indian Agent Joshua Bryan, but later released him in an abortive peace effort. The Carolinians reported, "At length his Master, being called the Woospau (Huspah) King, having under his command about Fifteen Men, sent him in to us, to desire a Peace with us."[51]

The Yamasee War once again shifted the indigenous geopolitics of the Southeast, and Spanish documentary sources pick up the Yamasee narrative in Florida. Only a month after the outbreak of the war, and in response to the perceived weakness of the English, Coweta's Chief Brims urged his subjects to switch their allegiance to the Spaniards. He sent a delegation of four chiefs to St. Augustine to relay this offer: Istopoyole, "heathen" cacique of Nicunapa, in the province of Apalachicola; Yfallaquisca, "heathen" war captain of Sadketche, in the same province of Apalachicola; Alonso, Christian mico and governor of Ocute in Tama; and Gabriel, "heathen" son of the Christian Yamasee, Santiago Sule. On May 28, 1715, they met with Governor Francisco de Córcoles y Martínez, the royal accountant Captain Francisco Menéndez Márquez, and the royal treasurer Don Salvador Garzía at the Nuestra Señora de Tolomato mission. Through translator Antonio Perez Campaña of the Guale nation, who was also able to speak Uchise and Yamasee, Yfallaquisca, known in Spanish records as the "heathen" Perro Bravo, related the reasons for Coweta's political realignment.[52]

Through his interpreter Perro Bravo told the Spanish officials that for more than three years the governor of San Jorge (Charles Town) had taken Yamasee children from their parents and shipped them away to be sold as slaves. Perro Bravo cast the Yamasee slaughter of the English traders at Pocotaligo as proactive self-defense, repeating an oft-cited report the Huspah king had made to Charles Craven that white settlers intended to kill their head men, enslave the rest of the Yamasee and send them away from their homes.[53] In an interesting inversion of the story told in English narratives, Perro Bravo also stated that English trader William Bray's indigenous wife had alerted the caciques of Sadketche and Pocotaligo to this danger.[54] Perro Bravo's account supports William L. Ramsey's supposition that Bray's wife was indigenous, and it is possible, even probable, if Bray's wife had relatives living at Pocotaligo, she did not share Cuffy's warning with her husband. Perro Bravo's account did not mention Cuffy, but as Ramsey notes since Cuffy or Kofi is an Akan day name for a man born on Friday, the alleged "Indian Cuffy" may well have been one of the Africans allied with the Yamasee confederacy.[55] William Bray's account from English records stated that because of "his great love for her and her two sisters," a "Yamasee" man warned his wife that the Creeks were going to attack Charles Town, that he would return right before the event, and that "they must goe (sic) immediately to their town," probably either Pocotaligo or Sadketche. Despite this warning, Bray left for St. Augustine "after some of his slaves." For his supposed loyalty in warning of the forthcoming attack, as Ramsey recounts, Carolina's Commons House of Assembly rewarded "the Indian Cuffy with 10 lbs of Carolina currency and a coat."[56]

Continuing his narrative, Perro Bravo told that Spanish officials that fearing for their own lives, the Yamasee decided to kill the English traders and an Englishman who arrived the next day allegedly bearing their execution orders. Perro Bravo did not name that Englishman nor the person able to read the English letters, but the Spanish reported that the Yamasee were "capaces en la idioma ynglesa por la frequencia del trafico" (capable in English for the frequency of their exchanges).[57] As Reverend Le Jau had earlier reported, some enslaved Africans were also able to read English and may have translated this letter for the Yamasee. Perro Bravo stated that the English governor's letter was also said to divulge his plans to lead troops to Pocotaligo, so the Yamasee hid their women and children inland near the Ysabel River, deployed groups of warriors to lie in wait, and were able to rout the English forces. Perro Bravo added that once the war began, Spanish prisoners "and other Blacks and mulattos" as well as some Spanish women held prisoner on English plantations fled to Yamasee towns and subsequently joined their exodus to Spanish Florida.[58] Some of the "Blacks and mulattos" may have been the later founders of Gracia Real de Santa Teresa de Mose in Spanish Florida, but I have found no other reference to Spanish women held prisoner by the Carolinians.[59] This reference to Blacks and mulattos confirms Chief Jospo's testimony some twenty years later, that Africans, like other indigenous groups, had been incorporated into the multicultural Yamasee confederacy prior to their removal to Florida. The reputedly warlike Yamasee must have recognized and respected the military skills of these escaped slaves, as did the Spanish, who formed them into frontier militias. In this manner the Mandinga man who became Francisco Menéndez and led the first free Black town in what is today the United States, Gracia Real de Santa Teresa de Mose, escaped enslavement in Carolina.

Governor Córcoles welcomed his new allies with gifts, firearms, and foodstuffs and also sought and received a significant increase in the annual subsidy for Indian gifts.[60] During their parlay Perro Bravo laid eight chamois cords full of knots before the Spaniards, telling them that each knot denoted a town promising to switch allegiance to the Spaniards (a total of 161 towns) and that towns of fewer than 200 persons were not even represented on the cords. Perro Bravo thus offered the Spaniards approximately 32,000 new indigenous allies, and he asked that the cords be sent to the king of Spain as a missive from Chief Brims.[61]

As was customary when Native delegations visited St. Augustine, Yfallaquisca or Perro Bravo and the others were housed among the city residents, and Perro Bravo and his subjects stayed in the house of Sergeant Juan de Ayala y Escovar. In Perro Bravo's retinue were four African "slaves," who after fighting with the Yamasee for several years surely considered that they had liberated themselves. Perro Bravo gifted Sgt. Ayala with one of his Black slaves as compensation for the food and expenses of his stay, but he stated in subsequent complaints that he expected to be paid for the three others.[62] The African Perro Bravo "gifted" to Ayala may have been the most significant of them, later to be baptized as Francisco Menéndez, and the remaining three may have been Menéndez's later subordinates at Mose, Antonio Eligio de la Puente, Francisco Escovedo, and Pedro Graxales, whose names always appear right after his on Spanish village lists.[63]

Spanish officials settled their new Indian allies in ten villages on the periphery of St. Augustine, generally grouping them by language. A census of 1717 conducted by Joseph Primo de Rivera shows that 430 Yamasee were grouped into three villages: Nuestra Señora de Candelaria de la Tamaja, Pocosapa, and Pocotalaca. Chief Jospogue was assigned to Nuestra Señora de Candelaria de la Tamaja along with other Yamasee caciques, while Perro Bravo, now don Francisco Yfallaquisca, ruled the Yamasee village of Pocotalaca (after Pocotaligo).[64]

All did not go smoothly in this resettlement. In December 1716 Chief Jospogue and other chiefs petitioned for Governor Córcoles, their old patron, who had gifted them and treated them with affection (*cariño*), to be returned to office. The caciques stated that Chief Brims had told them to obey Córcoles and that they did not like either don Pedro de Olivera y Fullana, who served only briefly before dying in 1716, or Juan de Ayala y Escobar, who became interim governor (1716–18). Translating for the recently arrived Chief Jospogue was the Spanish woman María Garzia de Labera (La Vera), who had been captured by unidentified Indians as a little girl and spent more than twelve years living among them. María's captors may have been Yamasee since she translated for Chief Jospogue, but she earned a soldier's *plaza* (salary) serving as interpreter of five or six indigenous languages.[65]

More complaints from the Yamasee followed. In the fall of 1717

Spanish officials held a hearing at the Mission of Nombre de Dios to investigate the ongoing complaints of the Yamasee cacique Perro Bravo. Present were Father Phelipe Osorio Maldonado, caciques Juan Rodríguez de Espinosa, don Joseph de Fuentes, and Francisco Navarro, and St. Augustine's public notary, Juan Solana. Cacique Bernardo de Yspolea, who headed the nearby village of Nuestra Señora de Guadalupe de Tolomato, composed of remnants of the Yamasee, Guale, Chiluque, and Uchise nations, served as translator at this session. Yspolea was said to speak Perro Bravo's language so may have been Yamasee, but he also spoke good Castilian and could sign his name. Don Bernardo reported that he had heard Perro Bravo say many times that he still had not been paid for the African slaves he had brought into Florida years earlier. Perro Bravo had also told him he had asked Governor Pedro de Olivera y Fullana many times for payment, but because the governor was a friend of Ayala's, Ayala was not made to pay. Perro Bravo threatened that if this debt were not satisfied, he would kill the slaves and that he had many other lands in which he could live. Next, Spanish officials also took the testimony of cacique don Joseph de Fuentes at Ayachin, where Perro Bravo had a *bohio* and slept although he was by then cacique of the mission town of Capuaca. Don Joseph swore on the cross and by God to tell the truth and repeated don Bernardo's account, adding that Ayala also owed Perro Bravo for an arroba and a half weight silver bar.[66] Finally, on August 31, 1718, in the presence of Father Osorio, cacique don Joseph de Fuentes, and various soldiers and residents of St. Augustine, the then acting governor of Florida, Juan de Ayala y Escovar, paid Perro Bravo the 600 pesos owed him in corn and liquor.[67]

Among the slaves whom Perro Bravo claimed and for whom the Spanish paid were Francisco Menéndez and his Mandinga wife, who had fled with him from Carolina three years earlier. Spanish slavery was not what either sought, but it would be different than the slavery they had experienced in Carolina. And although their purchase by the governor seems to have made them Crown slaves, Menéndez and his wife must have lived for some time with Ayala since Menéndez's wife took the name Ana Maria de Escovar.[68] Thus the soon to be Spanish governor acquired valuable intermediaries.

Meanwhile, in Carolina an ever growing African population and the fear that slaves might ally with Spaniards in Florida led planters to obsess about slave rebellion. Carolinians discovered alleged slave plots in 1711 and 1714, leading the Colonial Assembly in that year to establish a new Act for Governing Negroes that read: "the number of negroes do extremely increase in the Province, and through the afflicting providence of God, the white persons do not proportionately multiply, by reason whereof, the safety of the said Province is greatly endangered." The new act placed duties on all slaves imported from Africa "twelve years and upward."[69] Despite their efforts at control, in 1720 the townspeople of Charles Town uncovered a major slave conspiracy in which at least some of the participants "thought to gett to Augustine." Fourteen got as far as Savannah before being captured and executed.[70] In 1724 ten more runaways reached St. Augustine, assisted again by English-speaking Yamasee Indians, and they stated they knew that the Spanish king had offered freedom for those seeking conversion and baptism.[71]

Following the precedent first set in 1687, in 1725 Florida's new governor, Antonio de Benavides (1718–34), offered to purchase the runaways for two hundred pesos apiece, and he sent Don Francisco Menéndez Márquez and Captain Joseph Primo de Rivera to Charles Town to negotiate with their owners, who angrily rejected the offer as insufficient.[72] Although Governor Benavides wrote to his superiors to determine if sanctuary was still in force, since the runaways had appeared during a time of truce between Spain and England, as often happened, he received no reply, and after the English threatened to reclaim their lost slaves by force, Benavides sold the unlucky fugitives at public auction to the leading creditors of the St. Augustine treasury. In this way don Francisco Menéndez Márquez acquired the Mandinga namesake for whom he served as godfather during Catholic baptism.[73]

Don Francisco Menéndez Márquez was sent on repeated diplomatic and military missions to Carolina, and it seems likely he would have taken with him the slave who had fought his way through that terrain and who also knew so well the Yamasee and English geopolitics. In 1725 he was sent to Charleston to demand the destruction of Fort King George, and the following year Governor Benavides named don Francisco Menéndez's slave and namesake the captain of St. Augustine's Black militia. Thereafter the Mandinga Captain Francisco Menéndez led important military engagements against the English from whom he had fled, each of which would have enhanced his status in the Spanish community.[74]

In 1728 the Spanish governor named Menéndez the captain of the slave militia, and the same year planters near Stono "had fourteen Slaves Runaway to St. Augustine." Governor Arthur Middleton of Carolina complained to London that the Spaniards not only harbored their runaways but had "found a New way of sending our own slaves against us, to Rob and Plunder us."[75] Yamasees from St. Augustine joined the former slaves in these operations, and Middleton reported that "Six of our Runaway slaves and the rest Indians" in two canoes attacked near Pon Pon in the fall of 1727 and carried away white captives. A second account of that raid added that "Ten Negroes and fourteen Indians Commanded by those of their own Colour, without any Spaniards in company with them" had been responsible and that they had also taken one Black man and a mulatto boy back to St. Augustine. That year Florida's multiracial raiders hit again at a plantation on the Edisto River, carrying away seven more slaves.[76] In fact, Governor Antonio de Benavides had offered thirty pieces of eight for every English scalp and one hundred pieces "for every live Negro" the multiracial raiders brought back to St. Augustine.[77]

The repeated raids from Florida triggered an English response, and in 1728 Colonel John Palmer led a retaliatory attack against St. Augustine. By this time the Yamasee village of Pocotalaca had moved from a location at Ayamón, six leagues south of St. Augustine, to "the distance of a rifle-shot," and people were living in their *bohios* only during the day and sleeping within the Castillo at night. Palmer's forces, which included approximately two hundred Indians of unstated nation, set fire to the mission village of Nombre de Dios and "did some nasty damage to the statues" of the village church.[78] On that occasion the Black militia led by Captain Francisco Menéndez proved one of the city's most effective defense forces. By this time Governor Antonio de Benavides was so convinced of the Black militia's ability that in 1733 he proposed sending the runaways north to foment rebellion in

Carolina and, once again, planned to pay them for English scalps, but the Council of the Indies rejected this design.[79] The Spanish Crown commended the enslaved forces for their bravery in the 1728 invasion and in 1733 also issued a new decree reiterating its offer of freedom to runaways from Carolina.[80]

Despite his repeated military service Captain Francisco Menéndez, however, was still a slave and so he persisted in his efforts to achieve the freedom repeatedly promised by the Spanish king. On behalf of his community, he presented several petitions to the governor and to the auxiliary bishop of Cuba, who toured Florida in 1735, but uncertain of the legalities, these officials wrote to Spain seeking guidance, as had Governor Benavides, and Menéndez and his community remained enslaved.[81]

The Africans' fortunes changed in 1737 with the arrival of the new governor, Manuel de Montiano, and the advent of renewed hostilities with the English. Once more Captain Francisco Menéndez solicited freedom for himself and others in a petition that listed thirty-one individuals unjustly enslaved, including some who had been taken to Havana, and the names of the persons who claimed ownership over them. This time Menéndez's petition was supported by another from an indigenous ally, the Yamasee chief Jospo. Jospo claimed to be the chief who had led the Yamasee uprising against the British in 1715 and stated that he and the other Yamasee chiefs "commonly" made "treaties" with the slaves. The use of the terms *allies* and *treaties* implies Yamasee recognition of the slaves' autonomy and utility. Jospo confirmed that Menéndez and three other Africans (probably those who at baptism became Antonio Eligio de la Puente, Francisco Escovedo, and Pedro Graxales) had fought bravely with him until they were ultimately defeated and headed to St. Augustine, hoping to receive the Christian sanctuary promised by Spain. Jospo also testified that in St. Augustine Perro Bravo had betrayed the Africans by selling them into slavery, but Jospo excused Perro Bravo, saying that as a "heathen" he knew no better. Instead, Jospo blamed the Spaniards who bought the unlucky Blacks, who in his estimation had been patient and "more than loyal."[82]

Governor Montiano was expecting war with England at any moment, and the combined petitions and stated alliance of Africans and Yamasees must no doubt have made an impression on a governor in need of their services. He wisely chose to investigate. After reviewing all relevant documentation on the issue, on March 15, 1738, Governor Montiano granted unconditional freedom to all fugitives from Carolina. The powerful men, like the royal accountant don Francisco Menéndez who had received the slaves in payment for loans to the cash-strapped government, vehemently protested their emancipation, but Governor Montiano ruled that the men had ignored the royal determination expressed in repeated decrees, and therefore all deals were null and void and all the enslaved were free.[83] After reviewing Governor Montiano's actions, the Crown approved and ordered that not only all the Blacks who had come from Carolina to date "but all those who in the future come as fugitives from the English colonies" should be given prompt and full liberty in the name of the king. Further, so that there be no further pretext for selling them, the royal edict should be publicly posted so that no one could claim ignorance of the ruling.[84]

Following the preexisting model for Indian towns, Governor Montiano assigned the newly emancipated Spanish subjects lands two miles north of St. Augustine and recognized the Mandinga Captain Francisco Menéndez as leader of the new free Black town of Gracia Real de Santa Teresa de Mose. Further, in his official correspondence the governor described the almost one hundred residents of the new town, composed of nations as diverse as Mandinga, Carabalí, and Congo, as Menéndez's "subjects."[85] Menéndez was, in effect, the cacique, or natural lord, of Mose. His newly freed subjects promised to be "the most cruel enemies of the English" and to spill their "last drop of blood in defense of the Great Crown of Spain and the Holy Faith," and Captain Francisco Menéndez headed the new Mose militia that would carry through on that vow.[86]

The War of Jenkins' Ear (or the Guerra del Asiento) broke out in 1739, raged through 1742, and only concluded in 1748. Throughout this era of conflict African and Indian militias proved crucial assets to the defense of the Spanish colony. Together they patrolled the frontier, gathering information on the encroachments of hostile English and Indian attackers, rounding up cattle and horses, and herding them to the safety of Anastasia Island. Governor Montiano offered them rewards of twenty-five pesos for every Indian or English person captured. On some of the larger expeditions don Pedro Lamberto Horruitiner commanded twenty-five Spanish cavalry, an equal number of Spanish infantry, thirty Indians, and "free Blacks of the fugitives from the English colonies." On others, don Romulado Ruiz del Moral commanded twenty-five Spanish cavalrymen, twenty-five Indians, and twenty-five free backs. But the Indian and Black militias also operated independently, and among the most active Indian leaders were the Caciques Chislala, Juan Savina, Geronimo, and Juan Ygnacio de los Reyes, of Nuestra Señora de la Concepción de Pocotalaca, about which Amanda Hall writes in her essay in this volume.[87]

Reyes offers an example of the cultural exchanges taking place in Spanish Florida in these years. After his return from a successful mission to assess Charleston's defenses, Governor Montiano ordered Reyes to Havana to report to the captain general, but "Juan Ygnacio having declared to me that he had made a certain promise or vow, in case of happy issue, to Nuestra Señora de la Caridad de Cobre, I was unwilling to put him aboard with violence, and I let him go at his own free will to present himself to Your Excellency." La Caridad de Cobre was and still is the Black patron saint of Cuba, whose miraculous discovery was attributed to two Cuban Indians and an African who were fishing together, and was also the syncretic symbol for Ochun, the Yoruba goddess of fertility. That Reyes prayed to her on such an important issue offers tangible proof of the cultural assimilation between Africans and Yamasees on the Florida frontier.[88]

Over the next two decades, Africans and Indians reinforced their military, political, and sociocultural ties, some of which had origins stretching back to Carolina. They also formed families together. In 1745 Francisco Buenaventura y Texada, the bishop of Tricale, reviewed St. Augustine's ecclesiastical records from 1640 to 1707 for examples of racial intermarriage, both between Spaniards and Indians and between Indians and Africans. Father Pedro Lorenzo de Asevedo's notations show that Catholic marriages between men of African descent and indigenous women become more frequent after 1670. In 1690 Francisco Joseph, the drummer and Black slave of Captain Antonio de Argüelles, married Micaela, a Native of Mayaca. The following year another of Argüelles's slaves, Pedro Aponte, married María Lucia, a Native of Santa Catalina in Guale, and in 1702 Juan de los Santos, the slave of Ayudante Geronimo Rexidor, married Marta Maria, described as an "yndia ladina y natural de Guale." The priest reported many other examples, concluding approvingly that by "marrying Spaniards, Blacks or mulattos, slowly their children will stop being Indians" and more easily enter into the "true knowledge of the mysteries of our Catholic faith."[89]

As newly introduced Africans or *bozales* escaped from Carolina or Georgia to claim religious sanctuary in Florida in the 1750s, Spanish officials considered them "new Christians" in need of evangelization, as Indians continued to be. In 1752 Governor Fulgencio García de Solís reestablished the free Black town of Gracia Real de Santa Teresa de Mose, near its original location, and Father Andres de Vilches, formerly assigned to the Yamasee village of Pocotalaca, now worked to evangelize these newcomers.[90]

Although Florida continued to attract runaway slaves from Carolina, its Indian populations continued to dwindle in the final years of Spanish dominion. Spanish censuses of 1752, 1759, and 1763 record this decline and the resulting amalgamation of Indian towns. To illustrate, by 1759 the Yamasee cacique Juan Sánchez, who in 1752 had headed the Yamasee village of Pocotalaca, had been relocated with his subjects to Nuestra Señora de la Leche, there joining cacique Antonio Matichaiche, who in 1752 had lived at La Punta serving as captain of Florida's Indian troops. And Miguel de los Santos, who in 1752 lived at Palica, by 1759 lived at Tolomato.[91]

When the English enemy finally acquired Florida by the Treaty of Paris in 1763, Spain relocated all its subjects, including its diverse Indian and African allies, to Cuba at royal expense. Captain Francisco Menéndez and the Black villagers of Mose received new lands to settle on the Matanzas frontier, at San Agustín de la Nueva Florida. Florida's amalgamated Indians were instead settled at Guanabacoa, a former Indian reserve across the bay from Havana. Sadly, Spanish census lists show that many of the Yamasee did not survive this final relocation, and their deaths are recorded in Spanish parish and treasury records in Cuba.[92]

Notes

1. Important accounts of the Yamasee and the 1715 War from which I draw include among others Steven J. Oatis, *A Colonial Complex: South Carolina's Frontiers in the Era of the Yamasee War, 1680–1730* (Lincoln: University of Nebraska Press, 2004; William L. Ramsey, *The Yamasee War: A Study of Culture, Economy, and Conflict in the Colonial South* (Lincoln: University of Nebraska Press, 2008); Verner W. Crane, *The Southern Frontier, 1670–1732* (New York: Norton, 1981), ch. 8.

2. Jane Landers, *Black Society in Spanish Florida* (Urbana: University of Illinois Press, 1999), ch. 2. English records use variants of Huspaw, Huspah, and Jospogue for the Yamasee village and its chief, or "king" as they sometimes called village chiefs, but as Susan Parker does in this volume, I use Jospo.

3. John E. Worth, "Yamassee Origins and the Development of the Carolina-Florida Frontier," paper delivered at the Omohundro Conference, Austin, Texas, 1999.

4. Steven C. Hahn, "The Mother of Necessity: Carolina, the Creeks, and the Making of a New Order in the Southeast, 1670–1763," in *The Transformation of the Southeastern Indians, 1540–1760*, ed. Robbie Ethridge and Charles Hudson (Jackson: University Press of Mississippi, 2002); Oatis, *A Colonial Complex*; Ramsey, *The Yamasee War*; Alan Gallay, *The Indian Slave Trade: The Rise of the English Empire in the American South, 1670–1717* (New Haven: Yale University Press, 2002).

5. John E. Worth, *The Struggle for the Georgia Coast: An Eighteenth-Century Spanish Retrospective on Guale and Mocama*, Anthropological Papers of the American Museum of Natural History, no. 75 (Athens GA: University of Georgia Press, 1995), 23, 181.

6. Herbert E. Bolton and Mary Ross, *The Debatable Land: A Sketch of the Anglo-Spanish Contest for the Georgia Country*, repr. (New York: Russell and Russell, 1968). See also Crane, *The Southern Frontier*, 6–10, and John J. TePaske, *The Governorship of Spanish Florida, 1700–1763* (Durham NC: Duke University Press, 1964).

7. Landers, *Black Society*, ch. 1.

8. Elizabeth Donnan, *Documents Illustrative of the Slave Trade to America* (Washington DC: Carnegie Institution of Washington, 1931), vol. 4, 242.

9. Peter H. Wood, *Black Majority: Negroes in Colonial South Carolina form 1670 through the Stono Rebellion* (New York: W. W. Norton, 1974), 95–130.

10. Roster of Black and Mulatto Militia for St. Augustine, September 20, 1683, Archivo General de Indias, Santo Domingo (hereafter cited as AGI SD), 226, legajo 157A, John B. Stetson Collection, microfilm, P. K. Yonge Library of Florida History, University of Florida, Gainesville hereafter cited as SC, PKY). On the history of Black military service in Florida and the Spanish circum-Caribbean see Luis Arana, "Military Manpower in Florida, 1670–1703," *El Escribano* 8, no. 2 (1971): 40–63; Jane Landers, "Transforming Bondsmen into Vassals: Arming the Slaves in Colonial Spanish America," *Arming Slaves in World History*, ed. Philip Morgan and Christopher Brown (New Haven: Yale University Press, 2006), 120–45; and Paul Lokken, "Useful Enemies: Seventeenth-Century Piracy and the Rise of Pardo Militias in Spanish Central America," *Journal of Colonialism and Colonial History* 5, no. 2 (2004).

11. Indian trader Caleb Westbrooke reported in more detail the following month that more than one thousand Yamasee accompanied by "3 nations of the Spanish Indians that are Christians, Sapella, Soho, and Sapicbay" had also moved into Carolina's orbit. W. Noel Sainsbury, *Records in the British Public Record Office Relating to South Carolina*, Sainsbury transcripts, 36 vols. (Columbia: Historical Commission of South Carolina, 1928–47), 2: 8–9 (hereafter cited as BPRO-SC).

12. David Hurst Thomas, "The Archaeology of Mission Santa Catalina de Guale: Our First 15 Years," *The Spanish Missions of Florida*, ed. Bonnie G. McEwan (Gainesville: University Press

Yamasee-African Ties in Carolina and Florida   185

of Florida, 1993), 1–34; John H. Hann, *Summary Guide to Spanish Florida Missions and Visitas, Americas* 46, no. 4 [1990]: 417–13 (repr., Oceanside CA: Academy of American Franciscan History, 1990), 471–72.

13. William Green, Chester B. DePratter, and Bobby Southerlin, "The Yamasee in South Carolina: Native American Adaptation and Interaction along the Carolina Frontier," in *Another's Country: Archaeological and Historical Perspectives on Cultural Interactions in the Southern Colonies*, ed. J. W. Joseph and Martha Zierden (Tuscaloosa: University of Alabama Press,), 11–29; Rebecca Saunders, "Architecture of the Missions of Santa María and Santa Catalina de Amelia," in McEwan, ed., *Spanish Missions of Florida*, 35–61; Hann, *Summary Guide to Spanish Florida Missions*, 1990, 472.

14. John Worth has gathered, translated, and published the most pertinent documents for this Spanish attack on Carolina. Worth, *Struggle for the Georgia Coast*, 146–71.

15. Morton's "stolen" slaves included Peter, Scipio, Doctor, Cushi, Arro, Emo, Caesar, and Sambo. The women were Frank, Bess, and Mammy. "William Dunlop's Mission to St. Augustine in 1688," *South Carolina Historical and Genealogical Magazine* 43 (January 1933): 1–30. For unknown reasons, two of the thirteen captured slaves escaped the Spaniards and returned to their English masters. Landers, *Black Society*; Crane, *Southern Frontier*, 31–33; Wood, *Black Majority*, 50; Worth, *Struggle for the Georgia Coast*, 146–71; Edward Randolph to the Board of Trade, March 16, 1699, BPRO-SC, 2: 88–95.

16. Helen Hornbeck Tanner, "The Land and Water Communications Systems of the Southeastern Indians," in *Powhatan's Mantle: Indians in the Colonial Southeast*, ed. Peter H. Wood, Gregory A. Waselkov, and M. Thomas Hatley (Lincoln: University of Nebraska Press, 1989), 6–20; Larry E. Ivers, "Scouting the Inland Passage, 1685–1737," *South Carolina Historical Magazine* 73, no. 3 (July 1972): 117–29.

17. Interrogation of the Black corsair, Diego, by Governor Don Juan Márques Cabrera, St. Augustine, Florida, 1686, in the John Tate Lanning papers, Thomas Jefferson library, University of Missouri, St. Louis, 13–18. I am indebted to John H. Hann, of the San Luis Archaeological and Historical Site in Tallahassee, Florida, for this reference and his generosity. Royal Officials of Florida to the crown, St. Augustine, September 30, 1685, cited in Luis Arana, "Grammont's Landing at Little Matanzas Inlet, 1686," *El Escribano* 9, no. 3 (1972): 107–12.

18. Case of the *Turtle*, 1697, Elizabeth Donnan, *Documents Illustrative of the History of the Slave Trade to America* (Washington DC: Carnegie Institution, 1931), vol. 4, 245, 135.

19. Donnan, *Documents*, 4: 242–43.

20. Cited in Donnan, *Documents*, 4: 243; Edward Randolph reports to Board of Trade, 1699, *Calendar of State Papers*, 104. I am indebted to both Denise Bossy and Steven Hann for copies of the South Carolina Shipping Records, CO5/508, Public Record Office, London, that document additional Black slaves imported to Charles Town from the Caribbean and from Africa in the years following the Yamasee War.

21. Calendar of State Papers, Colonial, 1699, cited in Donnan, *Documents*, 4: 104, 243, 249; Frank J. Klingberg, *An Appraisal of the Negro in Colonial South Carolina* (Washington DC: Associated Publishers, 1941), 13–19, 24–25.

22. Census reports for Carolina indicate a significant increase in slave imports between 1709 and 1711. By 1713 St. John's parish planter William Cantey Jr. and a crew of thirteen slaves produced two hundred barrels of pitch per year. Wood, *Black Majority*, 108–10.

23. Wood, *Black Majority*, ch. 4. Steven C. Hann in this volume describes a Yamasee Indian attack on William Stead's cowpen near the Edisto River in 1717 that resulted in Stead's death.

24. The men were named Conano, Jessie, Jacque, Gran Domingo, Cambo, Mingo, Dicque, and Robi. Dunlop did not name the women. Samuel Bordieu claimed Mingo, his wife, and daugh-

ter; John Bird claimed two of the men; Joab Howe claimed another; John Berresford claimed one woman; Christopher Smith claimed one man, and Robert Cuthbert claimed three other men. "William Dunlop's Mission," 1–30.

25. On June 13, 1710, the Reverend Francis le Jau reported, "There are 3 or 4 Portuguese slaves in this parish very desirous to receive the communion among us." Later he specified that the Portuguese-speaking slaves were from Madeira. Klingberg, *An Appraisal of the Negro*, 13–19.

26. Among the acts of charity that a good Catholic was urged to perform were to offer protection to the miserable and to shelter fugitives. Maureen Flynn, "Charitable Ritual in Late Medieval and Early Modern Spain," *Sixteenth-Century Journal* 16 (Fall 1995): 1–30; on Catholicism in Kongo see Linda M. Heywood and John K. Thornton, *Central Africans, Atlantic Creoles, and the Making of the Foundations of the Americas, 1585–1660* (New York: Cambridge University Press, 2007).

27. The governor assigned the men to work as ironsmiths and laborers on the new stone fort, the Castillo de San Marcos, and the women became domestics in the governor's own household. He claimed to have paid all of them wages; the men earning a peso a day, the wage paid to male Indian laborers, and the women earning half as much. Royal officials to Charles II, March 3, 1699, cited in Irene Wright, "Dispatches of Spanish Officials Bearing on the Free Negro Settlement of Gracia Real de Santa Teresa de Mose," *Journal of Negro History* 9 (1924): 151–52. In April 1687 Captain Dunlop had tried to convince the Altamaha king to attack the Spanish at Amelia, but Altamahaw refused, saying the Spanish had never killed his people. Green, DePratter, and Southerlin, "The Yamasee in South Carolina."

28. Royal decree, November 7, 1693, AGI SD 58-1-26, SC, PKY. Despite the royal decree of 1693, in 1697 Governor Laureano de Torres y Ayala returned six newly arrived Blacks and an Indian "to avoid conflicts and ruptures between the two governments." Joseph de Zúñiga to Charles II, October 10, 1699, AGI SD 844 on microfilm reel 15, PKY.

29. TePaske, *Governorship;* and John H. Hann, *A History of the Timucuan Indians and Missions*, Florida Museum of Natural History, Ripley P. Bullen Series (Gainesville: University Press of Florida, 1996).

30. Green, DePratter, and Southerlin, "The Yamasee in South Carolina."

31. TePaske, *Governorship*, 197.

32. The inability of the Spaniards to protect even the Nombre de Dios mission outside their very walls led many of their once loyal Indian allies to defect to the English. Charles W. Arnade, *The Siege of St. Augustine in 1702* (University of Florida Monographs, Social Sciences, no. 3, Summer 1959), 35; TePaske, *Governorship of Spanish Florida*, 110–16, 130–32, 196–97.

33. Kenneth R. Jones, "A 'Full and Particular Account' of the Assault on Charleston in 1706," *South Carolina Historical Magazine* 83, no. 1 (January 1982): 1–11; TePaske, *Governorship*, 116–22; Hahn, *Invention of the Creek Nation*, 460. "Mustee" was a term used for persons of mixed African and Indian heritage. William L. Ramsey, "A Coat for Indian Cuffy: Mapping the Boundary Between Freedom and Slavery in Colonial South Carolina," in Rosemary Brana Shute and Randy J. Sparks, *Paths to Freedom: Manumission in the Atlantic World* (Columbia: University of South Carolina Press, 2009).

34. Governor and Council to Proprietors, Board of Trade, September 17, 1708, in *The Colonial South Carolina Scene: Contemporary Views, 1697–1774,* ed. H. Roy Merrens (Columbia: University of South Carolina Press, 1977), 32.

35. Governor Edwards reported only 1,100 families (presumably white) in the province in 1709. Calendar of State Papers, 1708–1709, cited in Donnan, *Documents*, 255, 259, 444–54. A colonial census of 1719 reported the same Black:white ratio with a colonial population of "9580 souls including 1360 freemen, 900 free women, sixty white servant men, sixty white servant women,

1700 slaves, 500 Indian men slaves, 600 Indian women slaves, 1200 negro children slaves and 300 Indian children slaves." The report added that "negro men slaves [are increased in the last five years] by importation 300, negro women slaves 200 and negro children 600." Edward McCrady, *The History of South Carolina under the Proprietary Government, 1670–1719* (New York: Macmillan, 1897). McCrady cited what seem to be low slave import figures of 24 in 1706, 22 in 1707, 53 in 1708, 131 in 1709, 170 in 1710, 419 in 1711, and 81 in 1712. http://www.slavevoyages.org/tast/database/search.faces.

36. Governor and Council to Proprietors, Board of Trade, September 17, 1708, 32.

37. *Journals of the Commissioners of the Indian Trade: Sept. 20, 1710–August 29, 1718*, ser. 2, The Indian Books, vol. 1 ed. W.L. McDowell Jr. (Columbia: South Carolina Archives Department, 1955), 11; hereafter cited as JCIT.

38. Chapman J. Milling, *Red Carolinians* (Chapel Hill: University of North Carolina Press, 1940), 137.

39. On April 17, 1712, John Cochran and William Bray reported to the Commissioners of the Indian Trade that Samuel Hilden had intercepted and bought slaves from the Yamasee Indians before they got to their towns, in JCIT 1: 23.

40. Milling, *Red Carolinians*, 137; Hewatt on Carroll, *Historical Collections*, Alexander Hewatt, *An Historical Account of the Rise and Progress of the Colonies of South Carolina and Georgia*, 2 vols. (London, 1779), 1: 192–94.

41. Huspah King to Charles Craven, 1715, quoted in William L. Ramsey, "'Something Cloudy in Their Looks': The Origins of the Yamasee War Reconsidered," *Journal of American History* 90, no. 1 (June 2003): 44–75, and *The Yamasee War*, 228; Denise I. Bossy, "Godin & Co.: Charleston Merchants and the Indian Trade, 1674–1715," *South Carolina Historical Magazine* 114, no. 2 (April 2013): 96–131.

42. TePaske, *The Governorship of Spanish Florida*, 197–204; Hewatt, *An Historical Account*, 1: 215.

43. Ramsey, "A Coat for Indian Cuffy"; Ramsey, "'Something Cloudy in Their Looks'"; Ramsay, *Yamasee War*.

44. Klingberg, *An Appraisal of the Negro*, 16–19.

45. George Rodd, "Relation," BPRO-SC, 6: 74; Milling, *Red Carolinians*, 141–42. Also see Ramsey, "'Something Cloudy in their Looks,'" and "A Coat for Indian Cuffy."

46. On the body of one of the enemy dead, a man named Smith, who may have been of mixed race, Carolinians found a letter warning Governor Craven to leave the country and boasting that all the nations on the continent were united to take it. Charles Rodd to his employer in London, May 8, 1715, Calendar of State Papers, 1714–1715, 28: 166–68.

47. Society for the Propagation of the Gospel in Foreign Parts, Series, vol. 4, 23, cited in Edgar Legaré Pennington, "The South Carolina Indian War of 1715, as Seen by the Clergymen," *South Carolina Historical and Genealogical Magazine* 32, no. 4 (October 1931): 251–69. On millenarian aspects of the Pueblo Revolt see David J. Weber, ed., *What Caused the Pueblo Revolt of 1680?* (Boston: Bedford–St. Martin's, 1999).

48. Landers, *Black Society*, ch. 1.

49. A report by Commissary Johnston, however, reported that George's father and family were "taken and sold as slaves." Pennington, "The South Carolina Indian War."

50. BPRO-SC, 6: 236–37, cited in Milling, *Red Carolinians*, 153.

51. BPRO-SC, 6: 239, cited Milling, *Red Carolinians*, 153.

52. Testimony of the four caciques, May 28, 1715, and subsequent report by Governor Francisco de Córcoles y Martínez to the king, January 25, 1716, AGI SD 843 (SC 58-1-30), PKY. In Spanish records Sadketche (Salkahatchie) is also spelled Satiquicha, Salquicha, or Salaquiliche.

53. Testimony of the four caciques, May 28, 1715; Huspah King to Charles Craven, 1715, quoted in Ramsey, "'Something Cloudy in Their Looks,'" and *The Yamasee War*, 228; Bossy, "Godin & Co."

54. Testimony of the four caciques, May 28, 1715.

55. John C. Inscoe, "Carolina Slave Names: An Index to Acculturation," *Journal of Southern History* 49, no. 4 (November, 1983): 527–54.

56. George Rodd, "Relation"; Ramsey, "'Something Cloudy in their Looks,'" and "A Coat for Indian Cuffy."

57. Testimony of the four caciques, May 28, 1715.

58. Testimony of the four caciques, May 28, 1715.

59. Testimony of the four caciques, May 28, 1715.

60. To secure the allegiance of their new subjects, the Spanish government almost tripled the Indian gift allotment from 2,063 pesos to 6,000 pesos annually. TePaske, *Governorship*, 198.

61. TePaske, *Governorship*, 198; Mark F. Boyd, "Diego Peña's Expedition to Apalachee and Apalachicola in 1716," *Florida Historical Quarterly* 28 (July 1949): 1–27; John H. Hann, "St. Augustine's Fallout from the Yamasee War," *Florida Historical Quarterly* 68 (October 1989): 180–200; Alejandra Dubkovsky, "One Hundred Sixty-One Knots, Two Plates and One Emperor: Creek Information Networks in the Era of the Yamasee War," *Ethnohistory* 59, no. 3 (Summer 2012): 489–513.

62. Governor Francisco de Córcoles y Martínez to the king, January 25, 1716, AGI SD 843 (SC 58-1-30), PKY.

63. See Census of Father Ginés Sánchez, February 11, 1759, AGI SD 2604, and Landers, *Black Society*, Appendix 5.

64. The variants of this name in English and Spanish records include Yaquisca and La Quisca. John H. Hann, "St. Augustine's Fallout"; April 1717 Census of Captain Joseph Primo de Rivera, included in Governor Juan de Ayala y Escobar to the King, April 18, 1717, AGI SD 843, SC, PKY. In the 1718 hearing regarding his African slaves, Perro Bravo is described as the cacique of the Yamasee Pueblo de Capuaca. Susan R. Parker has described the frequent relocations of these Indian villages and also of their inhabitants. She theorizes that Chief Francisco Jospogue was born on or near St. Catherines. In 1702 he was chief of Nombre de Dios Chiquito. His loyalty to Spain and Christianity cost him dearly when the English attacked and enslaved his family in 1715. He was then assigned to "shepherd" the Yamasee refugees at Nuestra Señora de Candelaria. Don Francisco Yospogue, Cacique del Pueblo de el Nombre de Dios Chiquito, October 18, 1728, AGI SD 2584; Susan R. Parker, "The Second Century of Settlement in Spanish St. Augustine, 1670–1763," PhD diss., University of Florida, 1999, ch. 3.

65. Testimony of Cacique Jospo de los Yamasees, December 12, 1716, included in Governor Juan de Ayala y Escobar to the King, January 18, 1717, AGI SD 843, SC, PKY.

66. Governor Antonio de Benavides to the King, August 25, 1718, Buckingham Smith Papers, Reel 1, frames 747–66, PKY. I am indebted to James Cusick for a copy of this material. Franciscan census and copy by Gelabert, January 10, 1752, Havana, AGI SD 2604.

67. Franciscan census and copy by Gelabert, January 10, 1752. Domingo, of the Chachis nation, also held a Black woman in slavery for whom he demanded 200 pesos.

68. Crown slaves in Cuba were primarily single males assigned to public works who lived in communal barracks. Evelyn Powell Jennings, "War as the 'Forcing House of Change': State Slavery in Late-Eighteenth-Century Cuba," *William and Mary Quarterly*, 3rd ser., vol. 62, no. 3, The Atlantic Economy in an Era of Revolutions (July 2005): 411–40. This couple, however, were always listed together, and the Spanish seem to have recognized their union. They later lived together in Cuba. List of individuals from the presidio of St. Augustine housed in Regla in the house of Don Gonzalo de Oquendo; AGI, Cuba 1076, f. 395.

69. Donnan, *Documents*, 257.

70. The following year Carolina enacted a new and harsher slave code. Wood, *Black Majority*, 298–99, 304.

71. Memorial of the fugitives, 1724, AGI SD 844, on microfilm reel 15, PKY.

72. For the exchange on this mission see the letters of Governors Arthur Middleton (Carolina) and Antonio de Benavides (Florida) in *Documentos históricos de la Florida y la Luisiana, Siglos XVI al XVII* (Madrid, 1912), 252–60.

73. The governor gave the proceeds to the envoy from Carolina who would have preferred to reclaim the former slaves. Other buyers included several military officers and even some religious officials. Governor Antonio de Benavides to Philip V, November 11, 1725, cited in *Documentos históricos*, 164–66. Carolinians charged that the Spanish governor "Makes Merchandize of all our slaves, and ships them off to Havanah for his own Profit," and they were at least partially correct. Accord, June 27, 1730, AGI SD 844, on microfilm reel 15, PKY; Wood, *Black Majority*, 305. Some of the slaves sold at the 1729 auction were taken to Havana by their new owners. Nine years later Governor Manuel de Montiano would try to retrieve them. Decree of Manuel de Montiano, March 3, 1738, AGI SD 844, on microfilm reel 15, PKY.

74. Francisco Menéndez to the king, January 1, 1740, AGI SD 2658.

75. June 13, 1728, BPRO-SC, 12: 61–67, cited in Wood, *Black Majority*, 305.

76. Four slaves who fled or were taken from a plantation near Port Royal in 1726 were later spotted in St. Augustine. Governor Arthur Middleton, June 13, 1728, BPRO-SC, 13: 61–67, and John Pearson, October 20, 1727, BPRO-SC, 19: 127–28, cited in Wood, *Black Majority*, 305.

77. Wood, *Black Majority*, 305.

78. Fray Joseph de Bullones to the King, October 5, 1728, AGI SD 865 (58-2-16/8), SC, PKY.

79. Governor Antonio de Benavides to King Philip V, April 27, 1733, AGI SD 833.

80. The crown actually issued two separate edicts in 1733. The first, on October 4, 1733, forbade any future compensation to the British, reiterated the royal offer of freedom, and specifically prohibited the sale of fugitives to private citizens, no doubt in response to the auction of 1729. The second, on October 29, 1733, commended the Blacks for their bravery against the British in the invasion of 1728 but also stipulated that the enslaved would be required to complete four years of royal service as an indenture prior to being freed. Royal decree, October 4, 1733, AGI SD 843 (58-1-24), SC, PKY; Royal decree, October 29, 1733, AGI SD 843 (58-1-24), SC, PKY.

81. Report of the Visita of Bishop Francisco de San Buenaventura, April 29, 1736, AGI SD 5543, PKY; TePaske, *Governorship*, 167–69. Memorial of the Fugitives, included in Governor Manuel de Montiano to King Philip V, March 3, 1738, AGI SD 844, on microfilm reel 15, PKY.

82. Memorial of Chief Jospo, included in Governor Manuel de Montiano to Philip V, March 3, 1738, AGI SD 844, on microfilm reel 15, PKY. In earlier works I misread this very blackened microfilm to read Jorge. Jospo is also spelled Jospe and Jospogue in other Spanish documents. Since Chief Francisco Jospo, about whom Susan R. Parker writes, was already deceased by 1737, this is a different Chief Jospo. It is still possible, however, that this Jospo was father of the Yamasee youth educated in England to be a native missionary for the Society for the Gospel in Foreign Parts who returned to Carolina with Commissary Gideon Johnston in 1715 in the midst of the Yamasee War. The young Prince George returned and later wrote, "I have had noos that my Father as gone in Santaugustena and all my Friends." A later account reporting that the father had been killed proved untrue, and another report that he had been captured, returned to Charles Town and then sold with the rest of his family as slaves was unconfirmed. There are no further reports about the young Prince George after Commissary Johnston's death in 1716. Frank J. Klingberg, "The Mystery of the Lost Yamasee Prince," *South Carolina Historical*

and Genealogical Magazine 63 (1962): 18–32. Also see Denise I. Bossy, "Spiritual Diplomacy, the Yamasees and the Society for the Propagation of the Gospel: Reinterpreting Prince George's Eighteenth-Century Voyage to England," *Early American Studies: An Interdisciplinary Journal* 12, no. 2 (2014): 336–401.

83. Petition of Diego Espinosa and reply by Governor Manuel de Montiano, May 5, 1738, AGI SD 845, on microfilm reel 16, PKY. Diego de Espinosa was a successful mulatto cattle rancher whose fortified ranch twenty miles north of St. Augustine on the Diego Plains served as an important outpost guarding the Spanish city.

84. King Philip V to Governor Manuel de Montiano, July 15, 1741, AGI 58–1–25, SC 5943, PKY.

85. Scholars hotly debate the origins and meaning of these African ethnonyms. I have used them throughout as they appear in Spanish documents. See for example, Paul E. Lovejoy, "Identifying Enslaved Africans in the African Diaspora," in Paul E. Lovejoy, ed. *Identity in the Shadow of Slavery* (London: Continuum, 2000); Gwendolyn Midlo Hall, *Slavery and African Ethnicities in the Americas: Restoring the Links* (Chapel Hill: University of North Carolina Press, 2005); Philip D. Morgan, "The Cultural Implications of the Atlantic Slave Trade: African Regional Origins, American Destinations and New World Developments," *Slavery and Abolition* 18, no. 1 (1997): 122–45.

86. Memorial of the Fugitives, included in Governor Manuel de Montiano to King Philip V, March 3, 1738, AGI SD 844, on microfilm reel 15, PKY.

87. Governor Manuel de Montiano to the King, January 31, 1740, AGI SD 2658. Montiano counted only 366 Indian subjects (men, women, and children) at the eight nearby and allied Indian towns of Nombre de Dios (43), San Antonio de la Costa (22), Nuestra Señora de Guadalupe de Tolomato (29), San Juan del Puerto de Palica (52), Nuestra Señora de la Concepción de Pocotalaca (44), Nuestra Señora del Rosario de la Punta (51), Santo Domingo de Chiquito (55), and San Nicolás de Cacepullas (70). Governor Manuel de Montiano to the King, May 9, 1740, AGI SD 2658.

88. Jane Landers, "An Eighteenth-Century Community in Exile: The Floridanos in Cuba," *New West Indian Guide*, 70, nos. 1 & 2 (Spring 1996): 39–58.

89. Letters and reports of ecclesiastics, January 8, 1642–July 23, 1759, AGI SD 864.

90. Father Andres de Vilches recounts his services, December 8, 1757, AGI SD 864. For examples of continuing intermarriage see Landers, *Black Society*, 47–53.

91. Censuses of Gelabert, 1752, AGI, SD 2604; Ginés Sánchez, 1759, AGI SD 2595; and 1763 Exit Census AGI, Cuba 416.

92. Lista de las familias de Indios venidos de Florida que se hallan alojados en Guanabacoa, AGI, Cuba 416, f. 728–63. Cacique Juan Sánchez died at age forty, one of many. The many orphaned children became part of amalgamated Indian families in Guanabacoa.

7

The Long Yamasee War
Reflections on Yamasee Conflict in the Eighteenth Century

STEVEN C. HAHN

The massacre of South Carolinians at the Yamasee town of Pocotaligo on April 15, 1715, has been unambiguously recognized as the beginning of the Yamasee War. In contrast, the war's end point remains difficult to identify with similar precision. South Carolina's restoration of peace with the Creeks in 1717, along with John Palmer's 1728 raid against Yamasees near St. Augustine, are commonly cited as final acts, but what of the violence that persisted for decades more? While some South Carolinians may have been eager to declare the war terminated as early as 1716, Indian peoples like the Yamasees experienced no such decisive moment of closure. Rather, conflict remained a persistent feature of Yamasee life, thereby requiring us to take a longer view of the war bearing their name. Divisive from the start among Natives who fought against the South Carolinians, the necessity for Native communities to redefine their alliance commitments with regional European powers gradually widened this breach further, particularly as the British extended their settlements southward into the "debatable land" that became Georgia. One result was a decades-long war of attrition between Yamasees, particularly those who lived near St. Augustine, and certain groups of Creeks and their British allies. Yamasee-Creek conflict, in fact, was one of the war's most durable legacies, making it plausible that the war did not so much conclude as gradually burn out following the War of Jenkins' Ear. This was not a quarrel between entire Indian nations but rather the kind of reciprocal small-scale warfare between clans and towns rooted in southeastern kinship systems. That the Yamasee and Creek combatants were former allies and shared kinship ties made animosities between them all the more bitter, personal, and persistent.

As with many longstanding quarrels between closely related people, the rift between Creeks and Yamasees grew gradually and was marked by periods of relative calm punctuated by phases of violence. In what might be called the first phase of postwar violence (ca. 1716–22), Yamasees made incursions into South Carolina to attack plantations and liberate slaves who were now living on lands some Yamasees still considered to be theirs. Meanwhile, a group of Creeks and Yamasees (known to colonists as "Pon Pon Indians") moved onto land owned by John Musgrove in Colleton County, South Carolina, serving as intermediaries between invading Yamasees and a South Carolina government that was increasingly bent upon stopping them. The years 1723–28 encompass a second phase, whereby South Carolina officials turned up the pressure upon the Pon Pon Indians, as well as the Creeks, to take more decisive action against the Yamasees. Gradually the Creeks living at Pon Pon, and a few living within the nation, decided to throw in their lot with the British, culminating in the 1728 raid on St. Augustine led by John Palmer. That attack, in which many Yamasees died or fled, marked a decisive turning point, for many of Pon Pon's Indians, as well as a few Creeks, played key roles in the attack. From that point forward, Yamasee-Creek conflict entered a long third phase (ca. 1732–45), in which cyclical violence between Indians merged with a broader imperial war between Spain and Britain. Although recorded acts of violence between Yamasees and Creeks diminished after the mid-1740s, in reality war between the two did not cease until the Yamasees at St. Augustine departed with the Spanish for Cuba in 1763.

Looking back at a previous century of scholarship, historians have often hedged when attempting to assign an ending to the Yamasee War. In his pioneering study of the southern frontier, Verner Crane posited that the war "in a real sense" ended by the fall of 1715, citing Maurice Moore's march to the Cherokees (which produced a lasting peace agreement between them and the South Carolinians) and Robert Daniel's foray into Guale, which spurred Yamasees to relocate to St. Augustine. While acknowledging that the Creeks would not come to peaceful terms until over a year later, and that "sporadic forays" continued for many years, Crane nevertheless concluded that by the spring of 1716 the war was more or less over, and that South Carolina "had begun to count the costs and to plan reconstruction."[1]

Historians following in Crane's wake have been less inclined to dismiss continued Yamasee attacks as "sporadic forays," which has led them to expand of the war's temporal parameters. Stephen Oatis observes that the Yamasee War "ended for most South Carolinians in the fall of 1717," yet its legacy "continued to weigh heavily on most of South Carolina's frontiers for at least another decade." Oatis identifies the construction of Ft. King George on the Altamaha River in 1721 as a catalyst for the war's "reescalation" in the 1720s, culminating in John Palmer's 1728 raid. For Oatis, Palmer's attacks finally "broke the back of Yamasee resistance," and he cites depopulation figures indicating that the Yamasees had "disintegrated as a distinct nation." While he entertains the question of the war's end, at the same time Oatis seeks to reframe it by pondering Native rather than European viewpoints. "It would be better," he explains, "to emphasize the continuation of Indian resistance," as Indians asserted their autonomy through peaceful and warlike means for decades to come.[2] Oatis's reframing of the question seems particularly useful when taking the long view of violence in the region, although it is to be observed that Oatis and most other scholars tend to terminate their studies around the year 1730.[3]

One notable exception to that rule is William Ramsey, who in the provocative conclusion to his 2008 book pondered the long-term implications of the Yamasee War. Ramsey casts the war as a formative experience for the Georgia trustees, who recognized that the need for a "racially cohesive defensive zone" required regulating market relations with the Indian tribes. Going beyond that, Ramsey points out that the plantation system may not even have existed without the suppression of certain threats, notably that of Indian wars. In this light the Yamasee war may be regarded as "one of the first and greatest . . . winnowing events" that contributed to the making of the antebellum South.[4] Looking at the repercussions of the Yamasee War from indigenous perspectives, it would seem that taking a longer view of the war is just as essential for understanding various facets of tribal histories, ranging from migration to trade to diplomacy with Europeans.

Returning to some of the Yamasee War's major events, it is reasonable to suggest that the conflict instigated on April 15, and which continued through the fall of 1715, ought to be characterized unambiguously as war, for that is how contemporaries understood it. While a detailed account of battles falls beyond the scope of this essay, it is worth mentioning a few highlights. Following the Good Friday massacre at Pocotaligo, Yamasees laid waste to several of South Carolina's outlying southern parishes, such as St. Bartholomew's and St. Paul's, Stono. In the weeks that followed, the combatants engaged in some of the most intense of the war's battles. In late April Governor Charles Craven led the Colleton County militia against the Yamasees at their encampment on the Combahee River, driving them southward through the Salkahatchie swamp. Although Craven's expedition momentarily checked Yamasee incursions, by early June the South Carolinians faced attacks from the north along the Santee River, most notably the disaster at Schenkingh's Cowpen, where Indians managed to take the makeshift fort after tricking its commander into admitting them under a flag of truce. In mid-July governor Craven directed troops northward, thereby exposing the colony's southern flank to a massive Creek invasion, which resulted in the destruction of more farmsteads and notably the burning of a key bridge on the Edisto River. While the South Carolinians were largely left to their own devices in these first stages of the war, relief from other colonies—in the form of men and war materiel—began to trickle in by fall. In December Colonel Maurice Moore led three hundred men into the heart of Cherokee country. Moore's intentions were twofold: ratify a peace agreement made with Cherokees, and then attack the Creeks. It so happened that a delegation of Creeks from Coweta arrived in Cherokee country at about the same time. Courted by both sides, the Cherokees threw in their lot with the South Carolinians and murdered the Coweta diplomats at the Cherokee town of Tugaloo.[5]

As Crane, Oatis, and others have noted, the Cherokees' bold act proved to be a pivotal turning point in the war, at least as the South Carolinians saw things. By siding with the Carolinians rather than the Yamasees, Creeks, and their allies, the Cherokees (then the most numerous Indian nation in the region) foreclosed the possibility of

The Long Yamasee War

sustaining a truly pan-Indian revolt, and their regional influence seems to have had a ripple effect of convincing smaller tribes in the Carolina piedmont to make peace with the colony. Consequently, South Carolinians began to sense that the worst was over. Observing this shift in attitude firsthand was navy captain Samuel Meade, who arrived in Charles Town harbor in May 1715 while making a routine mail delivery. Upon discovering that South Carolina was at war with Indians, Meade ferried messages for several months between Charles Town and Virginia, as the former sought the latter colony's assistance in the war effort. What Meade found in late December astonished him. "I was very much surprised to see Charles Town left so thin of men," Meade wrote, observing that "a great many" had gone to the Florida coast in an attempt to salvage what remained of the Spanish treasure fleet that had been destroyed in a July hurricane.[6]

With even the local citizenry feeling secure enough to neglect the defense of their capital in favor of diving for Spanish gold, it is perhaps understandable that by 1716 colonial administrators had begun to perceive that the war was "near an end."[7] Governor Craven, who had postponed his return to England in order to organize the colony's defenses, addressed the Commons House of Assembly one last time on July 13, 1716. Reminding assembly members that his return to England was long overdue, Craven justified his decision to leave, stating that, "thro' God's blessing on our endeavours, the clouds that then threatened ruine and destruction to this colony are now blowne over and dissipated." "Our enemies," Craven added, "for the most part [are] defeated and fled way, and the war itself in a manner [is] extinguish'd."[8] The assembly howled in protest at Craven's remarks, insisting that the colony was still in danger and in need of assistance from the Crown.[9] Nevertheless, South Carolinians were in a position to plan for the future by passing a new Indian trading act and erecting forts on the colony's frontiers. By late August the commissioners of the Indian trade issued instructions to Charlesworth Glover to return to the falls of the Savannah River, where he was to oversee the Indian trading operation centered at Fort Moore.[10] By the spring of 1717, South Carolina's fortunes further improved when the Creeks began floating peace proposals, which eventually led to a treaty and a restoration of trade.[11] While Yamasees continued to make incursions into South Carolina for another decade, a "new normal" had set in, whereby colonial officials worked to keep Yamasee violence at manageable levels and began rebuilding and repopulating frontier parishes.[12]

Although nowhere near as dramatic as the Pocotaligo attack, Yamasee reprisals against South Carolina in the late teens and 1720s are noteworthy for their persistence and indicate that the Yamasees remained very much at war. In March 1717 a war party made a brazen incursion into the heart of St. Bartholomew's parish, killing trader William Steads at his "cowpen" near the Edisto River, afterward murdering William Saunders and his wife.[13] Rumors of a "small parcel of sculking Indians" operating on "the other side of Pon Pon" continued to haunt colony officials well into April, with circumstantial evidence suggesting that they were responsible for an attack on a supply boat headed up the Savannah River toward Fort Moore.[14] One colonist opined that the Indian war was "so hard upon us," because "stocks [of corn] are almost destroyed," leaving them in a starving condition.[15] Occasionally Yamasees picked off members of the Port Royal garrison, as was the case in an August 1719 incident when two men were killed.[16]

Importantly, Yamasee incursions provided opportunities for African slaves to escape from their masters. As Jane Landers has demonstrated (this volume), escaped Africans from South Carolina plantations "had been incorporated into the multicultural Yamasee confederacy" prior to the war and subsequent exodus to Florida, where governing authorities had repeatedly issued proclamations offering freedom to escaped slaves. Africans and Yamasees not only "rose in revolt together" against South Carolina, but they also relocated together to Florida, where some Africans rose to prominence in St. Augustine's Black militia, while others managed to live in freedom at the village of Gracia Real de Mose. For several decades, escapees from South Carolina continued to make their way to Florida, and Africans and Yamasees engaged in common in Florida's defense against British attacks during the War of Jenkins' Ear.[17]

When viewed in this light, in the postwar period, Yamasee raids into South Carolina plantations to promote the liberation of slaves establishes a pattern of continuity, perhaps indicating that one of the further goals of these raids was to promote incorporation of Africans or perhaps even to reunite with enslaved kinsmen on the plantations. The frequency with which South Carolinians complained of escaped slaves is telling. In June 1718 Yamasees invaded the territory surrounding Port Royal (their recent homeland) and plundered the plantation of one Mrs. Edwards, absconding with four of her slaves and causing some of her white tenants to flee.[18] Slave "stealing" (as South Carolinians reckoned it) continued for several years thereafter. In the years 1720–21, South Carolina officials counted nineteen slaves taken from nine different plantations, including those of eminent residents Col. John Barnwell and John Cochran.[19] Albeit on a lesser scale, the taking of white hostages (who were often ransomed in St. Augustine) also continued, such as the August 1719 kidnapping and ransoming of Mrs. Augustine Burrows, the wife of a Hilton Head Island planter.[20]

Yamasee attacks in South Carolina are well documented for the 1720s and have been described elsewhere by historians.[21] It is worth recalling, however, that a Yamasee named Istoweekee led several incursions during the years 1721–23, and Indians scored memorable blows against the colonists in August 1726, targeting Hilton Head Island and plantations along the Ashepoo River.[22] To put a stop to these incursions, South Carolina officials routinely pleaded with the Creek Indians to attack the Yamasees, thereby pitting the former allies against each other. These attempts were largely unsuccessful, however, because the two peoples had intermarried extensively during the preceding decades. Moreover, several noteworthy Creek leaders, including the Coweta "Emperor" Brims, and the Tuckabatchee leader Tickhonabe, had made peace with the Spanish, who were obliged to protect the Yamasees living near them. When pressured by South Carolina's Indian agents, Creek leaders repeatedly made promises to attack the Yamasees, but rarely kept those promises. Still, as Creek political authority rested primarily within individual towns, some persons capitulated to South Carolina demands. In 1723, in the midst of a trade embargo, a Cussita warrior named Cusabo led a party that killed one Yamasee man and captured a woman, and later killed another Yamasee diplomat in the Creek nation. Upper Creeks living on the Coosa and Talapoosa Rivers, increasingly disinclined to follow Coweta's lead, managed to recruit several war parties that descended upon La Florida to attack Yamasees. Although reports sometimes indicated that war parties returned without success, in 1725 Creeks and Yuchis did manage terrorizing strikes against the Yamasee villages of Tamaja and Pocotalaca.[23]

Finally, after years of pleading with the Creeks and making small retaliatory attacks, the August 1727 murder of trader Matthew Smallwood on the Altamaha River prompted the South Carolina government to take decisive action. Several months later a force of more than one hundred South Carolina volunteers and mostly Creek Indian allies marched to the Yamasee mission of Nombre de Dios, located within sight of the Castillo at St. Augustine. On March 7, 1728, Palmer and his men launched a surprise attack at dawn, killing thirty Yamasees, wounding scores more, and capturing fifteen. Surviving Yamasees scrambled to the Castillo, where they found safety. Palmer and his men spent several more days harassing those inside the Castillo, and then he returned to Charles Town a war hero.

Interestingly, although the Creeks seem to have played only a limited role in Palmer's raid, they remembered it as the "last decisive battle" against the Yamasees. Decades later they would cite it as one of the many conquests that enabled them to expand their territorial base into Florida. When William Bartram toured Creek country in the 1770s, informants pointed out to him Yamasee burials or "tumuli" that contained the bones of their slain foes. As the Creeks would have it, they exterminated their dogged Yamasee foes because they "would never submit on any terms." Creeks recalled that the extermination of the Yamasees was nearly complete, except for the forty or fifty persons who escaped the "last decisive battle" by "throwing themselves under the protection of the Spaniards at St. Augustine." Evidently, the descendants of these survivors were still carrying on in Bartram's day; Creeks told one story about a "fugitive remnant" of Yamasees living in the Okefenokee Swamp and another among the Apalachee Seminoles.[24]

That the memory of Palmer's raid would find a place in these oral traditions is indicative not only of eighteenth-century Creek territorial ambitions but also of the centrality of the Yamasee-Creek alliance in the saga of the Yamasee War. Taking the long view, one discerns that the breach between these two Native groups is one of the war's central plot lines, and it helps explain why fighting continued many years after the supposed "last decisive battle" in 1728. But whereas neither the Yamasees nor Creeks were monolithic entities with centralized political leadership, it becomes necessary to place Yamasee-Creek conflict under the proverbial microscope to track its origins and explain how and why warfare endured. Surprisingly perhaps, such an investigation leads to the heart of Colleton County, South Carolina, where John and Mary Musgrove established a mixed settlement of Creeks and Yamasees on their land. Dubbed "Pon Pon Indians" by South Carolinians, their experience illustrates in microcosm the bitterness generated when politics gets in the way of familial connections.

In order to understand how these former allies became foes, it is necessary to recognize that the war was divisive from the start. Even among the Yamasees we find hints of disagreement. SPG minister Gideon Johnston reported that some Yamasee warriors refused to partake in the war against the South Carolinians. Among them, Johnston observed, was the father of the young "Yamasee Prince," who was erroneously thought to have been "kill'd by the Indians for not Joyning with them in the war against us."[25] A degree of divisiveness can also be seen between the Yamasees and Creeks, who may have planned the attack at Pocotalico. Two years later Creek leaders tried to absolve themselves of responsibility by blaming the Yamasees, as if they had had second thoughts all along about resorting to military force. Emperor Brims accused the Yamasees of "having driven them into a war" against the English, and he vowed to "destroy" them "under the walls of St. Augustine."[26]

Although Johnston's story may be apocryphal, and one can perhaps accuse Brims of revising history to exonerate his people, it is nevertheless the case that Creek and Yamasee alliance commitments began to diverge in 1716, when both peoples relocated in order to evade reprisals from South Carolina. Yamasees dispersed from the homes they had occupied on the southern border of South Carolina. Some joined the Creeks, while others migrated to western Florida, taking up lands north of Pensacola and San Marcos. Perhaps the greatest number fled to St. Augustine, and it was this core group—comprising some of the leading foes of the English—who would later come to blows with

Creek and other Indians allied with British colonists. Meanwhile, the Creeks, many of whom had lived in the Ocmulgee River basin for a generation, elected to return to their ancestral territories on the Chattahoochee. From that point onward, the diplomatic histories of the two peoples grew further apart; Yamasees enmeshed themselves firmly within the fabric of La Florida, while the Creeks developed a neutrality policy that helped to reopen trade and diplomacy with the English. As further evidence that their commitments were diverging, as Creeks floated peace proposals to Carolina officials in the spring of 1717, the Yamasees renewed their campaign against South Carolina in the spate of attacks against the parish of St. Bartholomew's in March and April 1717.

As part of that broader reshuffling of peoples, a Creek and Yamasee Indian community formed in 1717 within the borders of that same South Carolina parish, on land recently purchased by John Musgrove. Why they chose to settle there, and why South Carolina officials grudgingly allowed them to remain within colony borders, is difficult to determine. The most plausible scenario is that there were a number of Creek and Yamasee individuals who longed for the pre-war years, when they had found living on the margins of British settlements to their liking, because it placed them in an advantageous position to conduct trade and diplomacy. As might be expected, their loyalties lay somewhere in between the two. In fact, it would appear that the "Pon Pon Indians" were playing a double game; sometimes they assisted the colony in keeping the Yamasees at bay, while at other times the Pon Pon Indians served as a conduit for Yamasee raids. Among the first colonists to recognize the Pon Pon Indians' potential utility in warfare was Capt. John Barnwell, commander of a small garrison at Port Royal, who had the unenviable task of defending the colony's southern frontier. In April 1719 Barnwell employed several of these Creek Indians to accompany him to the St. Mary's River to invite the Huspah king to make peace and return to his vacated town in South Carolina.[27] The Huspah king refused, however, and the Yamasees struck again on Hilton Head Island, requiring Barnwell to organize a second, more punitive, expedition to Florida. At Port Royal Barnwell gathered an impressive contingent of Creek Indians, who traveled with him by water to St. Augustine that September. The composition of the Creek leadership, which Barnwell identified in some detail, reveals the Pon Pon community's kinship ties to John and Mary Musgrove. The main fighting force consisted of forty to fifty "Creek Indians," all commanded by Oweeka. Musgrove's uncle, Whitlemico, was Oweeka's "second" in command. Also fighting under their leadership were John Musgrove and his wife Mary's brother, Edward Griffin.[28]

Like many Creeks, Pon Pon's Indians were well connected to the Yamasees through intermarriage, as indicated by the presence of one Wehomee, a Yamasee man who lived there.[29] In fact, their forays against the Yamasees seem to have been conducted for reasons that were personal and familial, and suggest a kind of nostalgia for the past, in which Yamasee and Creek Indians lived amicably in proximity to the South Carolinians. Concerning the April foray to Florida, for instance, three Creek men described as being "related to the Huspaw King," initiated the proposal to venture to St. Mary's, assuring South Carolina officials that they "could prevail with the Huspaw King to desert the Spaniards & bring over the Yamasee Indians with him to come & make a Peace with us [the English] & return to their former obedience under this Government."[30] They failed, but the September expedition is even more revealing in that Oweeka's war party attempted to retrieve "relatives" who still lived among the Yamasees. Among them was one of Barnwell's Creek spies, who sought his "wife and family." In so doing, however, he tipped off the Yamasees to the Creek war party's advance, enabling them to flee safely to St. Augustine. A Spanish prisoner later reported that about sixteen of the Creeks who lived among the Yamasees had, in fact, "come away," perhaps because Creek warriors had vowed to "not leave one alive" that chose to stay.[31]

Sporadic attacks in the Port Royal area, and knowledge that kinship ties and commerce united the Creeks and Yamasees, convinced South Carolina officials that the Yamasees and Pon Pon Indians were allies. In fact, South Carolina officials briefly entertained the prospect of expelling Whitlemico from the colony.[32] Whitlemico and his followers were allowed to stay, but the troubles between the South Carolinians and Pon Pon Indians persisted. Nor does it appear that Whitlemico was ever willing or able to stem the flow of Indians into

South Carolina, in particular a small band of Creeks and Yamasees led by an Apalachicola man named Cherokeeleechee. On record boasting of the "harm" he had done to the English, Cherokeeleechee remained something of a renegade, settling with a pro-Spanish band of followers at the convergence of the Flint and Chattahoochee Rivers. Although the Creeks and Carolinians were officially at peace, Cherokeeleechee carried on a clandestine war against the English by using the pretense of trading to gain admission to the area surrounding Port Royal, which he did repeatedly in the early 1720s. Providing cover were the Pon Pon Indians, who may have assisted Cherokeeleechee directly, or at least served him as unwitting accomplices. Why the Pon Pon Indians were willing to tolerate, perhaps even conspire with Cherokeeleechee's band may be partly explained by the common Apalachicola origins that members of both groups shared. Most important, one of Cherokeeleechee's "relatives" was none other than Oweeka.[33] We may infer, then, that many members of the Pon Pon community, possibly even John Musgrove, were in some way related to Cherokeeleechee's Creek and Yamasee followers.[34]

Although South Carolina officials remained wary of the Pon Pon Indians, they tended to blame others for the various insults committed by Indians against the plantations. It became difficult for the Pon Pon Indians to evade suspicion, however, when in the middle of August, 1726, six Indians descended upon Hilton Head Island, where they murdered a man and his wife. Two weeks later the same party moved inland, killing John Edwards and absconding with the slaves at his Ashepoo River plantation.[35] South Carolina officials almost immediately suspected Cherokeeleechee and made plans to "bring in [his] head."[36] But by then Carolina officials had begun to connect the dots in a way that suggested the Pon Pon Indians' complicity in the murders. Edwards's plantation, for instance, was less than a day's walk from the Musgrove lands in St. Bartholomew's, which must have raised suspicions.[37] Council President Arthur Middleton likewise perceived that "the mischief is done by the stragling Creeks, that live in those lower parts & seldom go up to their nation." Middleton identified the leader as "the relation of one [Oweka]," a discovery which seemed to implicate the Pon Pon Indians. To prevent future attacks,

Middleton instructed Indian agent Tobias Fitch to urge the Creeks to call home "all their people up that live about Pon Pon, and all other parts." This was no idle threat on the part of Middleton, who warned that he would take "another course with them [i.e., one involving force]" if they failed to do so.[38]

How was it possible for the Musgroves and other Indians living at Pon Pon to avoid suspicion when government authorities implicated them in so many recent murders and violations of settler property? The answer can be seen in John Musgrove's response, and that of the Pon Pon Indians, to the Smallwood murder and the military planning that culminated in Palmer's 1728 raid on the Yamasees. Caught between the warring Yamasees and South Carolinians, John Musgrove demonstrated his loyalty to the latter, and his choice caused an irreparable rift between the Musgroves' Creek kin and the Yamasees, one that was familial, personal, and thus not easily repaired. Whether or not it was the "last decisive battle," Palmer's raid may have been decisive in carving a permanent fault line between Yamasees living near St. Augustine and the Creeks connected to the Musgroves.

As alluded to previously, the origins of Palmer's raid can be traced to August 1727, when it was reported that Matthew Smallwood's trading house located near the forks of the Altamaha River had been robbed, resulting in the deaths of Smallwood and several others.[39] Immediately the Commons House of Assembly dispatched John Musgrove and the half-Chickasaw trader James Welch (one of several prominent mestizos who lived at Pon Pon) to the Forks of the Altamaha to investigate.[40] Meanwhile, colonial officials named Colonel Charlesworth Glover as agent to the Creeks, and had Musgrove and Welch recruit Indian warriors to punish the Yamasees, who were leading suspects in Smallwood's murder.[41]

If at one level the involvement of Pon Pon's mestizos and Indians seems to suggest a willingness to serve the South Carolinians, it should be stressed that they had their own reasons for fighting the Yamasees. As inhabitants of St. Bartholomew's parish, it is possible that the Pon Pon Indians had also been victims of Yamasee attacks, and likely found common cause in suffering along with their white neighbors. This applied particularly in the immediate context of the

1728 campaigns and may explain the zealous service of Musgrove and Oweeka. In fact, by late August 1727, reports surfaced of Indians "lurking upon the borders of our settlements on Pon Pon River," where they had begun "harassing" the people who lived there. The same party that killed Smallwood, it seems, later advanced into Colleton County, killing two planters named Henry Mushoe [Michaux] and Hezekiah Wood and carrying away ten of their slaves. Shortly thereafter Capt. John Bull, one of St. Bartholomew's more eminent planters, organized a retaliatory party that chased the Yamasees, killing six (and one Spaniard) and earning the approbation of the colony's leaders. The Indian threat continued well into the following year, and by February, St. Bartholomew's residents had to abandon their homes and live "three four or five families together," leaving their plantations exposed to plunder.[42]

Musgrove served the colony loyally during Glover's agency, as did several others drawn from Pon Pon's mestizo and Indian community. Musgrove worked in the employ of Glover for six months beginning in November 1727, presumably assisting him in turning the Creeks against the Yamasees. The following February Glover commissioned him and one other Indian known as the "Tuckesaw King" to command a party of thirty warriors to attack the Yamasees at St. Augustine. Although they arrived two days after Palmer's larger force destroyed the Yamasee village, they nevertheless returned that April to Glover with two Yamasee scalps.[43] Oweeka, who served along with several other Indians as auxiliaries to John Palmer, played an important role in bringing the Yamasees to heel. Colonial officials, in fact, singled him out for being "serviceable in several expeditions against the Yamasees" and rewarded him with a new gun, a fine sword with a brass handle, and a new suit of clothes, for which the House paid a bit extra to have it trimmed in lace.[44]

Although South Carolinians and Creeks both wishfully thought of it as the "last decisive battle," it is erroneous to think Palmer's raid entirely put an end to hostilities. In fact, Yamasees struck back almost immediately, when one of their war parties invaded and attacked the crew of a South Carolina scout boat at Daufuskie Island. In the process, the Yamasees killed the entire crew and kidnapped their captain, one Mr. Gilbert, who was taken to St. Augustine and later released.[45]

Four years later Yamasees killed two South Carolina traders operating on the Flint River, which drew John Musgrove yet again into government service to investigate and recruit Indians to punish the offenders.[46]

By that time, around June 1732, John Musgrove and his wife Mary had already settled at Yamacraw Bluff, on a site that became Savannah, Georgia, just one year later, in 1733. The Musgroves may have moved there in order to exploit economic opportunities—expanding their rice and cattle ranching operation, as well as the Indian trade. But their timing suggests that South Carolina officials who encouraged them to do so may have had frontier defense in mind, as the new Yamacraw settlement conformed to Governor Robert Johnson's "township" scheme, which involved creating several buffer towns along the colony's southern frontier, including the Swiss settlement at Purrysburg (also on the Savannah River) and a proposed settlement on the Altamaha that never materialized. Meanwhile, the Yamasees, already accustomed to making offensive forays to the north, found new opportunities—and new reasons—to seek revenge. Yamasees had scores to settle with John Musgrove, in particular, for bringing in Yamasee scalps and for enslaving two young persons who most likely were Yamasees.[47] Yamasees also would have targeted the Musgroves' Indian neighbors, Tomochichi's band of one hundred or so Creeks (commonly referred to as "Yamacraws"), who had settled in the vicinity of Musgrove's trading post. The arrival of the first settlers of Georgia in 1733 only exacerbated tensions between Yamasees and these British-allied Indians.

A detailed look at the Georgia records reveals the cycle of violence that involved the Yamasees of St. Augustine and Georgia's Indian allies—Yamacraws, Yuchis, Savannah River Chickasaws, and occasional Creeks. In July 1734, when the colony was little more than a year old, a rumor circulated that Yamasees and Spaniards had landed on Skidaway Island, prompting Georgia authorities to form a search party.[48] A few months later Yamasees returned for real, killing nine Yuchis living near the Palachacola fort on the Savannah River. Around June 1735 the Yamasees struck again when they encountered Yamacraws hunting near the Altamaha River. Reports indicated that the Yamasees had killed seven relatives of a Yamacraw man named Tallapholeechee, and continued "sculking" near the Argyle River several weeks more.[49]

Georgia's Indian allies struck back, and on balance, probably meted out more attacks than they received. One colonist, Joseph Hetherington, described the fever pitch of the Yamacraw Indians, who proposed to "fetch all the Spanish Indians scalps" and bring them to Georgia officials.[50] Hetherington politely declined that request, but just months later the Osuche *mico* named Licka killed one Spanish sentinel near St. Augustine, purportedly an act of vengeance for his dead brother, "out of whose scull they drink at St. Augustine."[51] Licka's action earned him a reward from the Georgia government, but the murder of the sentinel also seems to have prompted the Yamasees to kill the seven Yamacraws on the Altamaha River, those identified as "relatives" of Tallapholeechee. Eager to revenge his deceased kinsmen, in the summer of 1735 Tallapholeechee initiated his own war against the Yamasees, with several credible reports indicating that he had made forays into Florida.[52]

Observing this war of attrition firsthand was Mary Musgrove, who kept Georgia officials informed of Tallapholeechee's undertakings throughout the spring and summer of 1735. Mary was also aware that some Creek Indians living within the nation had scores to settle with the Yamasees. Around February 1737, some Creeks who had been hunting "southward" of the Altamaha River arrived at her cowpen with seven Spanish horses and other items they had plundered. They explained that while hunting, they had encountered a party of Spaniards, Yamasees, and "mulattos," who had tried to lure the Creeks to St. Augustine promising trade and friendship. The Creeks considered the offer but then realized that the Spanish Indians possessed property belonging to their "friends" who had been killed a year before. The Creeks turned on them, killing the Yamasee man and his accomplices before heading north to trade with Mary.[53]

Georgia's southward expansion, particularly the new installation on St. Simons Island, brought Creeks and Yamasees more frequently into proximity to one another, thereby increasing the likelihood for armed conflict. In 1736 James Oglethorpe had returned to the colony after spending more than a year in England promoting the Georgia project. Soon after arriving, Oglethorpe expanded upon England's land claims by building a series of forts along the coast, including Ft.

The Long Yamasee War

Frederica on St. Simons Island. Yamacraw Indians not only accompanied Oglethorpe on his journey south to survey potential fortification sites but also remained nearby to hunt and scout for him. Knowing that conflict between Indian allies threatened to bring Britain and Spain themselves to the brink of war, Oglethorpe and the governor of Spanish Florida Francisco de Moral Sanchez prohibited their Indian allies from attacking each other. These efforts were unsuccessful. In April 1736 Lower Creeks and Tallapoosas attacked Ft. Pupo, during which another Spanish soldier was killed, and Governor Moral Sanchez reported yet another attack the following year.[54]

Georgia's Indian allies continued to mount small-scale attacks on Yamasees and Spaniards as Florida's newly installed governor, Don Manuel de Montiano, took the helm. In January 1738, Montiano reported that English-allied Indians murdered the Yamasee cacique Pujoy and several others, while taking fourteen persons prisoner. Their fates are unknown. Six months later Yuchi Indians killed two Spanish soldiers who were manning a post at Fort Pupo, a few miles north of St. Augustine.[55] Still technically at peace with Spain, Georgia officials recognized that these attacks by their Indian allies could have repercussions. Writing from Savannah, secretary William Stephens observed that the colony's "greatest danger" came from "Indians in the Spanish interest," namely Yamasees. Although Stephens confided that he found it "pretty hard to distinguish" between them, he noted that Georgia's "neighboring Indians know them well," and that several parties had volunteered their services at the outbreak of the War of Jenkins' Ear.[56]

Taking this pattern of reciprocal violence into consideration suggests that the War of Jenkins' Ear, which began in the fall of 1739, manifested itself locally first as a war between the Creeks or Yamacraws and other allied tribes, on the one hand, and the Yamasees on the other. Only later was an imperial war grafted onto this ongoing conflict. As I have argued elsewhere, James Oglethorpe's most reliable allies derived from Native communities living in proximity to Savannah, although some Creeks also engaged in the action, thanks in part to Mary Musgrove's recruitment of war parties. With war declared, Oglethorpe's first move was to send Indians into Florida to assist with the destruction of forts Pupo and Picolata, which Montiano described as existing "solely for the purpose of defending and sheltering from the continual attacks of Indian allies of the English." On January 13, 1740, a party of forty-six "Uchise" Indians (the Spanish moniker for Creeks) led by Jacob Mathewes attacked the Yamasee town of Ayamón, killing its cacique named Yfallaquisca. Following that attack, Montiano continued to complain about "harassment" from the Uchises. He observed that they had penetrated far to the south of Florida looking for slaves, then backtracked north to attack Ayamón and Las Rosas, causing the inhabitants to scramble to the fortress.[57] Many other such attacks probably went unrecorded. One Spanish prisoner confessed he heard "that the Creeks are out and often kill of their Yamasee Indians [adding] that almost every week have heard of their killing some men and women that they took near Augustine."[58]

Yamasees and Creeks squared off again in two of the war's most dramatic contests, the 1740 British siege of St. Augustine and the 1742 Spanish invasion of St. Simons Island. Despite months of recruiting, Oglethorpe managed only to amass 100–300 Indians as part of the 1740 siege army. Meanwhile, at St. Augustine, Montiano counted 50 Indians as part of the militia. Although the Indian combatants seem to have spent relatively little time fighting, parties on both sides were involved in the showdown. On May 9 Oglethorpe sent Creek Indians ahead of the main forces to "reconnoiter the country," which resulted in their detaining one "negro" and confiscating some Spanish documents.[59] Subsequent reports from Florida indicated that Indians were involved in like deployments: spying, confiscating Spanish horses and cattle, patrolling. On one memorable occasion a Chickasaw warrior returned to Oglethorpe's camp bearing the head of a Spanish Indian, a trophy which Oglethorpe refused to accept.[60] Indians also formed part of the siege forces that camped on Anastasia Island, from which the English lobbed cannon fire into the town.[61] Montiano's Indians engaged in similar acts of espionage and diversion, and also engaged in direct combat, sometimes against Indians. In one instance, as Oglethorpe advanced toward Ft. Diego (a small outpost on the outskirts of Spanish Florida), Spanish Indians fired upon them from the woods, killing Oglethorpe's servant and cutting off his head.⁶² Spanish Indians accompanied a detachment that overran the rangers and Highlanders stationed at Ft. Mose, which Oglethorpe had recently captured, and which had been manned, in part, by some Creek relatives of Mary Musgrove.⁶³

Whereas Oglethorpe's reluctance to stage a frontal assault limited the number of direct skirmishes in 1740, British and Spanish records chronicling Spain's 1742 attack on St. Simons Island independently confirm direct encounters between English- and Spanish-allied Indians. In a preemptive strike that March, a sloop captain named David Braddock recruited a party of sailors and Indians, who advanced by water to St. Augustine, returning to Charles Town on March 20 with a prize ship. The *South Carolina Gazette* reported that Braddock's Indians had taken five Yamasee prisoners.⁶⁴ When the Spanish landed on St. Simons that July, Creek Indians brought in five Spanish prisoners as Oglethorpe's army retreated northward to stage a defense at Ft. Frederica. On July 7 the combatants engaged in a contest known as the "Battle of Bloody Marsh," in which British forces turned back the advancing Spaniards, who abandoned the invasion and eventually left the island on July 25. Indians on both sides faced each other in this now legendary battle. Forty-five Yamasees are reported to have fought alongside the Spaniards, who also employed them as scouts; meanwhile, three small companies of Yamacraw, Tomohetan, and Chickasaw Indians, totaling between fifty and one hundred men, fought for the British. The most noteworthy exploit was that of Tooanahwi, the Yamacraw war leader, who received a gunshot wound in his right arm, and then shifted his gun to his left hand to kill the Spaniard who had wounded him.⁶⁵

Although these battles were the most significant encounters between the combatants, Yamasee and Creek Indians exchanged blows in the sporadic fighting that continued for several years more. One of the most daring attacks came in November 1742, when a war party raided Mary Musgrove's trading post (recently converted to a fort) at Mount Venture, killing most of the garrison and taking several others prisoner.⁶⁶ It may simply have been a convenient target, but the history of animosity between the Musgroves, the Yamacraws, and the Yamasees suggests that the raiders intentionally targeted Mary. One informant who escaped and reported his version of events was Mary's slave named Nottoway, who indicated that the Yamasees were veterans of the St. Simons invasion who had lost a great number of their kinsman during the fighting there.[67]

The attack on Mount Venture proved to be a pyrrhic victory, however, as the Yamasees' affront to Mary seems to have stiffened the resolve of Creek warriors to defend her. Mary responded by recruiting "a strong party" of Creek Indians that harassed Spanish installations on the St. Johns River in preparation for another siege of St. Augustine. In 1743 scores of Mary's Coweta kin, including her kinsman Malatchi, joined Oglethorpe, Tooanawhi and Captain Patrick Mackey at the walls of the Castillo, where they captured one boat, and in the process took five Yamasee scalps and a severed hand as war trophies.[68] One report indicated that Indians continued to invade the St. Augustine area to "knap prisoners."[69] Yamasees struck back in February 1744 by invading St. Simons Island and carrying off five British soldiers. Commander William Horton promptly sent a detachment of "regulars and Indians" to track down the Yamasees, eventually recovering the British prisoners and coming away with one Yamasee prisoner and five Yamasee scalps.[70] Fatefully, it proved to be the final military exploit for Tooanahwi, who died instantly after receiving a gunshot to the chest.[71]

Judging by the paucity of recorded instances of violence, by the mid-1740s the frequency of Creek attacks against the Yamasees seems to have abated. The lack of evidence, however, should not rule out the probability that small scale violence between the two continued. Don Pedro Griñán's 1756 Report on Florida, for instance, illustrates the defensive posture that characterized the Yamasee villages during the last years of the first Spanish regime in Florida. According to Griñán, roughly fifty to sixty Indian men served in the militia, complementing the cavalry squads on their "frequent expeditions" patrolling the area. Griñán indicates, too, that the Yamasee villages were fortified; each had a small wooden fort with three or four small cannon manned by an artilleryman. Griñán also observed that Indians regularly "break the friendship pacts" contracted with the Yamasees, attacking them while they were out hunting, fishing, or collecting firewood.[72] Amanda Hall's excavations at the Duero site (the Yamasee town of Pocotalaca) seem to confirm the militarized posture of one important Florida Yamasee settlement, where artifacts associated with armaments, including a gunflint, lead shot, and a sword hilt have been found.[73] While sparse, the paper trail also substantiates Griñán's claims. One report from August 1748 indicated that Creeks hunting south of Ft. Frederica killed a Yamasee headman named Chillawlee and three others, taking another ten as prisoners.[74] During the French and Indian War, hostilities between Creeks and Yamasees occurred sporadically, despite the fact that Britain and Spain remained at peace until its final phases. In February 1759, near St. Augustine, Creeks killed five Spaniards and at least two "Spanish Indians," and then killed five members of the Spanish cavalry detachment sent to apprehend them.[75] Two years later Yamasees retaliated by killing three persons in the Lower Creek "point towns" (Ocmulgee, Osuche, and Chehaw).[76]

The question to ponder, then, is why Yamasee and Creek violence seems to have dwindled to relatively miniscule proportions. One possibility is the passing of the generation that lived through the Yamasee War and the War of Jenkins' Ear, most notably individuals such as John Musgrove, Tomochichi, and Tooanahwi, Perro Bravo (Yfallaquisca), and Francisco Menéndez, captain of St. Augustine's Black militia. Demographic changes certainly played a role. By that point the Yamacraws ceased to be a community in any meaningful sense, as settler pressure compelled the remaining villagers—increasingly at odds with Georgia officials about land and the distribution of presents—to migrate elsewhere. The Yamasees' demographic profile tells a similar story; if the five Yamasee villages could field no more than fifty warriors, their total population probably did not exceed three hundred persons. As for Mary Musgrove, even if she had wanted to revenge herself against the Yamasees for destroying Mt. Venture and killing her friend Tooanahwi, by then her concerns had drifted to her infamous land case, which consumed the final two decades of her life. Moreover, the imperial intrigues that provided the context for Native warfare shifted westward, as Britain's chief concern, and perhaps that of the Creeks, was the French colony of Louisiana and its Native allies, culminating in the Great War for Empire that engulfed North America in 1754.

When did the Yamasee War end? In view of the evidence presented here, it would seem that its scope gradually narrowed and evolved into an intermittent retaliatory war with Britain's closest Indian allies, many of whom, coincidentally or not, were connected to the Musgroves. Technically speaking, this war did not "end" until most Yamasees living near St. Augustine evacuated Florida in 1763, with many winding up in Cuba and Mexico.[77] Historians have long recognized the lasting significance of the war, as a means of reorienting Creek diplomacy and South Carolina trade and defense policy. But the Long Yamasee War suggests that perhaps it is wrong to attribute an end to any colonial-era war in the Americas. The test of a war's durability, it seems, is not what deals are struck at European courts and inscribed on paper. Nor can the end of a war be seen in the ceremonial burial of war implements, as occurred between South Carolina and the Cowetas in 1718. Rather, when we zoom in to look closely, we find the persistence of warfare rooted in local and sometimes personal grievances, a situation at odds with the grand diplomatic narrative. For that reason, such warfare needs to be acknowledged if we are to capture a sense of the personal politics, along with the horrors and emotions that perpetuated it. That the Yamasees were willing for the better part of three decades to convert to Catholicism, endure attacks by other Indians, and aid the Spanish in offensive warfare, underscores the lengths to which they were willing to go to extricate themselves from the British colonial regime, which had prompted the 1715 uprising at Pocotaligo in the first place.

Notes

1. Verner W. Crane, *The Southern Frontier, 1670–1732* (New York: G. E. Stechert and Company, 1929), 184.

2. Steven J. Oatis, *A Colonial Complex: South Carolina's Frontiers in the Era of the Yamasee War, 1680–1730* (Lincoln: University of Nebraska Press, 2004), 263, 284.

3. A cottage industry of Yamasee War studies emerged in the 1990s, mostly exploring the origins of the conflict. In addition to Oatis's work, see William Ramsey, *The Yamasee War: A Study of Culture, Economy, and Conflict in the Colonial South* (Lincoln: University of Nebraska Press, 2008); Bradley S. Schrager, "Yamasee Indians and the Challenge of Spanish and English Colonialism in the North American Southeast, 1660–1715," PhD diss., Northwestern University, 2001; David T. Rayson, "A Great Matter to Tell: Indians, Europeans, and Africans from the Mississippian Era through the Yamasee War in the North American Southeast, 1500–1720," PhD diss.,

University of Minnesota, 1996; Richard Durschlag, "The First Creek Resistance: Transformations in Creek Indian Existence and the Yamasee War, 1670–1730," PhD diss., Duke University, 1995; Richard L. Haan, "The 'Trade Do's Not Flourish as Formerly': The Ecological Origins of the Yamassee War of 1715," *Ethnohistory* 28, no. 4 (Autumn 1981): 341–58. For a narrative of the military conflict, see Larry Ivers, *This Torrent of Indians: War on the Southern Frontier, 1715–1728* (Columbia: University of South Carolina Press, 2016).

4. Ramsey, *Yamasee War*, 222–24.

5. Crane, *Southern Frontier*, 169–73, 179–83. For a recent work on military history, see Ivers, *This Torrent of Indians*.

6. For Meade's observations of Charles Town at the beginning of the war, see Samuel Meade to Josiah Burchette, May 15, 1715, Admiralty Department: Captains' Letters, ADM 1/2095, British National Archive, Kew. On the Charlestonians' wrecking activities, see Meade to Burchette, December 27, 1715, ADM 1/2095.

7. Governor Robert Hunter of New York was also enlisted to come to South Carolina's aid. Hunter responded by arming the Five Nations Iroquois and giving them orders to attack the "Indians in warr with Carolina." Iroquois warriors returned the following April with "several scalps and some prisoners." Interestingly, in his correspondence in September, Hunter pondered the means of "putting an end to ye Carolina war," whereas by April, Hunter perceived the war to be "near an end." See Robert Hunter to the Board of Trade, September 29, 1715, *Calendar of State Papers Colonial: America and West Indies*, vol. 12: *1685–1688 and Addenda 1653–1687*, ed. J. W. Fortescue (London: Her Majesty's Stationery Office, 1899), British History Online, http://www.british-history.ac.uk/cal-state-papers/colonial/america-west-indies/vol12 (hereafter cited as CSP-AWI), vol. 28, no. 629; Hunter to the Board of Trade, April 30, 1716, CSP-AWI, vol. 28, no. 133.

8. Gov. Charles Craven's Speech to the Assembly of South Carolina, July 13, 1716, CSP-AWI, vol. 28, no. 239ii.

9. Reply of the Assembly of South Carolina, July 13, 1716, CSP-AWI, vol. 28, no. 239iii. Historian Verner Crane points out that the assembly's protest should not be taken at face value. At the time, South Carolina assembly members sought to exploit the war as a means of discrediting the proprietary government, which eventually fell in 1719. See Crane, *Southern Frontier*, 184.

10. Entry for August 27, 1716, *Journals of the Commissioners of the Indian Trade: September 20, 1710–August 29, 1718*, ed. William L. McDowell Jr. (Columbia: South Carolina Archives Department, 1955), 106.

11. Steven C. Hahn, *The Invention of the Creek Nation, 1670–1763* (Lincoln: University of Nebraska Press, 2004), 94–96.

12. The reconstruction of Colleton County's southwestern areas seems to have commenced in 1717. At that time John Musgrove was among several who braved the Yamasee threat and purchased land there. Also a 1721 census indicates that forty-seven heads of household were living in St. Bartholomew's Parish. Modest numbers, to be sure, but indicative that the parish was on the rebound. On Musgrove's land, see Thomas and Elizabeth Jones to John Musgrove, Lease and Release, February 4–5, 1716/17, South Carolina—Register of the Province, Conveyance Book F (unpaginated), South Carolina Department of Archives and History (hereafter cited as SCDAH), microfilm reel ST 0756. For St. Bartholomew's 1721 population, see South Carolina Census, January, 1721, Governor Francis Nicholson Papers, Houghton Library, Harvard University.

13. Lords Proprietors to the Board of Trade, March 29, 1717, in W. Noel Sainsbury, *Records in the British Public Record Office Relating to South Carolina*, Sainsbury transcripts, 36 vols. (Columbia: Historical Commission of South Carolina, 1928–47), 7: 17 (hereafter cited as BPRO-SC).

14. Lords Proprietors to the Board of Trade, April 24, 1717, BPRO-SC, 7:20.

15. Extract of Letters from South Carolina, April 25, 1717, CSP-AWI, vol. 29, no. 541.

16. Thomas Hasell to the SPG Secretary, August 1, 1719, Records of the Society for the Propagation of the Gospel in Foreign Parts, Series-A, Letterbooks, vol. 13, 239.

17. See Jane Landers, "Yamasee-African Ties in Carolina and Florida," this volume.

18. Extract of a Letter from South Carolina to Joseph Boone, June 8, 1718, CSP-AWI, vol. 29, no. 601.

19. A List of Negroes Taken in the Years 1720 and 1721, ca. 1721, Board of Trade and Secretaries of State: America and West Indies, Original Correspondence—South Carolina, CO: 5/358, f. 182, British National Archive, Kew.

20. John Barnwell to Gov. Robert Johnson [no date, ca. November 1719], "America and West Indies: January 1720, 1–15," in Calendar of State Papers, Colonial, America and West Indies *Calendar of State Papers, Colonial, America and West Indies*, vol. 31, 1719–1720, ed. Cecil Headlam (London: His Majesty's Stationery Office, 1933), 293–311, http://www.british-history.ac.uk/cal-state-papers/colonial/america-west-indies/vol31/pp293-311.

21. See Crane, *Southern Frontier*, 254–80; Oatis, *A Colonial Complex*, 264–98; Hahn, *Invention of the Creek Nation*, 121–48.

22. John Barnwell to Gov. Francis Nicholson, September 17, 1723, BPRO-SC, 10: 150; South Carolina—Council Journal (hereafter cited as SC-CJ), September 3, 1726, Arthur Middleton's Letter to Tobias Fitch [same date], CO: 5/429, p. 16; SC-CJ, December 1, 1726, CO: 5/429, f. 85; SC-CJ, November, 17, 1726, Letter of Tobias Fitch to Arthur Middleton, October 30, 1726, CO: 5/429, f. 76. The situation of John Edwards's plantation can be seen in John Washington, Plat for 640 Acres in Colleton County, August 17, 1711, Colonial Plat Books (Copy Series), vol. II, 523, SCDAH.

23. See Amy Turner Bushnell, "Living at Liberty," and Amanda Hall, "The Persistence of Yamasee Power and Identity at San Antonio de Pocotalaca, 1716–1752," this volume.

24. Kathryn E. Holland Braund and Gregory A. Waselkov, eds., *William Bartram on the Southeastern Indians* (Lincoln: University of Nebraska Press, 1995), 37, 48, 52, 92, 113, 255.

25. Edgar L. Pennington, "The South Carolina Indian War of 1715, as Seen by the Clergymen," *South Carolina Historical and Genealogical Magazine* 32, no. 4 (October 1931): 256–57. For the most recent and detailed account of the Yamasee Prince, see Denise I. Bossy, "Spiritual Diplomacy," this volume.

26. Journal of the South Carolina Commons House of Assembly, May 24, 1717, Green Transcripts, vol. 5, 275, SCDAH.

27. John Barnwell to Robert Johnson, April 20, 1719, BPRO-SC, 7: 186.

28. John Barnwell to Robert Johnson, [no date] ca. October, 1719, BPRO-SC, 8: 1.

29. South Carolina officials identified the Yamasee man by name and indicated that he was still living at Pon Pon as late as 1732. See SC-CJ, August 16, 1732, CO 5/434, f. 1.

30. William Rhett to William Rhett Jr., April 28, 1719, BPRO-SC, 7: 188.

31. John Barnwell to Robert Johnson, [no date] ca. October, 1719, BPRO-SC, 8: 5.

32. SC-CJ, January 5, 1721/22, CO: 5/425, f. 219. See also the governor's proclamation that same day banning Indians from coming into the settlements, f. 223; SC-CJ, March 8, 1721/22, CO: 5/425, f. 287.

33. Council president seems to have been rather confident in naming the culprit as "the relation of one Owe=cau, that was taken up about three years ago at Port Royall, and sent off the country." The "relation" in question could only have been one of two men, Cherokeeleechee or Istoweekee the Yamasee. Other reports tend to blame Cherokeeleechee for those particular murders, so my conclusion at this point is that he was the "relation" in question. It is possible, however, that Middleton was referring to Istoweekee, who was apprehended in 1723 on Parris Island and escorted out of the colony. For Middleton's statements, see SC-CJ, September 3, 1726,

Arthur Middleton to Tobias Fitch, (same date), CO: 5/429, 16. For evidence indicating Cherokeeleechee's culpability for the 1726 murders, see SC-CJ, November 17, 1726, Letter of Tobias Fitch to George Chicken, October 30, 1726, CO: 5/429, f. 76.

34. SC-CJ, February 11, 1722/3, CO: 5/425, f.; John Barnwell to Gov. Francis Nicholson, September 17, 1723, BPRO-SC, 10: 150.

35. SC-CJ, Sept. 3, 1726, Arthur Middleton's Letter to Tobias Fitch [same date], CO: 5/429, 16.

36. SC-CJ, November, 17, 1726, Letter of Tobias Fitch to Arthur Middleton, dated October 30, 1726, CO: 5/429, f. 76.

37. The situation of John Edwards's plantation can be seen in John Washington, Plat for 640 Acres in Colleton County, August 17, 1711, Colonial Plat Books (Copy Series), vol. 11, 523, SCDAH.

38. SC-CJ, September 3, 1726, Arthur Middleton to Tobias Fitch [same date], CO: 5/429, 16.

39. SC-CJ, August 2 and August 3, 1727, CO: 5/429, 2–5.

40. SC-CJ, August 3, 1727, CO: 5/429, 5. For confirmation of Musgrove's and Welch's remuneration, see SC-CJ, September 30, 1727, CO: 5/429, 25; JCHA-SC, July 15; South Carolina–Treasury. Reports of General Accounts, Ledger C, f. 29.

41. SC-CJ, August 26, 1727, CO: 5/429, 18. At one point President Middleton infers that the Pon Pon Indians had joined with the local militia, which he described as "the militia and Indians now at Pon Pon and other." See SC-CJ, August 24, 1727, CO: 5/429, 8. Quoted passage from Oboyhatchey, King of the Abecas to Arthur Middleton, September 13, 1727, BPRO-SC, 13: 71. Musgrove and Welch's intelligence can be found in SC-CJ, September 21, 1727, CO: 5/429, 10. For an overview of Glover's agency, see Hahn, *Invention of the Creek Nation*, 139–48.

42. Steven C. Hahn, "The Indians that Live about Pon Pon: John and Mary Musgrove and the Making of a Creek Indian Community in South Carolina, 1717–1732," in *Creating and Contesting Carolina: Proprietary-Era Histories*, ed. Bradford Wood and Michelle LeMaster (Columbia: University of South Carolina Press, 2013), 343–66.

43. Charlesworth Glover, Journal, BPRO-SC, 13: 113, 129, 163.

44. Quoted passage, JCHA-SC, May 3, 1728, CO: 5/430, 90. For payment records and the information that the government paid extra to one "Mr. Tilly" for trimming Oweeka's clothes in lace, see South Carolina–Treasury, Reports of General Accounts, Ledger C, f. 106, 110; Arthur Middleton to the Board of Trade, June 13, 1728, BPRO-SC, 13: 61; "The Representation and Petition of the Inhabitants of the Parishes of St. Paul's and St. Bartholomew's Conjoyned," April 5, 1728, BPRO-SC, 13: 19–25.

45. *Report of the committee of both houses of assembly of the Province of South-Carolina, appointed to enquire into the causes of the disappointment of success, in the late expedition against St. Augustine, 1741* (Charleston SC: Walker, Evans, Cogswell and Company for the South Carolina Historical Society, 1887), 15–16.

46. Musgrove's service in 1732 is poorly documented. Extant documents do indicate that he was again tapped to serve Charlesworth Glover, and "attend him with the head men of those Creeks who reside at Yamacraw." Glover kept a journal of their agency to the Creeks, who were suspected accomplices to the murders, but the journal has never been found. See SC-CJ, September 6, 1732, CO: 5/434, f. 2.

47. At the time of Georgia's founding the Musgroves held two Indian slaves, Wan and Nanny. Their tribal origins are not recorded, but "Wan" is most likely an Anglicized form of the name Juan, indicating that the individual in question derived from somewhere in Spanish Florida.

48. Thomas Gapen to the Trustees, June 13, 1735, in Kenneth Coleman and Martin Ready, eds., *Colonial Records of the State of Georgia* (Athens: University of Georgia Press, 1982), vol. 20, 391 (hereafter cited as CRG).

49. George Dunbar to James Oglethorpe, January 23, 1734/5, Thomas Causton to the Trustees, June 20, 1735, and Noble Jones to James Oglethorpe, July 6, 1735, CRG 20: 191, 398, 428.

50. Joseph Hetherington to James Oglethorpe, March 22, 1734/5, CRG 20: 277.

51. Licka's war party numbered about twenty-five individuals. It is also noteworthy that Licka conducted himself secretly in order to avoid repercussions back home, indicating that many Lower Creeks were averse to attacking the Yamasees. See Patrick Mackey to James Oglethorpe, March 29, 1735, CRG 20: 297.

52. On the Yamacraw-Yamasee violence, see Thomas Causton to the Trustees, June 20, 1735, CRG20: 398–99; Noble Jones to James Oglethorpe, July 6, 1735, CRG 20: 427–28. Mary later relayed information of the Yamacraws' military actions to Georgia officials. See Thomas Causton to the Trustees, CRG 21: 58.

53. Thomas Causton to Thomas Broughton, ca. February, 1737, CRG 21: 344.

54. Hahn, *Invention of the Creek Nation*, 176.

55. Manuel de Montiano to Juan Fernandes de Guemes y Horcasitas, February 3 and July 4, 1738, *Collections of the Georgia Historical Society*, vol. 7: *Letters of Montiano, Siege of St. Augustine* (Savannah: Georgia Historical Society, 1909), 11, 21.

56. Journal of William Stephens, November 22, 1739, CRG 4: 458.

57. The route taken suggests that the attacking Creeks were already familiar with the path southward, reminiscent of the slave raiding conducted against Calusas and other south Florida Indians prior to 1715.

58. Examination of Felix Aguilar, May 8, 1741, CRG 35: 373.

59. Oglethorpe often failed to mention the tribal affiliations of Indians he employed in military operations. Evidence suggests that the roughly 120 Indians involved in the 1740 siege consisted mostly of Cherokees, with some Creeks, Yuchis, and Savannah River Chickasaws. One report suggested that a mere nine individuals were Creeks, but the likelihood is that these men played a key role in reconnaissance, and thus were probably the ones involved in the May 9 incident. See General Oglethorpe's Journal of his First Proceedings, May 9–24, 1740, Deposition of Thomas Wright, June 25, 1741, and Deposition of Thomas Jones, April 9, 1741, in *Appendix to the report of the committee of both houses of assembly of the Province of South-Carolina, appointed to enquire into the causes of the disappointment of success, in the late expedition against St. Augustine, under the command of General Oglethorpe* (London: J. Roberts, 1743), 21, 24, 34–37; Thomas Eyre's Account, September 29, 1739–April 20, 1740, in John Juricek, ed., *Early American Indian Documents: Treaties and Laws, 1607–1789*, vol. 11: *Georgia Treaties, 1733–1763* (Frederick MD: University Publications of America, 1989), 100–1.

60. On the decapitation incident, see Depositions of Jonathan Bryan, March 25, 1741, William Steads, March 13, 1740/1, and Richard Wright, March 28, 1741, in *Appendix to the Report of . . . South-Carolina*, 33, 46, 50.

61. *View of the town & castle of St. Augustine*, ca. 1740, University of Georgia Hargrett Library Map Collection, http://www.libs.uga.edu/darchive/hargrett/maps/1740s5.jpg.

62. General Oglethorpe's Journal of his First Proceedings, May 9–24, 1740, in *Appendix to the Report of . . . South-Carolina*, 23.

63. Deposition of John Palmer, February 19, 1740/1, in *Appendix to the Report of . . . South-Carolina*, 41.

64. *South Carolina Gazette*, March 13–20, 1742, no. 417, p. 2.

65. Documentary references to Indians fighting during the 1742 invasion are scattered. For some examples, see *South Carolina Gazette*, July 12–19, 1742, no. 434, p. 2; Anonymous, "Diario de las Noticias a Recidas en el Puerto de Cartagena de Yndias desde el Principio de Junio de 1739," Huntington Library, San Marino, California.

66. Mary Bosomworth, "Memorial to Alexander Heron," August 1747, in Juricek, *Early American Indian Documents*, vol. 11: *Georgia Treaties*, 143.

67. The Declaration of Nottoway, November 22, 1742, CRG 36: 54.

68. Journal of William Stephens, February 9, 1743, in E. Merton Coulter, ed. *The Journal of William Stephens, 1741–1743* (Athens: University of Georgia Press, 1958), 169; William Horton to Mary Mathews, February 19, 1743, CRG 27: 5; James Oglethorpe to Mary Mathews, February 28, 1743, CRG 27: 4; Edward Kimber, *An Impartial Account of the Siege of St Augustine* (London: 1743), 15, 28, 29; Malatchi's Speech to Alexander Heron, December 7, 1747, in Juricek, *Early American Indian Documents*, vol. 11: *Georgia Treaties*, 150; James Oglethorpe to Mary Mathews, March 22, 1743, CRG 27: 4–5; Journal of William Stephens, March 30, 1743, in Coulter, *Journal*, 187.

69. Kimber, *Impartial Account*, 10.

70. William Horton to Mary Mathews, December 17, 1743, and February 19, 1744, CRG 27: 5, 6.

71. William Horton to Mary Mathews, March 20, 1744, CRG 27: 6.

72. Michael Scardaville and Jesus Maria Belmonte, "Florida in the Late First Spanish Period: The 1756 Grinan Report," *El Escribano* 16 (1979): 9, 11–12, 15–16.

73. See Hall, "Persistence of Yamasee Power," this volume.

74. *South Carolina Gazette*, August 15–27, 1748, no. 749, 2.

75. *South Carolina Gazette*, February 23–March 3, 1759, no. 1273, 2.

76. *South Carolina Gazette*, October 24–31, 1761, no. 1422, 2.

77. See John E. Worth, "The Yamasee in West Florida," this volume, for a detailed account of what befell the Yamasees after the transfer of power in 1763. Evidence suggests that the Yamasees remaining in West Florida, in particular, had played roles as "intermediaries and power brokers" between the Spaniards and Creeks, and therefore tended not to be targets of Anglo-Creek warfare directed at St. Augustine.

THREE

Surviving the Yamasee War

8

The Persistence of Yamasee Power and Identity at the Town of San Antonio de Pocotalaca, 1716–1752

AMANDA HALL

The Yamasee Indians who returned to Spanish Florida in 1715 inhabited a very different setting than what they had become accustomed to in South Carolina. Instead of occupying a network of confederated Indian villages, they dispersed and relocated to different areas of La Florida and Apalachicola. Some of the Yamasees who came to St. Augustine reestablished their South Carolina towns and resided near the Spanish and other Indian groups, such as the Guales, Timucuas, and Apalachees. Other Yamasees and their Indian allies, such as factions of the Lower Creeks, Tallapoosas, and Chickasaws, chose to keep their distance from the colony and live in the Apalachicola region.[1] Those Yamasees who came to St. Augustine faced bouts of epidemics, illnesses, and continuous British attacks on their villages, which over time resulted in the decline of their numbers and the fall of their towns.

Following their arrival in St. Augustine the Yamasees initially reestablished the towns of San Antonio de Pocotalaca (Pocotaligo), Nuestra Señora de Candelaria de la Tamaja (Altamaha), and Pocosapa. While in South Carolina, Pocotalaca (Pocotaligo) town was an influential place to the Yamasees, their Indian allies, and the British. Serving as a main location for negotiations between Indian groups, traders, and colonists, the town is best known as the place where the Yamasee War began.[2] When the Yamasees of Pocotalaca arrived in postwar St. Augustine, the Spanish were already aware of their significance and political position. Documents describing the decades of the postwar city leading up to British control of La Florida (1763) reveal that because of the Yamasees' influential status, the Spanish valued those at Pocotalaca.

Since the 1660s the Yamasees had managed to build a group identity within colonial landscapes based on their Indian alliances and sovereignty. In South Carolina (1683–1715) they and their Indian allies had formed a confederacy of multiethnic Indian towns under the Yamasee name that by the early 1700s numbered at least four thousand Indians.[3] Although the war weakened the confederacy's numbers and cohesion, Pocotalaca's Yamasees arrived in St. Augustine determined to remain an autonomous group within a colonial setting.

Using an ethnohistorical approach this chapter focuses on how the Yamasees at Pocotalaca maintained their group identity, influence, and many of their cultural practices regardless of living near the Spanish and other Indian groups. Just as the town held prominence as the upper head town in South Carolina, Pocotalaca maintained this status in St. Augustine, thus shaping Spanish relations with the town's inhabitants. Documents reveal that the political influence of the inhabitants, their connections to Indian groups in Apalachicola (greatly sought by the Spanish), and the willingness of the warriors to work closely with the Spanish against British forces afforded Pocotalaca's Yamasees a high level of sovereignty. Securing independence also resulted in the maintenance of Yamasee lifeways at Pocotalaca. The archaeological analysis of a Yamasee household at Pocotalaca (Duero site), when compared to the data from a second Pocotalaca site, Oneida, and various proto-Yamasee, as well as pre- and postwar Yamasee sites, suggests that those occupying the Duero site were maintaining some continuity in their material choices, subsistence, and structural design.[4]

The Yamasees' Return to La Florida

On May 27, 1715, two Yamasee and two Apalachicola (Lower Creek) leaders arrived in St. Augustine to solicit a pardon from Governor Francisco de Córcoles y Martínez for their actions against the Spanish colony while allied to the British. Representing a weakened yet vital confederacy, the delegates sought permission from the Spanish to return to La Florida.[5] The Yamasee diplomats were Alonso, the *cacique* of Ocute, and Gabriel, the son of Yamasee chief Santiago Sule. The

Lower Creek faction was Yfallaquisca (likely a Yamasee), the warrior chief of the town of Sadketche, and Istopoyole from Nicunapa, both from the province of Apalachicola.[6]

The delegation signifies the deep connections between the Yamasees and Lower Creeks that formed decades prior to the war. In this volume Steven Hahn discusses how intermarriages between the two resulted in an alliance profoundly rooted in kinship. He explains that because of these bonds, the British often failed at attempts during the postwar period to entice the Lower Creeks into siding against the Yamasees. However, since individual Creek towns maintained their own governance, occasionally town leaders chose to side with the British.[7] Despite these stray factions, the Yamasees and Lower Creeks maintained a postwar alliance.

The Yamasees and Lower Creeks made a unified decision "to establish diplomatic links with local Catholic powers."[8] Chosen and sent by the mico Brims and Coosa's mico Chislacaliche, the governor of all the towns in Apalachicola, Yfallaquisca clarified to Martínez the reasons why the Yamasees made war on the British.[9] He explained, "the causes . . . were many," but the most alarming was British plans to enslave their people in exchange for debts owed to the traders for their purchases of British goods.[10]

Yfallaquisca then handed eight leather belts to Istopoyole, who presented them to Martínez. Each belt was a strand of knots, and each knot represented one of 161 Native villages in South Carolina and Apalachicola willing to ally with the Spanish.[11] Yfallaquisca asked that Martínez deliver the belts to the king of Spain as a symbol of a new alliance.[12]

Eighteenth-Century St. Augustine and the Yamasee Mission Towns

St. Augustine was an unstable city by the early eighteenth-century, under the continuous threat of British and Indian attacks. The city had become a target for enemy raiding parties after the fall of the mission system in the late seventeenth century. Surviving mission Indians such as the Guales, Timucuas, and Apalachees regrouped and resided on the outskirts of St. Augustine in approximately seven mission villages, totaling around four hundred Indians.[13]

The Yamasees' arrival in 1717 was perfect timing for the vulnerable Spanish colony. Not only did their presence double the Indian population in St. Augustine, but it also increased the number of Indian mission villages from seven to ten.[14] Just as the other Indian groups were living on the fringes of the city acting as buffers against outside intrusions, Yamasee towns also provided some defense for the colony. However, because of British hatred for the Yamasees, their towns were more prone to attacks.[15]

The Yamasee towns of Pocotalaca and Tamaja initially settled south of the city in Las Rosas de Ayamón, located between four and twelve leagues from the city along the southern coastline of St. Augustine. The location of the town provided some protection for the city from the south while offering the Yamasees some distance from the Spanish.[16] However, following a British and Indian attack on the Yamasee towns in 1725, the Yamasees moved their towns closer to the Castillo to be under the protection of the guns. Pocotalaca's Yamasees settled "at a distance of a rifle-shot" outside the city's gates, inhabiting approximately twenty households dispersed over twenty-five acres (map 10).[17] Not only did living closer to the city gates offer the Yamasees temporary relief while under the guns of the Castillo; the new location also offered the city protection from outside intrusion.[18]

Pocotalaca's Yamasees remained near the Castillo from 1725 until 1738 before moving back to the area of las Rosas, perhaps to have access to more fertile land for growing food.[19] However, reoccurring harassment and attacks from enemy Indians, as discussed by Hahn in this volume, motivated them to return to their location near the city's gates in 1740.[20] Here Pocotalaca remained until the aggregation of St. Augustine's Indian populations into the mission settlements of Nuestra Señora de Guadeloupe de Tolomato and Nombre de Dios in the late 1750s.[21]

The Yamasees at Eighteenth-Century Pocotalaca

While moving between Spanish and British powers the Yamasees worked to remain a distinctive group.[22] A main characteristic of their determination to maintain group cohesion and identity is their choice to retain village names. Continuity in the town name Pocotalaca, a

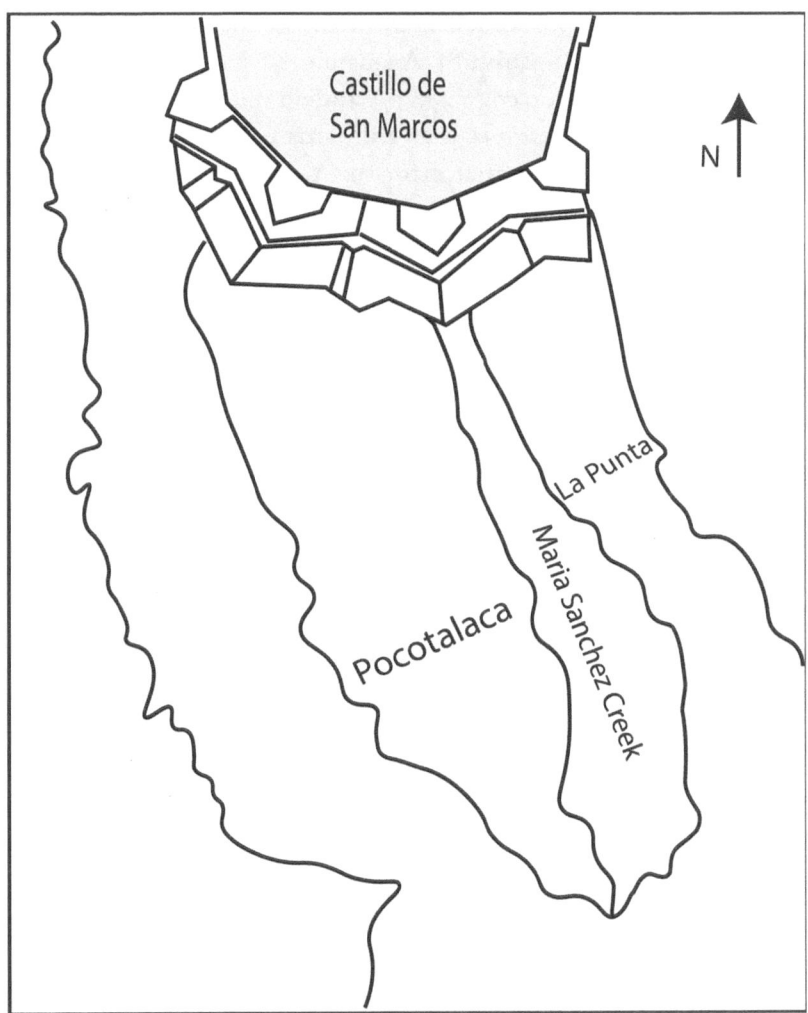

MAP 10. Adapted from the 1737 Arredondo map. Pocotalaca community, ca. 1737. Map by Amanda Hall.

phonetic rendition of South Carolina's Pocotaligo, reveals that regardless of the town's geographic location, retaining the name likely aided in preserving kinship ties and alliances associated with the town's inhabitants. Additionally, because Pocotalaca was a prominent town in South Carolina, keeping the name would also have been important for political purposes such as maintaining status for recognition upon their arrival in Spanish St. Augustine.

Surely the Spanish recognized the Indian dignitary Yfallaquisca, who was Pocotalaca's *cacique* when the Yamasees arrived in the city.[23] Serving as a trusted negotiator for the Yamasee-Creek delegation that came St. Augustine in 1715, Yfallaquisca "was the first to step forward to speak" on behalf of the absent micos Brims and Chislacaliche of Apalachicola.[24] Undoubtedly the Spanish would have acknowledged Yfallaquisca's connections to Apalachicola and Pocotalaca and, for political reasons, would have given preferential treatment to the town's residents.

Yfallaquisca's relations with the Yamasees at Pocotalaca extended back to South Carolina (and perhaps even further). In fact, he was a primary participant in the attack on the British at Pocotaligo at the opening of the Yamasee War on April 15, 1715. Following a meeting held between the Yamasees and British ambassadors, the Yamasees "appeared satisfied, shook hands [with the British] in a token of friendship and drank."[25] That night while the British slept, Yfallaquisca and two Yamasee headmen, one from Pocotaligo, one from Sadketche (a Yamasee upper town), and other Indians "painted their faces . . . with red and black streaks" and awoke the Carolinians with their "terrible war-whoop."[26] Yfallaquisca and the others attacked the agents then proceeded to "fire upon everybody without distinction."[27]

Yfallaquisca's dedication to the Yamasees prior to the war, throughout it, and during its aftermath suggests he was Yamasee and not Lower Creek. As mentioned earlier, some Yamasees relocated their towns from South Carolina to Apalachicola instead of St. Augustine. One of these towns was probably the town of Sataquica or Satiquicha, where Yfallaquisca was reportedly serving as war chief in 1715, and is likely a phonetic rendition of the South Carolina Yamasee upper town of Sadketche (Salkehatchie). Also notable is that during the attack on the British in Pocotaligo at the start of the war, a Sadketche headman accompanied Yfallaquisca in the assault.[28] A census of Pocotalaca penned by Captain Joseph Primo de Rivera taken in 1717 also suggests Yfallaquisca was Yamasee. Rivera refers to Yfallaquisca, who was serving as cacique, as a Yamasee and not Lower Creek, yet clearly distinguishes differences between the Yamasee groups living at Pocotalaca that included "four Christians of the Oapa nation."[29]

Considering Yfallaquisca's political connections with Apalachicola headmen, he likely served as a main dignitary for the Yamasees in St. Augustine during the early postwar period. The Spanish would have acknowledged him as a gateway for negotiations and securing additional Indian alliances in Apalachicola. Consequently his attachment to Pocotalaca surely would have aided in the continuation of the town's status as well as the independence of its inhabitants.

Because documents pertaining to Yamasee towns in St. Augustine lack insight about their political structures, it is unclear how Pocotalaca functioned politically and how much influence the caciques held over their people. It appears that Pocotalaca maintained a political system that required a cacique and perhaps a council. Rivera's census lists six other subchiefs under Yfallaquisca, who likely represented a council where each held an important position in the town.[30] Rather than holding significant power over their people, the town's headmen probably played important roles for retaining autonomy of the town, perhaps serving as mediators for Indian and Spanish relations.

The need for the Spanish to secure and maintain additional Indian alliances such as those in Apalachicola through the Yamasees also offered those at Pocotalaca, especially having Yfallaquisca as chief, a means for building and securing influence in St. Augustine. The Spanish, desperate to earn the Yamasees' trust and partnership, gave them "everything they asked for."[31] Documents reveal that the "Spanish presented them [Yamasee caciques] with gifts" such as "hats and coats" and even requested that they "dine with the Governor."[32] Shortly after negotiations took place between Martínez and the Yamasee–Lower Creeks in 1715, Martínez acted on securing the offered alliances of the 161 towns in Apalachicola by requesting that Spain send friars to live in the villages to offer the Indians religious instruction. However, likely due to Spain's poor financial position at the time, by 1724 only 11 of the 161 Indian towns had resident friars.[33]

Because Pocotalaca was a primary town in South Carolina, the Spanish showed even greater preferential treatment to the town's caciques—at times treating them like nobility. On the night of the 1725

British and Lower Creek attack on the Indian towns in las Rosas, one of St. Augustine's affluent Spanish citizens, Agustín Guillemo de Fuentes, brought Pocotalaca's "*Cacique principal*" at the time, Don Antonio Jospo and his family, into the Fuentes home, allowing them to stay for some time.[34] Despite the assaults on three other towns, the Spanish singled out Pocotalaca's cacique to receive this sort of superior treatment.[35] Meanwhile, other villages involved in the attack consisting of Yamasees, Timucuas, and Jororos were left to prepare temporary shelters near the city walls.[36] Although Fuentes's exact motivations for offering Pocotalaca's cacique and his family aid to such an extent are unclear, Susan Parker in this volume elucidates how his generosity was politically motivated.

The Yamasees at Pocotalaca also secured their positions in St. Augustine by building and maintaining strong bonds with the Spanish. One method possibly used was religious adoption. Unlike in their initial alliance with the Spanish, documents suggest that some of the Yamasees at Pocotalaca were engaging in some aspects of outside religious practices over the town's tenure. Since any evidence of the how the Yamasees regarded Christianity or their level of involvement at Pocotalaca comes solely from Spanish sources, it is impossible to say with certainty what Christianity meant to them or their sincerity in the practice. Rivera's 1717 census noted that over 80 percent of the townspeople were non-Christian.[37] However, as early as 1718, records regarding the baptisms of some of the inhabitants and the establishment of a church in 1726 suggest that some dabbling in outside religion might have occurred.[38] Although it can never be known for certain, the Yamasees might have adopted aspects of the Christian faith as a method for preserving their community and culture, as historian Daniel Silverman suggests was the case for the Wampanoag of Martha's Vineyard during the colonial period.[39] An alternative explanation could be that the Yamasees were engaging in what historian Denise Bossy refers to as "spiritual diplomacy" (this volume).[40] The Yamasees at Pocotalaca might have been adopting aspects of Christianity and using them as a form of negotiation for building and maintaining a strong alliance with the Spanish.[41] Southeastern Indians often used spiritual diplomacy as a means of obtaining influence in their alliances with colonial powers.[42] Because saving Indian souls was a primary concern to the Spanish, Pocotalaca's Yamasees might have used outside religion to their advantage.

The Yamasees at Pocotalaca also used their military skills for securing alliances with the Spanish. An unmistakable characteristic of the Yamasees noted by Don Pedro Sánchez Griñán in 1756 (recalling his tenure in St. Augustine from 1731 to 1742) is that the Yamasees were "brave" warriors who spent a good portion of their time "wag[ing] war."[43] By warring, the Yamasees could accumulate and assert power, which directly contributed to their ability to maintain group cohesion and identity. Just after the Yamasees departed La Florida in the early 1680s and aligned with the British, they gained influence among their new British partners by raiding the mission provinces. By the early 1700s, the Yamasees, serving as one of the main suppliers of Indian slaves for the British, grew to be one of the most powerful and feared Indian groups in the Southeast. Following their return to St. Augustine and realignment with the Spanish, they continued their roles as warriors, only this time they attacked the British. Griñán noted there were "50 to 60" Indians from the local mission villages who helped to secure the defenses of the town and "serve[d] on frequent expeditions" accompanying Spanish soldiers, which would have included the warriors from Pocotalaca, as there were twenty-three warriors listed by Antonio de Arredondo as capable of bearing arms for the town.[44] Many of the Yamasees' warring expeditions involved raiding Carolina plantations and collecting "bounties for English scalps and black slaves" with their Lower Creek allies.[45]

Some of the Indians from Pocotalaca held significant positions directly assisting Governor Montiano as runners and spies during British attacks and encroachment on La Florida. Montiano recognized one of Pocotalaca's Lower Creek Indians named Juan Ignacio de los Reyes for his military skills and dedication.[46] From 1739 to 1740, during English General Oglethorpe's preparation and failed siege on St. Augustine, Ignacio took the position as a spy and runner responsible for gathering and delivering information for the Spanish. Governor Montiano was very fond of Ignacio and often sent him on "important mission[s]" to areas in Spanish Florida overtaken by British forces, like Fort Pupo located on the west bank of the St. Johns River, to gather intelligence on Spanish enemies.⁴⁷ In addition, Ignacio spied on the British during their invasion of Fort Picolata, also on the St. Johns River, where he "observe[ed] the movements of the enemy" and provided important information to Montiano.⁴⁸ The governor was so pleased with Ignacio's assistance and allegiance that he wrote to his superiors stating that Ignacio was skilled at using his "native wit" to gather information pertaining to British numbers, whereabouts, and plans.⁴⁹

Interestingly, Ignacio was not the only one of Pocotalaca's inhabitants to assist Montiano against Oglethorpe's invasion. Chislala, noted on Arredondo's 1736 list of Yamasee warriors, was "an Indian of bravery and enterprise," as Montiano described him.⁵⁰ In 1739 Montiano also relied on Chislala, along with "eight Indians of his choice" to go to Picolata and capture a "hostile Indian or Englishman prisoner alive" to be brought back for interrogation.⁵¹ Though by the time Chislala arrived in the area the British camps were deserted, Montiano wrote that by using his skills to read the "signs left behind" by enemy forces, Chislala was able to provide him with the number of British allied Indians.⁵² Considering Montiano's admiration of Ignacio and Chislala for their assistance during Oglethorpe's siege, it is clear that they played crucial roles during this pivotal period by helping to hold back the British until January 1740, when Oglethorpe and his Indian allies seized and destroyed both Pupo and Picolata. However, just four months later the Spanish managed to regain their losses and took back the forts.⁵³

Because the Yamasees aided the Spanish maintaining their hold on La Florida, they were able to carve out a space near the city where they could remain a self-sufficient group and continue many of their lifeways. After the group arrived from South Carolina, the ethnic composition of Pocotalaca was predominantly Yamasee. According to Rivera, this village was of the "Yamasee Nation and tongue," totaling ninety-eight Yamasees, which was similar to the average size of Yamasee prewar towns in South Carolina discussed by Sweeney in this volume.⁵⁴ Many of the Yamasees living at Pocotalaca would have been the same men, women, and children who occupied the town in South Carolina.⁵⁵ Other documents spanning Pocotalaca's tenure reveal that the town remained Yamasee, which suggests that the occupants actively engaged in maintaining their identity as a group.⁵⁶

The Persistence of Yamasee Power and Identity

After returning to St. Augustine, most Yamasees generally remained detached from other Indian groups in the city, such as the Guales, Timucuas, and Apalachees.[57] This applies especially for Pocotalaca's occupants. Although other Indians such as Lower Creeks, Guales, and Costas occasionally lived in the town, they represented only small numbers.[58] A census reveals that as late as 1752, of forty-one inhabitants, thirty-three were Yamasees and the remaining eight were Costa.[59] The Yamasees at Pocotalaca did not fully aggregate with other groups until sometime after 1752, when only six Indian towns remained. By this time epidemics and British and Indian attacks on the city had wreaked havoc on the Indian populations, and to survive, the fragmented towns had to unite. In 1759 Pocotalaca's numbers totaled twenty-three before aggregating with a mix of Indian ethnicities at Nombre de Dios. Despite their small numbers and amalgamation with other Indians, the Spanish still identified them as Yamasees.[60]

The power and place that Pocotalaca's Yamasees secured for themselves in St. Augustine allowed them to maintain their identity as a group. Archaeological data from a Yamasee household at Pocotalaca suggests they were also able to retain aspects of their culture. Those occupying the site continued to manufacture and acquire ceramics and trade goods just as they did in South Carolina and maintained some of their indigenous practices, apparent in their choices of tool manufacturing and use, subsistence, and structural design.

Because the Yamasee Indians were a multiethnic group that formed in response to colonial pressures, while becoming Yamasee they established a collective identity within a colonial setting that reflects the persistence of traditional practices and materials as well as the incorporation of new materials.[61] From an archaeological perspective the Yamasees developed an "archaeological signature" that is visible across material assemblages.[62] This signature, characterized by a blended assemblage of Indian San Marcos with non-Indian ceramics and artifacts, formed during the late seventeenth century and early eighteenth century as the Yamasees negotiated their place and power in colonial landscapes.[63] Although the identification of this Yamasee signature is beneficial for the confirmation of Yamasee sites in South Carolina, it does not apply in the same manner to sites in postwar St.

Augustine since most groups living in the city used similar assemblages. However, Yamasee assemblages in South Carolina can be instrumental for exploring continuity and change in Yamasee culture prior to and after the war, especially when compared to a site documented as a Yamasee town. To interpret the archaeological data from the household at the Duero site, this study draws on the data from multiple sites, including Pocotalaca's Oneida site, La Punta, the prewar Yamasee sites of Altamaha, Chechessee, and Pocotaligo, and other sites associated with the Yamasees, such as proto-Yamasee sites in the Oconee River Valley of Georgia and Lower Creek sites in the Apalachicola region.

Pottery and Artifacts

The most common artifact recovered from the Duero site was Native American pottery, specifically San Marcos. Altamaha/San Marcos pottery is characteristic of Yamasee archaeological assemblages and is the most abundant ware recovered from Yamasee sites in both South Carolina and Florida.[64] As discussed by Keith Ashley in this volume, San Marcos and Altamaha pottery represent the same series, and from ca. 1625 to 1763 Yamasee, Guale, and Mocama (Timucua) Indians manufactured the series, referred to as San Marcos in Florida and Altamaha in South Carolina. Attributes establishing a significant difference between the two series remain inconclusive.[65]

Just as San Marcos pottery dominates other Yamasee pre- and postwar sites, the type is also the most abundant in the Duero assemblage, totaling 89.0 percent (table 3).

TABLE 3. The Duero site assemblage

ceramic group	frequency	percentage of category	percentage of group
Indian ceramics			
San Marcos	234	89	81.3
Colonoware	15	5.7	5.2
Other Indian	14	5.3	4.9
Total Indian ceramics	263	100%	91.4%

European ceramics			
Majolica	4	16	1.4
Spanish olive jar	1	4	0.3
Coarse earthenware	4	16	1.4
El Morro	11	44	3.8
Blue and white Delft	3	12	1
English slipware	2	8	0.7
Total European ceramics	25	100%	8.6%
Total ceramics	288	100%	100%
Kitchen group			
Ceramics	288	98.6	94.7
Bottle glass	4	1.4	1.3
Category total	292	100%	96.1%
Arms group			
Gunflint	1	25	0.3
Lead shot	2	50	0.7
Sword hilt	1	25	0.3
Category total	4	100%	1.3%
Tobacco			
Kaolin pipe stem fragments	7	100	2.3
Category total	7	100%	2.3%
Architectural hardware group			
Nails	1	100	0.3
Category total	1	100%	0.3%
Total assemblage	304		100%

Note: Artifacts from the Duero site are placed in functional groups solely for the purposes of organizing the data.

San Marcos from the site displays various surfaces with the most common being cross simple stamped (table 4). Over half the San Marcos surfaces exhibit stamping and only 12 percent have plain surfaces (table 5). Differing from the Duero site, Gifford Waters's analysis of

San Marcos pottery surfaces from Pocotalaca's Oneida site investigated in 2001 indicates that plain sherds, totaling 69.1 percent, represent the main surface finish (table 5).[66] Although working with limited data at the time, Waters's research focused on the maintenance of pottery traditions among the amalgamated mission Indians. He suggested that because stamped San Marcos pottery appears more frequently at Guales sites and plain (and check stamped) surfaces were more common at Altamaha, the higher proportion of plain sherds recovered from Pocotalaca might reflect preference or tradition among Yamasees. However, he does not rule out that because of stress during this period, Guale potters may have been producing more plain surfaces.[67]

TABLE 4. Count and percentage of San Marcos surface treatments from the Duero site

surface	count	percentage of count
Check stamped	16	6.8
Complicated line block	26	11.1
Complicated curvilinear	11	4.7
Complicated rectilinear	8	3.4
Cross simple stamped	42	17.9
Simple stamped	36	15.4
Plain	19	8.1
Unidentified	76	32.5
Total	234	100%

TABLE 5. Stamped and plain San Marcos surfaces from the Duero and Oneida sites

	Duero		Oneida	
surface	number	percentage of count	number	percentage of count
Stamped	139	88.0	42	30.9
Plain	19	12.0	94	69.1
Total	158	100%	136	100%

Note: Table does not include UID stamped or UID San Marcos surfaces (Unidentified stamped = the stamping cannot be identified; Unidentified San Marcos = the surface cannot be identified).

Analysis of the more recent San Marcos data from the Duero site reveals a high percentage of stamped surfaces (88%) making attempts to isolate surface attributes of San Marcos pottery that distinguish Yamasee from Guale groups at Pocotalaca inconclusive (table 5). However, differences in stamped and plain surfaces at Duero and Oneida might indicate preferences or the maintenance of pottery traditions between Yamasee families. Because Pocotalaca consisted of approximately twenty family households, surfaces could vary by the family manufacturing the pottery.

The comparison of the combined San Marcos data from the Duero and Oneida sites (table 6) to the town sites of Altamaha and La Punta also blurs any attempts to delineate a Yamasee preference for a specific surface design. Stamped surfaces are more frequent at Pocotalaca (61.6%) and Altamaha (59.1%), whereas plain surfaces are more common at La Punta.

TABLE 6. Comparison of Pocotalaca, La Punta, and Altamaha/San Marcos stamped and plain surfaces

surface	Pocotalaca (Duero and Oneida)		La Punta		Altamaha	
	number	percentage of count	number	percentage of count	number	percentage of count
Stamped	181	61.6	640	43.2	88	59.1
Plain	113	38.4	840	56.8	61	40.9
Total	294	100%	1480	100%	149	100%

Note: Table does not include UID stamped or UID San Marcos surfaces.

Source: Oneida, La Punta, and Altamaha data is adapted from Waters, "Maintenance and Change," 148, 151, 153.

In addition to Altamaha town, stamped San Marcos is also more common at other prewar Yamasee towns in South Carolina. Alexander Sweeney's combined analysis of the type recovered from Pocotaligo and farmsteads at Huspah and Chechessee reveals that stamping was more frequently used.[68] If stamped San Marcos is indeed more common in Guale assemblages, then the higher rate of stamped sherds at some of the prewar towns could suggest that the Yamasees were engaging in trade with the Guales that involved the exchanging of vessels, or more Guales were living in the villages under the Yamasee name than what British documents reveal. The predominance of stamping at Pocotalaca could also be the result of trade or a larger number of Guales living in the town and making most of the pottery.[69] However, this is hard to discern at Pocotalaca because Spanish documents regarding postwar St. Augustine often differentiate between Indian groups and describe Pocotalaca over the decades as a Yamasee town occupied by only a few Guales.

Differences in San Marcos surface treatments could relate more to temporal factors than identity markers, especially when comparing assemblages from contemporaneous and non-contemporaneous Yamasee and Guale sites spanning decades. Moreover, it is nearly impossible to know if the Duero and Oneida sites were at any time occupied simultaneously over the three decades that Pocotalaca was near the Castillo, making the differences in San Marcos surface treatments even more ambiguous. Whether at the town level or on a broader scale, surface variations could relate to several circumstances, such as internal factors, women marrying into Yamasee groups and incorporating their pottery traditions, external factors like war and relocation, or other stresses might have influenced the need for change in pottery manufacturing techniques.

Colonoware, a pottery type rooted in the Yamasees' prewar material expression, is also part of the Duero site assemblage and suggests that the Yamasees occupying the household were likely manufacturing and using the type. Colonoware, a postcontact pottery, has red slip applied to the vessel's interior and represents a blended Aboriginal-European ware.[70] Although it was manufactured by Indian potters using local clays and techniques, certain characteristics of the pottery "clearly speak to a colonial influence" since vessels typically represent European forms (e.g., brimmed bowls, plates, handled mugs).[71]

The appearance of colonoware at La Punta and prewar Yamasee sites in South Carolina reveals a consistent presence in Yamasee assemblages.[72] As in other Indian groups living near the Spanish during the

The Persistence of Yamasee Power and Identity

prewar period, such as the Guale and Timucua, the introduction of colonoware among the Yamasees likely occurred during their initial alliance with the Spanish (1660s to 1680s). Interestingly, they continued to use and possibly manufacture the type even while living outside La Florida. However, its occurrence at pre- and postwar Yamasee sites makes up only small portions of the ceramic assemblages. At the Duero site colonoware represents 5.7% of the Native American ceramics (table 3).

Just as in their prewar South Carolina towns, the Yamasees occupying the Duero site also continued to incorporate Spanish and British ceramics into their lifeways. Making up 8.6 percent of the assemblage, types included Puebla and Aranama Spanish majolicas, English slipware, Delft, Spanish olive jar, El Morro, and coarse earthenwares (table 3). The addition of non-Indian wares probably originated during the Yamasees' initial alliance with the Spanish and over time became a more consistent part of their material make-up while allied with the British.[73]

Other non-Indian materials collected from the Duero site included a small number of glass fragments from bottles. Glass bottles in colonial St. Augustine are commonly associated with rum and according to Griñán, the Yamasees spent all their earnings on spirits.[74] However, the glass fragments representing the mission period recovered from the Duero site consist of only four pieces of light green glass, representing no more than one bottle. The Yamasees' reputation for rum consumption largely stems from their time in South Carolina. Many documents discuss that the Yamasees were incurring large amounts of debt "from their traffik in and dealing with the traders for rum."[75] Yet the recovery of glass from Chechessee in South Carolina only represents about four bottles, leaving one to question the amount of embellishment used in some of the documents pertaining to the Yamasees and their use of rum. Additionally, some documents discuss how South Carolina traders often fabricated claims for rum debts owed by the Yamasees.[76]

Kaolin pipe fragments recovered from the Duero site reveal that the inhabitants likely continued their traditional use of pipes for tobacco smoking. Interestingly, cigar smoking among the Spanish was more common than pipe smoking, which offered the Yamasees living at

Pocotalaca easy access to acquire cigars through Spanish channels. Regardless of convenient trade, they still chose to acquire and use kaolin pipes. For most Indians, pipe use was traditional, and using kaolin pipes was simply incorporating familiar items into old practices.[77] Kaolin pipe fragments recovered from Yamasee sites in South Carolina suggest that their use and perhaps transition from manufacturing and smoking traditional clay pipes to acquiring and using kaolin pipes might have originated during their alliance with the British.[78] Since the Spanish preferred cigars, the procurement of kaolin pipes by Yamasees in postwar St. Augustine would likely have been through illicit trade with the British or perhaps indirectly from other Indian groups allied with the British.[79]

Other trade items recovered from the Duero site were artifacts associated with armaments that included a gunflint, two lead shots, and a sword hilt. Armaments at the site suggest the Yamasees at Pocotalaca acquired weapons while in St. Augustine and, like their activities in South Carolina, continued to hunt and maintain their roles as warriors.[80] Documents describe how the Yamasees in eighteenth-century St. Augustine spent much of their time warring and hunting for wild game. The recovery of gunflints and shots, items used for operating flintlock muskets, suggests the Yamasees had arms at the site and were likely engaging in these sorts of activities.[81]

The hilt was part of a sword of Spanish origin manufactured between 1740 and 1760.[82] Because swords were standard issue for the Spanish military, Spanish soldiers often carried them.[83] Pocotalaca also had a garrison where at times Spanish soldiers served, which suggests that the hilt might have belonged to a soldier.[84] However, because the recovery of the hilt was near the structure with San Marcos pottery, it could also have belonged to a Yamasee, perhaps functioning as adornment solely worn to signify status, or used as a weapon since Yamasee warriors often aided the Spanish army.

Bone and Shell Tools

Modified animal bones and shells recovered from the Duero site indicate that the Yamasees occupying the household were manufacturing and using traditional types of tools to perform daily tasks. Ten percent of the animal bone assemblage appears to have signs of secondary human use.[85] That many of them reveal multiple damages suggests that the Yamasees were using bones for various tasks, such as piercing and scraping. These modifications included edge wear, polish, reduced tips, serrations, and pointed tips. In addition, five modified quahog clams reveal signs of edge wear, which could point to their employment as scrapers commonly used for tasks such as cleaning animal hides.

Subsistence at the Duero Site

Faunal remains from the Duero site suggest that the Yamasees at Pocotalaca preferred a local diet reflecting many of their subsistence patterns during their tenure in South Carolina. Griñán describes how the Yamasees engaged in hunting and small-scale farming. They had fields for planting, but they cultivated "only a small harvest."[86] Faunal and botanical remains from the Duero site also suggest this was the case. Only small amounts of fish remains and shellfish such as oyster and clam were present. Both wild and domestic species appear at the site, but the wild deer remains outnumber pig and cow remains (table 7). These differences might indicate a heavier reliance on mammals and a preference for indigenous over domesticated species. However, a larger faunal sample would be necessary to confirm this. A similar pattern is noted for Yamasee dietary choices while in South Carolina. Faunal remains from the Yamasee town of Chechessee reveal that species such as pig, cow, and chicken were present. However, indigenous animals such as deer, bear, raccoon, and squirrel appear to be the main sources of protein.[87]

The appearance of deer at the site could also relate to its "prestigious food" status among affluent households in St. Augustine.[88] Griñán described the Yamasees as avid hunters who "earned from their hunts," making the acquisition of deer for men and its processing by women an even greater part of Yamasee daily life in the city.[89] The Yamasees probably traded some of the meat and hides for goods in St. Augustine's city square. Not only does Griñán suggest that they profited from their hunts; considering their previous economic relationship with the British while in South Carolina, it would have been characteristic of the Yamasees to cultivate lucrative trade relations with the Spanish colony.[90]

TABLE 7. Faunal remains from the Duero site

taxon	count	percentage of count	w(g)	percentage of w
Odocoileus virginianus (white-tailed deer)	10	8.2	23.8	4.4
Sus scrofa (domestic pig)	5	4.1	28.8	5.3
Bos Taurus (domestic cow)	8	6.6	24	4.4
Mammal*	85	69.7	459	84.5
Bird*	6	4.9	1.61	0.3
Turtle*	1	0.8	0.3	0.1
Fish*	3	2.5	1.91	0.4
Pogonais cromis (black drum)	1	0.8	0.02	0.0
Paralichodes (flounder)	1	0.8	0.5	0.1
Bone*	2	1.6	3.1	0.6
Total	122	100%	543.04	100%

* Species unknown.

Griñán also mentions that the Yamasees practiced some farming. Although the only botanical remains recovered at the Duero site were charred corncobs from a smudge pit, their presence indicates the Yamasees were growing corn at Pocotalaca.[91] Griñán also states that the Yamasees were growing "corn" as well as "legumes on their respective plots."[92] His use of "plots" proposes that the Yamasee households tended small gardens and not large fields.[93] Growing small amounts of crops for subsistence or perhaps trade resembles Yamasee lifeways while in South Carolina. At Chechessee the recovery of botanical remains reveals that they grew maize, roots, berries such as chokeberry and sour cherry, and pepperweed, knotweed, and other nutritional plants for food.[94] The small amount of botanical remains at the Duero site is likely the result of limited excavations, preservation bias, or recovery methods used at the site.

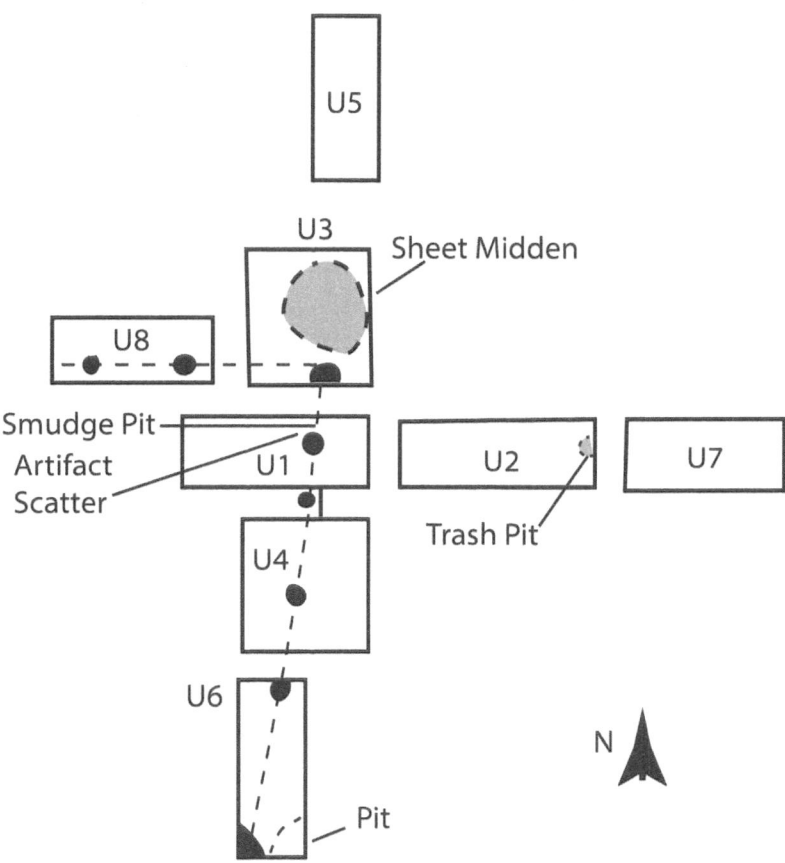

MAP 11. Map of the Duero site units, features, and structure. Created by Robert Thunen and Amanda Hall from original site map by Carl Halbirt.

Features at the Duero Site

Pits and middens at Pocotalaca offer information about how the Yamasees might have been living at the household and how they were using the space (map 11). Excavations at the Duero site revealed that in keeping with Native American practices, the Yamasees were using sheet middens and pits for discarding trash. A smudge pit found also suggests continuity of one or more activities taking place at the site and common among southeastern Indians, such as smoking hides, meats, and plants and smudging for ceremonies or repelling insects.[95]

Structural Remains

Posthole features at the Duero site reveal the presence of a structure that suggests the Yamasees used a traditional architectural design (map 11). Seven postholes represent the corner of a square or rectangular structure. At La Punta, in addition to circular structures, excavations revealed a square structure.[96] Because Europeans were the first recorded people to build rectangular structures in St. Augustine, rectangular or square architectural designs found in the archaeological record are commonly associated with European building styles.

However, for the Yamasee Indians, it was traditional to build both circular and rectangular or square structures, making the latter more reflective of Yamasee practices than European influence. Yamasee cultural origins are traceable to the towns of Altamaha, Ocute, and Ichisi in the Oconee River Valley of interior Georgia, where structural evidence reveals that their ancestors built both circular and rectangular structures.[97] Archaeological evidence and documents also demonstrate that Muskogee Lower Creek Indians in Apalachicola built their structures using both patterns during pre- and post-Yamasee War periods.[98] The Yamasees were in many ways connected to the Creeks. Both groups not only belong to the same Muskogean Indian language family, but as Steven Hahn discusses in this volume, during the colonial period they shared political alliances and kinship ties as well and often lived among one another.[99]

Archaeological evidence at Yamasee prewar towns in South Carolina also reveals that the Yamasees built circular and possibly rectangular structures. Alexander Sweeney in this volume discusses evidence of six circular structures found at Altamaha town, which are strikingly similar in design to pre-Yamasee Mississippian houses in the Oconee River Valley.[100] At Chechessee town, posthole features confirm the outline of a building that represents a rectangular shape or oval shape. Like the structure at the Duero site, posts at Chechessee appear individually set and lack a wall trench.[101]

The absence of wall trenches or daub associated with the structure at the Duero site suggests it was likely a pole-and-frame design with a palm thatched roof and thatched walls. Alternatively, the build-

The Persistence of Yamasee Power and Identity

ing may have been more open like a chickee. An artifact scatter surrounding the smudge pit in Unit 1 suggests this is the case. The scatter, extending beyond the eastern alignment of the structure and into the exterior area, implies that the excavated portion of the building did not have walls (map 11). Considering Florida's climate, it might have been practice for the Yamasees to construct and use an open or partially open structure during the hot summer months.

For Muskogean peoples, structural design often correlated with climate. During the winter, houses were circular and had daub walls for insulation, whereas summer houses were rectangular pole and frame structures that had thatched roofs, were designed for warmer temperatures, and were partially open or had windows for ventilation.[102] In the Oconee River Valley rectangular or summer structures had thatched walls often replaced by the inhabitants from season to season.[103]

Like the proto-Yamasees' building practices for warmer months, Lower Creeks also constructed rectangular structures. As described by botanist William Bartram in 1789, the Creeks constructed square ground public buildings that served as summer council houses thought to be similar in design to their summer houses. Appearing to be a pole and frame construction, they were rectangular and partially open.[104] Later the Seminoles (some of them Yamasees) used simple canopies referred to as chickees for houses.[105] Bearing in mind what the archaeological record and documents reveal about pre-Yamasee and Muskogean structural designs, the building at the Duero site was likely a building used during warmer weather, which in Florida is most of the year.

The structure at the Duero site reveals a rectangular or square building, which is consistent with Yamasee practices. The size of the assemblage suggests an ephemeral occupation at the site. Considering available excavation data, it appears some of the main activity at the site took place in and around the northeast area of the structure, since this area contained most of the artifacts and features. In view of the structure's location in relation to other cultural features and distribution of refuse, the structure appears to represent a partially enclosed area, perhaps a chickee (map 11). Because of its open design, it is questionable whether the Yamasees slept in the structure at night. It could represent a seasonal field house occupied only during the day or a briefly inhabited residence. Father Bullones wrote that following John Palmer's raid in 1728, some of Pocotalaca's Yamasees feared additional attacks on their town, so they built huts in the village for daytime use then retreated closer to the Castillo at night.[106]

Although the Duero site artifact assemblage is not very large, similarities to Yamasee assemblages at pre-sites and postwar sites reveal continuity in some of the material choices and traditions among the Yamasee group. San Marcos pottery remained the dominant ware, and some use of colonoware persisted for many decades following their initial alliance with the Spanish. The Yamasees continued to acquire non-Indian goods such as imported ceramics and British trade goods while maintaining various practices tethered to Yamasee tradition, including tool manufacture and use, subsistence choices, and structural designs.

Despite their ability to preserve aspects of their culture, the Yamasees at Pocotalaca faced continuous stress from enemy attacks and epidemics that eventually led to the decline in their population and town.[107] Because many Yamasees and their Indian allies did not come to St. Augustine after the war, the town's population could not replenish its losses (table 8).[108] By residing in St. Augustine, the Yamasees at Pocotalaca unintentionally isolated themselves.

Regardless of population decline at Pocotalaca, many of the town's inhabitants remained prominent and upheld their autonomy until the 1750s. By this time the number of Yamasees in the town was so small that to obtain protection and ensure survival of their people, they chose to aggregate with other Indians. Even then, they remained important in distinguishable ways. Pocotalaca's *cacique* Yamasee Juan Sanchez obtained the role of chief at Nombre de Dios in 1759 following the final aggregation of the six mission towns, where he governed not only Pocotalaca's Yamasees but also other Indian groups until the Spanish relinquished La Florida to the British in 1763.[109]

Collectively, the mid-seventeenth and eighteenth centuries were pivotal for the Yamasee Indians. Documents and archaeological data reveal the tenacity of those at Pocotalaca to remain Yamasee. The larger picture reveals that while being drawn into a colonial whirlwind, the

TABLE 8. Pocotalaca's population 1717 to 1752

source/date	date	men	women	children	total
Joseph Primo de Rivera	1717	42	31	25	98
Pablo Castillo	1728	22	19	14	55
Antonio de Arredondo	1737	23	44*		67
Antonio de Benevides	1738				62
Manuel de Montiano	1738	14	20	13	47
Güemes y Horcasitas	1739				54
Father Gelabert	1752	8	13	12	33

* Includes women and children.

Sources: John E. Worth, *Timucuan Chiefdoms of Spanish Florida*, 2 vols. (Gainesville: University Press of Florida, 1998), 2: 150–55; The Gelabert Report, Father Gelabert, General Mission List 1752, Archivo General de Indias, 87-1-14 (copy available at the St. Augustine Historical Society, St. Augustine, Florida).

Yamasees quickly adapted to a changing landscape while maintaining a firm grasp on their identity and practices. Reusing town names, remaining autonomous, and maintaining Indian alliances and cultural practices emphasize a group determined to persist. Although they may not have welcomed change, the Yamasees chose to remain flexible in their material choices, which would have aided them in acclimating to the changing colonial economy. That said, it is important to note that incorporating non-Indian materials into their lifeways did not make the Yamasees any less indigenous as we can never be fully certain how they used these objects or what values they placed on the items.

Notes

I gratefully acknowledge the input and support provided by many people who helped to bring this essay to fruition. First is Denise Bossy for her unlimited guidance. I would also like to thank both Denise and Chester DePratter for the opportunity to be a part of this significant anthology. Thanks go to my current advisor Charlie Cobb for his conversations and support as well as to the other contributing archaeologists and historians in this volume. I am grateful to Carl Halbirt for providing the archaeological data from the Duero site, Vicki Rolland for her assistance with the faunal analysis, and the St. Augustine Historical Society for their assistance with maps and documents.

1. Michael C. Scardaville and Jesús Mária Belmonte, *Florida in the Late First Spanish Period: The 1756 Griñán Report*, vol. 16 of *El Escribano* (St. Augustine Historical Society, 1979), 15. This chapter is a condensed study of "San Antonio de Pocotalaca: An Eighteenth-Century Yama-

see Indian Town in St. Augustine, Florida, 1716–1752," master's thesis: University of North Florida, 2016, by Amanda A. Hall.

2. Steven J. Oatis, *A Colonial Complex: South Carolina's Frontiers in the Era of the Yamasee War 1680–1730* (Lincoln: University of Nebraska Press, 2004), 125–26.

3. Joseph M. Hall Jr., *Zamumo's Gifts: Indian-European Exchange in the Colonial Southeast* (Philadelphia: University of Pennsylvania Press, 2009), 99.

4. Gifford J. Waters, "Maintenance and Change in 18th Century Mission Indian Identity: A Multi-Ethnic Contact Situation," PhD diss., University of North Florida, 2005, 94.

5. Francisco de Córcoles y Martínez to the King of Spain, July 5, 1715, Archivo General de Indias, Santo Domingo (hereafter cited as AGI SD), 843, trans. John Worth, March, 2007; Alejandra Dubcovsky, "One Hundred Sixty-One Knots, Two Plates, and One Emperor: Creek Information Networks in the Era of the Yamasee War," *Ethnohistory* 59, no. 3 (Summer 2012): 489.

6. Dubcovsky, "One Hundred Sixty-One Knots," 489.

7. Steven Hahn, "The Long Yamasee War: Reflections on Yamasee Conflict in the Eighteenth Century," paper presented at the Yamasee Indians: From Florida to South Carolina conference, St. Augustine, Florida, April 17, 2015; Steven Hahn, *The Invention of the Creek Nation, 1670–1673* (Lincoln: University of Nebraska Press, 2004), 83–84.

8. Hahn, *Invention of the Creek Nation*, 84.

9. Martínez to the King, January 25, 1716, attached "Testimony through interpreter Antonio Pérez Campaña, Christian Guale Indian, resident among the Guale [Yguaja]," May 28–29, 1715, AGI, SD, 843, trans. John Worth, 2007, 2.

10. Martínez to the King, January 25, 1716, 2.

11. Martínez to the King, January 25, 1716, attached "Testimony," May 28–29, 1715, 2.

12. Martínez to the King, January 25, 1716, 4.

13. John H. Hann, *A History of the Timucua Indians and Missions* (Gainesville: University Press of Florida, 1996), 306–11.

14. Hann, *Missions*, 306–7.

15. John H. Hann, *The Native American World Beyond Apalachee* (Gainesville: University Press of Florida, 2006), 289.

16. Susan Parker, "The Second Century of Settlement in Spanish St. Augustine, 1670–1763," PhD diss., University of Florida, 1999, 48; Petition of Agustín Guillermo de Funtes y Herrera, April 29, 1743, AGI 86–7–21/6, Stetson Collection, St. Augustine Historical Society, St. Augustine, Florida (hereafter cited as SC, SAHS).

17. Fray Joseph Bullones, "Testimony Relative to the Doctrinas of Florida," October 5, 1728, AGI 5–2–16/23, SC, SAHS; John Hann, "St. Augustine's Fallout from the Yamasee War," *Florida Historical Quarterly* 68, no. 2 (October 1989): 180–200, 186n38. I created this map by using information from Antonio de Arredondo, *Plano de la Ciudad de San Agustín de la Florida*, 1737, Historic St. Augustine Preservation Board Map Collection, University of Florida.

18. Petition of Agustín Guillermo de Funtes y Herrera, 1743; Parker, "The Second Century of Settlement," 48; Carl D. Halbirt, "Where the sea breezes constantly blow—an ideal place for a home . . .": The 18th Century Mission Community of Nuestra Señora del Rosario de la Punta," paper presented at the 2005 South Eastern Archaeological Conference, Columbia, South Carolina, 1.

19. Manuel de Montiano, "Letters of Montiano, Siege of St. Augustine," *Collections of the Georgia Historical Society* (Savannah: Georgia Historical Society, 1909), 33; Fray Bullones, "Testimony," October 5, 1728; Hann, "St. Augustine's Fallout," 194.

20. Fray Bullones, "Testimony," October 5, 1728.

21. Hann, *Missions*, 323.

22. John Worth, "Yamasee" in *Handbook of North American Indians*, vol. 14: *Southeast*, ed. Raymond D. Fogelson, gen. ed. William Sturtevant (Washington DC: Smithsonian Institution Press, 2004), 249.

23. Hann, "St. Augustine's Fallout," 186.

24. Hahn, *Invention of the Creek Nation*, 84.

25. Rodd to "a Gentleman in London," May 8, 1715, in W. Noel Sainsbury, *Records in the British Public Record Office Relating to South Carolina*, Sainsbury transcripts, 36 vols. (Columbia: Historical Commission of South Carolina, 1928–47), 6: 75.

26. Oatis, *A Colonial Complex*, 126; Rodd to "a Gentleman," May 8, 1715.

27. Rodd to "a Gentleman," 1715.

28. Oatis, *A Colonial Complex*, 126; in a conversation on October 1, 2015, Denise Bossy made the suggestion that Sadkatche and Sataquica might be phonetic renditions of the same town.

29. Hann, "St. Augustine's Fallout," 186.

30. Hann, "St. Augustine's Fallout," 186.

31. Joseph Ramos Escudero to the King, 1734, in *Early History of the Creek Indians and their Neighbors*, trans. John R. Swanton (Washington: Government Printing Office, 1922), 102.

32. James W. Covington, "The Yamasee Indians in Florida: 1715–1763," *Florida Anthropologist* 23, no. 3 (September 1970): 121.

33. Michael V. Gannon, *The Cross in the Sand: The Early Catholic Church in Florida, 1513–1870* (Gainesville: University Press of Florida, 1965), 81.

34. Petition of Agustín Guillermo de Funtes y Herrera, 1743; Parker, "The Second Century," 48.

35. Parker, "The Second Century," 48.

36. Susan Parker, "Nation's Oldest City: How Local Villages Were Devastated on Nov. 1, 1725," *St. Augustine Record*, November 2, 2003.

37. Hann, *Missions*, 310.

38. Hann, *Missions*, 314; Fray Bullones, "Testimony," 1728.

39. Daniel J. Silverman, *Faith and Boundaries: Colonists, Christianity, and Community among the Wampanoag Indians of Martha's Vineyard, 1600–1871* (New York: Cambridge University Press, 2005).

40. Denise Bossy, "Spiritual Diplomacy: The Tama Yamasees in and out of La Florida's Missions," paper presented at the Franciscan Florida in pan-Borderlands Perspective, St. Augustine, March 1, 2014.

41. Denise Bossy, "Spiritual Diplomacy, the Yamasees, and the Society for the Propagation of the Gospel: Reinterpreting Prince Georges Eighteenth-Century Voyage to England," *Early American Studies, An Interdisciplinary Journal* 12, no. 2 (Spring 2014): 369.

42. Bossy, "Spiritual Diplomacy, the Yamasees," 310, 314, 369.

43. Scardaville and Belmonte, *Griñán Report*, 11.

44. Scardaville and Belmonte, *Griñán Report*, 9; Antonio de Arredondo Pueblos Capases de Tomar Armas, November 27, 1736, AGI 87-1-1, SC, SAHS.

45. Covington, "Yamasee Indians," 122; Oatis, *A Colonial Complex*, 277.

46. Montiano, "Letters," 42.

47. Montiano, "Letters," 42.

48. Montiano, "Letters," 34. Jane Landers, "Fort San Francisco de Pupo (Florida)," *Colonial Wars of North America, 1512–1763: An Encyclopedia*, ed. Allan Gallay (New York: Garland, 1996), 663.

49. Montiano, "Letters," 25.

50. John Hann, "Demise of the Poyjoy and Bomto," *Florida Historical Quarterly* 74, no. 2 (Fall 1995): 193.

51. Montiano "Letters," 34.

52. Montiano, "Letters," 34–35.

53. Landers, "Fort San Francisco de Pupo (Florida)," 663.

54. Hann, "St. Augustine's Fallout," 186; Alexander Sweeney, "Cultural Continuity and Change: Archaeological Research at Yamasee Primary Towns in South Carolina," paper presented at the Yamasee Indians: From Florida to South Carolina conference, St. Augustine, Florida, April 17, 2015.

55. Oatis, *A Colonial Complex*, 180.

56. Fray Bullones, "Testimony," 1728; Hann, *Missions*, 311–23.

57. Oatis, *A Colonial Complex*, 180.

58. Hann, "St. Augustine's Fallout," 186; John H. Hann, *Indians of Central and South Florida 513–1763* (Gainesville: University Press of Florida, 2003), 103.

59. The Gelabert Report, Father Gelabert, General Mission List 1752, Archivo General de Indias, 87–1–14 (copy available at the St. Augustine Historical Society, St. Augustine, Florida); Hann, *Indians of Central and South Florida*, 103.

60. Hann, *Missions*, 323.

61. Kent G. Lightfoot, "Dynamics of Change in Multiethnic Societies: An Archaeological Perspective from Colonial North America," *Proceedings of the National Academy of Sciences for the United States of America* (2015), 5, doi: 10.1073/pnas.1422190112.5.

62. William Green, *The Search for Altamaha: The Archaeology and Ethnohistory of an Early 18th Century Indian Town* (Columbia: South Carolina Institute of Archaeology and Anthropology, 1992), 114.

63. Green, *Altamaha*, 114.

64. Alexander Y. Sweeney, "Investigating Yamasee Identity: Archaeological Evidence at Pocotaligo," master's thesis, Radford University, 2003, 118; Alex Y. Sweeney and Eric C. Poplin, "Perspectives on Yamasee Life: Excavations at Altamaha Town," paper presented at the Society of Early Americanists Biennial Conference, 2013, 8; Andrea P. White, "Living on the Periphery: A Study of an Eighteenth-Century Yamasee Mission Community in Colonial St. Augustine," master's thesis, College of William and Mary, 2002, 73; Green, *The Search for Altamaha*, 94; Bobby Southerlin, Dawn Reid, Connie Huddleston, Alana Lynch, and Dea Mozingo, *Return of the Yamasee: Archaeological Data recovery at Chechesy Old Field, Beaufort County, South Carolina* (Atlanta: Brockington and Associates, 2001), 168.

65. Keith Ashley, "Straddling the Florida-Georgia State Line: Ceramic Chronology of the St. Marys Region (A.D. 1400–1700)," in *From Santa Elena to St. Augustine: Indigenous Ceramic Variability (A.D. 1400–1700)*, eds. Kathleen Deagan and David Hurst Thomas, Anthropological Papers of the American Museum of Natural History, no. 90 (New York: American Museum of Natural History, 2009), 137; Rebecca Saunders, *Stability and Change in Guale Indian Pottery A.D. 1300–1702* (Tuscaloosa: University of Alabama Press, 2000), 152–53.

66. Gifford J. Waters, "Maintenance and Change in 18th Century Mission Indian Identity: A Multi-Ethnic Contact Situation," PhD diss., University of North Florida, 2005, 151.

67. Waters, "Maintenance and Change" 94, 119, 151, 159–60.

68. Sweeney, "Yamasee Identity," 48–50.

69. Waters, "Maintenance and Change," 119.

70. Waters, "Maintenance and Change," 78; Vicki Rolland and Keith Ashley, "Beneath the Bell: A Study of Mission Period Colonoware from Three Spanish Missions in North East Florida," *Florida Anthropologist* 53, no. 1 (2000): 36.

71. Keith Ashley, Vicki Rolland, and Robert Thunen, "Missions San Buenaventura and Santa Cruz de Guadalquini: Retreat from the Georgia Coast," in *Life Among the Tides: Recent Archaeol-*

ogy on the Georgia Bight, ed. Victor Thompson and David Hurst Thomas, Anthropological Papers of the American Museum of Natural History, no. 98 (New York: American Museum of Natural History, 2013), 417; Charles Cobb and Chester DePratter, "Multisited Research on Colonalwares and the Paradox of Globalization," *American Anthropologist* 114, no. 3 (2013): 453, doi: 10.1111/j.1548-1433.2010.01445.x.

72. Southerlin et al., *Return of the Yamasee*, 121, 170; Sweeney and Poplin, "Yamasee Life," 9; White, "Living on the Periphery," 72–73, 82; Green, *Altamaha*, 96.

73. Southerlin et al., *Return of the Yamasee*, 173; Green, *Altamaha*, 98.

74. Scardaville and Belmonte, *Griñán Report*, 11.

75. Southerlin et al., *Return of the Yamasee*, 131.

76. Board of Commissioners Meeting, August 3, 1711, in *Journals of the Commissioners of the Indian Trade: 1710–1715*, ed. W. L. McDowell Jr. (Columbia: South Carolina Archives Department, 1955), 14.

77. Kathleen Deagan, *Artifacts of the Spanish Colonies*, vol. 2: *Portable, Personal Possessions* (Washington DC: Smithsonian Institution Press, 2002), 310; White, "Living on the Periphery," 105.

78. Sweeney, "Yamasee Identity," 116; Sweeney and Poplin, "Yamasee Life," 6; Southerlin et al., *Return of the Yamasee*, 174; Green, *Altamaha*, 100.

79. White, "Living on the Periphery," 105.

80. Southerlin et al., *Return of the Yamasee*, 173–74; Sweeney and Poplin, "Yamasee Life," 9.

81. Ivor Noël Hume, *A Guide to Artifacts of Colonial America* (New York: Alfred A. Knopf, 1969), 213; Deagan, *Artifacts of the Spanish Colonies*, 2: 280; White, "Living on the Periphery," 97; Covington, "Yamasee Indians," 121.

82. John T. Powell, professor of history, curator of history, retired, e mail messages to author, July 31 and August 3, 2015.

83. Powell, emails; Carl D. Halbirt, pers. comm., June 2015.

84. Arredondo, *Plano de la Ciudad de San Agustín de la Florida*, 1737.

85. Faunal assemblage (n = 122).

86. Scardaville and Belmonte, *Griñán Report*, 11.

87. William Green, Chester B. DePratter, and Bobby Southerlin, "The Yamasee in South Carolina: Native American Adaptation and Interaction along the Carolina Frontier," in *Another's Country: Archaeological and Historical Perspectives on Cultural Interactions in the Southern Colonies*, ed. J. W. Joseph and Martha Zierden (Tuscaloosa: University of Alabama Press, 2001), 19–20. When working with faunal remains, there are many sample biases to consider. Hall, "San Antonio de Pocotalaca."

88. Elizabeth J. Reitz and Stephen L. Cumbaa, "Diet and Foodways of Eighteenth-Century Spanish St. Augustine," in *Spanish St. Augustine: The Archaeology of a Creole Community*, ed. Kathleen Deagan (New York: Academic Press, 1983), 159.

89. Scardaville and Belmonte, *Griñán Report*, 11.

90. Scardaville and Belmonte, *Griñán Report*, 11.

91. Scardaville and Belmonte, *Griñán Report*, 11.

92. Scardaville and Belmonte, *Griñán Report*, 11.

93. Scardaville and Belmonte, *Griñán Report*, 11.

94. Green, DePratter, and Southerlin, "Yamasee in South Carolina," 19–20.

95. Mary Theresa Bonhage-Freund, "Botanical Remains," in *Archaeology of the Lower Muskogee Creek Indians, 1715–1836*, ed. H. Thomas Foster (Tuscaloosa: University of Alabama Press, 2007), 146.

96. Carl D. Halbirt, A Synopsis of 76 Duero Street, unpublished report, 2013, 4; White, "Living on the Periphery," 56.

97. James W. Hatch, "Lamar Period Upland Farmsteads of the Oconee River Valley, Georgia," in *Mississippian Communities and Households*, ed. Daniel Rogers and Bruce D. Smith (Tuscaloosa: University of Alabama Press, 1995), 144–47.

98. H. Thomas Foster, ed. *Archaeology of the Lower Muskogee Creek Indians, 1715–1836* (Tuscaloosa: University of Alabama Press, 2007), 108.

99. Hahn, "The Long Yamasee War.

100. Sweeney and Poplin, "Yamasee Life," 5.

101. Southerlin et al., *Return of the Yamasee*, 90.

102. Foster, *Archaeology*, 108.

103. Hatch, "Lamar Period," 146–47.

104. Foster, *Archaeology*, 104.

105. Foster, *Archaeology*, 108.

106. Fray Bullones, "Testimony," 1728.

107. Deagan, *Spanish St. Augustine*, 32.

108. Hall, *Zamumo's Gifts*, 100; Worth, "Yamasee," 248.

109. Hann, *Missions*, 325.

9

Refuge among the Spanish
Yamasee Community Coalescence in St. Augustine after 1715

ANDREA P. WHITE

In 1728 Colonel John Palmer of South Carolina raided the refugee mission villages around St. Augustine in direct retaliation against the Yamasee people for their involvement in the 1715 Yamasee War. Before dawn on March 9, Palmer's party of around three hundred Carolinians and their Native allies attacked the village of Nombre de Dios. The raiding party killed thirty Indians, took fifteen captive, and wounded many more. "The rest of the Yamasee took refuge in the Spanish fort. For three days the little army lingered in front of St. Augustine, hoping to complete the destruction of the Yamasee."[1]

Palmer's raid offers two important pieces of evidence relevant to this chapter of the Yamasees' tenure in Spanish St. Augustine where some sought refuge after 1715. First, it demonstrates the effects raids had on the Yamasee population settled around St. Augustine. These frequent raids were part of the consequences associated with Yamasee actions that sparked the Yamasee War as well as the persistent violence associated with colonialism along the Spanish-English borderlands during the first half of the eighteenth century. One result of the raids was a declining number of Yamasees—and all indigenous groups—living among the Spanish after 1726. Second, a map portraying Palmer's attack illustrates the "Yamacy hutts" of Nombre de Dios and the location of three other refugee mission villages clustered around the colonial town. One "Indian town" marked on the map just south of the city walls corresponds to the Yamasee refugee settlement known as Nuestra Señora del Rosario de la Punta and provides the first evidence of this community.[2]

La Punta was a refugee mission village on the periphery of St. Augustine occupied primarily by Yamasees. As part of the diaspora of the Yamasee Confederacy following the outbreak of the Yamasee War, over four hundred Yamasee people eventually sought sanctuary in Spanish territory. They resettled in refugee mission villages. Following a series of raids and epidemics, surviving members from other refugee mission villages amalgamated to form La Punta sometime in the late 1720s.

During the time of occupation, La Punta was located south of the colonial town and its defensive system (map 12). The Rosario Line, a defensive line that surrounded part of St. Augustine, served as the community's north border. The Maria Sanchez Creek and the Matanzas River bounded La Punta on the remaining three sides, providing a good defensive vantage point. The refugee mission village once stretched across thirty acres, and the core of the community may have shifted on the landscape through time. Today numerous residential and commercial properties extend over the location of the original settlement, reflecting urbanization processes in modern St. Augustine. However, modern development had not destroyed all the remains of the community that once stood nearly three hundred years ago.

Through a series of excavation projects, the City of St. Augustine Archaeology Program, under the direction of City Archaeologist Carl Halbirt, examined portions of the La Punta settlement. The majority of the results discussed later in this chapter come from the 161 Marine Street property.[3] Between 1996 and 1997 Halbirt and his volunteer staff investigated the southern portions of the mission community and excavated over 150 square meters of the refugee mission settlement. Since the initial investigations, the City's Archaeology Program has documented additional components of La Punta at several other sites, including the identification of the mission church in 2004.[4] Combined, the La Punta excavations currently represent the largest dataset associated with the eighteenth-century refugee missions and with the Yamasees after the 1715 Yamasee War.[5]

Using both the archaeology and the ethnohistory of the La Punta community as a case study, I chronicle one thread of the Yamasee Confederation's diaspora following the Yamasee War. During their tenure

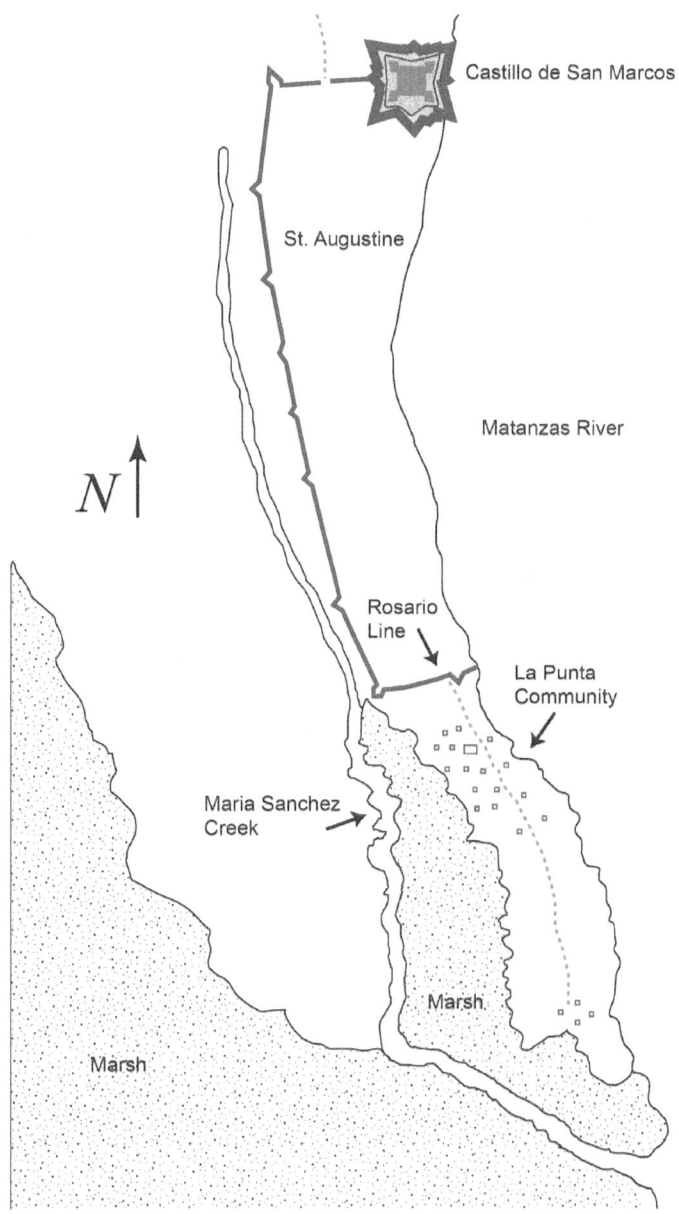

MAP 12. Location of the La Punta refugee community, south of St. Augustine and the Castillo de San Marcos. Courtesy of the City of St. Augustine Archaeology Program.

among St. Augustine's refugee mission communities, the Yamasees faced many pressures. These pressures included accelerated depopulation, village consolidation and resettlement, and intense multiethnic interaction living in close proximity to the Spanish and other Native groups. In this atmosphere of social stresses and instability, one Yamasee response was to enact community coalescence.[6] The establishment of La Punta and the increase of village membership through time—countering the overall demographic decline of the refugee mission villages—illustrate this coalescent response. Archaeology supports the notion that new members joined the community and that village location and occupation fluctuated through time. Furthermore, archaeological evidence demonstrates the La Punta Yamasees continued to replicate and practice some aspects of their traditional way of life, possibly as a way to ground themselves to their culture during tumultuous times despite being in a new geographic and multiethnic environment. Finally, the examination of La Punta via ethnohistorical and archaeological data provides a broader understanding of the Yamasees' legacy as they struggled to negotiate daily life after migrating close to St. Augustine and under the disruptive and often violent effects of colonialism.

The Struggle for Survival in St. Augustine's Eighteenth-Century Refugee Mission Villages

After the start of the Yamasee War in April 1715, the Yamasees retreated from their homes in the Upper and Lower towns in Port Royal Sound in South Carolina.[7] In May 1715 four Indian emissaries, including two (likely three) of Yamasee lineage, visited St. Augustine and petitioned the Spanish governor for sanctuary from the English.[8] Governor Córcoles y Martínez provided the delegates with gifts and sorely needed supplies. He hoped they would again become Spanish allies and was more than willing to grant them permission to relocate their people to lands near St. Augustine.

When around four hundred Yamasee people resettled on the outskirts of St. Augustine, they mingled with a large multiethnic Indian population. Many, like the Christianized Apalachees, Timucuas, and Guales, had sought refuge or been coerced to relocate near the safety of the town's presidio following the destruction of the Spanish mission system by English-led raiders a decade earlier.[9] The repercussions of the Yamasee War directly affected the composition of the Native populations in St. Augustine for a second time. A census taken in April 1717 chronicled the various tribal groups—including Yamasees—seeking sanctuary, essentially doubling the number of Native refugees.[10] Others documented in the 1717 roster included people from the Jororo, Mocama (Mocama-speaking Timucuas), Casapuya, Costa, and Alfaes groups.[11] Dispersed into ten *doctrinas* or *vistas*, most refugee villages were segregated initially by tribal affiliation, including three primarily occupied by the Yamasees. Over time the mixing of different ethnicities among the villages became more frequent. All told, between 1717 and 1726 more than a thousand Indians took refuge with the Spanish, many speaking different languages and having different cultural traditions and customs.

Sometime during the mid-1720s the refugees clustered around St. Augustine reached a zenith of 1,011 Native people. After 1726 the number of Natives residing in the mission villages decreased rapidly. Census records confirmed the overall reduction of Native populations, including the Yamasees. Between 1726 and 1738 the mission numbers fell by at least 600 people—more than half the total population—leaving less than 400 individuals.[12] Between 1739 and 1743 the War of Jenkins' Ear spilled over into the geopolitical landscape of the American South, pitting the English and Spanish, and their Native allies, against each other. In 1740 James Oglethorpe, governor of Georgia, attacked St. Augustine, forcing the abandonment of the refugee mission villages. Some Indians relocated to western La Florida, as John Worth discusses in chapter 11, or elected to abandon their alliance with the Spanish altogether.

The next mission census in 1752 documented only 155 village residents.[13] By 1759 there were only 95 Indians in two refugee mission communities.[14] In just over three decades nearly 90 percent of the Indian populations had either perished or elected to leave the refugee mission villages or were no longer counted by the census takers. The ethnohistorical records are unclear about the number of Yamasees who succumbed to death during this time, but the archaeology within the community cemetery confirms the fatality of at least some La Punta Yamasees, as discussed later in this chapter.

One main reason for dwindling population numbers was the raids on the refugee mission villages and the inability of the Spanish to protect those living in close proximity to the walled city. The English and their Native allies waged a war of terror specifically targeting the Yamasee settlements. These attacks endured throughout the first half of the eighteenth century and were particularly frequent during the 1720s. Raiding parties killed Yamasee men, captured Yamasee women and children for enslavement, and pursued the Yamasees for annihilation. Fray Joseph de Bullones noted that the Spanish-allied Yamasees were "hated by the rest of the nations. And they made war on them so much that they were being exterminated little by little."[15] These raids are examples of the violence aimed toward the Yamasees following the Yamasee War.

Violence and warfare had long been a part of the Mississippian world. However, violence in the late seventeenth and early eighteenth centuries had taken on a different role and appearance as colonial powers armed the South's Native people and encouraged the Indian slave trade. This new era of violence shattered indigenous populations of the American South but also provided new avenues to reorder their worlds. As a result, southern Natives continually adjusted their diplomatic polices and survival strategies. The Yamasees, once the victims of seventeenth-century slave-raiding parties, became prominent attackers and slave traders until they dissolved their alliance with South Carolina in 1715.[16] While there was much violence directed toward the Spanish-allied Yamasees after the Yamasee War, they were not merely passive actors. Many engaged in reciprocal skirmishes and raids on the English colonists and their Native allies, and the Yamasee War continued to drag out over several decades, as suggested by Steven Hahn in this volume.[17]

Other factors played a role in the decline of Native populations enumerated in Spanish records. In addition to death or enslavement by attacking parties, disease became an invisible exterminator. A smallpox epidemic in 1727 and a measles outbreak in 1732 quickly spread through the villages with a devastating effect on mortality rates.[18]

Decreasing mission populations also reflect the process of outmigration. Many Indians recognized the inability of the Spanish to provide adequate protection from English-backed raids, disliked the required *repartimiento* labor service, and grew weary of the marginal living conditions.[19] They deserted the refugee settlements to seek a better life, choosing to take up with other Native groups or rekindle old kinship ties. However, some Native Americans chose to remain with the Spanish and inserted themselves into the St. Augustine community. Susan Parker, in the following chapter, illustrates how a Native could become a *vecino*, a legal full member of society, either by marriage or through military service.[20] As a result of these processes, some might have lost their Indian identity in the documents and therefore were no longer counted among village populations. Outmigration within the refugee communities also included moving from one refugee mission village to another, often associated with marriage. In matrilineal societies this often involved the husband moving to reside with the wife's family. Regardless of which factor was in play, refugee mission populations continued to decline.

One important Yamasee response to waning populations—encouraged by the friars and government officials—was the amalgamation of refugee settlements. Community coalescence was mutually beneficial to the Yamasees, other refugee mission villagers, and the Spanish administration. Furthermore, the strategy dovetailed with Spanish *reducción* and *congregación* policies (adapted for the eighteenth-century circumstances).[21] In response to English aggression, Spanish officials attempted to place the refugee villages strategically to serve as a buffer around the city, effectively creating St. Augustine's first line of defense. The danger of raids resulted in a constant state of flux for the Native communities surrounding St. Augustine. Uncertainty and volatility resulted in the movement of villages, or what Susan Parker called a "concertina."[22] In times of strife, refugee settlements would migrate closer to the town's defenses and temporarily abandon their villages until the threat abated. The frequent movement of the mission settlements suggests that refugee Indians had some agency in determining their community's fate and a suitable village location. Perhaps village caciques and leaders based their decisions with regard to soil fertility, safety, and defensibility or with kinship ties and past alliances in mind. Communities reacted in different ways to frequent movement and heavy losses sustained during this time of instability. Occasionally surviving refugees from one village would join an existing community. Some village sites were destroyed or abandoned altogether. New communities formed as well, often in a new geographical location, when members from several communities coalesced, as in the case of La Punta genesis.

While community coalescence may have had some success as a mechanism for survival, it may have created additional challenges within the context of St. Augustine's refugee mission villages. The amalgamation of communities brought groups from an array of backgrounds, cultures, and languages into close proximity to one another and to Spanish society in an urban context. Residing in such intermingled contexts, mission Indians could be more susceptible to deadly diseases, which sometimes affected whole communities. Furthermore, living with disparate Native groups and the loss of community members disrupted Native social organization and family structure. In the next section I examine La Punta's persistence despite these challenges.

The Genesis and Decline of La Punta

The formation of La Punta is a direct example of a coalescent response to survive the unstable and volatile refugee mission landscape. During its existence across three decades, the community membership continually increased, thus affirming the success of the community to flourish by adopting newcomers, increasing numbers through birth, and/or extending the lifespan of existing residents. However, the eventual demise of La Punta sometime after 1752 illustrates the community's struggles to endure in the face of dwindling refugee mission society.

Community members with Yamasee lineage probably could connect some of their kinship ties back to precontact Mississippian chiefdoms in the American South. Scholars have attempted to understand the origins of the Yamasee Confederacy by correlating place names in the ethnohistorical record.[23] In South Carolina the Lower Yamasee towns of Altamaha, Okatee, and Chechessee can be traced back to the Lamar chiefdoms encountered by the Hernando de Soto entrada

Refuge among the Spanish

into the Oconee River Valley during the sixteenth century. John Hann extended some of the place-name correlates to the initial settlements around St. Augustine documented in 1717.[24] The persistence of settlement names, or town identities, as Yamasee populations moved from English South Carolina to Spanish La Florida suggests the movement of some of the same community members or at least those with close kinship ties. However, the connection of La Punta to these older place names is less clear.

It is possible La Punta originated from the splintered population of the predominantly Yamasee-occupied village Nuestra Señora de Candelaria de la Tamaja, established by 1717.[25] Based on part of the village name, Tamaja, and the name of the Yamasee cacique, Alonso Ocute, this settlement likely had ties to the Lower Yamasee towns of Altamaha and Okatee. Furthermore, the Candelaria name may be linked to community ties to the seventeenth-century Nuestra Señora de Candelaria, a former Yamasee mission in Apalachee province prior to 1704.[26] An attack in 1725 on Candelaria de la Tamaja is the last mention of this community's existence in the ethnohistorical records.[27] By 1728 evidence indicated many surviving Candelaria residents moved to Nuestra Señora de Rosario de Moze.[28] Moze, a predominantly Apalachee-occupied mission village, had recently undergone a devastating smallpox epidemic in 1727.[29] It is plausible that sometime before or just after John Palmer's raid in 1728, the remnant populations of Candelaria and Moze amalgamated to form Nuestra Señora de Rosario de la Punta. A map based on Palmer's attack illustrated a Native village just south of St. Augustine in the vicinity of La Punta's location.[30] How many people survived the raids and epidemics to form La Punta's initial population is unknown, as is their tribal heritage.

The genesis of La Punta certainly occurred before 1736, based on the earliest known reference to the mission by name in a document containing the names of Native American villages in service to the Presidio of San Augustin. Enumerations for La Punta listed the names and ages of the cacique and sixteen additional men.[31] A year later the 1737 Antonio de Arredondo Map provided both the location and population of La Punta (map 12).[32] The map shows details of the community, including a large structure—presumably the mission church—and twenty farmsteads scattered across thirty acres. The two clusters of farmsteads could have corresponded to the seventeen men and seventeen women and children living at the settlement.

Table 9 illustrates the aggregated data of the La Punta population. La Punta experienced an increase of inhabitants over time. Some historical descriptions provided clues to the composition of the La Punta community. In addition to residents identified as Yamasee, the mission population included at least one Apalachee person, which is to be expected if the village included Yamasees and Apalachees from remnant Moze and Candelaria villages, as previously noted.

TABLE 9. La Punta population estimates

source	year	population				total	reference
		men	women	children	families		
Anonymous (likely Arredondo)	1736	17	—	—	—	17	Swanton 1922: 105
Arredondo	1737	17	17*	*	—	34	Arredondo 1737
Benavides	April, 1738	15	26*	*	—	41	Hann 1996: 316
Montiano	June, 1738	10	13	20	—	43	Hann 1996: 316
Güemes y Horcasitas	1738	—	—	—	14	51	Hann 1996: 317
Friars	1752	25	34	—	—	59	Hann 1996: 323

* Indicates combined sum of women and children.

Sources: Antonio de Arredondo, *Plano de la Ciudad de San Agustín de la Florida*, 1737, Historic St. Augustine Preservation Board Map Collection, University of Florida; John R. Swanton, *Early History of Creek Indians and Their Neighbors* (1922; repr., Gainesville: University Press of Florida, 1998); John H. Hann, *A History of the Timucua Indians and Missions* (Gainesville: University Press of Florida, 1996).

Keen observers will note the lack of data during the 1740s. In fact historians have found very little documentary information relating to mission-village demographics during this twelve-year gap.[33] One

Refuge among the Spanish

possible explanation is the outbreak of the War of Jenkins' Ear and James Oglethorpe's siege of St. Augustine in 1740. To avoid death or enslavement, mission residents who did not flee took refuge inside the Castillo walls. For three months, English-led forces besieged the town. During the attack, La Punta residents would have abandoned their community—as the archaeology clearly demonstrates. It is possible the abandonment of La Punta continued throughout the duration of the war. Kathleen Deagan noted a similar archaeological pattern of abandonment associated with the siege at the free African community of Fort Mosé.[34]

Furthermore, the archaeology indicates La Punta was reoccupied. By 1752 La Punta boasted its largest population, numbering at least 59, including 25 men and 34 women—no number for children was included. It was the largest of six remaining refugee villages, under the leadership of Chief Antonio Juta. John Hann suggested La Punta's inhabitants remained predominantly Yamasee because in 1736 two Yamasee villages had chiefs with the name Juta (Yuta): Nombre de Dios Chiquito and Pocotalaca.[35] Given the reduction of refugee mission villages between 1738 and 1752, the La Punta population enumerated in the 1752 census probably included members from disbanded mission villages, among them those destroyed during the 1740 siege.

While La Punta's population increased over time, it is not a true reflection of the Yamasee or other Indian populations near St. Augustine as a whole. This upward trend stands in stark contrast to the demographics at other refugee mission communities, which were more unstable. As previously discussed, between 1726 and 1759 a massive depopulation of the refuge mission villages occurred, both in the total number of communities and in the number of Indian residents. What does La Punta's ability to counter the overall demographic trend observed in refugee village populations tell us? At La Punta the increase of community members over time strongly suggests a coalescent response by incorporating newcomers into the community.

By 1759 historical records no longer referred to La Punta and do not speak to the fate of the community members. Most likely the two remaining mission villages of Tolomato and Nombre de Dios absorbed the La Punta residents who chose to remain in the Native villages, thus continuing the process of village consolidation. The 1763 Pablo Castelló map illustrated the ruins of the mission church near the area of La Punta.[36] That same year, as part of the treaty ending the French and Indian War, Spain ceded La Florida to the British in exchange for Havana, Cuba. When St. Augustine residents departed for Cuba, at least 89 Indians elected to join them. Of the 89, at least 11 were Yamasee evacuees.[37] Presumably the ones who chose to stay behind formed their own communities or joined other regional tribes.

Archaeology of the La Punta Community

The preceding discussion of the ethnohistorical records provides a contextual framework to understand the tenure of the Yamasees near Spanish St. Augustine. The archaeological record can be a different dataset to examine the daily life of the Yamasee people as they resided within the La Punta community and navigated St. Augustine's multiethnic society. Archaeology offers a more tangible connection to the Yamasees, including the items they made and consumed, the material evidence of the communities they constructed, and even their physical remains. I use the archaeology of La Punta to illustrate four ideas. First, at the most basic level, the archaeological record documented at La Punta is the physical manifestation of community coalescence; that is to say, the outcome when remnant populations join together to create a new community. Second, excavation results provide evidence for the movement of the settlement on the landscape and the abandonment and reoccupation of the village, corroborating ethnohistorical research and the concept of refugee mission villages being in a fluctuating state of disruption. Third, through coalescence, the Yamasee people not only persisted; they were able to create a sense of stability through the replication of cultural traditions. Comparisons to archaeological data from other Yamasee sites illuminate how closely related Yamasee kinfolk continued certain traditional practices even as they migrated into an environment that was different geographically and socially. Finally, the archaeology provides a glimpse of daily life, including the creation of domestic and communal spaces, community health and composition, and production of and access to material goods. This is essential information not just about the La Punta community but about the Yamasees as a whole following the diaspora of the Yamasee Confederacy.

Community Features

One important clue archaeologists used to confirm the remains of the La Punta community was the presence of numerous features—such as postholes, trash pits, and a well—remaining in the ground. The types and spatial arrangement of these features illustrate the layout of the refugee mission village. During the 1997 investigations archaeologists documented one Yamasee structure, and possibly two additional ones, relating to the mission occupation.[38] A total of six uniformly spaced postholes and postmolds delineated the perimeter of a circular structure approximately six meters in diameter with a center support post (Structure 1, in map 13). A cluster of eight features on the north side of the house likely represented a discrete household task space. The presence of five daub pits near the exterior of the residence pointed to traditional wattle-and-daub construction for the walls. Around two hundred nails were recovered from the site, suggesting nails and cordage were used to affix wattle or wooden framing before applying layers of daub plaster. Additionally, the nails may have functioned as hooks within the structure. Ethnographic data described roofs as thatched with palm fronds. The circular pattern of postholes in two other locations could represented two other structures, although their footprint extended beyond the limits of excavation (Structures 2 and 3, in map 13). The placement of the dwelling on the landscape showed that the La Punta Yamasees lived within a small, nucleated community along on a relict dune ridge with agricultural fields scattered in between the dwellings.

When comparing the La Punta residential data to other Yamasee sites, well-defined patterns of architectural replication emerged, including post-in-ground construction methods and wattle-and-daub walls. In previous chapters Alexander Sweeney and Amanda Hall have compared architectural features and structural design from La Punta with archaeological data from Yamasee sites in La Florida and South Carolina as well as the ancestral Yamasee homeland in the Oconee River Valley of interior Georgia.[39] Their research argued for the per-

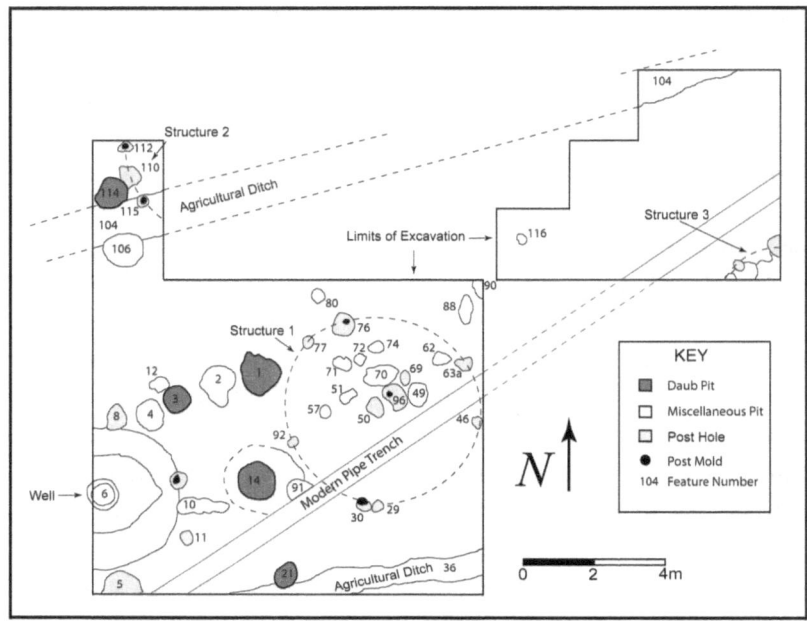

MAP 13. Site map of the 1997 excavations of La Punta located at 161 Marine Street, St. Augustine, Florida. By Andrea P. White.

sistence and continuity of Yamasee domestic architectural traditions spanning more than two hundred years, through multiple migrations across geographical space.

Other archaeological features not only confirm the mission's existence but illustrate the migratory nature of the community. The most intriguing feature to emerge during the 1997 excavations was a communal well that residents constructed out of a single large barrel (figs. 4 and 5). Posthole placement indicated that an open structure extended over the well to protect it from rain and debris. It has been dubbed a "walk-in well" because one had to descend down into a depression to collect water at the barrel's edge.[40] The construction of the La Punta well is unique when compared to other wells documented at colonial sites in St. Augustine, which were typically constructed out of a series of stacked barrels extending from the water table to the ground surface.[41] Recently Carl Halbirt has located a second well within the historical boundaries of La Punta, which displayed similar walk-in characteristics, suggesting this well-construction pattern was repeated within the community and could be a distinct style associated with the Yamasees.[42]

Careful archaeological excavation of the community well provided clear evidence of two different episodes of use, separated by a period of abandonment. These episodes were evident when examining the well profile and interpreting the different layers of soil that accumulated within the well shaft. At the very bottom of the well was a layer of fine sediment that collected during the first episode of use (B in fig. 4). Just above the layer of fine sand was a second layer of soil (C in fig. 4) containing the articulated remains of a bird and a rat—indicators of well abandonment. With the community abandoned and the well unattended, the rat and the bird became trapped inside the barrel, where they eventually died. Over time, sand collected around the decomposing creatures. The archaeological evidence of this deposit signifies that the well went unused for a time, and by extension the community of La Punta was vacated for a period of time, possibly during the 1740 siege. Once the Yamasee residents returned, they put the well back into service by sealing the earlier deposits with a coquina and clay lens (D in fig. 4), capping off the decomposing pests from their drinking water. During the second period of community use, small amounts of sediment accrued inside the barrel (E in fig. 4). With the final abandonment of La Punta in the 1750s, sands and trash from later occupation periods began to accumulate in the open well shaft (F through I in fig. 4), and the wooden barrel began to rot.[43]

Other archaeological evidence corroborates the abandonment and reoccupation of the La Punta community and the changing use of the village landscape. At the 161 Marine Street property two agricultural or irrigation ditches (features 36, lower right, and 104, upper left, in map 13), presumably constructed by village residents, extended across the site.[44] A thin layer of mottled sands, void of artifacts, settled at the bottom of the ditches while they were in use. Similar to the what was seen in well, a period of possible settlement abandonment is insinuated by an accumulated layer of sand (although without trapped creatures) that accrued in the trench due to lack of use and maintenance. Upon the reoccupation of the refugee mission village, residents filled

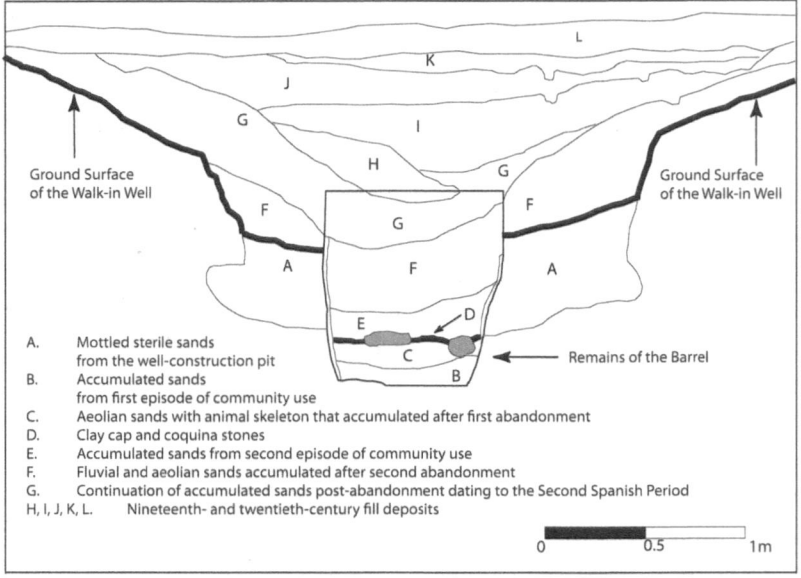

FIG. 4. Profile of La Punta's community well illustrating two episodes of use, separated by a period of abandonment. By Andrea P. White.

in the remaining portion of the northern ditch (feature 104) and constructed Structure 2 over the top of it. The layering of features over one another marked a shift in land use from agricultural to residential. Additionally, the superposition of the domestic and agricultural features confirms the "concertina" movement of the population and even abandonment and reoccupation of the La Punta community. Similarly, there are multiple layers of fill documented in the southern ditch (feature 36). Carl Halbirt has documented similar patterns of superimposed features and ditches with multiple fill layers on other properties within the historical boundaries of La Punta.[45]

Life and Death in the Community

Additional archaeological work at La Punta provided information about the village population. In 2004 excavations in another portion of the site uncovered the remains of the mission church and the cemetery contained with its floors.[46] To date the La Punta church and cemetery are the only documented example of a La Florida mission ceme-

FIG. 5. The remains of the community well, post-excavation. By Andrea P. White.

tery dating solely to the eighteenth century. The results of the church excavations confirmed the site as the La Punta refugee mission village. The osteological examination of some of the individuals interred illustrated the biological manifestation of physical and dietary stress, suggested ethnic variability among community members, and attested to the high mortality associated with a refugee village. Finally, mortuary patterns provide information about the continuity and accommodation of ritual practice within the fold of the Spanish friars.

The discovery of human remains was the first clue as to the location of the La Punta church. Due to state regulations regarding unmarked burials, archaeologists and physical anthropologists were able to examine only a limited number of interments to ascertain ancestry and confirm the extent and age of the cemetery prior to reburial. A total of ten individuals were laid to rest in an extended position on their backs, their bodies oriented with head to the east. Most individuals did not have funeral objects such as jewelry, other adornments, or personal items buried with them. The mortuary pattern of La Punta's deceased appeared to follow the traditional custom of laying Christianized mission Indians to rest. Archaeologists have reported uniformity of mortuary patterns at other La Florida mission churches. Typically interments occurred within the earthen church floor, or just outside the church walls, and aligned along the long axis of the building.[47] Bodies were usually in an extended position with the head to the east. The excavation for each new interment could disturb the previous grave, often resulting in multiple, overlapping burial pits. This was the case at La Punta, where the overlapping graves and limited excavation made it difficult to identify the complete skeleton belonging to some individuals. An estimated 50 to 100 individuals were buried in the cemetery. This is a fairly high number considering that the village was occupied no more than thirty years, the total population never reached more than 59 men and women, and the community appeared to have been abandoned for an extended period of time. Yet the high mortality is not surprising, considering the overall census data for the refugee mission villages and the role disease and raids played in depopulation.

However, the demographic pattern at La Punta did not reflect the overall pattern observed for refugee mission populations as previously discussed. In fact, La Punta's numbers swelled over time. Assuming those buried within the La Punta church were community residents, there appears to be a positive ratio of new community members to the number of deceased.[48] In other words, the population of La Punta still grew over time even though an estimated 50 to 100 community members perished. It is important to note the community lost members not only due to death but also via other means, such as outmigration (either away from or into the city, or via marriage) or being taken captive as human capital, whereby members were not included in the cemetery numbers. When combining the archaeological and census evidence, the La Punta demographic increase is quite remarkable. While it is possible births outnumbered deaths, it is more likely that La Punta increased community membership through coalescence.

Although the remains available for preliminary osteological examination were limited, results provided insight into the daily life and composition of the La Punta community. Some of the individuals had distinctive shovel-shaped incisors, typically indicative of American Indian heritage, while others did not. The lack of shoveled incisors associated with some of the interred individuals insinuates that potential ethnic mixing occurred between indigenous populations and those of European or African ancestry. This is not surprising; mixed marriages and relationships—whether consensual or forced—that resulted in offspring were not uncommon. Furthermore, research by Jane Landers and Susan Parker has documented multiethnic households in St. Augustine.[49] The incisor of one individual displayed signs of enamel hypoplasia indicative of growth disruption associated with childhood stress. Absent from the dentition were dental carries (i.e., cavities), which have been documented in other pre-1704 indigenous mission populations and attributed to a high carbohydrate-based diet, such as corn. Although speculative, the absence of dental carries could confirm that La Punta community members enjoyed a traditional Yamasee diet, which appears more varied than in earlier mission populations.[50] The examination of the skeletal remains revealed osteoarthritis was common. At least three individuals experienced leg fractures (the femur of one individual and fibula of two separate individuals) during their lifespan.[51] The fact that the fractures had healed prior to death signifies a community support system existed for the healing and caring for the injured. These wounds and conditions also speak to the physical stresses of life in colonial contexts.

Finally, data from the mission church support the notion of some similarities related to the ritual burial of the deceased across Yamasee-related sites, albeit slightly adapted for Christianized practice. Located four meters outside the church walls and oriented in a different direction than church burials, archaeologists uncovered a single adult male interred with a shell necklace and a greenstone celt, or axe.[52] These objects were common burial items traditionally associated with southern Native Americans. The male was in an extended position instead of the traditional flexed or semi-flexed position (i.e., knee up to the chest). The placement of this individual outside the church, with his more traditional funerary items, suggests that even in death, his caretakers or descendants resisted some aspects of Catholic customs, perhaps in accordance with the deceased's wishes. However, they recognized the overall space around the church as sacred. Upon initial review, the placement of the dead in the La Punta church floor appears to be in contrast to earlier Yamasee-related sites. At sites in the Oconee River

Valley and at Altamaha Town, family members interred the deceased in flexed or semi-flexed positions within or near the walls of their domestic structures, as Sweeney highlights in this volume.[53] However, while the locational placement of the deceased might have changed with regard to the function of the building (domestic versus ecclesiastical), it might not have been such a dramatic shift in ritual practice from burying family members in the floor of their residence to the floor of their community church. After all, the La Punta Yamasees likely saw both as sacred spaces.

Material Culture

Another way the Yamasees maintained cultural traditions was through the production of pottery. Native American pottery was the most abundant material recovered from La Punta, accounting for 70 percent of the 161 Marine Street collection (figs. 6 and 7). The majority of the indigenous ceramics—62 percent—exemplified Altamaha/San Marcos-series characteristics.[54] Numerous Indian groups crafted Altamaha/San Marcos ceramics, including the Guale, Yamasee, and Mocama-speaking Timucuan people. Beginning in the mid-seventeenth century it became the dominant ware produced at eastern mission sites. Archaeological evidence suggested Yamasee potters were quick to adapt to Altamaha/San Marcos production during the seventeenth century when they settled among the Guale missions. And they continued to craft it while in South Carolina despite being no longer under the influence of the Spanish mission system.[55] A homogenized ware might make it difficult to differentiate group identity based on the ceramics they produced, and Keith Ashley in this volume argues it presents a challenge when distinguishing Yamasee- from Guale-occupied sites.

While a full discussion of the La Punta pottery assemblage is beyond the scope of this chapter, two observations warrant mention with respect to possible correlates to population losses and intermingling of groups at multiethnic refugee mission villages. The first is the variety of indigenous ceramics with regard to types, decorative designs, and tempers. In addition to the Altamaha/San Marcos wares, the collection included sand-tempered, St. Johns, San Pedro, Mission Red Filmed, and unidentifiable shell-tempered and fiber-tempered pot-

FIG. 6. Examples of decorated ceramics recovered from La Punta. Courtesy of the City of St. Augustine Archaeology Program.

tery. Although there was a prevalence of the dominant Altamaha/San Marcos series, the varieties within this series observed in the collection could reflect the consolidation of disparate Indian populations, each bringing with them their own ceramics to the community, as well as certain ceramists' traditional knowledge in ceramic production and artistic ability. When compared to urban St. Augustine *mestizo* households, both La Punta and Pocotalaca, another refugee village site, the eighteenth-century mission villages appeared to have a greater range in indigenous ceramic types, thus reinforcing other indications of variety.[56]

Second is the question of how, if at all, coalescence and depopulation—in particular the loss or new introduction of pottery producers—might affect a community and in what ways this could manifest in the archaeological record. Enumerations detailed the rapid overall decline of the refugee settlements, but census takers were more often concerned with the number of able-bodied men in the community. Consequently, it is difficult to grasp fully the changes to the female population at La Punta and within the refugee mission villages as a whole. As previously illustrated, several forces affected the number of community females—and presumably female potters: death, enslavement, community abandonment, adoption of new members, and the

FIG. 7. A reconstructed Mission red filmed bowl recovered from La Punta. Courtesy of the City of St. Augustine Archaeology Program.

practice of *mestizaje* (the marriage of Indian women to Spanish men). As part of a larger research program to investigate group variation among eighteenth-century refugee-mission ceramic assemblages, Gifford Waters noted a high percentage of plain wares—with a variety of tempers—and postulated that the prevalence of undecorated wares could be an indicator of disruption in traditional production patterns. Conversely, he noted that the high frequency of plain wares may signify a Yamasee preference or tradition.[57] At the time of study Waters was working with a limited dataset of comparative material. With data from recent excavations, this concept warrants additional exploration using comparative material from other Yamasee-occupied sites. Clearly more work is needed (such as Poplin and Marcoux in this volume) to understand what, if anything, ceramics can reveal about the adaptive strategies of the Yamasee people in colonial contexts.

In addition to constructing ceramic vessels for household use, potters produced indigenous wares for a market economy.[58] The selling of ceramic wares was one way Indians participated in the Spanish economy. In eighteenth-century St. Augustine, mercantile opportunity was on the rise, and some Yamasees certainly took advantage by offering their services and selling their products and wild game to town residents.[59] Goods entered the town through various means, including the *situado* supply ships as well as illicit and sanctioned commerce with merchants and traders.[60] Archaeologically, one's access to commodities is manifested in the material culture. Kathleen Deagan illustrated the availability of English goods in St. Augustine and their prevalence in Spanish households of lower socioeconomic status, at least until after 1740 when the English trade was no longer illegal.[61] Items such as glassware, tobacco pipes, and European table and utilitarian wares recovered from La Punta demonstrate that village residents had an active participation in the local economy and were able to acquire a variety of both Spanish- and English-manufactured goods.

Examination of the abandoned and discarded material at La Punta, of the physical remains of the village, and of those community members interred in the soil has provided valuable information about the lives of the Yamasees who lived along the periphery of St. Augustine following the Yamasee War. When this information was combined with the ethnohistorical record, several historical processes were evident at La Punta. First is settlement migration in response to external forces. Historical records indicated movement of the mission villages, and the superimposed features combined with the archaeology of the community well confirm at least one episode of community abandonment and reoccupation. Second, La Punta underwent demographic growth through coalescence. The mixed ethnicity of some of the interred individuals and the variety of ceramics styles suggest the addition of new community members. Moreover, I have used the archaeological record to illustrate the continuation (and some accommodation) of some Yamasee traditional customs, such as in domestic architecture, pottery production, and burial practice, even after multiple migrations and multiethnic interactions.

The period following the diaspora of the Yamasee Confederacy was a challenging time for the Yamasee living on the fringes of Spanish St. Augustine. Electing to settle among various other Indians populations in refugee mission villages, they contended with frequent attacks, a concertina-like migration of refugee settlements, demographic collapse, and village consolidation likely resulting in social disruption caused by these pressures. When faced with an unstable refugee mission landscape, one way the Yamasees responded to these pressures was through community coalescence. La Punta provides a case study of a coalescent response, including the genesis of the community from the remnants of past communities and the growth of the village in an environment of overall population decline. Examining the archaeology of La Punta affirms the establishment and occupational fluctuations of the settlement and helps illuminate Yamasee daily life. Furthermore, research demonstrates the persistence and practice of several Yamasee cultural traditions by La Punta residents. In their chapters Sweeney and Hall provided additional support for Yamasee cultural replication in subsistence practices, structural design, settlement patterning, and material choices. Replication and maintenance of traditional customs was one way the Yamasees anchored their culture when they were not tied to a specific geographical place.

While the examination of La Punta highlights community coalescence and cultural replication, the Yamasees relied on a myriad of survival mechanisms throughout their history. Additionally, the examination of La Punta also speaks to how some Yamasees employed agency and migration. Historical research shows how Indians took advantage of their close proximity to Spanish St. Augustine to improve their economic and social standing. Yamasee men secured military positions, Indian women married Spanish men, and some became *vecino*, while still maintaining familial ties to their Native communities. In other acts of agency, some refugees decided to abandon their alliance with the Spanish and take up with other Native groups living in the region.

As demonstrated throughout this anthology, migration and diaspora were important survival strategies utilized by the Yamasee people. Through the process of migration the Yamasees geographically positioned themselves to take advantage of the changing colonial landscape in order to acquire protection, create alliances, strengthen kinship ties, and elicit trade from various European, African, and Native groups. This included the choice to relocate to St. Augustine. Here, on the periphery of the city, the Yamasees continued their pattern of settlement migration by relocating and reformulating their communities, albeit on a smaller scale, to provide the best opportunity for survival.

Over three hundred years ago, when several Yamasee chiefs led their people to St. Augustine seeking refuge among the Spanish, it is difficult to say for certain the life they envisioned for themselves and their people. However, the ethnohistorical and archaeological record is providing clues about how the Yamasees adapted to a new life on the outskirts of St. Augustine following the Yamasee War and giving voice to those who called La Punta home.

Notes

Thanks are extended to Denise Bossy and Chester DePratter for organizing the first Yamasee conference and for the invitation to contribute to this volume. Denise and other anonymous reviewers enhanced the clarity of my work. Special thanks to Carl Halbirt, who provided value information and ideas about the archaeology of the La Punta community. He persuaded me to volunteer during the 161 Marine Street excavations and convinced me to study the archaeology of the Yamasee people for my master's research. I am forever grateful for his keen archaeological insight and friendship. Numerous volunteers participated in the 1997 excavation project and analysis of the 161 Marine Street artifacts; all deserve a warm thank you. Helen Gradison and Pauline Larrivey earned special mention for assistance analyzing the La Punta material. Of course all omissions and errors are my own.

1. Quoted from Verner W. Crane, *The Southern Frontier 1670–1732* (Ann Arbor: University of Michigan Press, 1929), 250. Also see John Jay Tepaske, *The Governorship of Spanish Florida 1700–1763* (Durham: Duke University Press, 1964), 130–32; John R. Swanton, *Early History of Creek Indians and Their Neighbors* (1922; repr., Gainesville: University Press of Florida, 1998), 341; Jane Landers, "Black-Indian Interaction in Spanish Florida," *Colonial Latin American Historical Review* 2, no. 2 (1993): 152; Steven J. Oatis, *A Colonial Complex: South Carolina's Frontiers in the Era of the Yamasee War 1680–1730* (Lincoln: University of Nebraska Press, 2004), 283–84.

2. Colonel John Palmer, "St. Augustine and Its Harbor," 1730, Historic St. Augustine Preservation Board Map Collection, map on file at the Dr. Sue A. Middleton Archaeology Center.

3. White first synthesized the 161 Marine Street excavations; see Andrea P. White, "Living on the Periphery: A Study of an Eighteenth-Century Yamasee Mission Community in Colonial St. Augustine," MA thesis, College of William and Mary, 2002. The first archaeological evidence

of La Punta was documented during the surveys of 159 and 161 Marine Street; see Carl D. Halbirt, "Nuestra Señora del Rosario de la Punta: Phase 1 Archaeological Survey of an 18th-Century Yamassee Mission Community in St. Augustine, Florida," City of St. Augustine Archaeological Program Occasional Series Paper no. 2, 1996; "'Where the sea breezes constantly blow—an ideal place for a home . . .': The 18th-Century Mission Community of Nuestra Señora del Rosario de la Punta," paper presented at the 62nd Annual Meeting of the Southeastern Archaeological Conference, Columbia, South Carolina, 2005.

4. Through subsequent excavations Halbirt documented additional deposits associated with La Punta on several properties within the known boundaries of the mission; see Carl D. Halbirt, "Archaeology of 18th-Century Yamassee Sites in St. Augustine, Florida," paper presented at the Yamasee Indians: From Florida to South Carolina conference, St. Augustine, Florida 2015.

5. Cumulatively, the La Punta investigations have been reported in White, "Living on the Periphery"; Halbirt, "Phase 1 Archaeological Survey," " Ideal Place for a Home," and "Archaeology of 18th-Century Yamassee Sites"; Willet A. Boyer, "Nuestra Señora del Rosario de la Punta: Lifeways of an Eighteenth-Century Colonial Spanish Refugee Mission Community, St. Augustine, Florida," MA thesis, University of Florida, 2005; City of St. Augustine Archaeology Program, "Nuestra Señora del Rosario de la Punta," http://www.citystaug.com/archaeology/NuestraSenora.php; Gifford J. Waters, "Aboriginal Ceramics at Three 18th-Century Mission Sites in St. Augustine, Florida," in *From Santa Elena to St. Augustine: Indigenous Ceramic Variability (A.D. 1400–1700): Proceedings of the Second Caldwell Conference, St. Catherines Island, Georgia, March 30–April 1, 2007*, ed. Kathleen A. Deagan and David Hurst Thomas (New York: American Museum of Natural History, 2009); Gifford J. Waters, "Maintenance and Change of 18th Century Mission Indian Identity: A Multi-Ethnic Contact Situation," PhD diss., University of Florida, 2005.

6. Native South scholars usually used the term *coalescence* on a larger scale, describing the formation of many groups, such as the Yamasees, Creeks, Cherokees, Chickasaws and others as coalescent societies. Coalescence is just one possible response to demographic pressures and social stresses, although the actual process is less clear. In the example of La Punta, my focus is less on how the process of coalescence worked at La Punta and more on recognizing coalescent responses in the combined archaeological and ethnographical datasets. Examining coalescence at a community scale could help us understand how the processes of coalescence operate on larger scales. For an overview see Robbie Ethridge, "Introduction," in *Mapping the Mississippian Shatter Zone: The Colonial Indian Slave Trade and Regional Instability in the American South*, ed. Robbie Ethridge and Sheri M. Shuck-Hall (Lincoln: University of Nebraska Press, 2009), 38–39. Many authors discussed coalescent groups in the edited volume by Robbie Ethridge and Charles Hudson, eds., *The Transformation of the Southeastern Indians, 1540–1760* (Jackson: University Press of Mississippi, 2002). For a broader discussion on coalescent societies see Stephen A. Kowalewski, "Coalescent Societies," in *Light on the Path: The Anthropology and History of the Southeastern Indians*, ed. Thomas J. Pluckhahn and Robbie Ethridge (Tuscaloosa: University of Alabama Press, 2006).

7. William L. Ramsey, *The Yamasee War: A Study of Culture, Economy, and Conflict in the Colonial South*, Indians of the Southeast (Lincoln: University of Nebraska Press, 2008), 117–18; Oatis, *A Colonial Complex*, 178–79.

8. The delegation included both Yamasee and Creek representatives. See Tepaske, *Governorship*, 198; Steven C. Hahn, *The Invention of the Creek Nation, 1670–1763* (Lincoln: University

of Nebraska Press, 2004), 84–85; Oatis, *A Colonial Complex*, 113; Ramsey, *Yamasee War*, 103–4; Alejandra Dubcovsky, "One Hundred Sixty-One Knots, Two Plates, and One Emperor: Creek Information Networks in the Era of the Yamasee War," *Ethnohistory* 59, no. 3 (2012): 490–93.

9. The raids included the destruction of the Guale province, the 1702 siege of St. Augustine, and the 1704 attack on the Apalachee province by the English and their Indian allies, who included some Yamasees. For a summary see Jerald T. Milanich, *Florida Indians and the Invasion from Europe* (Gainesville: University Press of Florida, 1995), 222–27.

10. A 1711 census listed 401 inhabitants living in the refugee mission villages close to St. Augustine. A 1717 census of native villages documented 946 inhabitants. A translation of Primo de Rivera's 1717 census appeared in both Hann's works. John H. Hann, "St. Augustine's Fallout from the Yamasse War," *Florida Historical Quarterly* 68, no. 2 (1989): 182–86, and his *A History of the Timucua Indians and Missions* (Gainesville: University Press of Florida, 1996), 303–11; Ramsey, *Yamasee War*, 117–18; Oatis, *A Colonial Complex*, 180.

11. Hann suggested the possibility that as many as nineteen tribes may have been represented in the refuge mission populations. Hann, "St. Augustine's Fallout."

12. Hann suggested the demographic "high point" for the native villages might have occurred just before 1726. Governor Montiano's 1738 report indicated 354 Indian allies. Tepaske, *Governorship*, 213–14; Hann, *Missions*, 314–17.

13. Hann, *Missions*, 322–23.

14. Hann, *Missions*, 325.

15. Joseph de Bullones letter to the King, Havana, October 5, 1728, in Hann, trans., *Missions to the Calusa* (Gainesville: University of Florida Press, 1991), 376.

16. For an overall discussion of violence, especially as it pertains to the Yamasees, see Matthew H. Jennings, "Violence in a Shattered World," in *Mapping the Mississippian Shatter Zone: The Colonial Indian Slave Trade and Regional Instability in the American South*, ed. Robbie Ethridge and Sheri M. Shuck-Hall (Lincoln: University of Nebraska Press, 2009).

17. For raids see Tepaske, *Governorship*, 208–9; Oatis, *A Colonial Complex*, 182; James W. Covington, "The Yamasee Indians in Florida: 1715–1763," *Florida Anthropologist* 23, no. 3 (1970); Paul Kelton, "Shattered and Infected: Epidemics and the Origins of the Yamasee War, 1696–1715," in *Mapping the Mississippian Shatter Zone*, 328.

18. Tepaske, *Governorship*, 67; Henry Dobyns, *Their Numbers Become Thinned* (Knoxville: University of Tennessee Press, 1983), 283–85; Kathleen A. Deagan, "St. Augustine and the Mission Frontier," in *The Spanish Missions of La Florida*, ed. Bonnie McEwan (Gainesville: University Press of Florida, 1993), 94. Dobyns noted that the mortality rate for the 1727 epidemic was around 16 percent.

19. Tepaske, *Governorship*, 209; 213–14; Hann, *Missions*, 321; Covington, "Yamasee Indians in Florida."

20. Susan Parker illustrated the fluidity of racial identification by Spanish administrators in the historical record of colonial St. Augustine. See Susan Parker, "The Second Century of Settlement in Spanish St. Augustine, 1670–1763," PhD diss., University of Florida, 1999, 54; "Spanish St. Augustine's "Urban" Indians," *El Escribano* 30 (1993).

21. Kathryn Sampeck stated that scholarly literature has conflated *reducción* and *congregación* policies to refer to the forced or directed relocation of people and communities. However, she argues *reducción* more broadly refers to establishing a Christian order to daily life, which could include *congregación*, the aggregation of dispersed and dwindling settlements. See Kathryn E. Sampeck, "Chronology and Use of Guatemalan Maiolica Ceramics as *Reducción* in the Izal-

cos Region of El Salvador," *Historical Archaeology* 49, no. 2 (2015): 18-49. For the implementation of these policies for the seventeenth-century Timucuas, see chapter 2 in John E. Worth, *Timucuan Chiefdoms of Spanish Florida*, vol. 2: *Resistance and Destruction* (Gainesville: University Press of Florida, 1998).

22. Parker, "Second Century of Settlement," 47-49.

23. William Green, Chester B. DePratter, and Bobby Southerlin, "The Yamasee in South Carolina: Native American Adaptation and Interaction Along the Carolina Frontier," in *Another's Country: Archaeological and Historical Perspectives on Cultural Interactions in the Southern Colonies*, ed. J. W. Joseph and Martha Zierden (Tuscaloosa: University of Alabama Press, 2002); Alexander Sweeney, "Investigating Yamasee Identity: Archaeological Research at Pocotaligo," MA thesis, University of South Carolina, 2003; John E. Worth, "Yamasee," in *The Handbook of North American Indians*, vol. 14: *Southeast*, ed. Raymond D. Fogelson (Washington DC: Smithsonian Institution Press, 2004); Ramsey, *Yamasee War*, 105-10.

24. Hann, "St. Augustine's Fallout." Also see Amanda Hall, "The Persistence of Yamasee Power and Identity at the town of San Antonio de Pocotalaca, 1716-1752," this volume.

25. Hann, "St. Augustine's Fallout," 184-86, and *Missions*, 308-9.

26. Hann, "St. Augustine's Fallout," 188.

27. Hann, *Missions*, 314, 318.

28. Hann, *Apalachee: The Land between the Rivers* (Gainesville: University of Florida Press–Florida State Museum, 1988), 289; Hann, "St. Augustine's Fallout," 192; Hann, *Missions*, 314-15. This Moze mission is not to be confused with the free African community of Gracia Real de Santa Teresa de Mosé established later in 1738.

29. John Hann noted that Moze was also known as Nuestra Señora de Rosario de Jabosaya in 1717 and San Luis de Talimali in 1711. Clearly there were ties between Moze and an earlier Mission San Luis de Talimali in Apalachee province, destroyed in 1704. Furthermore, both the seventeenth-century Candelaria and San Luis missions were near each other in Apalachee, suggesting possible ties between the Apalachee and Yamasee residents. See Hann, *Apalachee*, 287, "St. Augustine's Fallout," 184, 193, and *Missions*, 318.

30. Palmer, "St. Augustine and Its Harbor."

31. Swanton, *Creek Indians*, 105.

32. Antonio de Arredondo, *Plano de la Ciudad de San Agustín de la Florida*, 1737, Historic St. Augustine Preservation Board Map Collection, University of Florida.

33. Hann, *Missions*, 322.

34. Kathleen A. Deagan and Darcie Macmahon, *Fort Mose: Colonial America's Black Fortress of Freedom* (Gainesville: University Press of Florida, 1995), 23.

35. Hann, *Missions*, 323. Nombre de Dios appears to be omitted from the 1752 list but was likely still in existence.

36. Pablo Castelló, *Plan[o] del Presidio de San Agustín de La Florida y Sus Alrededores* (Madrid: Archivo del Museo Naval, 1763). The map denoted the ruins of the mission "Yglesia arruinada qu la fuée del Pueblo de Indios de la Punta."

37. Robert L. Gold, "The Eastern Florida Indians under the Spanish and English Control: 1763-1765," *Florida Historical Quarterly* 44 (1965): 108; Covington, "Yamasee Indians in Florida," 126; Worth, "Yamasee," 252.

38. White, "Living on the Periphery," 56-59.

39. Additional site data comparisons included Bobby Southerlin et al., "Return of the Yamasee: Archaeological Data Recovery at Cheechesy Old Field, Beaufort County, South Carolina" (Prepared for Chechessee Land and Timber Company, 2001), 166; Alexander Swee-

ney, "The Archaeology of Indian Slavers and Colonial Allies: Excavations at the Yamasee Capital of Altamaha Town," paper presented at the 42nd Annual Conference on Historical and Underwater Archaeology, Toronto, Canada, 2009, 7–9; James W. Hatch, "Lamar Period Upland Farmsteads of the Oconee River Valley, Georgia," in *Mississippian Communities and Households*, ed. J. Daniel Rogers and Bruce D. Smith (Tuscaloosa: University of Alabama Press, 1995), 144–46.

40. White, "Living on the Periphery," 50–54.

41. Kathleen A. Deagan, *Spanish St. Augustine: The Archaeology of a Colonial Creole Community* (New York: Academic Press, 1983).

42. Halbirt, "Archaeology of 18th-Century Yamassee Sites."

43. White, "Living on the Periphery," 53–55.

44. White, "Living on the Periphery," 65–67.

45. This includes data from the 159 Marine Street excavations. Boyer, "Nuestra Señora del Rosario," 53–56. Boyer referenced the 1997 excavation field notes; however, the notes have gone missing from the Dr. Sue A. Middleton Archaeology Center.

46. Halbirt, "Ideal Place for a Home," 10–11, and "Archaeology of 18th-Century Yamassee Sites"; City of St. Augustine Archaeology Program, "Nuestra Señora del Rosario de la Punta"; Boyer, "Nuestra Señora del Rosario," 85. Florida law protects those interred in the cemetery. The owners of the property preserved the La Punta cemetery with a conservation easement in agreement with the City of St. Augustine and the St. Augustine Archaeological Association. Today an interpretive marker next to the cemetery highlights the history of the Yamasee and Apalachee community.

47. Clark Spenser Larsen provided an overview of documented La Florida mission cemeteries in "On the Frontier of Contact: Mission Bioarchaeology in La Florida," in *The Spanish Missions of La Florida*, ed. Bonnie McEwan (Gainesville: University Press of Florida, 1993).

48. This also assumes the majority of deaths in the cemetery did not occur within a short span resulting in the final demise of the community. The overlapping nature of the burials suggests the cemetery was in use for an extended period of time.

49. Kathleen A. Deagan, "A New Florida and a New Century: The Impact of the English Invasion on Daily Life in St. Augustine," *El Escribano* 39 (2002): 107. For examples of this research, see Kathleen Deagan and Jane Landers, "Fort Mosé: Earliest Free African-American Town in the United States," in *I, Too Am American*, ed. Theresa Singleton (Washington DC: Smithsonian Institution Press, 1999); Parker, "Second Century of Settlement." For a specific example of recorded intermarriage at La Punta, read Landers, "Black-Indian Interaction in Spanish Florida," 158. For a general discussion about multiethnic households and archaeology in St. Augustine, see Kathleen A. Deagan, "*Mestizaje* in Colonial St. Augustine," *Ethnohistory* 20 (1973): 55–65; and see her "Sex, Status and Role in the Mestizaje of Spanish Colonial Florida," PhD diss., University of Florida, 1974, and *Spanish St. Augustine*.

50. For a subsistence discussion, see White, "Living on the Periphery," 105–19.

51. For the results of the osteological examination, see Anthony B. Falsetti, "Report of Osteological Examination Caphil Case Number 5e04," C. A. Pound Human Identification Laboratory, University of Florida, Report on file with the City of St. Augustine Archaeology Program, 2004; "Report of Osteological Examination Caphil Case Number 2d04," C. A. Pound Human Identification Laboratory, University of Florida, Report on file with the City of St. Augustine Arcaheology Program, 2004.

52. Halbirt, "Ideal Place for a Home," 11, and "Archaeology of 18th-Century Yamassee Sites"; Boyer, "Nuestra Señora del Rosario," 74.

53. Hatch, "Lamar Period Upland Farmsteads," 148–52; Sweeney, "Altamaha Town."

54. White, "Living on the Periphery," 71–82.

55. Rebecca Saunders, *Stability and Change in Guale Indian Pottery A.D. 1300–1702* (Tuscaloosa: University of Alabama Press, 2000), ch. 3, 248; Rebecca Saunders, "Stability and Ubiquity: Irene, Altamaha, and San Marcos Pottery in Time and Space," in *From Santa Elena to St. Augustine: Indigenous Ceramic Variability (A.D. 1400–1700): Proceedings of the Second Caldwell Conference, St. Catherines Island, Georgia, March 30–April 1, 2007*, ed. Kathleen A. Deagan and David Hurst Thomas (New York: American Museum of Natural History, 2009); Kathleen A. Deagan and David Hurst Thomas, "Epilogue," in *From Santa Elena to St. Augustine*; John E. Worth, "Ethnicity and Ceramics on the Southeastern Atlantic Coast: An Ethnohisorical Analysis," in *From Santa Elena to St. Augustine*.

56. Waters, "Aboriginal Ceramics," 176.

57. Waters, "Aboriginal Ceramics," 174.

58. Saunders, "Stability and Ubiquity"; Jennifer A. Melcher, "More Than Just Copies: Colono Ware as a Reflection of Multiethnic Interaction on the 18th-Century Spanish Frontier of West Florida," MA thesis, University of West Florida, 2011.

59. Deagan, "St. Augustine and the Mission Frontier," and "A New Florida and a New Century"; Waters, "Maintenance and Change," 52–53.

60. Joyce Elizabeth Harmon, *Trading and Privateering in Spanish Florida 1732–1763* (St. Augustine: St. Augustine Historical Society, 1969); Amy Turner Bushnell, *The King's Coffer: Proprietors of the Spanish Florida Treasury 1565–1702* (Gainesville: University Press of Florida, 1981); Amy Turner Bushnell, *Situado and Sabana: Spain's Support System for the Presidio and Mission Provinces of Florida*, Anthropological Papers of the American Museum of Natural History, no. 74 (Athens GA: Distributed by University of Georgia Press, 1994).

61. Deagan, "A New Florida and a New Century"; Kathleen A. Deagan, "Eliciting Contraband through Archaeology: Illicit Trade in Eighteenth-Century St. Augustine," *Historical Archaeology* 41, no. 4 (2007): 98–116.

10

Chief Francisco Jospogue
Reconstructing the Paths of a Guale-Yamasee Indian Lineage through Spanish Records

SUSAN RICHBOURG PARKER

In the 1680s a significant number of the Guales began to abandon ties with the Spanish and to migrate from their lands along the Georgia coast and its river deltas toward South Carolina, becoming Yamasees. By then many of the Guales and the Spanish had developed an ambivalent relationship. Guales began interacting with the Spanish soon after the 1565 founding of a permanent European settlement at St. Augustine, Florida, and with the promising but short-lived settlement of Santa Elena (1566–76, 1577–87) in today's South Carolina. Within the first decade or so fissures appeared in the Guales' relations with the Spanish. In 1576 war erupted between the Spaniards at Santa Elena and the Guale. Successful attacks by the Guale and Orista on the Spanish settlement forced the Spanish to evacuate Santa Elena. After a period of relatively peaceful missionization, in 1597 the Guales killed five Franciscan missionaries. Florida Governor Gonzalo Méndez de Canzo retaliated, destroying the Guales' villages and burning their maize crops, thereby creating a famine. He further intended that the Guales be distributed as bound laborers among Spanish residents, combining retribution and control. A royal order in 1600 stymied outright enslavement, but the Guales were subjected to the *repartimiento* labor system and renewed missionization.[1]

In the 1660s Westos (also called Chichimecos) moved against coastal Georgia, attacked northern Guale towns, but also brought a viable alternative to Spanish allegiance as refugee Yamasee Indians began to settle in Guale-Mocama. Disaffected and, no doubt, fearful Guales would later join the Yamasees in the 1680s and emigrate toward a new force in the southeast: the English in Carolina. These unhappy Guales turned away from the Spanish, away from Christianity, away from its missions and its friars. They turned away from Spanish demands to provide food and labor. They turned away from "the devil they knew."

Others, among them leaders of the Guale lineage of Opso/Jospo or Jospogue, persisted as Guale mission villagers and thus remained allied with the Spanish. Émigré Guales joined with the Yamasees to attack Guale missions and to capture Spanish-allied Guales as slaves. Among the Guale-Yamasees were also Ospos, who became Huspahs in South Carolina. The assaults forced the Spanish-allied Guales to new locations southward toward St. Augustine. Already weakened in numbers by the slave raids and destruction of villages, the Spanish Guales could not counter with slave hunting. Spanish policy prohibited the taking of Indian slaves, placing the Guales not just in a weak survival position but in a comparatively weak economic position as well.

The different paths taken by the Guales who joined the Yamasees and those who remained in Spanish Florida are illuminated by the story of one segment of the Ospo lineage. In 1702, 1717, and again in 1728, the Guale *cacique* Francisco Jospogue (pronounced "Hos-po-gay" in Spanish), requested sustenance from the king of Spain for his service and loyalty to the Crown and recognition of the tremendous losses he had suffered as a result. His signature on his petition is legible and straightforward, not displaying the flourishes and rubrics of colonial officials and scribes. Still the mere act of fashioning a legible signature in that place and time was extraordinary and placed Francisco Jospogue among the few literate persons at that time. In the first half of the 1700s about one in eight of Florida's soldiers could sign his name, and even fewer, one in twelve, could write. There is no similar information for Indians, Blacks, or women.[2] Cacique (chief) Francisco Jospogue and his family were indeed exceptional. But even more exceptional is that we can follow this Guale Indian family for a century, from the early 1660s into the 1760s and from the coast of today's Georgia to the island of Cuba. John Worth asserts in his 2002 essay "Spanish Missions and the Persistence of Chiefly Power" that chiefly lineages lasted far longer on the southeast coast than they did in the deep interior.[3] After Chief Jospogue's death (by the year

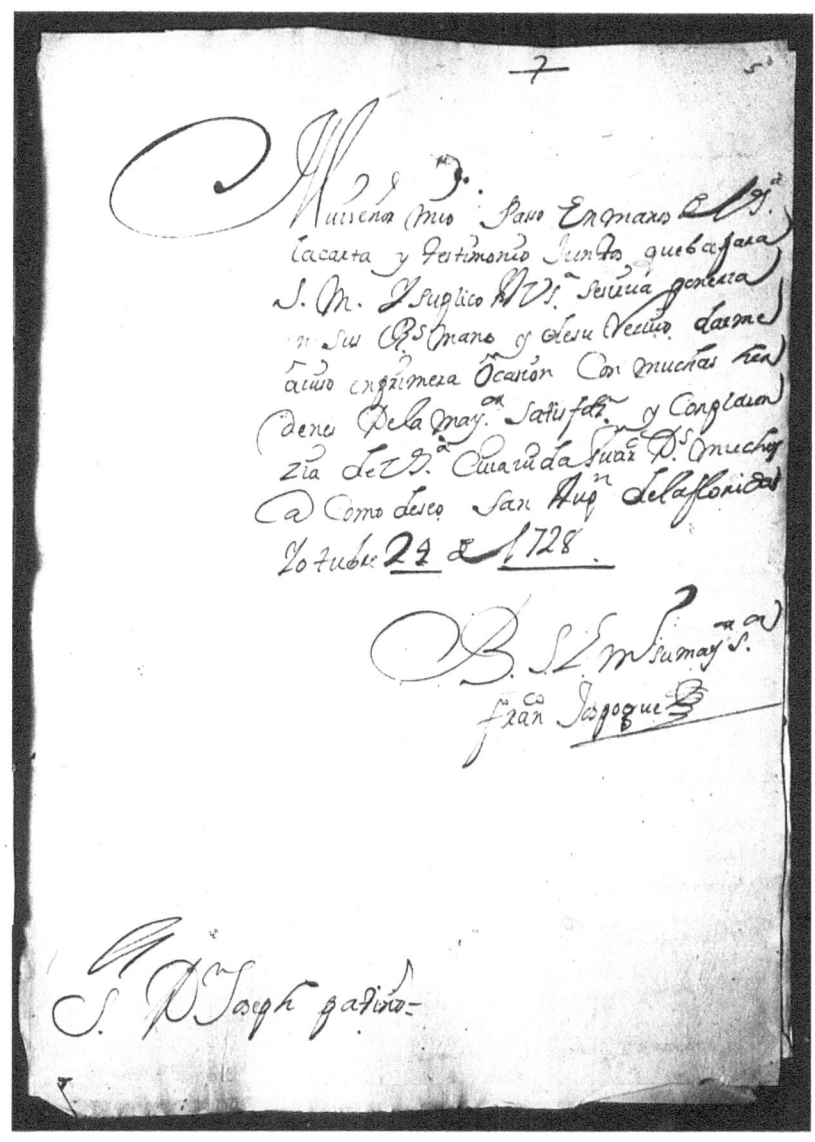

FIG. 8. Cacique Jospogue's signature. Petition of Francisco Jospogue, October 18, 1728, with transmittal correspondence dated January 12, 1734, Archives of the Indies, Seville, Spain. Courtesy of the Collection of the St. Augustine Historical Society.

1737), members of his family attested to their respect for their own noble lineage(s) by choosing "noble" marriage partners while living among Spanish residents in the city of St. Augustine. The priests of St. Augustine's parish included the noble, or chiefly, ancestry in records of marriages and baptisms. Tracing the lives of Francisco Jospogue and his family members through these exceptional documents and the St. Augustine church records reveals how Jospogue and other Guales tried to survive colonial shatter zones by strategically allying with the Spanish even as the majority of Guales joined the Yamasee Indians.

For his years of service and sacrifice Francisco Jospogue in 1728 requested a monetary award, a *plaza* (the pay of a soldier) for the rest of his life and then passing to his heirs. With this Chief Jospogue moved for direct support from the funds of Florida's defense budget. Payments would be in cash or goods directly to him or his heirs, not sustenance via the funds allotted for missions and their villagers. Jospogue was following a long-established practice in Spanish Florida of requesting a soldier's space and pay (plaza) without having to perform guard duty. In January 1734 Florida's Governor Antonio de Benavides recommended a pension or alms (*limosna*) be awarded to Chief Francisco Jospogue of two *reales* per day, the daily wage for a skilled worker and about three-fourths the pay for an infantryman.[4]

Florida's colonial officials provided supporting testimony for Jospogue's request, giving the petition a veracity that a single-person recollection might not enjoy or merit. Based on their own observations, Florida's governors Francisco de Córcoles y Martínez (1706–16) and José de Zúñiga y Cerda (1699–1706) affirmed Jospogue's leadership position, loyalty, and actions to protect Florida for Spain. Zúñiga, writing on behalf of his predecessor Governor Diego de Torres y Ayala (1693–99), verified that Torres recognized the hereditary position of chief that Francisco held. In the petition Jospogue is described with the broad term "*indio*" (Indian). But his history places him geographically as Guale as a child and young adult.

Chief Jospogue made his first petition, for recognition of his service and loyalty, in January 1702. In his second petition, dated February 7, 1717, he declared that he had been among the first to leave his house and defend against the enemy heathen Indians when they attacked on November 2, 1715. It appears that during this assault he lost his family. The attackers captured his wife and four children. Chief Jospogue made a third petition on October 18, 1728. The latter two petitions, made over eleven years apart, illustrate how long Jospogue waited for compensation for his services. The 1728 petition reiterated the earlier petition and did not include additional acts about his defending Florida and the Catholic Church. Jospogue was already in his fifties when he made his 1717 petition and in his sixties at the time of the 1728 request, and possibly by then too old to take up arms effectively. In 1730 Governor Antonio de Benavides described Jospogue as "of advanced age."

The typical practice of using formulaic language makes it difficult for researchers to parse the role of agency in Jospogue's actions or those of many other Indians. While Chief Jospogue could actually read the documents that he signed, it was royal scriveners and Crown officials who composed and oversaw the form and content of his petition. Spanish scribes and officials emphasized Jospogue's compliance with *Spanish* concerns and the role of officials in Jospogue's "career" as a Native American leader.

Jospogue seems to have initiated both petitions and, as he claimed, he signed both petitions with his own hand. The closing words of Francisco's petition show that he was literate, for there are no remarks that the petition was read to him. Nor did he sign with a cross, accompanied by the requisite language for use of the symbol in lieu of a signature. Jospogue sought to demonstrate his level of Hispanization and acculturation, especially his religious fervor, to show that he had taken to heart the teachings of the friars in the missions, how he had evangelized, how he had aligned his actions and desires with those of the Spanish Crown—who he hoped would be his benefactor—and had eschewed and even fought against heathen Indians.

The language of Jospogue's petition for an award presents his connection with Christianity as one of religion or religious affiliation, not of faith or beliefs. The question of conversion was not likely one faced by Francisco Jospogue. He was probably "born into" Christianity. His parents were probably Christians when he was born, and a Franciscan friar would have baptized him as an infant in the early 1660s. It is likely that his grandparents were Christians as well, given the association of the Ospo lineage with Spanish missions dating to the late 1500s. Kenneth M. Morrison examines the meaning and language of Christian conversion and changing worldviews in the middle of the 1600s among Algonkians in French Canada and David J. Silverman does so for Wampanoags of Martha's Vineyard—contemporaries of Francisco or his parents. But Jospogue simply offers us a recitation of his actions to defend Catholicism and to evangelize.[5]

The Spanish of Florida had a long history with the Ospo/Ospogue. There were Ospo individuals who fled *to* the Spanish after the Yamasee War. Some (or their offspring) were earlier defectors *from* the Spanish missions, who had bolted after Westo attacks in the 1680s or perhaps during the first decade of the eighteenth century, when they faced English invaders led by Carolina Governor James Moore. Still others might have emigrated several generations earlier, in the late 1500s, following reprisals by Spanish troops for the 1579 and 1597 revolts. (In 1579 the Spanish retaliated against Indian attacks on Santa Elena and to ferret out Frenchmen harbored in Guale. In 1597 the Spanish attacked to punish Indians for the killing of Franciscan friars stationed in Guale and to eliminate future resistance.) Ospo was among the towns that the Spanish assailed in 1597, located at that time on the mainland west of St. Catherines Island. There might have been an Ospo town between Santa Elena and Charles Town in the 1670s, suggesting, according to ethnohistorian John Worth, that at least some of the settlements "comprising the emergent Yamassee confederacy had originated on the Georgia coast to the south." Not only Indians from interior Georgia, but also Guales from Ospo and other coastal Indians were early participants in the ethnogenesis of the Yamasees.[6]

Divided over the question of how best to navigate the shatter zone, the Ospo chiefdom split on a number of occasions. In the early 1670s, for example, the Spanish reported that the brother of the chieftainess of Ospo had offered to lead the English Carolinians in an attack on Santa Catalina. In the 1670s and 1680s, as many Ospos moved north to ally with the English and Yamasees, Francisco Jospogue's lineage remained in Spanish La Florida. The chiefly lineage of Ospo or Ospogue persisted both *beyond* Spanish-controlled territory and *within* the Spanish missions of the Guale province.[7]

Francisco Jospogue was born at the beginning of this geopolitical upheaval in the Guale chiefdom of Aluste, between 1657 and 1663.[8] Later in life he declared that his parents, Francisco José and Agustina María, were "noble Christian Indians," and he claimed to be the hereditary chief of his community. Although he noted his parents' elite status, he did not call either of them a "chief" (*cacique* or *cacica*), suggesting that matrilineal succession was still in place and that he inherited his chief's position from an uncle, probably his mother's brother.

As a child Francisco Jospogue likely lived at the Spanish mission of Santa Catalina on the barrier island of that name or possibly at San José de Zápala (on Sapelo Island). The body of water at the south end of Sapelo Island was known as the *barra de Ospogue* in the sixteenth and seventeenth centuries.[9] In chiefly fashion, Native "family" names and the name of the area were often the same. Today Ospogue Bar is called Doboy Sound. It was here that the young Jospogue would first have encountered Yamasee Indians, who in the 1660s began to settle along the coast and on the islands of Sapelo, St. Simons, and Cumberland.

Francisco's very signature on his pension application tells us about his childhood. He was educated by Franciscan friars as a student in a mission school, and his signature is a testament to his literacy and education. Bishop Gabriel Díaz Vara Calderón reported in 1675 that at the La Florida missions "the children, both male and female go to the church on work days, to a religious school where they are taught by a teacher." Native American leaders noted that the friars taught "*muchachos y muchachas*" (boys and girls) at the mission of Nombre de Dios in St. Augustine in 1682. Scholars Timothy Johnson and Aaron Broadwell note that girls were included in the classes so that later in life, both Indian men and women would be prepared to evangelize.[10]

From the beginning Jospogue's life was one of relocation and dislocation. Around the time of his birth, Westo Indians in 1661 began attacking the Spanish mission towns of the middle Georgia coast. (See Amy Turner Bushnell's essay in this volume.) The attackers were on the move in response to displacement and pressures from English settlement farther north, in Virginia, and sought to capture Spain's

Native allies to sell as slaves to the English. Historians and anthropologists have re-created a chronology of the movements and realignments forced on the Guale towns of the Georgia coast in order for their residents to survive.[11] Chief Francisco Jospogue and his family offer a perspective where we can see the drama in the Southeast and for the mission villages unfold at the family and individual level.

While Francisco was learning to write, English schemers were making their first settlement attempts in today's South Carolina. Westo Indians already moving southward brought even more immediate danger and indeed attacked the coastal missions while Francisco was a young child. Chief Jospogue's signature testifies that the friars, even in the face of disruption and danger, continued to educate and acculturate the children in the mission to be Spanish Catholics.

Indians of the Southeast relocated in both directions. Hundreds of Yamasees seeking to escape these raids settled in Guale-Mocama territory, while some Ospos moved north near Santa Elena, where they could be closer to the English in Carolina. Francisco was about twenty years old when a round of Indian attacks in 1680 led to the abandonment of Santa Catalina. The Ospo villagers moved to San Felipe mission on Sapelo Island.[12] Spanish Florida Governor Pablo de Hita Salazar wanted the Santa Catalina town reoccupied, but its refugee inhabitants balked and even threatened mass suicide if they were forced to return, as they feared for their lives.[13] Francisco Jospogue was about twenty-five years old when pirate attacks in 1684 completed the destruction of the coastal missions along the middle Georgia coast, and he retreated southward with other refugees while many Guales went north to South Carolina with the Yamasees. He most likely relocated to Amelia Island. In 1685 Sergeant Major Domingo de Leturiondo made an official visitation to the mission villages. The villagers had just retreated to south of today's Florida-Georgia border, and the visitation was during "the most turbulent years of the history of the Guale and Mocama." In the village of San Felipe, Leturiondo recorded "Antonio, cacique of Ospogue," and four other chiefs. Antonio may have been Francisco's maternal uncle, from whom Francisco would inherit the chieftaincy.

Ten years later, in 1695, Juan de Pueyo on another visitation found that there was still a cacique of "Juzpo" at San Felipe, but now there was also a cacique of "Azpogue" at the Santa María village.[14] Jospo's petition notes that at some time between 1693 and 1699 Florida Governor Laureano Torres y Ayala "chose" Francisco Jospogue to be the cacique of what was an amalgamated Guale community. Was Governor Torres's act of "choosing" an attempt to resolve a breach or split among the Ospo lineage? Perhaps defections by the Guales had left no clear heir to the chieftaincy. On the other hand, perhaps Governor Torres was simply trying to stamp Spanish authority on what was in reality a Guale decision or practice. By the late seventeenth century at the age of thirty-six, Franscisco Jospogue was a cacique in his own right and would go on to serve as a cacique for almost forty years.[15] In 1701 Governor Zúñiga, successor to Torres y Ayala, during his own visitation of the missions, noted the presence of "the cacique of Jospo" at the San Felipe mission, by then located on Amelia Island. Early the following year, in January 1702, Zúñiga, who used both "Jospo" and "Jospogue" for Francisco, affirmed that Francisco Jospogue was the cacique of Nombre de Dios Chiquito. Was there still dissension in 1701 about Francisco's leadership position that required the governor's authority to clarify and undergird it?[16]

Faced with decades of attacks, the Spanish increasingly armed surviving mission Indians. In the late seventeenth century Governor Torres had charged that, in addition to governing, Jospogue was to teach his men how to handle firearms. Francisco Jospogue asserted that he spent much of his life fighting "the enemy heathen Indians" whom the English had induced to menace and destroy the residents of Florida. Chief Jospogue's petition does not refer to any specific Native group, although he was surely referring to the Yamasee. Chief Francisco Jospogue reported that he made many sorties fueled by his "love of God and of Your Majesty."[17] Jospogue said that he continued to try to bring Indians to Christianity and that his greatest reward was new baptisms. The converts joined with "my [Jospogue's] people" in defending against heathen Indians. Spanish officials in Florida (as elsewhere) justified raids and harboring runaways with the explanation that it was the obligation of the Spanish to ensure that Christians had access to the sacraments. Spanish Florida officials had justified their 1688 refusal to the return the first documented Black enslaved laborers to run away from Carolina to Florida by saying that they could not permit the escapees' "losing [the opportunity] to live as Christians" after the runaways had received baptism in St. Augustine.[18] Petitioner Jospogue appealed to royal officials by pointing out his efforts to achieve Spain's primary goals: evangelize the Native peoples, fight against non-believers, and maintain Spain's territorial claims on the North American continent.

On November 3, 1702, Creek and Yamasee invaders led by South Carolina's Governor James Moore and Captain Robert Daniel began an attack on the missions north of St. Augustine, burning them as they moved south, "mak[ing] their way down the coast virtually unhindered."[19] The English destroyed the missions and captured those residents who were not able to escape toward St. Augustine or to the backcountry. Others, with their mission towns under attack, ran to the Carolinians and the Yamasees. After a fifty-two-day unsuccessful siege of St. Augustine, the English departed St. Augustine on December 29, 1702. Only a few residents of St. Augustine died during the siege from war-related injuries, and Florida remained Spanish, but the city was devastated. St. Augustine residents emerged from Castillo de San Marcos on December 29 to no sheltering homes in the city just as winter began, which even in Florida can be miserably damp and windy. Mission refugees in St. Augustine faced the same scenario.

Guales and other Indians who had hunted, farmed, and fought for Spain now had to cluster around the outskirts of St. Augustine for protection and provisions supplied by the Crown, although some were located as far as five leagues (twelve or thirteen miles) from the capital. As historian Amy Bushnell says, Spanish Florida's main asset, the mission villagers, now became its main liability. Chief Francisco Jospogue's petition is silent about his migration to St. Augustine itself and its protection. Nor does the petition speak of his relocations or whether he lived in the villages of refugees around St. Augustine during the years immediately after 1702.[20]

Native Americans and Euro-Americans who were already living in St. Augustine when the English invaded also had to rely on Crown charity to survive. Twenty-six thousand pesos arrived in December 1707 for rebuilding the town, of which 6,000 pesos were designated to support the needy. Governor Francisco de Córcoles y Martínez used the funds mostly for supplies for soldiers and to pay back salaries. In 1716 another allocation of 19,000 pesos arrived for rebuilding the church; again it was diverted for the needs of the residents. "Córcoles would not and could not use the money for the purposes laid down by the king," wrote historian John Jay TePaske. St. Augustinians survived because the governor misapplied the monies. Studies, such as that of John Hann, have focused on the plight of the Native Americans and their dependence on royal largess, but there were periods as well when the situation of the Spanish residents was precarious and dependent, the difference being the matter of degree.[21]

In 1715 Yamasees as well as Creeks, Choctaws, and Cherokees revolted against Carolinians in dissatisfaction with English traders, in the uprising known as the "Yamasee War." Yamasees (including Huspahs) who had forsaken the Spanish and the Guale region for the English in Carolina during the 1670s and 1680s turned back to their old Spanish allies for protection after the uprising.[22] Historian John Hann noted the paradox of the refugees' running to Spanish Florida from the Yamasee War when only a decade earlier they had "played prominent roles in the destruction of the Florida missions." They or their forebears might well have played a role in destruction of missions that took place over the two or three decades before the attacks by Carolinians in 1702, 1704, and 1706.[23]

Chief Francisco Jospogue paid a high price for his allegiance to the Spanish Crown. Although not explicit in the petition, it seems that the capture and loss of Chief Jospogue's family took place during a November 1715 raid. On All Souls Day (November 2), 1715, enemy Indians in Jospogue's words "hurled themselves" at St. Augustine, seeking "to burn the city of Florida." Governor Córcoles certified that Chief Jospogue again defended Florida and was "one of the first to take up arms when the enemy Indians flung themselves on the presidio." English-led raiders typically separated the strong Indians at knifepoint, then "gather[ed] up the women and children to conduct them away to be sold as slaves in other British lands." Often the head chiefs of these violated villages banded together to offer food and other products to ransom their captured families. But with Chief Jospogue, it was the

English doing the asking. Three times the English offered to return Chief Jospogue's family in exchange for his alliance with the English side and abandonment of Catholicism. Three times he refused. He believed that his wife and four children had been dispersed and separately "perished," in foreign lands, probably sold as slaves to work on sugar plantations in Jamaica or Barbados.[24]

English-allied Indians captured Natives who were allied with Spain under the justification of war, and delivered them to Carolina traders, who then sold them as slaves. The recently enslaved Indians were sent most likely to the British islands of Barbados or Jamaica, although other British colonies also had Indian slaves, including colonies in the northeastern mainland. Jospogue's choice to remain with the Spanish made him vulnerable to enslavement as a war enemy of the English. As Spain had abolished Indian slavery in 1542 and over the years several monarchs reaffirmed the decision, Natives allied with the English were not subject to enslavement by the Spanish, although that would not preclude capture as belligerents. The Spanish Council of the Indies in Madrid in 1716 regretted the situation in which the English "offer[ed] arms, munitions, foods and clothing to those Indians who will capture Christian [that is, Catholic] Indians found within Carolina's jurisdiction." Great Britain's claims by this time overlapped Spain's territorial claims for Florida.[25]

After the outbreak of the Yamasee War, more Indians appeared in Spanish Florida or in St. Augustine with a family or lineage name similar to or the same as Francisco Jospo(gue): Hoospau, Tospo, Tospe. Parsing who was who among those with a version of the name Jospo is complicated by the orthography itself and inconsistency of spelling in the documents, but it is possible to make some conjectures nonetheless. Chief Francisco Jospogue was a Christian, spoke Spanish, and by the end of the year 1715, as more refugees arrived, he had lost his family. The information recorded about the refugee mission villages in 1711, 1717, 1723, 1728, and 1734 (and after Jospogue's death, in 1738, 1739, and 1759) focused on similar sorts of information—gender, language, Christian or not, and name(s) of chief or other leader.[26]

Perhaps the most famous of the Ospos to return to Spanish Florida was the "Huspaw king," the Yamassee *mico* (chief) of Huspah town in

South Carolina. At that time it was believed that the Huspah king was the man who had actually initiated the Yamasee War.[27] After retreating to southern Georgia during the Yamassee War, the Huspah king headed to the Spanish in Florida, probably in November 1715. (Steven Hahn discusses the "long" Yamassee War in detail in this volume.) Was this new arrival bearing a Jospo/Huspah name a distant cousin of Chief Francisco Jospogue? It seems likely that he was.

What is certain is that both the English and the Spanish wanted him on their side. Suggesting their own awareness of the historic links between the Huspahs and the Spanish, the Carolinians accused the Spanish of giving the Huspah king control over more than five hundred Indians to attack South Carolina, "to come against us." Was the Carolinian gossip correct that the Spanish cosseted the Huspah king by permitting him to keep as slaves several white persons that he had brought to Florida with him? "What is still more barbarous in the Spaniards is that they suffer the Yamasees to keep diverse of our white women and children as slaves amongst them." The Spanish officials in Florida found themselves in a quandary, and geopolitical concerns carried the day. At the same time that the Spanish offered possible freedom to enslaved Blacks who fled Carolina, the Spanish, in order to keep Huspah as an ally, ignored that Huspah held white slaves almost under the noses of the officials. In August 1716 Carolinians reported that the "Hoospau king, having under his command about 15 men" was in St. Augustine and sending messages that he would consider leaving his new home in Spanish Florida and returning to the British fold. The Carolinians indeed came to Florida to try to parlay with the Huspah king, but they reported that the Spanish "had some notice of it and they had sent him out of the way on purpose." The Carolinians chafed that the Spanish of Florida considered the Yamasees "as the subjects of Spain who a long time ago revolted from the Crown but were now returned again to their former allegiance.[28]

Mission refugees as well as Yamasee "pagans" fleeing the English settled themselves in villages around St. Augustine. Indians from several villages and language groups mixed together within a single organizational enclave.[29] What happened to Jospogue during this period? The 1717 report made by Captain José Primo de Rivera of the refugee missions located around St. Augustine noted that a Chief Tospe was attached to the Yamasee village of Our Lady of Candelaria. Primo de Rivera recorded that Tospe spoke the Yamasee language, was not the principal chief of the town, and was not Christian. Why was someone of such high worth to the Spanish and high rank among the Indians not the head of the mission? Perhaps because he was not a Christian, and the Spanish could not permit a "heathen" to head a Christian village. Perhaps the Spanish feared that if Tospe/Huspah headed the village, he might lead its residents away to Carolina.

By late 1725 Huspah (by then known as Antonio Jospo/Tospo) was living about fifteen miles south of St. Augustine seemingly without the entourage or followers reported a year earlier by the Carolinians and without the "white slaves" or his Black compatriots from Carolina. Forty years earlier, in 1685, Leturiondo had listed "Antonio, cacique of Ospogue" at the San Felipe village on Amelia Island. Was this the same chief Huspah or a son or a nephew? Had he been a Christian, moved away from the Spanish, and then returned to the Catholic Church (at least nominally) after arriving in St. Augustine? It seems that he had indeed chosen to be baptized, like the majority of the Yamasees who came to Spanish Florida after 1715. The Christian name of "Antonio" implies his baptism. The Franciscans would have taught the precepts of Catholicism to the Yamasees in the missions, such as Our Lady of Candelaria. The Yamasees who followed Antonio Huspaw/Jospo/Huspsaw likewise would have followed him into baptism and incorporation into the Roman Catholic Church in Florida. Governor Benavides reported that in Our Lady of Candelaria eighty-two adults and twenty-three children were baptized between 1718 and 1723.[30] The converts would have received baptism shortly after Easter, when adults were baptized, and received a Christian baptismal name. Entries in the church books recorded only the name given at baptism, and not a prior name, making it difficult centuries later to identify individuals. With baptism, the former Yamasees could become members of Spanish society, opening the way for marriage with those who were not mission villagers and possibly to paid positions with the military. With baptism came some protection, for the Spanish were obligated to ensure converts' access to

Catholic Christianity and thus could not bargain the Yamasees away to the Carolinians.

But the act of conversion and alliance with the Spanish made Huspah and the Yamasees more generally the target of decades of attacks by the English and by other southeastern Indians, as discussed by Steven Hahn in this volume. On November 1, 1725 (All Saints Day), at seven in the morning, "Uchises, Uches and Apiscas" (Abihikas?) attacked the Spanish villages of the "Xororos, Timuqua, Lactama, Jospo, and Pocotallac," which stretched along two leagues (five miles) of the bank of the estuary south of Matanzas Inlet in an area known as Las Rosas de Ayamón. The attackers brought with them artillery and guns. St. Augustine resident Agustín Guillermo Fuentes y Herrera headed to the enclave of villages to provide relief and provisions and to rescue at least its most valuable members: the (formerly) principal chief of the Yamasee, Don Antonio Jospo (as spelled in the Fuentes y Herrera petition), with all of his family—his wife, three children, father- and mother-in-law, nephew, and a servant boy. Fuentes y Herrera reported that the "*pueblos* were very ruined . . . and there was much loss of life." Many of the Candelaria villagers (Lactama) who did survive were badly wounded, and were left "without their arms (*ramos*)." Fuentes y Herrera claimed that he supplied the survivors with flour and corn, for they "had escaped with nothing of their crops." In his large canoe Fuentes y Herrera carried the Jospo family group to St. Augustine, where the Spaniard "gathered them to my own house for three months, maintaining them with what [I] could." Fuentes y Herrera's offering his home as a refuge to Cacique Antonio Jospo and his family combined charity and the ability to keep an eye on an important Native leader with fluid allegiances, and it reflected an established pattern. Jane Landers notes in this volume that it was customary for visiting Native delegations to reside in the homes of citizens of St. Augustine.[31]

Here was at least the second time that enemy Indians attacked St. Augustine or its surrounding mission villages on a holy day. November 1, All Saints' Day, was one of the most important days in the liturgical cycle. Did the "enemy Indians" purposefully plan the two attacks in 1715 and 1725 on holy days, when they might expect St. Augustine's residents or the residents of mission villages to be at prayer, particularly in the early morning, and thus unprepared? Was the attack at seven o'clock in the morning on the aggregated villages at Our Lady of Candelaria calculated not just to surprise during a Christian ritual but to demonstrate the heathen attackers' disregard for Christian rituals or possibly to underscore the disavowal of Christianity among once-Spanish mission Indians? Religious scholar Timothy Johnson notes that friars and priests sought to use these "two holy days [November 1 and 2] throughout New Spain" in order "to replace pre-Columbian common Indian celebrations tied to spirits."

Meanwhile Chief Francisco Jospogue was putting the pieces of his own life back together, after losing his wife and children, probably in the raid of November 2, 1715. Chief Francisco Jospogue and Agustina Pérez married some time before 1728. Their marriage record is not in the St. Augustine parish books, and the books of the marriages written at the missions are not extant. We don't know where Agustina came from. Only one entry appears in the parish records that includes a racial description for Agustina Pérez: *mestiza*. All of the entries for Agustina reside in the books for non-whites (*pardos y morenos*), but the records offer no mission village affiliation for her or her parents, Diego Pérez and María Cruz. Perhaps, like her sister Francisca Xaviela Pérez, Agustina was a native of the village of Nombre de Dios Chiquito, at one time headed by Chief Francisco Jospogue.[32]

The year 1728 was momentous for Chief Jospogue: he had a new son, and the English accompanied by a small number of Indian allies made another devastating attack on St. Augustine. Colonel John Palmer arrived in Florida with three hundred South Carolina militia and Indian forces in early March 1728. A Spanish scout warned that he had detected the British forces north of St. Augustine, and the Spanish concentrated their defense at Mission Nombre de Dios, half a mile north of St. Augustine. On March 9 Palmer's men won a decisive victory at the mission. The Indians who survived Palmer's attack fled into Castillo de San Marcos. Governor Benavides refused to mount a counter-attack, and Palmer withdrew four days later. The Palmer raid had been a decisive move, and the Carolinians bragged "we now have balanced account with them," and the Spanish "never will come near us more."[33]

Seven months after the attack by Colonel Palmer, Francisco Jospogue revived his request for a pension, now with a new family to protect. Francisco Jospogue appealed to the king's royal officials to reward his decades of loyalty and sacrifice on behalf of Spain and Christianity, emphasizing the latter. He noted that even when lured by overtures from the English about returning his first family if he allied with them, he had refused. He refused English offers three times! By 1734 Chief Francisco Jospogue's value to the Spanish in Florida was his example of loyalty and his reputation as a leader, not as a now elderly warrior. An award would not only support Chief Jospogue and his family but would serve as an example to other Indians of Spain's treatment and consideration for years of service. After the Palmer raid, Spain could not afford to lose any more Native allies as the number of Indians counted in the missions surrounding St. Augustine had fallen, victims of both raids and epidemics.

Between 1734 and 1737 the Spanish finally granted Francisco Jospogue his pension. The Jospo(gue) family took advantage of the purchasing power that came with the granting of Francisco's pension of two *reales* daily to acquire a lot and a tabby house on St. George Street. It was a decisive move. From this point forward, the Jospo family would live among the Spanish residents of St. Augustine, identifying themselves as citizens of the Spanish city and leaving behind their association with whatever remnants of their mission lives remained. By the latter half of the 1730s neighbors of Francisco Jospo's family and the priest who performed the marriage of Francisco's widow had dropped the final syllable "gue" from Francisco's name, shortening it to "Jospo."[34] For Indians, integration or incorporation through economic means—in Spanish Florida usually through a paid position or in the Jospos' case through a veteran's pension, in a manner speaking—was much quicker than through intercultural or interracial marriage (miscegenation, *mestizaje*).

Francisco Jospogue lived in his home inside the defense walls of St. Augustine for only a short time. His family moved onto the property between 1734, when Francisco's petition was finally forwarded to the proper authorities, and before February 1737, when neighbors referred to Jospo as deceased. His widow Agustina Pérez still owned

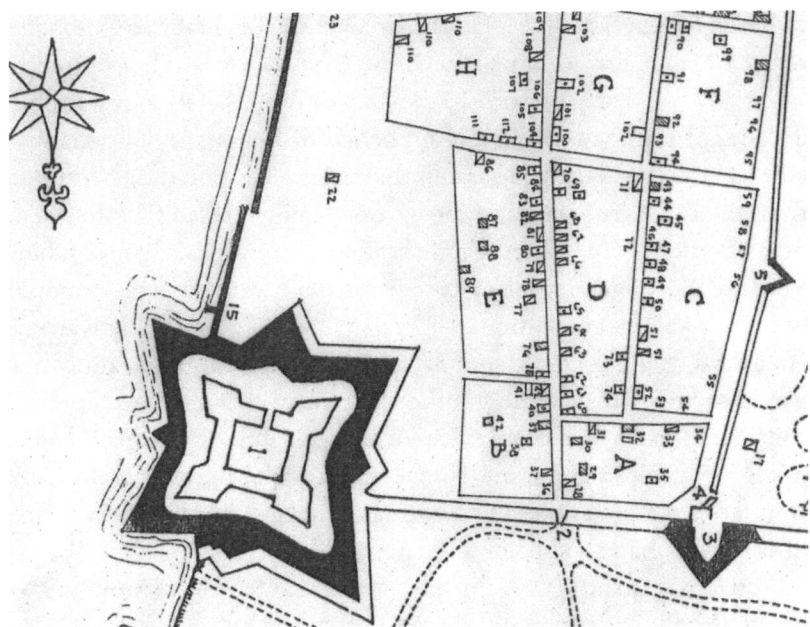

MAP 14. Location of the Jospo home in St. Augustine. Northeast section depicted in Plan of St. Augustine by Juan Jose Elixio de la Puente, hand drawn by Buckingham Smith, July 21, 1858, from the original in Royal Depository of Hydrography, Madrid, Spain. Courtesy of the Collection of the St. Augustine Historical Society.

the property, lot number 62 in block D, at the time that she evacuated St. Augustine in 1763. The Jospos' lot spanned the width of the block, 191 feet (70 *varas*) east to west. The house is at the head of a small street running perpendicular from it: today's St. George Street (then the "street to San Jorge," the Spanish name for Carolina), meeting the east side of the property for 41 feet (15 *varas*). When Agustina stood in front of her house, she could look directly down the street at the southwest bastion of Castillo de San Marcos.[35]

In June 1738 Francisco Jospogue's widow Agustina Pérez married Juan de Fuentes, the son of Chief José de Fuentes. Agustina again made an elite marriage. Perhaps upon marriage to Agustina Pérez with her home in the city and her pension, Juan de Fuentes was able to move from a mission and into Spanish society. Agustina's new husband found employment with a salary paid by the military budget allocation as a sailor and later as an artilleryman. Meanwhile, Agustina and the offspring of Francisco contributed money to the household as the heirs to Chief Jospogue's pension, secured by virtue of his loyalty. Thus Agustina Pérez provided income for her family through the same pension mechanism that supported many of St. Augustine's Euro-American widows and orphans. Agustina bore children as late as 1751, more than twenty years after her marriage to Francisco. Over the twenty-two years at least that Agustina was giving birth, the parish records suggest that the newborns whom she buried outnumbered the babies who survived, a common occurrence at the time.[36]

Chief Francisco Jospogue, his wife, her second husband, and other "urban" Indians joined the social fabric of St. Augustine through the foremost institutions of the Spanish world: the church and the military. The priest who recorded the nuptials of Juan de Fuentes and Agustina Pérez described both the groom and the bride in terms of their relationships to Indian nobles: son of a chief and widow of a chief, respectively. Indian or mestizo/a identity for these two would not appear again in the parish records. While her pension and his soldier's pay supported the family materially, Agustina Pérez and her husband, Juan de Fuentes, looked to their family's social relationship to the Church to verify independence and citizenship. The Fuentes family and their (Indian) neighbors, Pedro Tomás de Ribera and María de la Cruz, resisted the efforts of Franciscan friars to consider them mission Indians and argued that the missionaries were wrong by including these families with mission Indians in the Franciscans' census in 1745. Fuentes argued that he was a citizen of the town and that he and his family were communicants of the parish church, not residents of the missions. Distinction between full-fledged parishioner and mission Indian meant the difference between independence and dependency, between being a legally full member of the society, a *vecino* (citizen), and being a ward under the jurisdiction of the friars. The Fuentes' neighbors, the Ribera–de la Cruz family, faced the same contentions with the friars' claims. Ribera's situation mirrored that of Juan de Fuentes. He had been married and received a nuptial benediction in the parish church, and his children likewise had all been baptized in the parish church. Ribera objected and claimed that the friar's action in including him in the mission census was "against my wishes." The formal objections by Fuentes and Ribera might well have been instigated and orchestrated by the secular clergy—the parish priests—who wanted to retain as many parishioners as possible and their tithes or donations. Ribera's statement, however, illustrates the importance of this distinction to him and to his family. Natives had the option or, in the language of the day, the privilege granted by the king to choose their parish. The Fuentes and Ribera families chose the parish church of St. Augustine, not a mission church. The controversies between the friars and the priests—regular clergy versus secular clergy—were debates that involved the crown, but the former mission Indians living within the city limits of St. Augustine viewed the debate at the personal individual level; for them the distinction was about autonomy and access to the mainstream economy.[37]

That Francisco's pension was a turning point in the lives and direction of his family and descendants cannot be overemphasized. The funds to purchase a home and thus live in the city of St. Augustine set the family and descendants of Francisco Jospogue on a path away from their mission village origins and the diminished circumstances of the mission Indians in Spanish Florida in the 1700s. The pension serves as a major difference and point of departure between Francisco's life (more so that of his heirs) and that of his contemporary, the Yamasee Prince George. Their actions and those of their respective kin rather resembled each other in their use of spiritual diplomacy in seeking negotiation with the European powers in the Southeast for safety and authority. (See Denise Bossy's remarks about spiritual diplomacy in her essay in this volume.)

Even as the husband of Francisco Jospogue's widow and his neighbor sought to protect their social and economic status, they reshaped the St. Augustine community with their example of boldly contesting the tactics and actions of the Franciscan churchmen in a highly religious society. Not only did Fuentes and Ribera offer an example to the town's residents of resistance to religious "officials," but they made the point that in the disputes between the friars and the parish priests, the Indians who had moved into the town would cast their lot with the parish priests. While the intention was, no doubt, to maintain their status as citizens, their refusal to comply with the friars affected the level of support in the decades-old contest. It was a strong statement that they were no longer mission Indians.

For Indians who were memorialized in the parish records and military muster lists, the recorders frequently replaced racial identification or cultural group affiliation, such as *mestiza* or *cacique*, with an occupational role, such as sailor or artilleryman. The new (and changing) categories for persons, such as Francisco Jospogue or Agustina Pérez, obscured their Indian origins and affiliations, effectively hiding them from modern-day researchers. These Indians had blended into Spanish society in St Augustine, at least in the words of the documentary record. But the documentary blending was not total; entries for Francisco Jospogue, Agustina Pérez, Juan de Fuentes and their kin after 1735 appeared in the books for those who were not white but were *pardos y morenos* (literally "Blacks and browns"). Despite the multiplicity of racial terms, the replacement of racial categories with occupational ones moved the focus away from race to inclusion in the military budget and the community. "Living inside the walls" was about inclusion. In addition, priests could be inconsistent when assigning racial categories, and different priests did denominate the same person with varying racial classifications in the records.[38] The inconsistencies in racial classification were often intentional. Anthropologist Marvin Harris has observed in *Patterns of Race in the Americas* that even into modern times, throughout Latin America terms that denote racial identification have been applied to individuals with fluidity, contingent upon the benefits to either the recorder or the subject. Fluid identification might be invoked in the interest of community and stability, perhaps to narrow the racial and social distance between a bride and groom. Historian Patricia Seed found such occurrences in the middle of the eighteenth century in parish and census records from Mexico City. In 1759 Father Juan José Solana recorded the baptism in St. Augustine of newborn Ildefonso Ribera in the book of non-whites and denominated the baby's father as a *mestizo*, although Solana had made several earlier entries for family members in the books of whites and with no racial classification. It would seem that Father Solana used the baptism as an opportunity to demonstrate his antipathy toward Florida Governor Palacio y Valenzuela. The priest could dishonor the colony's highest official by recording Palacio's kinship through marriages with a racially inferior relative.[39]

Native American families in St. Augustine penetrated the city's Euro-American society through fictive kinship (godparental relationships) as well as corporate and commercial connections. The opportunity to move into the cash economy through military enlistment or civilian support positions for the presidio provided the means to advance socially into the city's mainstream (Euro-American) society and improve materially. Choices of sponsors and witnesses at personal religious rites of baptism and marriage established and formalized obligations that could carry over into the profane parts of life.

St. Augustine's Indian families chose Spanish neighbors to be witnesses or sponsors and in a few instances the Indians themselves served the same role for Spanish families. When María Antonia, daughter of Agustina Pérez and the deceased Chief Francisco Jospogue married a man from Cartagena de Indias (today Colombia) in 1750, Lt. Don Francisco Navarro, a Spaniard and entrepreneurial next-door neighbor, served as a witness of record. Father Francisco Xávier Arturo described the bride as a *natural vecina* (natural-born citizen [of St. Augustine]). When Agustina's sister had married in 1747, the sponsors at the nuptials were the Hitas, a locally important white couple who lived only a few doors from Agustina's house.[40]

Godparents of high standing offered social and economic opportunities for a godchild or for the child's parents. Jane Landers has noted the importance of ritual kinship and the dynamics associated with godparenthood as practiced by Blacks in Spanish St. Augustine. Religious kinship linked all three races. Artillery Sergeant Martín Martínez Gallegos, who lived directly across the street from Agustina Pérez and Juan de Fuentes, stood as godfather for their infant daughter in 1741. A sailor at the time of the baptism, Fuentes subsequently advanced economically and no doubt socially when he was able to enlist in an artillery company. Did godfather Sergeant Martínez Gallegos facilitate Fuentes's entry into the artillery corps? Not only did the artillery corps pay better (180 pesos annually) than infantry service (158 pesos), but the artillery also offered its members exemptions and privileges not available to the infantry or cavalry. Several Latin American historians who have studied the practice of godparenthood (*compadrazgo*) concluded that in Spanish America the relationship between parents and godparents was more important than the connection between godparent and godchild, while the latter was the primary relationship in Spain.[41]

The efforts of Francisco Jospo, Agustina Pérez, and a number of other Indians who left the missions to live in St. Augustine proper were largely successful for survival and economic opportunity. Through godparentage, "salaries," and pensions paid through the military budget they became Spanish citizens. The Spanish crown continued to view Agustina Pérez as a *vecina* (citizen) and eligible for crown support as an individual. When the Spanish evacuated Florida in 1763, these "urbanized" Indians were not included among the eighty-nine "Christian Indians," which was the paltry number of surviving mission villagers. Between April 1763 and January 1764 Agustina Pérez left Florida on one of the ships that carried Spanish St. Augustine's residents to Cuba. Spain transferred Florida to Great Britain at treaty negotiations at the end of the Seven Years' War and evacuated Spanish Florida residents. Agustina Pérez was not counted among those denominated as "Indians" in the departures rosters. The "Indians" were the mission villagers, not persons of Indian origin who had become citizens. In Cuba Agustina continued to be eligible to receive Francisco's pension, but like so many other evacuees, she did not survive for long on that island.

Chief Francisco Jospogue's repeated decisions to remain with the Spanish rather than ally himself and his villagers with the English set him on a different path than many other Guales and Yamasees. Spanish Florida officials supported Jospogue's claims to hereditary Indian leadership. The Spanish rewarded his fighting "heathen Indians" and his chiefly status with protection from enemies and with sustenance. Guales who chose to become Yamasees and allies of the English relocated and changed their lives to participate in colonial markets by hunting hide animals and enslaving other Native Americans. Even with the changes they retained their identity as Indians.

Meanwhile Chief Jospogue and his family moved ever nearer to St. Augustine for protection and then into the city to become citizens of the Florida capital. As they did so, they lost their Indian affiliation, at least in extant records created by Europeans, in exchange for livelihoods through participation in Spain's military organization. Native Americans who moved into St. Augustine moved from being mission villagers to residents and citizens of St. Augustine and parishioners of the parish church. Francisco Jospogue and his family moved physically and culturally, accomplished through his pension. After years of service in the Indian militia, by 1728 Jospogue was too old to fight. He relied on his record of action, loyalty, and evangelizing to acquire what younger (formerly mission Indian) men could acquire through a paid position with the Spanish Crown. Economic integration brought racial integration—at least in the documents. St. Augustine's parish records do not provide any association, such as Guale or Yamasee, for Chief Jospogue, his wife and later widow Agustina Pérez, her subsequent husband Juan de Fuentes, and her children of these two marriages. Royal funds continued to support Chief Jospogue's family after his death, not as social dependents but as the result of meritorious service, just as Euro-American families were supported.

From the Spanish perspective, Francisco Jospogue, his widow Agustina Pérez, and her subsequent husband Juan de Fuentes accomplished the goal of the mission system in which they were born and raised. They arrived at the status of *vecino*, a resident of a city, and became parishioners of a parish church, moving from mission Indian and ward status under the friars to full members of Spanish colonial society—*sui juris*.

Notes

1. Amy Turner Bushnell, *Situado and Sabana: Spain's Support System for the Presidio and Mission Provinces of Florida*, Anthropological Papers of the American Museum of Natural History, no. 74 (1994), 60–64; John E. Worth, "Guale," in *Handbook of North American Indians*, vol. 14: *Southeast* (Washington DC: Smithsonian Institution Press, 2004), 238–44.

2. Petition of Francisco Jospogue, October 18, 1728, with transmittal correspondence dated January 12, 1734, Archives of the Indies, Sevilla, Spain (AGI), 86–7–21/5, Stetson Collection microfilm (SC), P. K. Yonge Library, University of Florida, Gainesville; Council of the Indies, Madrid, 1716 January 8, AGI 58–1–24/18, SC; Juan Marchena Fernández, "St. Augustine's Military Society, 1700–1820," *El Escribano* 22 (1985): 54–59.

3. John E. Worth, "Spanish Missions and the Persistence of Chiefly Power," in *The Transformation of the Southeastern Indians*, ed. Robbie Ethridge and Charles Hudson (Jackson: University of Mississippi Press, 2002), 39–42, quote on 53.

4. José Antonio Gelabert to the Crown, General list of all who serve and are paid by the king at the presidio of San Agustín, 1752, Havana, AGI 87-1-14/2, SC.

5. Kenneth M. Morrison, *The Solidarity of Kin: Ethnohistory, Religious Studies and the Algonkian-French Religious Encounter* (Albany: State University of New York Press, 2002); David J. Silverman, "Indians, Missionaries and Religious Translation: Creating Wampanoag Christianity in Seventeenth-Century Martha's Vineyard," *William and Mary Quarterly*, 3rd series, 62 (2005): 141–74.

6. John E. Worth, *The Struggle for the Georgia Coast* (1995; repr., Tuscaloosa: University of Alabama Press, 2007), 24–25.

7. Pedro Menéndez Marquez led expeditions to Guale and Santa Elena. Eugene Lyon, "Santa Elena: A Brief History of the Colony, 1566–1587," Research Manuscript Series 193 (South Carolina Institute of Archaeology and Anthropology, University of South Carolina, 1984), 13; J. Michael Francis and Kathleen M. Kole, *Murder and Martyrdom in Spanish Florida: Don Juan and the Guale Uprising of 1597*, Anthropological Papers of the American Museum of Natural History, no. 95 (New York: American Museum of Natural History, 2011), 83–85, map locating the town of Ospo on 84.

8. This is based on his statement that he was thirty-six during the term of office of Governor Torres, who served from 1693 to 1699.

9. Charles W. Arnade, *Florida on Trial* (Coral Gables: University of Miami Press, 1959), 47.

10. George Aaron Broadwell, "Shadow Authors: The Texts of the Earliest Indigenous Florida Writers," in *Francisans and American Indians in Pan-Borderlands Perspective: Adaptation, Negotiation, and Resistance*, ed. Jeffrey M. Burns and Timothy J. Johnson (San Francisco: Academy of American Franciscan History, 2017).

11. Amy Turner Bushnell, *Situado and Sabana*, and John E. Worth, *Struggle for the Georgia Coast*, carefully assessed censuses and reports of visitations made by Spanish Florida military officials and by Franciscan missionaries to trace the fate of the mission villages in the latter decades of the seventeenth century.

12. Worth, *Struggle for the Georgia Coast*, 31–33.

13. Worth, *Struggle for the Georgia Coast*, 32–33.

14. Worth, *Struggle for the Georgia Coast*, 201, quote on 106.

15. Worth, *Struggle for the Georgia Coast*, 201, quote on 106. He also noted a cacique of "Azpogue" at the Santa María village, suggesting that the Ospos once again had divided into different lineages or factions.

16. Worth, *Struggle for the Georgia Coast*, 201; Petition of Francisco Jospogue.

17. Worth, *Struggle for the Georgia Coast*, 201.

18. Susan R. Parker, "Uncertain Freedom: Africans in Spanish Florida," presented at Fort Mose Historical Society Speaker Series, February 13, 2013, quote in Irene A. Wright, "Dispatches of Spanish Officials Bearing on the Free Negro Settlement of Gracia Real de Santa Teresa de Mose, Florida," citing the document from Royal Officials to the King, March 8, 1689, 151.

19. Bushnell, *Situado and Sabana*, quote on 192.

20. Bushnell, *Situado and Sabana*, quote on 194.

21. Robert L. Kapitzke, *Religion, Power and Politics in Colonial St. Augustine* (Gainesville: University Press of Florida, 2001,) 148–50; Charles W. Arnade, "The Architecture of Spanish St. Augustine," *Americas* 18 (1961): 152; John Jay TePaske, *The Governorship of Spanish Florida, 1700–1763* (Durham: Duke University Press, 1964), 91–92.

22. J. Leitch Wright Jr., *Anglo-Spanish Rivalry in North America* (Athens: University of Georgia Press, 1971), 56.

23. John H. Hann, "St. Augustine's Fallout from the Yamasee War," *Florida Historical Quarterly* 68 (1989): 186.

24. Petition of Francisco Jospogue; Council of the Indies, Madrid, January 8, 1716, AGI 58-1-24/18, SC.

25. Petition of Francisco Jospogue; Council of the Indies, Madrid, January 8, 1716, AGI 58-1-24/18, SC.

26. Regarding spelling of names, uppercase J, F, and T often appear similar at this time. See compilation of refugee villages by Hann in "St. Augustine's Fallout."

27. The Huspah King's Letter to Charles Craven in William L. Ramsey, *Yamasee War: A Study of Culture, Economy, and Conflict in the Colonial South* (Lincoln: University of Nebraska Press, 2008), 227–28; Alan Gallay, *The Indian Slave Trade: The Rise of the English Empire in the American South, 1670–1717* (New Haven: Yale University Press, 2002), 340–42.

28. Quotes in "Records in the Public Record Office Relating to South Carolina, 1663–1782," microcopy no. 1, reel 2 (Columbia: South Carolina Department of Archives and History), August 6, 1716, vol. 10, 295, 234–39.

29. Hann, "St. Augustine's Fallout," 180. Mario Góngora, *Studies in the Colonial History of Spanish America*, trans. Richard Southern (Cambridge: Cambridge University Press, 1975), 161–62.

30. Hann, "St. Augustine's Fallout," 192.

31. Statement of Juan Ascensio de Florencia in petition of Agustín Guillermo Fuentes y Herrera, March 27, 1727, AGI 86-7-21/6, SC.

32. Statement of Governor José de Zúñiga, January 11, 1712 [sic], in Petition of Francisco Jospogue. When Francisca Xaviela married in 1747, the marriage records noted that she was a native of Nombre de Dios Chiquito; see Marriage of Francisca Xaviela Pérez to Lorenzo de Selva, October 30, 1747, Cathedral Parish Records (CPR), Books of non-whites (Pardos y Morenos, P&M), Archives of the Diocese of Saint Augustine, St. Augustine, Florida, and Burial of Miguel Jospo, January 3, 1744, P&M.

33. TePaske, *Governorship*, 131–32; Quotes in "Records in the Public Record Office Relating to South Carolina, 1663–1782," microcopy 1, reel 2, March 27, 1728, enclosed in June 13, 1728, vol. 13, 187.

34. Petition of Francisco Jospogue; Marriage of Francisca Xaviela Pérez, CPR, P&M; Burial of Miguel Jospo, P&M.

35. Juan José Elixio de la Puente, *Plano de le Real Fuerza, Baluartes, y Linea de la Plaza de San Agustin de la Florida*, January 22, 1764, Royal Depository of Hydrography, Spain; Pablo Castelló, *Plano del presidio de San Agustín de la Florida*, July 21, 1763, Library of Congress (original in Spanish Ministry of War, LM 8a-1a) copy at St. Augustine Historical Society. Gerónima Rodríguez in her will of February 14, 1737, described her southern neighbors as "the heirs of Francisco Jospo" in Claim of Juana Navarro, Bundle 359, East Florida Papers, Library of Congress Manuscript Collection (microfilm copies at St. Augustine Historical Society).

36. Marriage of Juan de Fuentes and Agustina Pérez, June 12, 1738, and burial of Juana [de Fuentes], August 3, 1741; burial of a small nameless child of Juan de Fuentes and Agustina [Pérez], August 7, 1751, CPR, P&M. Petition of Francisco Jospogue; Don José Antonio Gelabert to the Crown, General list of all who serve and are paid by the king at the presidio of San Agustín, 1752, Havana, AGI 87-1-14/2, SC; Statements of Juan José de Fuentes, February 5 and 9, 1745, Archivo General de Indias, Audiencia de Santo Domingo (AGI SD) 846; Juan José Eligio de la Puente to Governor of Cuba, Havana, January 27, 1770, AGI 87-1-5/4, SC.

37. Statement of Juan José de Fuentes and of Pedro Tomás de Ribera, February 9, 1745, AGI SD 846.

38. See Susan R. Parker, "Spanish St. Augustine's 'Urban Indians,'" *El Escribano* 30 (1993): 1–15, for examples of other individuals and families; Robert L. Gold, *Borderland Empires in Transition: The Triple-Nation Transfer of Florida* (Carbondale: Southern Illinois University Press, 1969), 69.

39. Marvin Harris, *Patterns of Race in the Americas* (New York: W. W. Norton, 1974). See Parker, "Spanish St. Augustine's 'Urban Indians,'" for an elaboration on the insult to the governor, 11–13.

40. Marriage of Crespin Díaz to María Antonia Jospo, July 1750, and Marriage of Francisca Xaviela Pérez to Lorenzo de Selva, October 30, 1747, CPR, P&M.

41. Baptism of Juana [de Fuentes], August 3, 1741, CPR, P&M; Gelabert to Crown, General list; Jane Landers, *Black Society in Spanish Florida* (Urbana: University of Illinois Press,1999), 120–21, esp. 326n60.

The Yamasee in West Florida

JOHN E. WORTH

Although the Yamasee Indians have played a prominent role in scholarly study relating to European colonialism in the American Southeast, their origins and identity have always remained somewhat murky, despite considerable progress in recent decades.[1] As presently understood, the Yamasee were actually a product of the early colonial era, a completely new society that emerged within the contested frontier between Spanish Florida and English Carolina between the 1660s and the 1715 Yamasee War. Coalescing from the ruins of a number of indigenous chiefdoms impacted by more than a century of previous European exploration and settlement, Yamasee identity was a direct product of the tumultuous colonial borderlands, and much of their subsequent history reflects this initial pattern. It is no coincidence that the Yamasee bounced back and forth along the Spanish-English frontier for the first half century of their existence, allying themselves first with the Spanish against English-sponsored slaving, and then with the English as slave raiders themselves after 1684. And while the Yamasee War led most of the Yamasee to return to Spanish dominion and settle away from the frontier in the environs of St. Augustine, other Yamasee bands chose a different path, once again situating themselves precisely in the borderlands, though this time in West Florida. There, over the course of the next half century and beyond, the West Florida Yamasee actively styled themselves as middlemen and cultural brokers along the frontier between the Spanish and the interior Creek Indians to the north. A detailed examination of two bands, the Tamasle and Punta Rasa Yamasee, illustrates the fact that not all southeastern Indians chose to live on one side of the colonial frontier or the other. Some, like the West Florida Yamasee, voluntarily chose a life in the middle and consciously manipulated their social environment to their own advantage.

The impetus for the Yamasee migration to West Florida was the 1715 Yamasee War, which is widely acknowledged to have resulted in what might be described one of the most significant reorganizations of the social geography of the lower Southeast, and which is well documented to have resulted in the relocation of the majority of the Yamasee Indians from lower South Carolina both to Spanish St. Augustine along the Atlantic coast of northeast Florida and to the Lower Creek territory along the Chattahoochee River between modern Georgia and Alabama.[2] As noted, however, what is not so well explored is the subsequent settlement of several groups of Yamasee in western Spanish Florida, including one community named Tamasle that settled near San Marcos de Apalache after 1718, and another named Punta Rasa that settled near the Pensacola presidio after 1740. An ethnohistoric exploration of these two groups not only illuminates a poorly understood chapter in the broader history of the Yamasee but also provides an opportunity to examine the nature of colonial borderlands groups who consciously sought out and inhabited active frontiers between European colonists and indigenous Native American groups.

Tamasle

The first Yamasee to move back into West Florida seem to have come from among those who were living among the Lower Creeks following the 1715 Yamasee War. The first Spanish expeditions to traverse the abandoned mission provinces of the western interior and head north into the heartland of the Lower Creeks (known as Uchises to the Spanish of this era) during this period were led by Diego Peña in 1716 and 1717.[3] Although he visited no major towns explicitly identified as Yamasee, Peña did note during both expeditions that the inhabitants of the town of Tasquique, situated among the northern towns of the Lower Creeks, spoke the Yamasee language and were of the "Yamas nation," and somewhat to the south during his second voyage he also made note of "some fields or a little village governed by a Christian Indian named Augustín, of the Tama

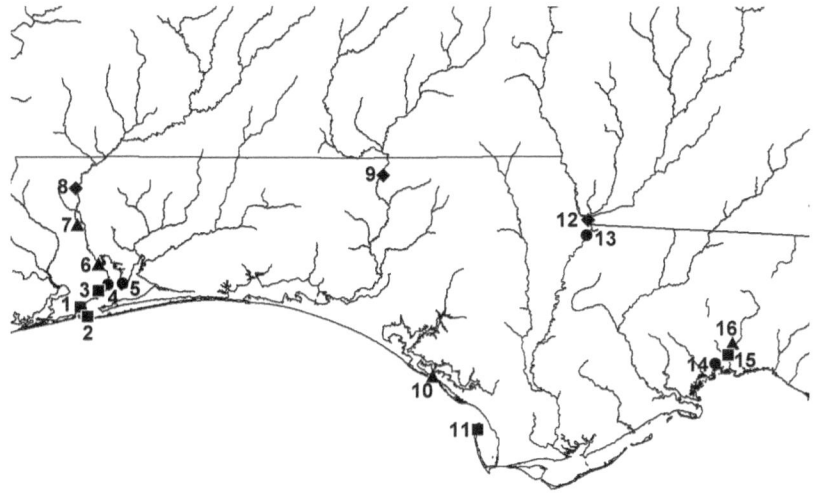

MAP 15. The Yamasee in West Florida. Map by John E. Worth.
(1) Presidio Santa María de Galve, 1698–1719
(2) Presidio Isla de Santa Rosa, Punta de Sigüenza, 1722–1756
(3) Presidio San Miguel de Panzacola, 1756–1763
(4) Yamasee Town, ca. 1740–1749
(5) San Antonio de Punta Rasa, ca. 1749–1761
(6) Nuestra Señora de Soledad y San Luis, 1718–ca. 1741
(7) San Joseph de Escambe, ca. 1741–1761
(8) Los Tobases, 1759–1761
(9) Talacayche, 1759–1761
(10) Apalachee Town, ca. 1719–1722
(11) Presidio San Joseph, 1719–1722
(12) Chilacaliche, ca. 1715–1763+
(13) Old Tamasle, ca. 1718–1818+
(14) New Tamasle, ca. 1723–1763+
(15) Presidio San Marcos de Apalache, 1718–1763+
(16) Apalachee Town, ca. 1719–1723

nation of Apalachee," which suggests that these may have been from the earlier Yamasee mission of Nuestra Señora de la Candelaria de la Tama within the Apalachee province, overrun and abandoned some thirteen years earlier.[4] Nevertheless, despite the limited appearance of Yamasees among the Lower Creeks during the Peña expeditions, a small group of them soon broke away to join the Spanish along the Gulf coast.

Renewed contact between the Lower Creeks and Spanish officials in St. Augustine was fomented in no small way by the intermediation of the Lower Creek chief named Chislacaliche, who had recently settled at the confluence of the Chattahoochee and Flint Rivers at the location of a prior mission called Savacola, and who came personally to St. Augustine in 1716 to escort Diego Peña on his first expedition.[5] He also subsequently accompanied the most important Upper and Lower Creek chiefs, who journeyed together to St. Augustine in the spring of 1717 to render obedience to the Spanish Crown and formally proposed the establishment of a Spanish outpost at the previously abandoned site of San Marcos de Apalache during a meeting in the governor's house on April 4.[6] By the end of his second mission into Creek country, Diego Peña reported that six chiefs had promised to move with their towns south toward the Spanish, either to the mouth of the Guacara (Wakulla) River near San Marcos or at Calistoble (Blue Springs) to the west, including three towns of the Uchise language (Apalachicolo, Oconi, and Achitto), Chislacaliche's Apalachee-speaking town at Sabacola, one town of the Yuchi language (Yuchi), and the sole Yamasee town of Tasquique.[7] Plans to rebuild and garrison the fort were put into motion early the next year, and on April 28, 1718, cavalry captain Joseph Primo de Rivera wrote back to the governor detailing the successful completion of his mission to reestablish San Marcos de Apalache.[8]

Over the course of the first five years after the founding of San Marcos, the documentary record is sparse and somewhat ambiguous as to which new towns were actually established, where, and exactly when, though only two towns, one Yamasee and one Apalachee, seem to have remained by the 1720s, with only the Yamasee town named Tamasle surviving through the 1730s and afterward. The first indications of impending Yamasee settlement in the vicinity of the new fort came on April 28, 1718, when the *cacique* of the Yamasee town of Tamasle, who had remained behind after a visit by the Lower Creek chiefs, came to the Spanish captain complaining about the chief Chislacaliche, who had evidently usurped the majority of his people.[9] Feel-

The Yamasee in West Florida

ing harassed by the Creeks, the chief said he had decided to relocate from where he had been setting up a new town at the *chicasa* of the Chacatos (presumably the old mission Santa Cruz along the upper Apalachicola River just below the confluence of the Chattahoochee and Flint Rivers), and settle instead at a location in the "Monte de Sartucha," only a league and a half away from the new Spanish fort. Though documentation from the late 1720s confirms that Tamasle did indeed settle at that distance from the fort, evidence from 1723 suggests that the town had actually remained near Chislacaliche along the Apalachicola until that time (see later discussion).

At least two other short-lived towns were established at locations named La Tama and Guacara during the years prior to 1723, when Captain Peña penned a detailed report to the governor of Florida regarding British machinations that year among the Upper Creeks to convince the Lower Creeks to come south into Florida and attack the Yamasees, offering prizes for each scalp.[10] Despite resistance among some Lower Creek towns, many took up the cause, and by the date of his August letter, four had been killed and scalped, including two Christian Yamasee in Apalachicola, and a Yamasee woman each in Oconi and Yufala; as a result, Peña held it as "very certain that they will now come down for the town of Tamasle, and that of Chislacaliche."[11] Despite initial promises to the contrary while at Chislacaliche's town, during the night the chief completely abandoned his town and embarked with his family and relatives on the river, sending the rest of the families across land toward the town of La Tama, presumably located at the site of the Tama mission in the old Apalachee mission province. Peña also remarked that "those from the village of Tamasle will have embarked; I believe they will come to La Tama or to this garrison," later wondering whether the chief of La Tama would be willing to support the populations of three towns.[12] Details are lacking regarding the final disposition of this move, but subsequent testimony from soldiers garrisoned at San Marcos suggest that Tamasle did indeed relocate near the fort, though apparently at the original location indicated in 1718, just a league and a half from San Marcos. Neither La Tama nor Guacara was mentioned again in subsequent decades, suggesting that both were abandoned during or after the

1723 threat, their inhabitants perhaps consolidating with other towns, such as Chislacaliche, which appears to have remained at the fork of the Apalachicola River.

Details regarding Tamasle and the earlier Apalachee settlement were provided by both a 1726 mission census and a set of 1727–28 declarations by military officers previously stationed at the fort. In the 1726 census Yamasee Indians were actually among the residents of both villages near San Marcos, including one named San Antonio "of the Yamaze nation" with forty-eight recently converted Christians and ninety-eight non-Christians, and another named San Juan "of the Apalachina and Yamases nation" with forty-five Christians and one non-Christian.[13] The military declarations compiled observations by seven officers based on their various stays dating between 1720 and 1727 and generally agreed with the previous census data.[14] Witnesses located the larger of the two towns (presumably San Antonio) at between 1.5 and 2 leagues from the fort, and variously described its population as being comprised of 200 persons, 60–80 gun men, or 70 *vecinos* (residents, probably including only heads of household). The smaller town, actually omitted by two of the seven officers (and presumably San Juan), was said to be located between half a league and one league from the fort (with one witness locating it only a quarter league away), and was stated to contain 30–40 persons, 18–20 gun men, or 19 *vecinos*. Though one witness described both towns as having resident missionaries during his stay in the garrison in 1721–22, he confirmed other witness testimony that these were both withdrawn shortly thereafter, leaving only the Franciscan chaplain at San Marcos to administer sacraments to the Christian residents of these towns. This might have resulted from the documented Creek aggression of 1723. A 1723 summation of Indian baptisms in all of Spanish Florida included a total of 18 Yamasee adults and 7 children by one friar, and 79 adults and 12 children by another, even though the "nation" indicated for the latter group was said to be "Amapiras."[15]

Additional information is found in the recollections of Franciscan missionary activity among the West Florida Yamasee penned more than a decade later by Fray Joseph Ramos Escudero, who recounted regarding "my Indians, who are called Llamasses"[16] that apart from the

Yamasee who settled around St. Augustine following the 1715 Yamasee War, some seven or eight chiefs initially settled in the depopulated Apalachee province. Upon the chiefs' request, two missionaries were sent after 1721, remaining there just three years until attacks from the Uchises forced their relocation closer to the Spanish, though subsequent attacks occurred in 1725 or 1726 in their new location.[17] Although the language is ambiguous, this account may be describing the establishment of the new Yamasee town of Tamasle close to the San Marcos fort, which would explain the reason why only a single friar may have been required after the move. There are few direct references to the exact location where Tamasle was established other than its distance from the fort (most commonly noted as 1.5 leagues, or just under 4 miles), but a map of the area around San Marcos de Apalache dating to about 1760 shows a road heading due west from the fort into the swampy lowlands, with the legend "Road from the town of Tamasle, very obstructed."[18] Moreover, a 1779 Spanish maritime expedition sent from Havana to meet surreptitiously with the Creeks after war was declared with Britain included detailed instructions specifying that the Indian emissary for the Spanish was to reach the "Pueblo of Tamasle" by traveling by canoe from the Punta de Casina (modern St. Marks Lighthouse) to the "Port of Tamasle" located two leagues from the fort.[19] Triangulating the distances between San Marcos and Tamasle (1.5 leagues) and Punta de Casina and Tamasle (2 leagues), the town was most likely located about 4 miles to the west-southwest of San Marcos, probably in the coastal lowlands somewhere in the zone between modern Wakulla Beach and Florida Highway 98 to the north.

By the mid-1730s only the Yamasee town of Tamasle seems to have remained as a distinct mission community near San Marcos, with the conventual name of San Antonio de la Tama, with separate friars typically stationed there and as chaplain of the fort.[20] It is unclear whether the Apalachee Indians who had been living at San Marcos in 1719 and 1726 had relocated to join their fellow Apalachees at Pensacola Bay or had simply become subsumed within the general population at the Yamasee town of Tamasle. In a 1738 overview by the governor of Florida, a single friar served both as chaplain of the thirty-two-man garrison at San Marcos and "for the instruction of eight families of Indians who live at a short distance from it in a small town named Tamasle."[21] That same year, however, extended and detailed documentation from a visiting Spanish officer from Havana provides the first unequivocal indication that there were two inhabited towns called Tamasle at that time. On April 3 the officer recorded the visit of "Yfamico, cacique of Tamasle," along with "Bigotes, war captain."[22] But in the formal record of gifts distributed to all the provincial chiefs of the "Province of the Uchises and Cavetas" later that same month, there were two towns listed with this name, one named "Tamaxle el Viejo" (with 12 gun men) represented by a *principal* named Juchufca, while the town of "Tamaxle el Nuevo" (with 26 gun men) was represented by its cacique Jupuififli Ymagla.[23] The "old" Tamasle was listed first, immediately before Chislacaliche and its daughter town Chaschave, founded by Chislacaliche's nephew, while the "new" Tamasle was listed last, after the northernmost towns of the Lower Creeks, and clearly out of geographical place. While this division into two towns by the same name appears in no other document of the era, when combined with other information, it confirms that there were actually two locations for Tamasle, one of which (the "new" town) was established near the fort at San Marcos, and the other of which (the "old" town) was located on the upper reaches of the Apalachicola River below the confluence of the Chattahoochee and Flint Rivers, which was where Tamasle's chief had originally been setting up his town before the arrival of the Spanish in the spring of 1718. There is even evidence from 1745 testimony that the site of Tamasle nearest to the fort may not have been cultivated every year; a soldier stationed there that year made specific note of the arrival at the fort of "three canoes of Indians who said they were going to farm this year in Tamasle, which is two leagues from it."[24] The soldier suggested that this was proof that Uchise hostility had diminished, which suggests that the use of this town site was at least partially contingent on Creek relations at the time. While these projected locations of "old" and "new" Tamasle cannot yet be confirmed beyond strong circumstantial evidence, later documentation confirms that the main town of Tamasle did indeed relocate or consolidate back on the upper Apalachicola River after the 1763 transfer of Spanish Florida to Britain, where it would subsequently remain at or near its "old" location into the American period after 1821 (discussed later).

Throughout the next decade Tamasle clearly remained an established mission post, and available Franciscan chapter meeting records for the province of Santa Elena de la Florida reveal the continual presence of a single missionary assigned to the convent recorded in Latin as "Sancti Antonij de la Tama" on five separate lists between 1748 and 1754.[25] The absence of an official post as chaplain of the fort at San Marcos suggests that both duties were shared by the Franciscan assigned to the San Antonio mission. The Tamasle Yamasee seem to have continued to assist the Spanish garrison as couriers, as highlighted by an incident during the French and Indian War (1754–63), when during a series of Creek raids against San Marcos in the summer and fall of 1757, the Spanish commander Juan de Cotilla requested aid from the chief of Tamasle in the form of messengers to penetrate the seige and send word to St. Augustine.[26] On August 20, six Yamasees sent by chief Natumayche arrived at the fort, among whom the commander selected one named Mestizo, and another named Nicasaya along with his son, to carry the messages, including Cotilla's detailed diary of the attacks.

Following the end of the war, at which time the Spanish delivered Florida to British control in exchange for the return of Havana, most of the Christian Yamasee attached to the St. Augustine and Pensacola presidios relocated to Cuba and Mexico with their Spanish allies. This was not the case with the Tamasle Yamasee, however; during the 1764 Spanish evacuation of the fort at San Marcos de Apalache, only two residents of the Yamasee town of Tamasle requested permission to accompany the Spanish soldiers to Havana: a Christian named Antonio Alvaro and his wife, accompanying two unconverted Indian porters and the wife of one from the Creek town of Sabacola.[27] Though their purported intent was to investigate whether they liked Havana in order to return later for their families, there is presently no evidence for any further migration, and indeed every reason to believe that most of the Yamasee inhabitants of Tamasle remained in West Florida. One reason for this may have been the enticements of English trade, since the Spanish commander of San Marcos also reported a visit in June 1763 by an English trader already established in Tamasle, who noted that the English had decided not to take formal possession of the Spanish fort due to its poor port.[28] The general lack of interest by British forces in maintaining the San Marcos garrison, which was ultimately withdrawn by 1769, could well have prompted the remaining Yamasees living in Tamasle to relocate inland to the upper Apalachicola, where they seem to have been established by no later than 1767. Regardless, a British trader seems to have been maintained in Tamasle, including one named James Burgess noted to be there in 1772.

During a 1767 trek from Pensacola to San Marcos, the town of the "Tomothlies" was documented by British Lieutenant Philip Pittman to have been located along the east bank of Apalachicola River just two miles below the confluence of the Chattahoochee and Flint Rivers.[29] Just a decade later the Stuart-Purcell map of 1778 clearly shows "Tomotley" located on the west side of the river below some "Old Fields," possibly at the same location where it remained through the rest of the British and Second Spanish Periods, and even into the American Period after 1821.[30] A second, smaller town, called "Hyhappo or Savannah" located five and a half miles downriver from Tomatly on the same side, was led by "Tomatly Warrior," suggesting a connection with the main town. The same map shows another location called "Ockcheeses Old Field" downriver, next to a note "Intalgees," clearly the same name as the headman listed for Tomatly. These apparent connections between multiple nearby towns extending several miles downriver from Tamasle would persist into the early nineteenth century (discussed later).

Even during the British occupation of Florida (1763–83), however, the Tamasle Yamasee nonetheless were able to maintain contact with their former Spanish allies via the emerging Cuban fishing industry, which ultimately led to frequent maritime interaction between the Lower Creeks and Spanish vessels cruising the Gulf coast of Florida.[31] This interaction continued unabated through the Second Spanish Period (1783–1821) and is documented by frequent references to Tamasle and its residents in Cuban sources. Visits to Havana during the British Period included a February 1775 party accompanying the Coweta chief Escuchape, among whom were war chiefs named Tamaslemiscu and Tamaslemisco.[32] Tamasle was also the first town visited by Spanish agents after finding the San Marcos fort uninhabited during two secret missions sent in 1779 to meet with the Creek chiefs,[33] and as noted, was reached by canoe through the "Port of Tamasle" two leagues from the Punta de Casina.[34] During these missions, Tamasle was one of twenty-one towns listed as part of the "Province of Cabeta [Coweta]," all of which received individualized gifts during the Spanish missions.[35]

After the return of Spanish control to West Florida following the American Revolution, Tamasle continued to appear in documentation for the Second Spanish Period. The town of Tamasle appears several times in the East Florida Papers in lists of gifts given to Indians visiting St. Augustine in the mid-1780s, and during this same period emissaries from Tamasle made several visits to Havana on Cuban-based fishing vessels. At least two small groups of Indians from Tamasle visited Havana during the first years of Spanish reoccupation of Florida, including nine in 1785, seven in the summer of 1786, and twenty-eight that December.[36] In addition during the early 1800s, a number of references to visiting Indians from the town of Tamasle receiving Catholic sacraments were recorded in the parish records of Nuestra Señora de la Regla in Regla, Cuba, home base of the Cuban fleet fishing in southern Florida.[37]

American records also include a number of references to Tamasle during the Second Spanish Period. In 1799, for example, Creek Agent Benjamin Hawkins listed seven Seminole towns in Florida, noting that they were "made from the towns" noted to include "Tum-maultlau."[38] While a detailed review of extensive documentation from the period of the 1813–14 Creek War or the 1817–18 First Seminole War is well beyond the scope of this review, several town lists of the era make reference to Tamasle and its cluster of immediate neighbors downriver along the west bank of the Apalachicola River, several of which seem to have had prior connections to Tamasle based on the 1778 Stuart-Purcell map (discussed earlier). An 1814 report by British marine Lieutenant George Woodbine included the following towns along the upper Apalachicola among those the British could count on against the Americans: "Tamathea or Tamathla and Ochesee, 150."[39] A detailed geographic description of the region penned by American

Captain Hugh Young in 1818 includes the following entry for a town located on the west side of the Apalachicola seven miles above another town located at what is still today called Ocheesee Bluff: "Tamatles [Tamasle]. Settled on some good river land seven miles above the Ocheeses numbers twenty-five warriors—chiefs Yellowhair and the Black King. In all other respects the same as the Ocheeses,"[40] as well as a separate reference to "a small clearing and the remains of some deserted Indian cabins of the Tamatle [Tamasle] tribe" on the east side of the river below Ocheesee.[41] Contemporaneous maps drawn up by Spanish surveyor Vicente Sebastian Pintado show these same towns in the proper position,[42] including the "Aldea de Tomathly" and "Aldea de Ochesees" as well as a town called "Yawolla" farther south, doubtless corresponding to the Young's Ehawhohasles,[43] identical to the Iola later belonging to John Blount (see later discussion).

The extent to which the original Yamasee town of Tamasle retained or even possessed a distinctive Yamasee identity and culture apart from that of their Creek/Seminole neighbors during this period is unclear, but based on these descriptions, by the end of the Second Spanish Period Tamasle had become part of a cluster of nearby towns along the upper Apalachicola River, all of which together seem to have emerged as a distinctive group known as the Apalachicola band, descendants of which persist even today. In an 1833 retrospective on later disputes between its various headmen, Florida territorial governor James Wescott recounted that the names of five towns under a principal chief named Yellow Hair, later replaced by a man named Blunt,[44] and his narrative is confirmed by documentation during the time of the 1821 transfer of Florida to United States control, including a meeting with General Andrew Jackson in Pensacola in September, when three chiefs named "[John] Blount, Nea-moth-la, and Mulatto King" expressed concerns about their fate under the American government and provided a list of fifteen Indian towns in Florida, including the following details on the cluster of towns previously described to be in the immediate vicinity of Tamasle.[45] Not insignificantly, the presence of Mulatto King along with Yellow Hair's successor John Blount at this early meeting underscored the importance of these leaders in ongoing negotiations and foreshadowed the

The Yamasee in West Florida

fact that two reservations were specifically parceled out for them in the 1823 Treaty of Moultrie Creek.[46] A list showing "the number of men retained by the chiefs who have reservations made them at their respective villages" included 43 men for John Blount, 45 for Cochran, 30 for the Mulatto King, and 28 for Emathlochee. All these towns were still inhabited as of 1833, when a census of residents was conducted, comprising a total of 605 individuals.[47] Their story after that point includes Blount's 1834 emigration to Texas and the 1839 removal of many others with the Seminoles to Oklahoma, but that is a separate chapter of the history of Tamasle's descendants.

Punta Rasa

Well over a hundred miles to the west of the Apalachicola valley, Pensacola Bay had been home to a Spanish presidio for two decades by the time the fort at San Marcos de Apalache was established in 1718. Largely bereft of indigenous Native American population by the time the Spanish settled there, the area around the Pensacola presidio of Santa María de Galve (1698–1719) soon became host to several hundred refugee Apalachee and Chacato Indians following the destruction of the Apalachee mission province by Creek and English attackers in 1704.[48] Though many of these pushed west and settled near the French colony at Mobile, some remained in the borderlands between the two European settlements, ultimately being joined by a second group of Apalachee who formed a new town at the mouth of the Escambia River at Pensacola Bay in 1718, as noted earlier. Apart from a brief visit by a "captain of the Yamace Indians who arrived at the same time with others of his nation" in the company of Apalachee chief Juan Marcos Isfani to Santa María in 1719, there is no evidence for a significant Yamasee presence at Pensacola until more than two decades later, when a group of East Florida Yamasee migrated from St. Augustine to Pensacola after the 1740 British attack on the city.[49]

The 1740 English siege of St. Augustine was a watershed event for all the refugee missions around St. Augustine, ultimately halving their number to only four, and provoking fear that ultimately led to the flight and relocation of many inhabitants far to the west, where they settled at Spanish Pensacola, as recounted several years later by Governor Manuel de Montiano.[50] While the exact date of their arrival is presently unknown, in 1741 the Franciscans in Presidio Isla de Santa Rosa (a new location occupied from 1722 to 1756) requested a complete set of supplies for what was called the "New Town of the Chiscas," including a one-time supplement of rations for thirty residents in the town.[51] Though elsewhere I have argued that this new town was actually a relocation of the earlier Apalachee village established in 1718 at the mouth of the river then known as the "River of the Chiscas" to the later site known as Mission San Joseph de Escambe,[52] it is nonetheless significant that the church furnishings requested actually include what seems to be a double set of every category of item being requested, and was unquestionably designed to equip two complete churches, especially when compared to similar lists for other new missions supplied elsewhere in New Spain during this same period. While this must remain speculation at this point, given the circumstances, one potential explanation is that the Franciscans intended to equip two mission churches, one of which could have served the Yamasee immigrants known to have moved to Pensacola at that time.

Several years later another group of Yamasee refugees appear to have joined the East Florida emigrants in Pensacola, this time from the Creek country. At least some Yamasee formerly resident among the Lower Creek towns along the lower Chattahoochee River were reported to have relocated to Pensacola during 1747 in response to Creek pressure for Yamasees to join their ongoing war against the Cherokee Indians, presumably joining the Yamasees already living there.[53] Additional detail is lacking, but this report suggests that during the 1740s Pensacola had clearly become a new aggregation point for refugee Yamasees, and later evidence confirms that they ultimately comprised an even larger population than the Apalachee residents of Mission San Joseph de Escambe, located some fourteen miles up the Escambia River.

The initial site of the Pensacola Yamasee settlement is not clear, but in 1750 the presidio's commander Captain Juan de Yarza y Ascona placed them just two leagues from the warehouse established in 1740 on the mainland at a location called San Miguel, which would later become the third and final Spanish presidio location on Pensacola Bay (San

Miguel de Panzacola, formally established in 1756). In a June letter to the viceroy of New Spain the commander had complained about the difficulty in restricting illicit trade between Pensacola's mission Indians and the Creeks trading with the English to the north and east, noting his attempts to impede "the communication that the Apalachee and Yamasee Indians have with the English, although at a distance of leagues, and the commerce that they have between them."[54] The viceroy reported that Yarza had complained that his efforts had failed "due to the domination of the Yamasees, and also because that presidio is distant, and by them being mixed with pagan Indians of different nations." The original *consulta* also noted that the "Apalachee and Yamasee Indians" had moved the pueblo they had on the mainland just two leagues (just over 5 miles) from the garrisoned warehouse at San Miguel, and relocated across the bay to a new location at Punta Rasa.[55] Certainly referring to the establishment of the mission that would be known as San Antonio de Punta Rasa on the southwestern side of modern Garcon Point,[56] this report also made note that the Yamasees made use of the more remote location to trade with "English Indians" who brought horses and skins to barter.

Later documents confirm that the Punta Rasa mission, like the Apalachee mission Escambe upriver to the north, was positioned precisely on the path between the Lower Creek Indians (the Uchises) and the garrisoned Spanish warehouse (and later presidio) at San Miguel. Punta Rasa's own Yamasee chief described it in 1758 as "one of the closest to this post [San Miguel], and they are in the location that serves as an out-guard between the Uchise Indians and the provinces of the English."[57] Indians traveling toward San Miguel from the east "passed through Punta Rasa since it was necessary, [where] they were provided lodging."[58] Governor Yarza y Ascona wrote to the viceroy of his as yet fruitless attempts to impede this illicit commerce, but was simply directed to use "the means that are suitable to prevent the commerce of the said Indians with the English."[59] The governor's solution seems to have been to establish small detachments of infantry soldiers to live in the missions; by no later than 1757, there was a small garrison of three soldiers and a corporal living at both Escambe and Punta Rasa.[60] Testimony from one of these soldiers named Antonio de Torres indicates that he must initially have been stationed at Mission Escambe in 1750, since he had been living there eleven years as of 1761.[61]

After 1750, then, Presidio Santa Rosa had two nearby garrisoned mission communities as out-guards and gateways to the Creek Indian provinces to the north and east: the Apalachee mission San Joseph de Escambe along the path to the Upper Creek towns near present-day Montgomery, Alabama, and the Yamasee mission San Antonio de Punta Rasa along the path to the Lower Creek towns south of Columbus, Georgia. Documentary evidence for this period indicates that these twin out-guards to the Spanish presidio were by this time the only Native American communities left in the immediate vicinity of Pensacola Bay, and this geographic configuration seems to have lasted through the violent end of both missions at Creek hands in 1761. In the meantime, however, Presidio Santa Rosa endured an extraordinary series of hurricanes during 1751 and 1752, culminating in a devastating hurricane that all but destroyed the settlement between November 3 and 5.[62] Following an extremely prolonged decision-making process that spanned a total of four years, the official transfer of Presidio Isla de Santa Rosa to its final mainland location at San Miguel de Panzacola was formalized in 1756, as was the establishment of a new cavalry company of fifty soldiers, to be formed using existing soldiers among the two infantry companies already present in the presidio.

In addition to bringing the entire Spanish garrison to the mainland just over 2.5 leagues (6.8 miles) closer to Mission Escambe, the creation of a new cavalry company would finally provide a degree of mobility and access to the mainland interior that had not been available before. However, given the difficulty in transporting so many horses from Veracruz, the viceroy approved their "purchase from the nearby Indians subject to our dominion, with much comfort in the price, and security in their subsistence."[63] The implementation of this decision by newly arrived Governor Miguel Román, however, would ultimately pave the way for considerable resentment and eventually outright hostility from Indian groups, leading to the total destruction of Pensacola's outlying missions and private haciendas. As it turned out, many or most of the horses purchased by the Spanish for the new cavalry company were purchased from Creek Indians through the agency of the Yamasee and Apalachee mission Indians. Easily the most important intermediary in these negotiations, as with all other diplomatic interactions with the Upper Creeks during this period, was the literate Yamasee chief of Punta Rasa named Andrés Escudero, whom Governor Román described to the viceroy in 1757 as "an able man, and instructed in the languages of these nations, and very much of my confidence."[64] In a later letter to a Spanish officer being targeted by Román as a scapegoat to take responsibility for the 1761 war that destroyed both missions, Punta Rasa's Yamasee chief Andrés Escudero suggested that the governor had ulterior motives for using him as an intermediary with the Creeks.[65] Escudero forwarded a copy of an original license issued by Governor Román granting Escudero "license to establish a store in his house, in which he can distribute it [the brandy], without excess, with other consumables that they need for their sustenance."[66] Many contemporary witnesses additionally confirmed that Governor Román spent only the minimum possible in acquiring the horses from the Indians, limiting the maximum purchase price for each horse to two *anclotes* (small barrels) of watered-down brandy, meaning that each horse was bought for 6 or 7 pesos, in comparison to the 20–22 pesos originally allocated by the viceroy.[67] Beyond this, Governor Román's treatment of Creeks visiting San Miguel was notoriously abusive, compounding the growing resentment and leading to violence in 1761 (discussed later).

The relocation of the presidio to the mainland may have provided greater security from the hurricanes that routinely scoured Santa Rosa Island, but it also increased vulnerability to Indian attacks, as had been experienced decades previously at Santa María de Galve. As if on cue, not long after Governor Román's arrival in 1757, tensions flared along the frontier with the Creek Indians to the north, following an incident in Fort San Marcos de Apalache to the east, in which a Yufala war chief had been killed by the Spanish.[68] On August 26 a letter arrived from the commandant of French Mobile relaying a report from Fort Toulouse that war parties had been dispatched from the Tallapoosa province to attack both San Miguel and San Marcos, and Governor Román immediately made defensive preparations, ordering a stockade to be constructed around the presidio, clearing the nearby woods, and dispatching the Yamasee chief of Mission Punta Rasa, Andrés Escudero, as a diplomatic envoy to the Creeks. Departing on September 10, Escudero successfully defused the situation, reporting in detail to Román by the end of the month from the Tallapoosa capital at Tuquipache (Tukabatchee) that the Upper Creeks had agreed to peace and promised to send a formal delegation to Pensacola the following February.[69] This visit did indeed occur in mid-April of 1758; the delegation included the principal chief of the Talapuces, Acmucaiche, thirteen other chiefs, and 126 other companions, including a representative of the principal Lower Creek town of Coweta.[70] As a result of the meeting, a general peace was established between the Spanish and the Tallapoosas and Abihkas (the Upper Creeks), and Yamasee chief Andrés Escudero was elected "governor general of the two provinces of the Talapuses and Apiscas," an appointment that was confirmed by Governor Román.[71] Thereafter, the twenty-nine-year-old Escudero played a very prominent role in all negotiations with the interior Creeks.[72] At the same time Román requested that Escudero gather all the Yamasees back to Punta Rasa "to congregate in my stated town the many Indians who were dispersed, and families who had moved to live in another place, considering how important it was to the service of God and the King to foment the said town, by being one of the nearest to this post."[73]

In the aftermath of the 1758 treaty Spanish and Creek interaction increased significantly, so much so that by the spring of 1759, two Creek towns had been established far to the south of their primary homeland in central Alabama, purportedly accepting vassalage to the king of Spain. One of these, Talacayche, was established some 30 leagues (just under 80 miles) to the east, and a second town was established just 4 leagues (just over 10 miles) north of Escambe, at a location known as Los Tobases.[74] Nevertheless, the peace established with the 1758 treaty was an ephemeral one, and early in 1761, rising tensions over trade abuses seem to have been the principal cause for the outbreak of war between the Upper Creeks and the Spanish, leading to the destruction of Punta Rasa and Escambe, as well as the withdrawal of both recently established Creek towns. The 1761 hostilities can be traced to a single event, in which abusive treatment of three Upper Creek Indians visit-

The Yamasee in West Florida

ing Presidio San Miguel to trade meat for brandy ultimately escalated into the murder of three soldiers and an entire Spanish family at Punta Rasa on their return northward.[75] Two men and a youth are reported to have brought several hundred pounds of meat to trade with the residents at San Miguel on February 11, but Governor Román evidently appropriated the meat for the use of the hospital, offering them only half their asking price in watered-down brandy, and when they complained about the price, the governor's majordomo was said to have abused them both verbally and physically. Before leaving, they spoke with an Indian woman at San Miguel, asserting that "if they couldn't take vengeance on the mico (which is what they call their leaders), his soldiers would have to pay."[76] After departing San Miguel, upon their arrival at Punta Rasa, and while the Yamasee residents were away hunting, on February 12 the three aggrieved Creek men attacked and killed the three remaining soldiers of the resident garrison there (two other men had not yet returned from San Miguel after escorting the Indians there from Punta Rasa). Murdered were Corporal Juan Joseph Gutierrez, his pregnant wife Rosalia Milán and five-year-old daughter, and soldiers Juan Nicolás Castillo and Simón Abellafuerte. Only Gutierrez's nursing infant daughter escaped despite her wounds.

Passing north along the Escambia River, the three attackers returned to their homes in the Upper Creek country, where they were later reported to have "exaggerated the horrors and offenses received in this presidio against their nations, with which they managed to stir up all their provinces."[77] Two months later, on April 9, 1761, a band of twenty-eight Alabama Indian warriors descended upon Mission Escambe, destroying the Apalachee village and killing two Spanish soldiers, leaving a third for dead, and capturing four.[78] In the aftermath of these two attacks on the missions, the entire population of Yamasees and Apalachees retreated to San Miguel, both in response to the threat and in defense of the presidio. Testimony is unclear regarding the exact circumstances and timing of the moves, especially in the case of Punta Rasa, since there is no evidence the Yamasee mission pueblo was burned at the time of the murders of the garrison there, and indeed it is likely that this occurred later, given that Governor Román persisted in the belief that the Punta Rasa incident was just an isolated incident until Mission Escambe was destroyed in April.[79] The destruction of Punta Rasa was apparently carried out with the help of the residents of the recently established Tallapoosa community of Talacayche, prompting the only known retaliation against the Creeks during this entire 1761 war. According to cavalry captain Luís Joseph de Ullate, the Yamasee warriors surreptitiously left in several different parties, attacking Talacayche before the governor could deny them permission.[80] Punta Rasa's chief Alonso Escudero later explained that he could not deny his war chiefs this satisfaction, since they might easily have abandoned the Pensacola presidio and moved elsewhere.[81]

By May 8 both of the Upper Creek towns established in 1759 had been abandoned, their inhabitants returning north to the Talapoosa province.[82] Pensacola's two mission communities had been destroyed and abandoned, the Creeks had retreated to the north, and the environs of Presidio San Miguel were an active war zone. Seven subsequent attacks are documented between April 23 and July 26, during which eleven more individuals were murdered, others wounded, and one additional soldier captured.[83] The casualties included not just murdered Spaniards, but also "a Yamasee or Christian Talapoosa Indian" as well as another Yamasee Indian named Acensio, both of whom were killed. While these later raiding parties were much smaller, consisting of only four to eight warriors, they nonetheless kept the Spaniards and their Indian allies in a state of constant terror during the late spring and summer of 1761.[84] The mission pueblos were not the only tangible losses; three of the most distant Spanish ranches were also left in ruins, marking a complete reversal of the incipient economic expansion that Presidio San Miguel had experienced since its formal establishment in 1756.[85] The 1761 war left Presidio San Miguel once again simply a fenced compound on the shore of Pensacola Bay.

Plans for resettling the refugees from the two destroyed missions began to be made soon after their arrival in San Miguel. Their initial stay inside the fort was documented on May 10, when the muster roll for the presidio listed a total of 184 "Christian Indians from the two pueblos of Punta Rasa and Escambe," who were given a daily ration of corn, beans, and chile, including ten in the hospital with unspecified illnesses or injuries.[86] Nevertheless, the refugees from both missions soon joined in their effort to establish a new town adjacent to the presidio. In an undated letter apparently written that same month, Yamasee cacique Andrés Escudero requested permission to establish a new town east of San Miguel at "a place called Punta Blanca, which is a cannon-shot distant from the said castillo."[87] Although a subsequent agreement regarding the location of a new settlement comprising twenty-six houses in a different location to the west of Presidio San Miguel was included in correspondence sent in October by Governor Román to the viceroy,[88] a subsequent British period map of the vicinity of the Spanish fort instead shows a tight cluster of some eighteen distinct structures just east of the fort, toward what the Spanish called Punta Blanca.[89] This residential cluster was known to the British as "Indian Town" no later than 1764, and the point as "Indian Point," making it likely that the refugees of Punta Rasa and Escambe actually settled in the eastern location they had first requested, instead of the area west of the fort toward the engineer's house.[90]

The reformulated Punta Rasa pueblo (including the survivors of both Punta Rasa and Escambe) survived two more years in its new location at Punta Blanca/Indian Town. In 1763 Spanish forces withdrew from Presidio San Miguel de Panzacola as part of the terms of the Treaty of Paris ending the Seven Years War (1756–63).[91] In a 1763 letter to the new governor, Punta Rasa's principal chief Andrés Escudero listed a total of 111 residents there who wished to immigrate to Mexico along with the evacuating Spanish.[92] By the time that they departed for Veracruz, just 108 were noted,[93] and after they disembarked in Veracruz on September 17, only 103 remained as of September 27–28.[94] Almost immediately upon their arrival in Veracruz, however, all of the Pensacola Indians were reported to have fallen ill, with 10 dead by October 19 alone, and 7 more by November 2, at which point 37 were still in the hospital, with others recovering.[95] Two years later a new town was laid out for the 47 surviving Pensacola Indian refugees just north of Veracruz, Mexico, called San Carlos de Chachalacas, where the residents elected twin mayors, one Yamasee and one Apalachee, each with two *regidores*, to serve under a single elected governor.[96] Although the overall governor named Francisco Gutierrez Vigia was still a Yamasee, Andrés Escudero had evidently perished during the previous two years.

A total of 30 heads of household then formally took possession of their plots of land, including all 7 leaders and 12 other men, and 11 women.[97] Just fifteen years later, however, there were just 5 original Pensacola Indian men surviving, 11 women, mostly widows and mothers, and a handful of local Indian ranchers who had married residents of the town.[98] By that time, just one of the original leaders was left as governor (Francisco Nolasco, from an Apalachee family), along with the sons of two others.[99] At least three Yamasee men were still living in the village, namely Antonio Lopez, Antonio Micón, and Lucas de Alcantara. In addition to the Indian residents, two men from the original Pensacola presidio were also living in the town, one of whom (Gervacio Rodríguez) had actually served as the town's governor in 1773.[100] The town was on the verge of ruin, having experienced smallpox plagues and even locusts, but despite several proposals to relocate the inhabitants and aggregate them to another community, the town nonetheless survives today. While a detailed history of the survival of this town remains for future research, the fact that at least a few of the Pensacola Yamasee survived that long offers some hope that at least a few of their descendants live today among the residents of modern San Carlos.

The story of the West Florida Yamasee is not one of helpless refugees fleeing the colonial wars along the Atlantic coastline. Both Tamasle and Punta Rasa were communities that willingly relocated toward Spanish outposts but generally kept them at arm's length. During their tenure in West Florida both groups seem best characterized as intentional intermediaries; they settled just close enough to the coastal Spanish garrisons to permit routine interaction and exchange, including resident Franciscan missionaries in both communities, but they remained far enough away to allow extensive interaction and trade with the interior Creek provinces, both as agents for the Spanish or Creeks and also for themselves. In this sense the West Florida Yamasee were truly borderlands communities, and not by accident. Just as their Yamasee ancestors had originally forged their social identity within Spanish-English borderlands between the 1660s and 1715, the Yamasee inhabitants of Tamasle and Punta Rasa deliberately chose to position themselves in the same type of social landscape, one characterized not just by perpetual diplomatic tensions and frequent warfare but also by almost unparalleled opportunities for trade and social mobility as middlemen and power brokers. Despite their small numbers, the West Florida Yamasee frequently played pivotal roles at the nexus of colonial interactions along the Spanish-Creek borderlands. And as products of a turbulent era that completely extinguished scores of other Native American groups in the Southeast, it is not insignificant to note that both these groups likely have living descendants today. The West Florida Yamasee serve as an object lesson in the fact that there was more than one path to survival during the colonial era, and that not all cultures chose to adapt to one side or the other of the dynamic Indian-European frontier. Some, like the Yamasee, actively sought out those cultural boundary zones, using these to their own advantage wherever possible. Far from being passive victims of colonial forces beyond their control, the Yamasee actively manipulated their own destiny, forging their own niche in a colonial landscape characterized by a continuous process of creation.

Notes

1. For example, John R. Swanton, *The Early History of the Creek Indians and Their Neighbors*, Bureau of Bureau of American Ethnology, Bulletin 73 (Washington DC: Government Printing Office, 1922), 80–109; Verner W. Crane, *The Southern Frontier, 1670–1732* (1929; repr., with introduction by Steven C. Hahn, Tuscaloosa: University of Alabama Press, 2004), 164; John E. Worth, *The Struggle for the Georgia Coast: An Eighteenth-Century Spanish Retrospective on Guale and Mocama*, Anthropological Papers of the American Museum of Natural History, no. 75 (Athens GA: Distributed by University of Georgia Press, 1995), 18–22; John E. Worth, "Yamasee," in *Handbook of North American Indians*, vol. 14: *Southeast*, vol. ed. Raymond D. Fogelson, gen. ed. William C. Sturtevant (Washington DC: Smithsonian Institution Press, 2004), 245–53.

2. See Crane, *Southern Frontier*, 162–86; Steven C. Hahn, *The Invention of the Creek Nation, 1670–1763* (Lincoln: University of Nebraska Press, 2004), 74–120; Steven J. Oatis, *A Colonial Complex: South Carolina's Frontiers in the Era of the Yamasee War, 1680–1730* (Lincoln: University of Nebraska Press, 2004); William L. Ramsey, *The Yamasee War: A Study of Culture, Economy, and Conflict in the Colonial South* (Lincoln: University of Nebraska Press, 2008); John H. Hann, "St. Augustine's Fallout from the Yamasee War," *Florida Historical Quarterly* 68, no. 2 (1989): 180–200; John E. Worth, "Razing Florida: The Indian Slave Trade and the Devastation of Spanish Florida, 1659–1715," in *Mapping the Mississippian Shatter Zone: The Colonial Indian Slave Trade*

and *Regional Instability in the American South*, ed. Robbie Ethridge and Sheri Shuck-Hall (Lincoln: University of Nebraska Press, 2009), 303–6.

3. Diego Peña, Diary of expedition, September 30, 1716, Archivo General de Indias, Santo Domingo 843, ff. 481v–498r (hereafter cited as AGI SD); Diary report to Governor Juan de Ayala Escobar, September 20, 1717, AGI SD 842, ff. 36v–55v; Mark F. Boyd, "Diego Peña's Expedition to Apalachee and Apalachicolo in 1716," *Florida Historical Quarterly* 28, no. 1 (1949): 1–27; "Documents Describing the Second and Third Expeditions of Lieutenant Diego Peña to Apalachee and Apalachicolo in 1717 and 1718," *Florida Historical Quarterly* 31, no. 2 (1952): 109–39.

4. John H. Hann, *Apalachee: The Land Between the Rivers* (Gainesville: University of Florida Press, 1988). The name of the Tama mission in Apalachee is rendered in several ways in documentation dating to the last quarter of the seventeenth century, including La Purificación de Tama, Nuestra Señora de la Tama, and simply La Tama.

5. John H. Hann, *The Native American World Beyond Apalachee: West Florida and the Chattahoochee Valley* (Gainesville: University Press of Florida, 2006), 95–105. The name Chislacaliche appears in many different variations in Spanish documentation, including Chislacasliche, Chalacaliche, Chalaquiliche, and others, while contemporary English documents commonly render the name Cherokeeleechee or Cherokee-killer; see also John H. Hann, "Late Seventeenth-Century Forebears of the Lower Creeks and Seminoles," *Southeastern Archaeology* 15, no. 1 (1996): 67.

6. Juan de Ayala Escobar, Letter and autos regarding the visit of the Creek chiefs, April 18, 1717, AGI SD 843, ff. 576v–577r.

7. Diego Peña, Diary, 496r; Letter to Governor Juan de Ayala Escobar, October 8, 1717, AGI SD 842, ff. 33r–v.

8. Joseph Primo de Rivera, Letter to Governor Juan de Ayala Escobar, April 28, 1718, AGI SD 843, ff. 689r–694r.

9. Joseph Primo de Rivera, Letter to Governor Juan de Ayala Escobar, April 28, 1718. AGI SD 843, ff., 693v–694r.

10. Diego Peña, Letter to Governor Antonio de Benavides, August 6, 1723, AGI SD 842, ff. 652r–654r.

11. Diego Peña, Letter to Governor Antonio de Benavides, August 6, 1723, AGI SD 842, ff., 652v.

12. Diego Peña, Letter to Governor Antonio de Benavides, August 6, 1723, AGI SD 842, ff., 653r–v.

13. Antonio de Benavides Vazan y Molina, Visitation and census of Florida missions, December 2–11, 1726, AGI SD 866, ff. 17r–v; John E. Worth, *The Timucuan Chiefdoms of Spanish Florida*, vol. 2: *Resistance and Destruction* (Gainesville: University Press of Florida, 1998), 151.

14. Pedro Lorenzo de Azevedo, Auto on the state of the missions, July 23, 1727–January 8, 1728, AGI SD 866, ff. 101r–108v.

15. Blas Pulido, Certification of Indian baptisms since 1718, February 25, 1723, AGI SD 866, ff. 44r–45v.

16. Joseph Ramos Escudero, Letter to the Conde de Montijo, October 10, 1734, AGI SD 2591, ramo 13, no. 1.

17. Joseph Ramos Escudero, Letter to the Conde de Montijo, October 20, 1734, AGI SD 2591, ramo 13, no. 4.

18. Anonymous, Plan of the fort of San Marcos de Apalache that is being constructed in the province of San Agustin de la Florida and the total reparation of the old fort which was very indefensible, Archivo del Centro Geográfico del Ejército, Florida (Estados Unidos), Fuerte de San Marcos de Apalache, Fuertes 1: 1700, 1760, image 71.

19. José Navarro, Instruction to Francisco Ruíz del Canto, July 20, 1779, Archivo General de Indias, Papeles de Cuba, 1290, f. 678v (hereafter cited as AGI CUB).

20. Pedro Morales, Antonio Navarro, Pedro del Corral, Ignacio Venegas, Francisco Gutiérrez, Joseph de Flores Rubio, Gabriel de Llerena, Chapter list, September 17, 1735, AGI SD 867, ff. 164r–169v; Antonio de Arredondo, State of the Indians who are at the devotion of the presidio of St. Augustine, Florida, with separation of towns able to take up arms, November 27, 1736, AGI SD 2591; Manuel Ojitos, Census of convents and missionaries of the province of Santa Elena de la Florida, their age, quality, and ministries in which they occupy themselves, October 17, 1736, AGI SD 867; Manuel de Montiano, Letter to the Spanish Crown, March 3, 1738, Biblioteca Nacional de Madrid (hereinafter BNM), MS 19508, ff. 186r–213v; Letter to the Spanish Crown, with attachments, June 4, 1738, AGI SD 866, ff. 342r–368v; Letter to the Spanish Crown, August 3, 1747, AGI SD 845, ff. 588r–599r.

21. Montiano, Letter, March 3, 1738, 200r.

22. Alonso Márquez del Toro, Diary of visit, April 17, 1738, AGI SD 2593, f. 11v. Mico is a Creek title for chief; see J. Leitch Wright Jr., *Creeks and Seminoles: The Destruction and Regeneration of the Muscogulge People* (Lincoln: University of Nebraska Press, 1986), 29–30.

23. Márquez del Toro, Distribution of gifts, April 16, 1738, AGI SD 2593, f. 48r. Ymagla is doubtless the Creek title Emathla.

24. Carlos Breson, Testimony, February 4, 1745, in Manuel de Montiano, Autos of testimony regarding the Uchises Indians, January 7–February 4, 1745, AGI SD 863, f. 213r.

25. Juan de la Rosa, Chapter list of the province of Santa Elena de la Florida, November 23, 1748, Biblioteca Nacional de Antropología e Historia, Fondo Franciscano, vol. 112, ff. 242r–245r (hereafter cited as BNAH, FF); Silvestre Ruíz, Chapter list of the province of Santa Elena de la Florida, October 17, 1750, BNAH, FF, vol. 112, ff. 247r–v; Andrés Menéndez, Chapter list of the province of Santa Elena de la Florida, October 16, 1751, BNAH, FF, vol. 164, ff. 254r–256v; Emanuel de San Antonio, Chapter list of the province of Santa Elena de la Florida, May 5, 1753, BNAH, FF, vol. 175, ff. 12r–14v; Chapter list of the province of Santa Elena de la Florida, October 12, 1754, BNAH, FF, vol. 112, ff. 248r–250v; all microfilm images from the Charles W. Spellman Collection, P. K. Yonge Library of Florida History, University of Florida, Gainesville.

26. Juan de Cotilla, Diary of the operations that the Talapuzes Indians of the French jurisdiction have executed against this presidio together with the town of Yufala of the province of the Uchizes, July 26–September 26, 1757, AGI SD 1504.

27. Bentura Diaz, Letter to the Viceroy of New Spain regarding the Indians, November 6, 1763, AGI SD 2574, ff. 442r–443r.

28. Bentura Diaz, Letter to the Viceroy of New Spain regarding the state of San Marcos de Apalache, November 6, 1763, AGI SD 2574, ff. 430r–v.

29. Mark F. Boyd, "Apalachee during the British Occupation," *Florida Historical Quarterly* 12, no. 3 (1934): 119; Mark F. Boyd, *Historic Sites in and around the Jim Woodruff Reservoir Area, Florida-Georgia*, River Basin Survey Papers, no. 13, Bureau of American Ethnology, Bulletin 169 (Washington DC: Smithsonian Institution, 1958), 228; Robert Right Rea, *Major Robert Farmar of Mobile* (Tuscaloosa: University of Alabama Press, 1990), 36, 85.

30. Mark F. Boyd, Map of the road from Pensacola to St. Augustine, 1778, *Florida Historical Quarterly* 17 (1938): 22.

31. John E. Worth, "Creolization in Southwest Florida: Cuban Fishermen and 'Spanish Indians,' ca. 1766–1841," *Historical Archaeology* 46, no. 1 (2012): 142–60.

32. Rafael de la Luz, Certification regarding expenses for visiting Indians, May 2, 1775, AGI CUB 1220, ff. 280r–281r.

33. Francisco Ruíz del Canto, Report of expedition to Apalachee, September 26, 1779, AGI CUB 1290, ff. 221r–223v; Report of expedition to Apalachee, February 14, 1780, AGI CUB 1291, ff. 79r–81v.

34. Navarro, Instruction, AGI CUB 1290, f. 678v.

35. José Navarro, Gift distribution list to Francisco Ruíz del Canto, July 27, 1779, AGI CUB 1290, ff. 682r–685r.

36. Antonio Moreno and Ignacio Peñalver y Cardenas, Libro Mayor de la Real Caxa de la Ciudad de la Havana del cargo de los Ministros del Exercito y Real Hacienda, AGI SD 1851; Joseph Bermudez, List of Indians from the town of Tamasle, December 21, 1786, AGI CUB 1397.

37. Worth, "Creolization"; Joseph María Cortés y Salas, Bautismos de Pardos y Morenos, Libros 1–3 (1807–1836), Archivo Parroquial del Santuario de Nuestra Señora de Regla, Regla, Cuba, in Ecclesiastical & Secular Sources for Slave Societies, Archives in Havana, Cuba, http://diglib.library.vanderbilt.edu/esss-cuba.pl; Alejandro Ramirez, 1816a, Letter to Governor José Cienfuegos, September 13, 1816, AGI CUB 1882; Letter to Juan Maria Echeverri, November 22, 1816, AGI CUB 1882; Letter to Juan Maria Echeverri, November 25, 1816, AGI CUB 1882.

38. Benjamin Hawkins, *Creek Confederacy and A Sketch of the Creek Country* (Savannah: Georgia Historical Society, 1848), 25–26, https://archive.org/details/creekconfederacy00hawk.

39. John Sugden, "The Southern Indians in the War of 1812: The Closing Phase," *Florida Historical Quarterly* 60, no. 3 (1982): 282.

40. Mark F. Boyd and Gerald M. Ponton, "A Topographical Memoir on East and West Florida with Itineraries of General Jackson's Army, 1818," *Florida Historical Quarterly* 13, no. 2 (1934): 82–104, see 86.

41. Boyd and Ponton, "A Topographical Memoir on East and West Florida with Itineraries," *Florida Historical Quarterly* 13, no. 1 (1934), 16–50, see 34.

42. Vicente Sebastián Pintado, Plano borrador de las posesiones los Señores Forbes y Compañia entre los Rios Apalachicola y San Marcos en la Florida Occidental (1817), Library of Congress, Geography and Map Division, Washington, D.C., http://hdl.loc.gov/loc.gmd/g3932a.lh000880; Plano del Rio Apalachicola, territorio é yslas adyacentes (1815), Library of Congress, Geography and Map Division, Washington, D.C., http://hdl.loc.gov/loc.gmd/g3932a.lh000883.

43. Boyd and Ponton, "Topographical Memoir," 86.

44. James B. Westcott, Letter to the Commissioner of Indian Affairs, November 13, 1833, in *Correspondence on the Subject of the Emigration of Indians, between the 30th November, 1831, and 27th December, 1833, with Abstracts of Expenditures by Disbursing Agents in the Removal and Subsistence of Indians* (Washington DC: Duff Green, 1835), 694–98; see also Boyd, *Historic Sites*, 228–29.

45. Andrew Jackson, Extract of a letter from General Jackson to the Secretary of War, with attachments, September 20, 1821, in *American State Papers, Class II, Indian Affairs, Volume II*, ed. Walter Lowrie and Walter S. Franklin (Washington: Gales and Seaton, 1834), 412–14.

46. William P. Duval, James Gadsden, and Bernardo Segui, Treaty with the Florida Indians, September 18, 1823, in *American State Papers, Class II, Indian Affairs, Volume II*, ed. Walter Lowrie and Walter S. Franklin (Washington: Gales and Seaton, 1834), 429–31.

47. James B. Westcott, Letter to the Commissioner of Indian Affairs and census of Apalachicola towns, November 13, 1833, in *Correspondence on the Subject of the Emigration of Indians, between the 30th November, 1831, and 27th December, 1833, with Abstracts of Expenditures by Disbursing Agents in the Removal and Subsistence of Indians* (Washington: Duff Green, 1835), 674–92.

48. James W. Covington, "The Apalachee Indians Move West," *Florida Anthropologist* 17, no. 4 (1964): 221–25; Hann, *Apalachee*, 264–83; Norma J. Harris, "Native Americans," in *Presidio Santa María de Galve: A Struggle for Survival in Colonial Spanish Pensacola*, ed. Judith A. Bense (Gainesville: University Press of Florida, 2003), 269–72.

49. Quote from González de Barcia Carballido y Zuñiga, *Ensayo cronológico para la historia general de la Florida* (Madrid, 1723, 347–48.

The Yamasee in West Florida 335

50. Manuel de Montiano, Letter to the Spanish Crown, July 20, 1747, AGI SD 866, ff. 549r–550r.

51. Juan de Urueña, Calculation of the situado for Presidio Isla de Santa Rosa, Punta de Sigüenza, Mexico, August 12, 1743, Archivo General de la Nación, Mexico City, General de Parte 33, Expediente 101, f. 121v–126v (hereafter cited as AGN).

52. John E. Worth, Jennifer Melcher, Danielle Dadiego, and Michelle Pigott, Mission San Joseph de Escambe: Archaeological Investigations 2009–2012, University of West Florida, Archaeology Institute, Report of Investigations (2015), Pensacola.

53. Juan Isidoro de León, Letter to Governor Montiano, June 26, 1747, in Montiano, Letter, August 3, 1747, AGI SD 866, 600r–607r.

54. Juan Francisco de Guëmes y Horcasitas, Order to Juan de Yarza y Ascona, February 10, 1751, AGN General de Parte 38, Expediente 4, ff. 9r–10r.

55. Juan de Yarza y Ascona, Report to the Viceroy, Presidio Isla de Santa Rosa, Punta de Sigüenza, June 30, 1750, AGI Guadalajara 104, translation by R. Wayne Childers on file, Archaeology Institute, University of West Florida, Pensacola.

56. John E. Worth, "Rediscovering Pensacola's Lost Spanish Missions," paper presented at the 65th Annual Meeting of the Southeastern Archaeological Conference, Charlotte, North Carolina, 2008.

57. Alonso Escudero, Letter to Governor Miguel Román de Castilla y Lugo, before December 18, 1758, transcribed in Joseph de Gorraez, "Testimonio de los Autos fechos a concerta del Coronel Don Miguel Roman de Castilla y Lugo, Governador del Presidio de San Miguel de Panzacola, en que da quenta a el mobimiento de guerra que los Yndios Ynfieles Talapuses intentaron contra aquella Plaza, y el Presidio de San Marcos de Apalache y sucesos de dicha commicion," Mexico, August 19, 1761, AGN, Marina 17, Expediente 19, ff. 317v–318v.

58. Andres Escudero, Letter to the Viceroy of New Spain, May 1761, in Pedro Ximeno, Petition to the Viceroy, with attachments, 1761, AGN Historia 571, ff. 359r–360v.

59. Guëmes y Horcasitas, Order, 1751.

60. Miguel Román de Castilla y Lugo, Letter to the Viceroy of New Spain, May 28, 1757, in Gorraez, "Testimonio," f. 341v.

61. Antonio de Torres, Testimony, July 9, 1761, in Miguel Román de Castilla y Lugo, Proceedings against Ensign Pedro Ximeno, July 9–14, 1761, AGN Marina 17, Expediente 9, ff. 122r–123r.

62. John J. Clune Jr., R. Wayne Childers, and April L. Whitaker, "Documentary History of Santa Rosa Pensacola (1722–1752): Settlement, Settlers and Survival," in Presidio Isla de Santa Rosa: Archaeological Investigations 2002–2004, by Norma A. Harris and Krista L Eschbach, 19–48, University of West Florida Archaeology Institute, Report of Investigations Number 133 (2006), Pensacola; John E. Worth, "From Island to Mainland: The Spanish Transfer from Presidio Santa Rosa to San Miguel de Panzacola," paper presented at the 65th Annual Meeting of the Florida Anthropological Society, St. Augustine, Florida, May 11, 2013.

63. Agustín de Ahumada y Villalón, Letter to Julián de Arriaga, with attachments, Mexico, August 30, 1757, AGN Correspondencia de Virreyes, vol. 3, series 1, Expediente 411, f. 128–128v.

64. Miguel Román de Castilla y Lugo, Letter to the Viceroy of New Spain, October 25, 1757, in Gorraez, "Testimonio," ff. 291r–v. Escudero was later documented to have been born about 1729, presumably in one of the St. Augustine Yamasee villages, from which most of the Punta Rasa Yamasee had fled in 1740; Andres Escudero, Testimony, July 9, 1761, in Román de Castilla y Lugo, Proceedings, f. 120v.

65. Andres de Escudero, Letter to Pedro Ximeno, May 15, 1761, in Ximeno, Petition, ff. 353r–355r.

66. Miguel Román de Castilla y Lugo, License for Andrés Escudero to open a public store, December 21, 1759, in Ximeno, Petition, ff. 366r. Copies of related correspondence sent between

Escudero and the governor were also included by Escudero in support of Pedro Ximeno's defense against accusations by Román; Andrés Escudero, Letter to Governor Miguel Román de Castilla y Lugo, May 16, 1759, in Ximeno, Petition, ff. 364r–v; Miguel Román de Castilla y Lugo, Letter to Andrés Escudero, May 4, 1760, in Ximeno, Petition, f. 367r.

67. Luis de Ullate, Report on the state of Presidio San Miguel de Panzacola and his company of cavalry, AGN Marina 17, Expediente 11, ff. 223r–224v.

68. Andrés Escudero, Letter to Governor Miguel Román de Castilla y Lugo, September 28, 1757, in Ximeno, Petition, ff. 362r–363r; Miguel Román de Castilla y Lugo, Letter to the Viceroy of New Spain, October 25, 1757, in Gorraez, "Testimonio," ff. 288r–293v.

69. Escudero, Letter, 1757.

70. Miguel Román de Castilla y Lugo, Letter to the Viceroy of New Spain, April 19, 1758, in Gorraez, "Testimonio," ff. 294r–302v; Miguel Román de Castilla y Lugo, Luis Quixano, Joseph Nodal, Juan de Goyeneche, Juan Antonio Hernández, Phelipe Feringan Cortés, Juan Joseph Cotilla, Santiago Benito Eraso, Juan Antonio Ytuarte, Carlos López, Joseph Escobar, Pedro Amoscotigui y Bermudo, Francisco Solano Garcia, Andrés Escudero, and Joseph Marín, Junta establishing peace with the Talapuses and Apiscas, April 14–15, 1758, in Gorraez, "Testimonio," ff. 305r–309v.

71. As pointed out by editor Denise Bossy in her review of this chapter, Andrés Escudero seems in this instance to have acted in the same role as a Fanni Mico, who for the Creeks of this era served as "a fictive relative who functioned as a spokesman for his adopted family or nation in the councils of his original family or nation," and who served as a "go-between, a person whose kinship ties allowed him to bring two peoples together in peace and harmony"; see Joshua Piker, *Okfuskee: A Creek Indian Town in Colonial America* (Cambridge: Harvard University Press, 2004), 22–27.

72. Apart from Escudero's appearance as an interpreter for virtually all direct meetings between Spaniards and Creeks in Pensacola during this period, Escudero also penned detailed accounts of several important negotiations he held with the Creeks, including the following: Andres Escudero, Copy of the Juntas held in Tuquipache, July 28, 1758, in Ximeno, Petition, ff. 361r–v; Letter to Governor Miguel Román de Castilla y Lugo, July 6, 1759, in Gorraez, "Testimonio," ff. 333r–336r.

73. Escudero, Copy of the Juntas, f. 361r.

74. Miguel Román de Castilla y Lugo, Consulta to the Viceroy of New Spain, February 12, 1759, in Gorraez, "Testimonio," f. 316r; Márquez del Toro, Diary; Román de Castilla y Lugo, Consulta to the Viceroy of New Spain, May 8, 1761, in Gorraez, "Testimonio," f. 338r.

75. Ullate, Report, ff. 245v–246v, 247r–v; Ximeno, Petition, ff. 349v–350r; Escudero, Letter, May 1761, ff. 354r–v and Letter, May 15, 1761, ff. 354r (see notes 58, 65).

76. Ullate, Report, ff. 246r–v.

77. Ullate, Report, f. 246v.

78. Ximeno, Petition, ff. 348r–v; Ullate, Report, ff. 242r–243v; Pedro de Alba, Testimony, July 10, 1761, in Román de Castilla y Lugo, Proceedings, ff. 125v–126r.

79. Ullate, Report, ff. 240v–242r.

80. Ullate, Report, f. 249v.

81. Andres Escudero, Testimony, July 9, 1761, in Román de Castilla y Lugo, Proceedings, f. 120v.

82. Román de Castilla y Lugo and Ytuarte, Consulta, f. 351r.

83. Santiago Benito Eraso, Report to Governor Diego Ortíz Parrilla, December 5, 1761, AGN Marina 17, Expediente 10, f. 197v–199r; Joseph Escobar, Report to Governor Diego Ortíz Parrilla, December 15, 1761, AGN Marina 17, Expediente 10, ff. 208r–209r.

84. Eraso, Report, f. 199v.

The Yamasee in West Florida   337

85. Miguel Román de Castilla y Lugo, Consulta to the Viceroy, May 8, 1761, in Gorraez, "Testimonio," ff. 338r.

86. Juan Antonio de Ytuarte, Muster roll of San Miguel de Panzacola, May 10, 1761, AGN Historia 571, ff. 41r.

87. Escudero, Letter, May 1761, ff. 360r–v.

88. Andrés Escudero and Thomás Micón, Petition to Governor Miguel Román, September 17, 1761, AGN Indiferente de Guerra, 260B, ff. 52r–v.

89. Elias Durnford, Plan of the New Town of Pensacola and Country adjacent, shewing the Gardens and situation of the Blockhouses, CO 700/FLORIDA20/1, Records of the Colonial Office, National Archives at Kew, London.

90. George Gauld, A Plan of the Harbour of Pensacola in West Florida, Surveyed in the year 1764 by George Gauld, M.A., The bar by Sir John Lindsay, Library of Congress, G3932.P45 1764 .G3, http://hdl.loc.gov/loc.gmd/g3932p.ar165600/.

91. Robert L. Gold, "The Settlement of the Pensacola Indians in New Spain, 1763–1770," *Hispanic American Historical Review* 45, no. 4 (1965): 567–76; Robert L. Gold, *Borderlands Empires in Transition: The Triple-Nation Transfer of Florida* (Carbondale: Southern Illinois University Press, 1969).

92. Andrés Escudero, Thomás Micone, Juan Joseph Micone, Nicolás Micone, and Luis Anacaliche, Letter from the caciques of the town of Punta Rasa, with list of families (1763), AGI SD 2574, Expediente 6.

93. Joseph Bernet, Presidio de San Miguel de Panzacola: Estado que manifiesta los oficiales, tropa, vecindario, y familias de que se compone dicha guarnicion, August 24, 1763, AGI SD 2574, Expediente 6.

94. Joseph de Araoz, Troops and people from Pensacola, September 27, 1763, AGN Carceles y Presidios 13, Expediente 4, ff. 85r–v.; Simón Joseph Vives, Joseph de Araoz, and Francisco Ignacio de Alarcón y Ocaña, List of the persons, men, women, and children, that comprise the town of Yamases Indians that came from the presidio of San Miguel de Panzacola, September 28, 1763, AGN Carceles y Presidios 13, Expediente 4, ff. 86r–87r.

95. Simón Joseph Vives, Joseph de Araoz, and Francisco Ignacio de Alarcón y Ocaña, Letter to the Viceroy of New Spain, October 19, 1763, AGN Carceles y Presidios 13, Expediente 4, ff. 126r–v.; Letter to the Viceroy of New Spain, November 2, 1763, AGN Carceles y Presidios 13, Expediente 4, ff. 138r–140r.

96. Pedro Amoscotigui y Bermudo, Lista de los Yndios de Panzacola que pasan a la Antigua Veracruz, y de alli a extablecerse en Zempola, January 16, 1765, AGN Tierras 911, Expediente 2, ff. 43r–v.; Letter to the Viceroy of New Spain, January 26, 1765, AGN Tierras 911, Expediente 2, ff. 54r–55v; Letter to the Viceroy of New Spain, February 26, 1765, AGN Tierras 911, Expediente 2, ff. 50r–51v.; Plano de las Tierras que se han medido para el establecimiento de las Familias de Yndios que salieron con la Guarnicion del Presidio de San Miguel de Panzacola, February 26, 1765, AGN Mapas, Planos, e Ilustraciones 876; Mapa del Pueblo nomobrado San Carlos que esta formando el Theniente de Ynfanteria Don Pedro Amoscotigui y Bermudo a la Orilla del Rio de Chachalacas, para el establecimiento de los Yndios de la Nacion Yamases, y Apalachinos, que salieron con la Guarnicion del Presidio de San Miguel de Panzacola, February 26, 1765, AGN Mapas, Planos, e Ilustraciones 877; Pedro Amoscotigui y Bermudo and Ignacio Sánchez de Mora, Certification of the election of officials for San Carlos de Chachalacas, November 21, 1765, AGN Tierras 911, Expediente 2, ff. 62r–v.

97. Joseph de Palacio Yvarros, Certification of heads of families taking possession of lands in San Carlos de Chachalacas, November 26, 1765, AGN Tierras 1085, Expediente 2, ff. 23v–24r.

98. Juan Marcos Sinjulo, Letter to the Viceroy of New Spain, July 17, 1780, with marginal notes by Josef Estephania de Thejada, August 5, 1780, AGN Tierras 1085, Expediente 2, ff. 1r–2r.

99. Josef Estaphania de Thejada, Relation of the number of persons who up to the day of this date find themselves living in the town of San Carlos, jurisdiction of Antigua Veracruz, January 16, 1781, AGN Tierras 1085, Expediente 2, ff. 28r–29r.

100. Gervacio Rodríguez and Manuel Sinjulo, Letter the Viceroy of New Spain, March 1773, AGN Tierras 1085, Expediente 2, ff. 169r–171r.

Contributors

Keith Ashley is assistant professor of anthropology at the University of North Florida. He is co-editor of *Late Prehistoric Florida: Archaeology on the Edge of the Mississippian World* (2012, University Press of Florida).

Denise I. Bossy is associate professor of history at the University of North Florida. Her recent publications include book chapters and journal articles in *European Empires and the American South*, *Native South*, *Early American Studies*, *South Carolina Historical Magazine*, and *Indian Slavery in Colonial America*.

Amy Turner Bushnell enjoys courtesy appointments in her retirement at the John Carter Brown Library and the Department of History at Brown University. Best known for her books and essays on Spanish Florida, a borderland without a constituency, she is currently writing a book about "The Indomitable Nations: Patterns of Security, Autonomy and Domain in the Indian Americas."

Alan Gallay holds the Lyndon B. Johnson Chair in U.S. History at Texas Christian University. He is the author of *The Indian Slave Trade: The Rise of the English Empire in the American South, 1670–1717*.

Steven C. Hahn is professor of history at St. Olaf College. He is the author of *The Invention of the Creek Nation, 1670–1763* and *The Life and Times of Mary Musgrove*.

Amanda Hall is a graduate student in the PhD program at the University of Florida. She is working on a degree in Southeastern Indian archaeological studies.

Jane Landers is the Gertrude Conaway Vanderbilt Professor of History at Vanderbilt and director of the Slave Societies Digital Archive (http://www.vanderbilt.edu/esss/index.php). Landers's award-winning monographs include *Black Society in Spanish Florida* (1999) and *Atlantic Creoles in the Age of Revolutions* (2011).

Jon Bernard Marcoux is the director of the Noreen Stonor Drexel Cultural and Historic Preservation program at Salve Regina University. He is the author of *Pox, Empire, Shackles, and Hides: The Townsend Site 1650–1715* (University of Alabama Press) and *The Cherokees of Tuckaleechee Cove* (Memoirs of the Museum of Anthropology, University of Michigan).

Susan Richbourg Parker specializes in the Spanish presence in the colonial Southeast. Her recent publications appear in the *Tulane European and Civil Law Forum, Signposts: New Directions in Southern Legal History* (University of Georgia Press), *The History of Florida* (University Press of Florida), and *From La Florida to La California: Franciscan Evangelization in the Spanish Borderlands (*Academy of American Franciscan History). She is writing a book on tri-racial Spanish St. Augustine.

Eric C. Poplin is senior archaeologist with Brockington and Associates with an intense interest in sixteenth- to eighteenth-century Native American material culture in South Carolina. Recent publications include "The Yamasee Indians of Early Carolina" in *Archaeology in South Carolina: Exploring the Hidden Heritage of the Palmetto State* (University of South Carolina Press), "In Much Smaller Things Forgotten: A Case for Microartifact Analysis in Cultural Resource Management" (*Southeastern Archaeology* 2016), "The Archaeology of the Wood Pottery: Confounding the 'Industrial' Transformation of Southern Stoneware Production after Edgefield" (*Historical Archaeology* 2017).

Alexander Y. Sweeney is an archaeologist directing cultural resource management projects and programs for Brockington and Associates. He has directed many archaeological projects throughout the U.S. Southeast, Midwest, and West and abroad in Japan.

Andrea P. White is a historical archaeologist examining the urban environment. She is the city archaeologist for St. Augustine, Florida.

John E. Worth is professor of historical archaeology at the University of West Florida, where he specializes in the archaeology and history of the Spanish colonial era in the southeastern U.S. He is the author of *Discovering Florida: First-Contact Narratives of Spanish Expeditions along the Lower Gulf Coast* (2014), *The Timucuan Chiefdoms of Spanish Florida* (1998), and *The Struggle for the Georgia Coast* (1995, 2007).

Index

Africans: alliances with Yamasees, xiv, 14, 19, 20, 163–64, 196–97; enslaved in Carolina, 165, 167–70; flee to Florida 37–38, 166–68, 171, 178, 289–90; negotiations with Spanish over, 168, 171, 177–79; serve in Spanish militia, 165–66, 169, 179, 181–82; slave rebellions, 178–79; Spanish Royal Proclamation of 1693, 168, 180. *See also* Menéndez, Francisco; Yamasee War

agriculture: Yamasee practices of, xiv, 29–30, 33, 61, 113, 123, 146, 239–41, 316; indigenous knowledge of medicinal plants, 30

Ais Indians, 121–22

Alonso (mico, Ocute, Yamasee), 173, 222, 259

Altamaha (mico, Yamasee), 31, 35–36, 100, 102, 110–11, 133, 135, 137, 169, 170

Altamaha Chiefdom (La Tama). *See* Mississippian progenitors of Yamasees

Altamaha River, 193, 198, 203, 205–6

Altamaha/San Marcos ceramic series, 8, 11–12, 23, 55, 85–87. *See also* Yamasee ceramics

Amelia Island, 24, 32, 55, 57–61, 63, 67–70, 102, 104, 121–22, 136, 288–89, 294

Anglicans and missionization, 118–20. *See* baptism; Society for the Propagation of the Gospel; Yamasees and Christianity

Apalachee Indians, xv, 4–5, 15–17, 19, 27–28, 34–35, 37, 39, 42–43, 45, 61, 135, 198, 223, 231, 254, 259–60, 311–15, 321, 323

Apalachicola band, 17, 320

Apalachicola Indians, 13, 19, 32, 34–37, 39, 43, 47, 135, 173, 202, 221–23, 226–27, 242, 313. *See also* Creek Indians; Uchise Indians

Apalachicola River, 312–13, 316–17, 319–20

Ashley ceramic series, 87–89, 94

baptism: Anglican, 131–32, 134, 155; Catholic, 17, 27, 47, 64, 168, 178, 180, 228, 289–90, 294, 299–302, 314

Barbados, 41, 162, 164–65, 167, 292

Barnwell, John (captain), 3, 111, 172, 197, 200–201

Bartram, William, 18, 198, 243

Benavides, Antonio de (governor), 44, 178–80, 284–85, 294, 296

Brims (mico, Coweta, Lower Creek), 21, 173, 175–76, 197, 199, 223, 226

British traders. *See* guns and Yamasees; Nairne, Thomas; Moore, James, Sr.; Wright, John; trade: Yamasee trade with the British

captives, European, 173, 175, 179, 293

Calusa Indians, 138, 216

Castillo de San Marcos. *See* forts, Spanish

Catawba Indians, 5, 93

Catholicism. *See* baptism; Franciscans; and Yamasees and Christianity

ceramic series. *See* Altamaha/San Marcos ceramic series; Ashley ceramic series; Lamar ceramic series; Yamasee ceramics

Chacato Indians, 35, 39, 313, 321

Chattahoochee River, 4, 200, 202, 310, 312–13, 316, 318, 322

Charleston (San Jorge). *See* South Carolina, colony

Charles Town. *See* South Carolina, colony

Cherokee Indians, 5–6, 75, 89, 192, 194, 216, 276, 291, 322; Cherokee-Yamasee chief, 45, 52

Cherokeeleechee. *See* Chislacaliche

Chichimecos. *See* Westo Indians

Chickasaw Indians, 3, 5, 203, 208, 209, 221
Chislacaliche (mico, Lower Creek), 43, 202, 214, 223, 226, 311–13, 315, 331
Chislala (Yamasee), 182, 230
Choctaw Indians, 5, 291
Colleton, James (governor), 34, 38–39, 168
Colon Indians, 31
conversion. *See* baptism; Franciscans; Yamasees and Christianity
Córcoles Martínez, Francisco (governor), 169, 171, 174–76, 222, 254, 284, 291
Costa Indians, 73, 169, 231, 255
Coweta, 36–37, 173–74, 194, 197, 210, 212, 318–19, 326. *See also* Apalachicola Indians; Brims; Lower Creek Indians
Craven, Charles (governor), 171–74, 187, 194–95
Creek Indians. *See* Apalachicola Indians; Lower Creek Indians; Upper Creek Indians; Yamasee and Creek affairs
Cuba, xv, 35, 169, 180, 182–83, 188, 192, 212, 262, 282, 303, 317–19
Cumberland Island, 58–59, 62, 287

diaspora, 12, 16, 22, 252, 263, 274–75, 284, 286–88. *See* mobility; Yamasee coalescence
Dickinson, Jonathan, 40–41
disease, 3, 7, 57, 59, 63, 90, 134, 221, 231, 244, 252, 256, 258–89, 268, 297

Edisto River, 5, 42, 179, 185, 194, 196
Escovar y Ayala, Juan de, 176–77

fanni mico, 138–39, 156–57, 159, 335
Flint River, 134, 202, 205, 311, 312, 316, 317
La Florida, 4, 9, 14–17, 31, 35, 39–40, 41–42, 44–45, 55, 62, 117, 122, 139, 156–57, 163–66, 168–73, 176, 178–80, 191–92, 196–99, 201, 204–12, 217, 221–24, 226–29, 231, 238–39, 242, 244, 251–52, 254–55, 257–58, 261–62, 264, 271–75, 284, 290–304, 310–11, 317–18, 321
forts, British: Frederica, 207, 209, 211; King George, 89–90, 178, 193; Moore, 195–96
forts, Spanish: Castillo de San Marcos, 16, 31, 41–42, 44, 122, 168, 179, 186, 198, 210, 224, 244, 253, 261, 290, 296, 298; Picolata, 45, 208, 230; Pupo, 45, 207–8, 229–30; San Marcos de Apalache, 43, 312–21
France, 35, 42, 61, 166, 169, 211, 286, 321, 325
Franciscan missions, 27–29, 31–32, 33, 38–40, 41–42, 55, 58–61, 117–18, 120–21, 132–34, 136, 227, 255, 281–87, 294, 299–300, 314–17, 323–24. *See also* baptism: Catholic
French and Indian War, 211, 262, 316

gender. *See* kinship; marriage; Yamasee ceramics and women; Yamasees in oral traditions
Georgia, 2–5, 44–46, 208–9, 216, 229–30, 255, 261, 321. *See also* forts, British: Frederica; Oglethorpe, James; War of Jenkins' Ear; Yamasee War
gift giving and Yamasees, 3, 8, 139, 150–52, 154, 171, 175–76, 188, 227, 254, 316, 319. *See also* trade
Guale Indians, 2–3, 11–13, 17, 19, 22, 29–31, 34, 36–40, 55–63, 66–70, 73, 77, 84, 87–91, 95–96, 103–5, 116–18, 132–36, 140, 157, 158, 174, 177, 183, 192, 223, 231–32, 234–37, 254, 270, 282–84, 286–91, 303. *See also* Huspah King; Ospo Indians
guns and Yamasees, 2, 12, 20, 34, 36–37, 42–45, 83, 92, 121–23, 151, 204, 209, 211, 224, 233, 238, 289, 295

Hilton Head island, 197, 200, 202
Huspah Indians (Yamasee). *See* Ospo Indians
Huspah King (Don Antonio Jospo), 163–64, 171, 173–74, 180–81, 184, 200, 228, 292–95, 295

Ichisi chiefdom. *See* Mississippian progenitors of Yamasees
Indian slavery, 3, 34–35, 39, 41–44, 292; of Indian women (and children), 36–37, 43, 45, 93, 136–38, 173, 175, 185, 208, 256, 285, 291–92, 313; indigenous practices of, 2, 4–5, 34–36, 44–45; by Yamasee Indians, 2, 36–37, 39, 41–42, 93–94; 120–23, 282, 289. *See also* Moore, James, Sr.; Westo Indians

Johnston, Gideon, 136–37, 139, 144–46, 148–52, 154, 156–57, 161, 187, 189, 199

INDEX

Jospogue, Francisco (chief; Guale), 16–17, 173, 176, 184, 188, 189, 281–304

King Lewis (mico of Pocotaligo, Yamasee), 100, 102–3, 118, 120, 170

Lamar ceramic series, 77, 85–88. *See also* Altamaha/San Marcos ceramic series
Lamar chiefdoms. *See* Mississippian progenitors of Yamasees
Lower Creek Indians, 1, 4–5, 8, 15–17, 20, 39, 43–46, 52, 63, 136, 157, 168, 174, 177, 207, 211, 216, 221–23, 226–29, 231–32, 242–43, 295, 310–18, 322–26. *See also* Apalachicola Indians

Márquez Cabrera, Juan (governor), 30–33, 36, 38, 60, 165–67
marriage: between different Indian communities, 236, 268–69, 296; of Indians and Spaniards, 138–39, 268–69, 274; of Indians and Africans, 182–83, 268–69; of Indians and British traders, 138–39
Menéndez, Francisco, 174–77, 178–81, 183, 211. *See also* Mose, Gracia Real de Santa Teresa de
Merenciana, Cacica (San Juan del Puerto, Mocama), 30, 58
mestizaje. *See* marriage
Middleton, Arthur (governor), 179, 189, 202–3, 214–15
Mississippian progenitors of Yamasees, 2, 29, 57, 62, 84, 104–5, 200, 258–59; abandon paddle-stamping, 87
mobility: as Yamasee practice and strategy, xiv, 9, 13, 18–19, 64–65, 134–35, 166, 257–58, 261, 264–66, 273, 324. *See also* diaspora; *vecino*; Yamasee coalescence
Mocama Indians, 2, 11, 24, 29–30, 37, 39, 55, 57–59, 61–62, 66–70, 74, 77, 83–84, 87–91, 94–96, 135, 232, 255, 270, 281, 288. *See* also Merenciana, Cacica; Timucua Indians
Montiano, Manuel de (governor), 44–46, 180–82, 207–8, 229–30, 321–22
Moore, James, Sr., 3, 41–42, 121–22, 168–69, 286, 290. *See also* Queen Anne's War
Mose, Gracia Real de Santa Teresa de, 175–76, 181, 183, 196, 209, 261. *See also* Menéndez, Francisco; Yamasee towns near St. Augustine: Nuestra Señora de Rosario de Moze
Musgrove, John, 192, 199–205, 211–12, 213, 215
Musgrove, Mary (Lower Creek), 199, 201–3, 205–7, 209, 211

345

Nairne, Thomas, 42, 100–102, 120–22, 140, 172
Niquisalla (mico, Yamasee), 36; Nicasaya, 317

Ocmulgee River, 57, 200
Oconee River, 87, 105, 106
Oconee-Ocmulgee River valley chiefdoms. *See* Mississippian progenitors of Yamasees
Ocute chiefdom. *See* Mississippian progenitors of Yamasees
Oglethorpe, James (general), 45, 206–10, 229–30, 255, 261. *See also* Georgia
Ospo Indians (Guale), 17, 282, 286, 288, 292, 305. *See also* Huspah Town; Huspah King; Jospogue, Francisco
Oweeka (Lower Creek), 201–2, 204

Palmer, John: assisted by Pon Pon Indians, 198, 204; 1728 attack on Yamasees, 44, 179, 191–93, 198, 203–4, 251, 259, 296–97
Peña, Diego de, 43, 310–13
Pensacola, 17, 46–47, 310, 315, 317–18, 320–24, 326, 328–30
pirates (corsairs), 35–37, 39, 41, 47, 61, 135, 166, 288
Pon Pon Indians, 15, 192, 196, 200–204. *See also* Musgrove, John; Musgrove, Mary; Oweeka; Whitlemico; Yamasee War
Port Royal, 2–5, 22, 35–38, 61, 87–88, 94, 103, 133–36, 139, 156, 189, 196–97, 200–202, 214, 254, 288. *See also* South Carolina, colony

Queen Anne's War, 41–42, 121–22, 168–69
Quiroga y Losada, Diego de (governor), 34, 38, 168

repartimiento (Spanish labor draft), 31, 257, 281; Yamasees involved in 30–31, 55, 58, 61, 257
Reyes, Juan Ignacio de los (Creek-Yamasee), 182, 229

Sanchez, Juan, Cacique (Pocatalaca, Yamasee), 16, 183, 190, 244
Santa Elena, 28, 134, 139, 165, 281, 286. *See also* Port Royal
Santiago Sule (mico, Yamasee), 174, 222
Sapelo Island, 89, 287–88
Savannah Indians, 5
Savannah River, xiii, 2, 31, 35–36, 57, 84, 195–96, 205
Scots. *See* Stuarts Town
Seminole Indians, xvii, 17, 75, 198, 243, 319, 321
situado (Spanish royal subsidy), 40, 43, 273
shatter zone. *See* diaspora
Society for the Propagation of the Gospel (SPG), 131, 136–37, 139, 141–57
South Carolina, colony, xiii, xiv–xv, 1–2, 34, 40–43, 47, 61, 65, 81–83, 92–93, 137–38, 164–65, 166–71. *See also* Africans; Moore, James, Sr.; Palmer, John; Stuarts Town; trade; Yamasee towns in South Carolina
St. Augustine. *See* La Florida
St. Catherines Island, 30, 39, 116–18, 188, 286
St. Helena Island, 166, 170. *See also* Santa Elena
St. Johns ceramic series, 11, 71, 121
St. Johns River, 30, 45, 55, 60–61, 71–72, 79, 121, 210, 229–30
St. Simons Island, 57, 58, 103, 206–10, 287
Stuarts Town, 35–38, 102, 166–67; William Dunlop and, 36, 168

Timucua Indians, 2, 28, 30–31, 34, 36–37, 39, 42, 55, 60–61, 71, 121–22, 135, 166, 169, 228, 255. *See also* Mocama Indians.
Toa Chiefdom. *See* Yamasee towns in South Carolina: Euhaw (Yoa) Town
Tomochichi (Yamacraw), 205, 211
trade: archaeological evidence of, 113–16, 120–21; Yamasee trade with the British, 41–42, 43, 81–83, 92–93, 100–103, 113–14, 120–23, 237, 317–18; Yamasee trade with the Creeks, 323; Yamasee trade with the Spanish, 34, 43, 45, 237, 273, 323; Yamasee women and processing of hides, 239
Tuscarora War, 3, 45

Uchise Indians, see Lower Creek Indians
Upper Creek Indians, 313, 324–28

vecino (Spanish citizen): Indians as, 16, 257, 274, 299–304

War of Jenkins' Ear, 43–45, 181, 191, 196, 207, 211, 255, 261. *See also* Georgia
Westo Indians (Chichimecos), xiv, 2–3, 29, 31, 46–47, 55, 57, 84, 134–35, 164, 281–82, 287–88
Whitlemico (Creek), 201
Wright, John, 1, 3–4, 100–102, 170–72
Woodward, Henry, 37

Yamacraw Indians, 205–7, 209, 211, 216
Yamasee: family structure of, 133–34; identity, 10–11, 12–13, 18–21, 27, 46–47, 62–67, 81–82, 87–88, 92–95, 123–25, 222, 224–25, 229–31, 244, 274–75, 303–4, 309, 330–31; kinship networks, 1, 3, 4, 11, 15, 18–19, 138–39, 144–45, 192, 201–2, 225, 262, 275, 302–3; in oral traditions, 18, 198–99; parenting by, 140, 146–48; population estimates, 33, 39, 60, 62–63, 108–11, 176, 183, 190, 222, 224, 230–31, 244, 255–56, 259–61, 313–14, 330; slaving by, 2–4, 120–23; sovereignty, 29, 33, 46–47, 56–57, 222, 230, 309–10; as victims of enslavement, xiii, 1–2, 3–4, 28; women and children as targets of slavery, 137–38; 256. *See also fanni mico*; marriage; Indian slavery; Yamasee ethnogenesis; Westo Indians
Yamasee and Creek affairs: before and during the Yamasee War, xiii, xv, 1, 4–5, 8, 13, 15, 39, 42, 63, 122, 136, 168, 174, 194; after the Yamasee War, 6, 16–18, 20, 43, 46, 75, 131, 157, 191–92, 197–211, 216, 223, 226, 256, 313, 310–28, 330. *See also* Lower Creek Indians
Yamasee ceramics: Altamaha/San Marcos, 11–2, 19–20, 66–67, 86–87, 232–34, 270–71; archaeological signature of, 8, 11–12, 66–67, 231–32; distinguishing from Guale-Mocama sites, 11–12, 55–56, 66–67, 69, 73–75, 88–90, 94, 96, 235–36; motifs, 85–86, 88; stamping, 12, 66, 73, 86–87, 89–91, 94–95, 233–36; women, as primary potters, 11–12, 19, 67, 88, 96, 236, 271–73
Yamasee coalescence, 8, 10, 16, 19, 55, 75, 254, 257–58, 262, 268, 271, 273–74, 276, 293
Yamasee Confederacy. *See* Yamasee towns in South Carolina

INDEX 347

Yamasee ethnogenesis, 2, 7, 10–11, 29, 35–36, 56–57, 63, 83–84, 99–100, 136, 139, 286; Apalachicolas join, 36–37; coalescence in Port Royal, 2, 36; land acquisition in La Florida, 30–31, 58; migration from La Florida to Port Royal, 2, 31, 35–36, 61, 84, 135; migrations to and within La Florida, 29, 57–58, 84; relations with Mocama in La Florida, 30, 58; some remain behind in La Florida, 39–40. *See also* Guale Indians; Yamasee towns in La Florida; Yamasee towns in South Carolina

Yamasee material culture: activity areas 112–13; adornments, 12, 83, 92–93; burials, 13, 70, 83, 100, 105–7, 114–18, 124, 267–70, 279; clothing, 37, 43–44, 46, 92, 144–45, 149–52, 154, 156; council houses, 59, 63, 109–11, 136, 170; diet, 239–40, 269; houses and buildings, 105–9, 242–44, 263–64; mission church, 266–67; pipes, 238; slaving, 120–23; tools, 237–39; trash and shell pits, 112–13, 241–42; weapons, 83, 92, 238; well, 264–67. *See also* agriculture; guns and Yamasees

Yamasee political organization, 32, 62, 63–64, 133–34, 223, 227; primary towns, the question of, 24, 39, 85, 89, 100–103, 111, 136–37, 222; Upper and Lower towns in South Carolina, 1–2, 12, 15, 17, 39, 62, 84–85, 99–100, 103–5; youth as ambassadors, 138–39

Yamasee Prince (George), 13, 131–33, 137–38, 142–43, 154–55. *See also* Yamasee towns in South Carolina: Euhaw (Yoa) Town

Yamasees and Christianity: reject Catholic baptism and/or conversion, xiii, 27, 29, 60, 64–65; reject Anglican baptism and/or conversion, 13, 119–20, 124, 134, 137, 155, 162, 228; spiritual diplomacy, 14, 132–35, 141–42, 149, 155–57; request SPG missionaries and schools, 139; little evidence of in burials at Altamaha Town, 114–18; conversion and nominal conversion to Catholicism, 163, 212, 285–86, 294–95, 314. *See also* Franciscan missions; Society for the Propagation of the Gospel; Yamasee material culture: burials

Yamasee towns in La Florida (circa 1663–83), 32–33, 55, 57–62, 69–74, 103–4, 134–35, 287; Anacape/Enacape, 32–33, 55, 60–61, 64, 71, 74; Ocotonico, 103–4; Ocotoque, 59, 62, 69; La Tama, 59, 62, 69, 104; Mayaca, 32–34, 55, 60–62, 64, 71–74, 76; Nuestra Señora de la Candelaria de la Tama (Apalachee), 77, 259, 278, 311; San Pedro, 30–31, 39, 59; San Simón, 31; Santa María, 24, 30, 32, 39–40, 58–59, 61, 63, 69–70. *See also* Amelia Island; Cumberland Island; Guale Indians; Ospo Indians; Sapelo Island; St. Simons Island

Yamasee towns in South Carolina (circa 1683–1715), 81–85, 89–94, 132, 135–37, 174–75, 196, 222, 252; Altamaha Town, 39, 85, 89–91, 92, 100–101, 105–18, 120–21, 123, 235, 242, 258–59, 270; Chechessee Town, 84, 93, 102, 104, 110, 232, 235, 237, 239–40, 242; Euhaw (Yoa) Town, 13–14, 84, 102, 104, 132–41, 156, 158, 159, 162; Huspah Town, 17, 84, 89–90, 102–3, 171, 184, 234, 282, 291; Okatee Town, 84, 102, 104, 110, 222, 258–59; Pocosabo Town, 84, 102; Pocotaligo Town, 1, 4–5, 39, 42, 84–85, 89–90, 100–103, 105, 109–11, 120, 123, 156, 159, 170, 172, 174–76, 188, 191, 221, 225–26, 235; Sadketche, 84, 102–3, 172–74, 187, 223, 226; Tomatley Town, 84, 102, 170, 318–19; Tulafina Town, 84, 102–3

Yamasees towns in West Florida (circa 1718+), 45–46, 309–31; San Antonio de Punta Rasa, 321–30; Tamasle, 310–21; visits to Cuba 318–19

Yamasee towns near St. Augustine (circa 1715–1763), 176, 221, 223–24, 229–30, 244–45, 251, 254, 256; Las Rosas de Ayamón, 79, 179, 208, 224, 294–95; Nombre de Dios Chiquito, 188, 190, 261, 289, 296; Nuestra Señora de Candelaria de la Tamaja (Tama), 16, 44, 176, 198, 211, 221, 224, 259, 295–96; Nuestra Señora de Rosario de Moze (Yamasee), 16, 44, 178, 259–60, 278; Pocosapa, 176, 221; Riverbend site (8vo2567), 73–74; San Antonio de Pocotalaca, 15–16, 74, 79, 162, 176, 179, 182–83, 198, 221–22, 224–32, 234–45, 261

Yamasee War (1715–1763), xiv–xv, 1–2, 4–6, 42–44, 156–57, 171–74, 179, 191–94, 196–97, 198, 202, 223, 226, 259, 291, 295; Africans as allies of Yamasees in, 14, 163, 172–75, 180; Africans liberated by Yamasees, 179,

Yamasee War (*continued*)
196; causes of, 137–38, 170–71; Cherokees, 5–6, 192–95; Creeks, 5–6, 15, 191–92, 194–95; Euhaws do not participate in, 156–57, 199–97; raids against the English, 178–79, 201–5; Yamasee-Creek delegation to the Spanish in 1715, 173–75, 222–23; Yamasees fission as a result of, 199–200, 221; Yamasee exodus (1763), to Cuba, 183, 262; to Veracruz, Mexico, 17, 212, 329. *See also* Africans: alliances with Yamasee; Brims; Georgia; Yamasee and Creek affairs; Yfallaquisca

Yfallaquisca (Perro Bravo; Yamasee), 14, 162, 172–77, 180–81, 208, 211, 223, 226–27

Yuchi Indians, 16, 198, 205, 207, 216, 312

Zúñiga y Cerda, José de (governor), 34–35, 41, 168–69, 284, 289

www.ingramcontent.com/pod-product-compliance
Lightning Source LLC
Chambersburg PA
CBHW030604230426
43661CB00053B/1833